Principles of Economics: Macro

THE IRWIN SERIES IN ECONOMICS

CONSULTING EDITOR   LLOYD G. REYNOLDS   *Yale University*

Principles of
ECONOMICS
Macro

WILLIS L. PETERSON, Ph.D.
University of Minnesota

1974   Revised Edition

RICHARD D. IRWIN, INC.   *Homewood, Illinois 60430*
Irwin-Dorsey International   *Arundel, Sussex   BN18 9AB*
Irwin-Dorsey Limited   *Georgetown, Ontario   L7G 4B3*

Revised Edition

First Printing, January 1974
Second Printing, May 1974
Third Printing, December 1974
Fourth Printing, March 1975
Fifth Printing, September 1975
Sixth Printing, January 1976
Seventh Printing, April 1976

ISBN 0–256–01509–0
Library of Congress Catalog Card No. 73–85664

Printed in the United States of America

LEARNING SYSTEMS COMPANY—
a division of Richard D. Irwin, Inc.—has developed a
PROGRAMMED LEARNING AID
to accompany texts in this subject area.
Copies can be purchased through your bookstore
or by writing PLAIDS,
1818 Ridge Road, Homewood, Illinois   60430.

Preface

As is all too evident to students during examinations, knowledge has a tendency to slip away with the passage of time. Not only do we forget a substantial amount of what we learn but part of what we do retain is likely to become obsolete in future years. It is important, therefore, that education be of a nature that facilitates retention of acquired knowledge and that this knowledge have a long lasting value. The kind of education that provides durability and lasting value is perhaps best described by Alfred North White-head in *The Aims of Education and Other Essays:* "Whatever be the detail with which you cram your student, the chances of his meeting in afterlife exactly that detail is almost infinitesimal; and if he does meet it, he will probably have forgotten what you taught him about it. The really useful training yields a comprehension of a few general principles with a thorough grounding in the way they apply to a variety of concrete details. In subsequent practice the men will have forgotten your particular details; but they will remember by an unconscious common sense how to apply principles to immediate circumstances."

In keeping with this philosophy of education, this text strives to strike a balance between principles and their application to current economic problems and decisions. Although circumstances will change with the passage of time, the principles contained in this volume should remain applicable to future economic problems that will confront the nation over the next 40 to 50 years.

This book is a twin. It is linked to my *Principles of Economics: Micro* in style and is complementary in content. Yet either can stand alone or be used with another text. The introductory material on demand and supply that has been added to chapter one of this revised edition of the macro text should make it easier to follow a macro-micro sequence than was the case for the first edition.

Among other changes that I believe make this a better book, it has been "fleshed out" (without becoming obese) in many areas and hopefully all of the "bugs" of the first edition have been removed. Much of the credit for the improvement should go to those who have offered detailed comments and suggestions on the first edition and on the first draft of the revised edition: Frank Child of the University of California at Davis, Barbara Henneberry and James Witte of Indiana University, William Hosek of the University of New Hampshire, Edward Kittrell of Northern Illinois, and Lloyd Reynolds of Yale. In addition I am indebted to many users of the first edition who have taken the time to offer comments and suggestions, many of which they will recognize in this revised volume. Special thanks also goes to Dorothy Peterson who probably learned more economics than she really wanted to know while assisting me with the proofreading.

December 1973   WILLIS L. PETERSON

Contents

1

Introduction to macroeconomics

"Micro" versus "macro" economics

During its relatively short history, economics has evolved into two major subdisciplines: microeconomics and macroeconomics. As its name implies, microeconomics is concerned mainly with small segments of the total economy—individual consumers and producers, or groups of consumers and producers which are known as markets or industries. The subject matter of microeconomics deals in part with allocating resources to their most valuable uses so as to maximize the total output of the economy. Considerable emphasis is also placed on wage and price determination, which bears upon the distribution of the total output.

Macroeconomics, the topic of this book, is concerned mainly with economic aggregates, or the economy as a whole. The subject matter of macroeconomics deals to a large extent with the problems of unemployment and inflation. In large part, these problems also bear upon the total output of society and upon the distribution of this output.

The existence of unemployment implies that the total output of society is smaller than it need otherwise be. Unemployment also has an effect on the distribution of society's output in that the unemployed suffer a reduction in income, which in turn means that they cannot place as large a claim on society's goods and services. Inflation also has distributional effects. Those whose wages or assets rise

1

less rapidly in value than the price level suffer a real loss during inflation.

At any rate we can say that both micro and macroeconomics deal with the size of society's output of goods and services and the distribution of this output. After completing the study of the micro and macro areas, however, it will become apparent that the methods of analysis used in each differ to a considerable degree.

We should also say at this point that macroeconomics can itself be divided into two major subdivisions. One is sometimes referred to as a study of income and employment theory; the other, as the study of monetary theory. The first deals to a large extent with the effects of government spending and taxation on the level of economic activity. The second is concerned mainly with the effect of the quantity of money and interest rates on the economy. As you might expect, then, the actions of government are very important in the study of macroeconomics.

Politics and economics—Political economy

In view of the importance of government in the study of macroeconomics, we should not be surprised to learn that politics and economics are closely related. Indeed, economics has sometimes been called the study of political economy. This was especially true during the 19th century. With the passage of time, political science and economics gradually emerged as separate, although closely related, disciplines.

We would expect, too, that much of the disagreement and controversy inherent in politics would carry over into economics, particularly in the macro area. This cannot be denied. People of a more conservative political outlook tend to prefer a society with a minimum of government intervention. Although it is unwise to generalize too much here, it seems reasonably safe to say that economists of a more conservative political philosophy also prefer a minimum of government intervention, particularly in the economic activities of society.

All, or virtually all, economists would probably agree on the need for a certain amount of federal government intervention. For example, there is little question about the need for government regulation of the money supply or the provision for certain public goods such as national defense or roads. Moving towards the liberal pole (and we should recognize various degrees of liberalism or conservatism rather than an all-or-none situation), we find people who are more willing to delegate more decision-making authority to government. Again, the more liberal economists would tend to fall within this category. Although most economists make a sincere attempt at being objective or "scientific" in their profession, it is important to recognize that their political philosophies may, to some degree, carry over into their economic analyses.

There are, of course, exceptions in each group. We find some economists, probably a growing number, who would be labeled as fairly conservative because of their objection to increased government intervention in the marketplace. But these same economists might at the same time appear quite liberal on other issues such as their support of a more equalitarian distribution of income or advocacy of a reduction in military spending. Thus, it is often misleading to label someone, particularly an economist, conservative or liberal solely on the basis of one or two criteria.

Positive versus normative economics

Economists, recognizing that they do have different political philosophies and that these divergent points of view may influence policy recommendations, have attempted to sort out as much as possible the "positive" from the "normative." We can think of positive economics as "what is" and normative economics as "what should be." For example, an economist may determine that a tax increase will take X billions of dollars away from the private sector. But it is a different matter to say that the X billion dollar tax increase is the best thing for the economy. The first statement would be considered positive economics, while the latter would be of a normative nature.

We should not conclude from this example, however, that all positive statements are devoid of value judgments and as such are purely objective. For in the process of formulating a study, a great deal of value judgment is involved. For example, the researcher must decide what data to collect, how to organize and analyze the data, etc. Beware of the person who says, "let the facts speak for themselves." What the facts say depends a great deal upon which facts are used and how they are presented.[1]

The individual versus society

Most of us are accustomed to looking at the world from the perspective of the individual. However, we find in our study of macroeconomics that what is true for the individual person need not hold true for society, or even for groups of people. Standing up to watch a touchdown run at a football game provides a good noneconomic example. If just one person stands up, he can gain a much better view, but if everyone in the stadium stands up, no one is much better off.

The distinction between the individual and society is especially important in monetary policy. Any individual would consider himself much better off if the amount of money he held were doubled, for this would mean he now has access to twice the amount of goods and services. But if the total quantity of money in the entire economy were doubled, the total quantity of real goods and services available to the people need not necessarily change. As we go along we will encounter other situations where circumstances are much different for the individual than for society.

Cause and effect

If two events happen in proximity to each other, there is a temptation to conclude that the second event was caused by the first. But whenever we observe two events such as these, we should always inquire whether there might have been a third event that caused both to occur. A good example is the stock market crash of 1929 and the ensuing Great Depression of the early 1930s. This order of events has prompted some people to argue that the stock market crash caused the Great Depression. But as we shall see later

---

[1] For an entertaining little book on the use of statistics, see Darrell Huff, *How to Lie with Statistics* (New York: W. W. Norton & Co., Inc., 1954).

a third independent event probably offers a better explanation for the Great Depression than the stock market crash, although the crash probably contributed to the depressed state of the economy once unemployment began to increase.

A rather interesting phenomenon that is somewhat related to this general topic is the relationship between women's skirt lengths and the state of the economy. With amazing regularity, women's skirts have shortened during economic booms and lengthened during periods of increased unemployment. The relationship again became evident during the 1960s. In the middle and latter part of the decade the economy boomed along with high employment, rising prices, and rising hemlines. Then as the economy experienced a slowdown in 1969 and 1970, the "maxi" and the "midi" appeared on the scene. Indeed, the aesthetic value of the "mini" provides incentive enough for maintaining a healthy, full-employment economy!

Seriously, though, there is no economic reason to expect a relationship between the state of the economy and women's fashions. It has been argued that with depressed economic conditions people become gloomy and turn to "dowdy" fashions, but this is mainly speculation. But perhaps there is a good lesson here. When attempting to explain economic phenomena it is always a good idea to look for economic reasons. Some of the early economists forgot this simple idea and attempted to explain business cycles (ups and downs in economic activity) by sunspots, which strikes us as quite silly today.

Unlearning preconceptions

One of the characteristics of studying economics, particularly macroeconomics, is that most people bring with them at the start at least some preconceived ideas of how the economy functions. In fact it is almost impossible not to form economic opinions in view of the vast amount of reporting of economics by the news media. This is both good and bad. It is good because people are becoming more aware of the importance of government economic policy in their lives. But it is bad to the extent that people form erroneous ideas of how the economy operates and the effect of government policy. Unfortunately many myths, half-truths, and misconceptions about the economy appear in the news media just about every day.

One of the major reasons for this problem is that there are many influential people both in government and in private industry who are carrying out economic analysis without the benefit of economics training. Few if any professional occupations can make this claim (or excuse). To practice law or medicine one must have the appropriate degree from an accredited college. Indeed, to be a plumber or electrician a person must complete a number of years of apprenticeship training. Not so in economics. Economics is practiced by everyone, and the importance of one's practice increases with his influence over the nation's affairs. Nations have paid a dear price for having leaders who have had little or no understanding of economics.

Throughout this book it is more than likely that you will come across ideas quite different from those you had previously learned and accepted. Understandably it is difficult to unlearn old ideas, but economics training will be of much greater value if you approach it with an open mind, allowing the new ideas you encounter to at least compete with your old preconceptions.

Economic models—A framework for thinking

Needless to say, the economy is very complex. Each day millions of economic decisions are made by millions of people. Some of these decisions, especially those made by the government, have far-reaching and long-lasting consequences. To study each decision, however, even the major ones, would be a hopelessly complicated task. We would soon be bogged down in a maze of dull and uninteresting detail. Thus, economists have found it useful to construct models of the economy. In a sense economic models provide a framework for thinking. They help us to identify and separate the important information for making economic decisions from the trivial or unimportant.

In Chapters 4 and 7 we will develop what has come to be known as the Keynesian model of the economy, named after its founder, a famous English economist, John Maynard Keynes. Here we will focus our attention on the effect of private and public spending decisions and the quantity of money on the level of employment and prices in the economy. We will see that the model makes it possible to explain the causes of economic events such as the Great Depression of the 1930s or the inflation of the late 1960s and early 1970s. Perhaps even more important, the model enables us to predict future levels of unemployment and inflation under certain government policies. In short, economic models facilitate explanation of past events and help us to predict future events.

Economic models also are known as economic theories or principles. Essentially all three mean the same thing. Thus, we could refer to the Keynesian model as the Keynesian theory or the Keynesian principle.

Unfortunately the word "theory" has suffered from a bad press for a long time. To students, the word often brings to mind abstract material devoid of any practical application. The feeling is probably justified if theory is learned purely for the sake of learning theory. But economic theory is not developed for its own sake; it is developed because it can be useful to explain and predict events. As we proceed, you will find that an attempt is made to apply the theories (models or principles) to real-world situations. Thus if you do not find the world dull, you should not find theory dull.

We should point out, too, that just about everyone utilizes theory of one kind or another from the time they are old enough to think. To take a very simple example, we know that if we touch a hot stove we will burn a finger. Essentially this is a theory. In essence, the "hot stove theory" both explains and predicts. It explains why you might have a sore finger and it predicts that should you touch another hot stove you will again burn a finger.

In the main, theories or models are developed by observing events and then generalizing from these events. Most of us formed the "hot stove theory" by touching a stove and observing (and feeling) what happened. From one or two observations we were able to generalize that touching all hot stoves results in burned fingers. Economic theories or models are developed in a similar manner. By identifying the prime causal factors of economic events, economists attempt to explain these events and thus predict future events.

The production possibilities curve

In studying the problems of unemployment and inflation, it is useful to have some understanding of how a market economy operates. In this and the following three sections we will present some of the basic facts of economic life. A much more thorough coverage of this material is found within the subject matter of microeconomics.[2] If you have already studied microeconomics, these sections should provide a brief review and refresh your memory. If this is your first exposure to economics, these sections should give you ample background information to pick up everything that is presented in the remainder of the book.

One of the more important economic facts of life to always bear in mind is that resources are scarce or limited, and therefore the output of goods and services is limited. This holds true for the individual, the state or region, and the nation. It also holds true regardless of the economic system—capitalism, communism, or any mixture.

Of course, the limited nature of output in itself need not be a problem. The rub comes because for all practical purposes human wants are unlimited, or at least are substantially greater than the goods and services that can be produced to satisfy these wants. Thus every person and every nation must "make do" with fewer goods and services than it would really like to have.

The phenomenon of unlimited human wants pressing against a limited output of goods and services gives rise to the necessity of making economic decisions. We cannot have everything we would like, so we have to choose the items that give us the most satisfaction for our effort or money. It is also true that when we choose more of one good or service, such as a more expensive automobile, we have to give up something else, such as a vacation trip or a new color TV set.

Exactly the same problem plagues us at the national level. If we decide to produce an extra $10 billion of military hardware, an

---

2 See Willis L. Peterson, *Principles of Economics: Micro* (rev. ed.; Homewood, Ill.: Richard D. Irwin, Inc., 1974), chaps. 1 through 6.

equal amount of something else, such as $10 billion in public transportation or education, must be given up.[3]

Economists have long used the concept of the "production possibilities curve" to illustrate the idea that output is limited and that choices must be made among alternative goods and services. One example of a production possibilities curve is presented in Figure 1–1. In this example we depict the possible levels of output of guns

FIGURE 1–1
A production possibilities curve

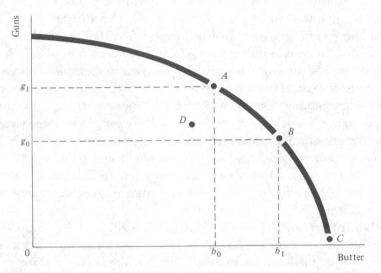

and butter that a nation can produce. In this case, "guns" illustrates military goods and services, whereas "butter" illustrates all other goods and services.

The curved line running from the vertical axis down to the horizontal axis is the production possibilities curve. It represents alternative combinations of the maximum possible output of these two goods that the nation can produce. For example, if the nation is at point A on the curve, it is producing g_1 quantity of guns and b_0 quantity of butter. The nation may want to have more of both guns

---

[3] We are assuming here that all available resources are employed in the most efficient manner possible. We will consider shortly the outcome when resource efficiency or employment can be increased.

and butter, but it cannot; the curve traces out the possible maximums that can be produced during a given year or time period.

It is possible, of course, for the nation to produce more butter if it is willing to decrease its output of guns. That is, it could move from point A to point B on the production possibilities curve. Now it would be producing g_0 of guns, a smaller amount, and b_1 of butter, a larger amount. (Keep in mind that points more distant from the origin represent larger quantities.) Point C represents the extreme case of zero guns and all butter. Here the nation is devoting all its resources to the production of nonmilitary goods.

Although we can be sure that a nation cannot be anywhere outside the production possibilities frontier (by definition this is impossible), there is nothing that guarantees that a nation will be on the surface of the curve. For example, a nation could be at point D. This means that it is not receiving the maximum possible output from its available resources. There are two reasons why this might occur: (1) the nation is not utilizing its resources in the most efficient manner, or (2) some of its resources are not employed. The subject matter of microeconomics deals in large part with achieving an efficient use and allocation of resources; in this book much of our discussion will be concerned with attaining a full employment of resources.

It is interesting to note that if a nation is able to move from a submaximum point, such as point D, it may be able to increase its output of both goods simultaneously. By moving to point A, for example, it could increase its output of both guns and butter.

We should make clear at this juncture that the production possibilities curve represents a country's output potential at a point in time. For example, it may represent output possibilities for a country during 1974. But there is nothing that requires the curve to remain fixed over a span of time. Indeed the production possibilities curve for most nations has been moving or shifting to the right over time, as illustrated by Figure 1–2. Economists call this economic growth. Economic growth has been pursued by most if not all nations because it provides the people with a larger total output of goods and services. Since just about everyone in the world today, especially the poor, would like to consume more goods and services than they currently do, economic growth remains a desirable goal.

We might mention here that a cleaner environment may well be part of the bundle of goods and services we desire more of.

The causes of economic growth are still not well understood. Some nations such as the United States, Canada, Japan, and the western and northern European countries have been quite successful in achieving growth; others, namely the so-called underdeveloped nations, have been less successful. We will consider the topic of economic growth in more detail in Chapter 12. For now we

FIGURE 1–2
Illustrating economic growth with a production possibilities curve

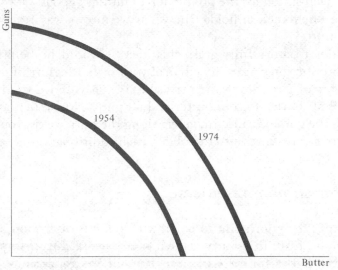

might just say that economic growth appears to be highly dependent on the growth of knowledge and technology. By increasing his knowledge, man has been able to conceive of and produce new, more productive inputs or resources that enable him to increase his total output of goods and services.

One additional aspect of the production possibilities curve may have caught your attention, namely the slight curvature that has been drawn into the line. Again this is a topic that is covered more thoroughly in Chapter 1 of the micro book. To satisfy your curiosity for the moment (or refresh your memory) we might mention that the curvature of the line implies that resources are not equally productive in all uses. In the context of the above example, it means that some resources are not as productive in the production of guns as they are in the production of butter. Agricultural land might be an example.

The curvature of the line reflects this idea because as we move away from butter toward guns, it is necessary to give up progressively larger amounts of butter to obtain each additional gun. In a way this makes sense, because some resources that are well suited to the production of butter will have to be pressed into service in the production of guns. As we mentioned, agricultural land is not particularly well suited for the production of military goods. Of course, the same phenomenon holds true when we move away from guns towards butter.

In order to more fully grasp this idea, it would be helpful to draw a production possibility curve of your own. Measure off equal increments of guns along the vertical axis. Then move from zero guns and all butter to zero butter and all guns. Notice that as you move up the gun axis and to the left along the butter axis, you give up progressively more butter to obtain each additional unit of guns.

The allocation of resources

Perhaps the major point to be drawn from our discussion of the production possibilities curve is that total output during any production period is limited, and an increase in one good can only be obtained by a decrease in the other if we are on the surface of the curve. Because of the two-dimensional nature of the diagram it is limited to presenting two goods, or two broad categories of goods, at a time. In addition to guns and butter, we could have depicted any number of different pairs of goods or services such as consumption versus investment goods, public versus private goods, or agricultural versus nonagricultural goods.[4] Which pair we choose to present depends on the point we wish to make or the question we want to analyze.

---

4 The first pair denotes the distinction between goods meant to be consumed at the present and goods that increase the output of consumption goods in the future. The second pair reflects the distinction between goods distributed by the government and paid for by tax money or special fees, and goods purchased by the individual.

Regardless of the pair of goods we choose to represent on the production possibilities curve, there is one thing the curve itself cannot tell us, and that is the particular mix of the two goods or categories of goods that will in fact be produced. In other words, the production possibilities curve only reflects the possible range of choices; it does not determine the exact choice that will be made. Nor does it explain fully why the choice may change over time.

In economies characterized by reasonably free markets, such as the United States and other noncommunist nations of the world, the mix of goods produced is determined in large part by the relative prices of goods and services. Prices are in large part determined by the forces of demand and supply. The topics of demand and supply and the price-making process constitute a major part, if not *the* major part, of microeconomics. Indeed microeconomics is often referred to as "price theory." In the following section we will present a brief introduction (or review) of demand and supply, the price-making process, and how prices determine the mix of goods and services produced.[5]

Introduction to demand and supply

Let us begin with demand. We can define demand as a relationship between price and quantity. For most goods and services we can observe an inverse relationship between price and quantity. That is, when price is relatively high the quantity of an item that people buy per week, per month, or per year, will tend to be relatively low. Conversely if price is relatively low the amount that people buy tends to be somewhat greater.

The idea that people buy less of an item when its price is high, and more when price is low, has a certain intuitive appeal. Generally what happens is that a relatively high price prompts people to look for less expensive substitutes that will satisfy their wants. For example, when beef is high, people tend to cut back on beef consumption and eat more pork, chicken, fish, cheese, etc. On the other hand, when the price of an item is relatively low, it becomes the substitute for other relatively more expensive items. In other words,

---

5 A more detailed account of this material is found in Chapters 1 through 6 of the companion micro book.

the inverse relationship between price and quantity demanded is just a reflection of consumers' trying to get the most for their money.

Economists will often illustrate this relationship with a diagram. Price is usually placed on the vertical axis and quantity on the horizontal axis. By choosing various possible prices and observing the amounts people will buy at these prices, we can trace out a downward sloping line, as illustrated by Figure 1–3. For example, if

FIGURE 1–3
A demand curve

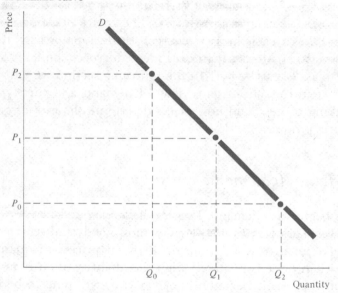

price is high, say at P_2, quantity will be low, say at Q_0. As price declines to P_1 and P_0, quantity increases to Q_1 and Q_2. If we assume that the same relationship holds between these points as on the points, we can connect them and obtain a downward sloping line. Economists call this a "demand curve," even though it is often drawn as a straight, downward sloping line.

Let us turn next to the concept of supply. We also can define supply as a relationship between price and quantity. For most goods and services we can observe a positive relationship between price and quantity. That is, when price is relatively high the quantity of an item that producers or sellers will place on the market will tend to be relatively large. Conversely, when price is relatively low the quantity supplied also will be low.

The idea that producers will place more on the market when price is high and less when price is low also is intuitively appealing. In this case, a high price provides an incentive for producers to increase output because their profits will be greater than when price is low, other things being equal. And the prospect of relatively high profits tends to result in producers' cutting back on less profitable activities and increasing the output of the high-priced item. For example, if shoes are high-priced, shoe manufacturers may build more manufacturing capacity for shoes and cut back on the production of other items. There will be a tendency for producers of other less profitable items to switch over to shoes in an effort to "get a piece of the action." The opposite occurs if shoe prices are low relative to other goods and services. Some shoe manufacturers may get out of the shoe manufacturing business entirely, while others cut back shoe production in an attempt to expand output of other more profitable things. After all, producers are consumers too. We would expect them to also try to get the most for their effort and money.

As in the case of demand, economists will often illustrate the supply relationship with a diagram, again placing price on the vertical axis and quantity on the horizontal axis. With a positive relationship between price and quantity, the observed points will tend to trace out an upward sloping line, as illustrated by Figure 1–4. For example, if price is relatively high, say at P_2, quantity supplied also will be high, as indicated by Q_2. As price declines to P_1 and P_0, quantity supplied also declines, to Q_1 and Q_0, respectively. Economists call the line that is traced out by his price-quantity relationship a "supply curve," even though it is often drawn as a straight, upward sloping line.

It is important to recognize at this point that demand alone, or supply alone, cannot tell us which price and quantity will actually exist. They only tell us the various possible prices and quantities that might prevail. But when we combine the two concepts, the exact market price and quantity can readily be determined. The demand and supply curves are something like two blades of a scissors; both are necessary to do the job.

The process of price and quantity determination can best be un-

FIGURE 1–4
A supply curve

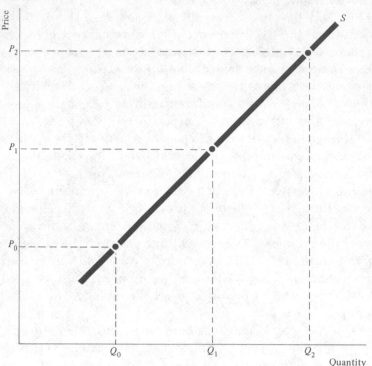

derstood by superimposing the demand and supply curves on the same diagram, as shown by Figure 1–5. This is possible because both have price on the vertical axis and quantity on the horizontal axis.

Perhaps the easiest way to see which price will prevail is to begin with a price that would not be likely to prevail, at least for long, say the high price P_2. At this price, consumers buy a relatively small amount, Q_1^d, but producers supply a relatively large amount, Q_2^s. As you can see, the outcome of this situation would be a buildup of unsold goods or services. As a result, there would tend to be a downward pressure on price. Some buyers, seeing the glut in the market, may press sellers to lower the price. And some sellers, seeing the buildup of inventories, may initiate some price reductions in an effort to entice buyers to take a larger amount of their output.

Alternatively, let's see what happens if price is relatively low,

FIGURE 1–5
Determination of equilibrium price and quantity

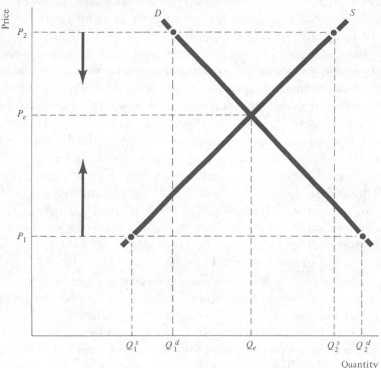

say at P_1. In this case quantity demanded, as shown by Q_2^d, is much larger than quantity supplied, Q_1^s. Now there will be a shortage of the item as demanders indicate a willingness to buy more than suppliers wish to sell. At this low price some buyers are not able to obtain all they would like to buy, while some sellers are experiencing empty shelves or drawing down their inventories. As a consequence some buyers will be likely to offer sellers a higher price in order to obtain some of the scarce good. Also we can be quite sure that at least some sellers will ask for a higher price as long as they can be sure of selling their entire stock.

So far, we have seen that neither the high price P_2 nor the low price P_1 could long prevail in the market. Forces would be present to drive P_2 down or P_1 up. By now it is probably evident that there is only one price, P_e, that can prevail without the presence of downward or upward pressure. For at price P_e buyers are willing to take off the market exactly the same quantity that sellers are willing to offer. In other words, the market will be in equilibrium. For this reason P_e and Q_e often are referred to as equilibrium price and quantity, respectively.

In summary we can say that the demand for and supply of a good or service determines the price and quantity of that good or service. In the context of the production possibilities curve, we can say that demand and supply determine where on the curve a nation will be. If the demand for and the supply of the good on the vertical axis is large relative to that of the good on the horizontal axis, the economy will be at some point on the upper portion of the curve.

One might conclude at this point that once a market gets into equilibrium, price and quantity should remain unchanged for all time to come. Right? Wrong! What generally happens in most markets is that the demand and supply curves themselves are con-tinually changing positions. Once they are in a new position, equilibrium price, quantity, or both are likely to be different. Once this occurs the equilibrating process must start over again.

In Figure 1–6, we illustrate the two possible changes that could lead to an increase in market price: (1) a shift to the right by de-mand or (2) a shift to the left by supply. A shift to the right by the demand curve represents an *increase* in demand. This means that buyers take a larger quantity at any given price. This can be seen by picking a price, P_e' for example, and noting that a larger quan-tity will be purchased under demand curve D' than under demand curve D Figure 1–6 (A). The shift to the left in the supply curve, illustrated by Figure 1–6 (B), represents a *decrease* in supply. This means that sellers offer a smaller quantity on the market at any given price. Again this is easiest to see by picking any price, P_e for example, and noting that a smaller quantity will be forthcoming under S' than under S.

Basically it is these shifts that cause adjustments to take place in the allocation of a nation's resources. The good illustrated by Fig-ure 1–6 (A) would exhibit an increase in quantity as producers responded to the increase in price caused by the increase in demand. The good illustrated by Figure 1–6 (B) would exhibit a decrease in quantity as consumers responded to the increase in price caused by the decrease in supply. Again in the context of the production pos-sibilities curve, an increase in demand for the good represented on

FIGURE 1–6
Changes in demand and supply causing an increase in equilibrium price

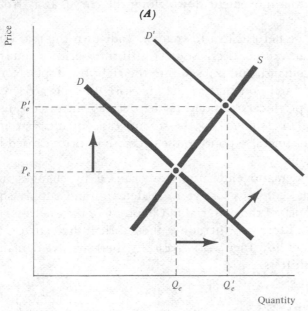

(A)

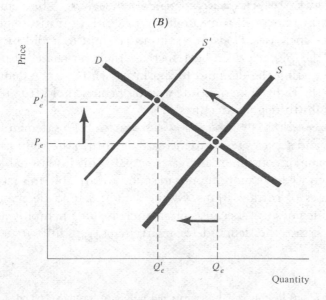

(B)

the vertical axis, for example, would be reflected as a movement up along the curve. In contrast a decrease in the supply of this good would lead to a movement down along the curve, away from this good.

It would be helpful to illustrate on your own the two kinds of shifts that can cause a decrease in equilibrium price: (1) a shift to the left by demand, and (2) a shift to the right by supply. Your diagrams should tell you that in the first case, there is a decrease in quantity as producers respond to the decrease in price caused by the decrease in demand. In the second case, quantity would increase as consumers respond to the decrease in price caused by the increase in supply.

Shifts in demand and supply are caused by changes in phenomena that economists refer to as demand and supply shifters. Although much of the material in Chapter 6 of the micro text deals with these shifters, we introduce them briefly here to provide a general idea of how they work. Basically there are five demand and five supply shifters.

DEMAND SHIFTERS

1. Changes in prices of related goods or services. The demand for a good, say pork, will increase if the price of a substitute good, such as beef, increases. Consumers, in an attempt to avoid buying as much of the higher priced beef, increase their purchases of pork, thereby increasing the demand for pork, i.e., shifting the demand for pork to the right. The opposite would of course hold true if the price of a substitute good declines.

2. Changes in money incomes of consumers. The demand for most goods and services tends to increase or shift to the right as the money income of consumers increases.[6] Again this is reasonable to expect; when we have more money to spend we are able to increase our purchases of certain items. By the same token, a decrease in consumer incomes, say because of an increase in unemployment, tends to decrease the demand for many items, i.e., shift it to the left.

---

6 Some exceptions include cold-water flats, old fashioned washboards, and starchy foods.

3. Changes in expectations of consumers regarding future prices and incomes. If consumers expect the price of an item to increase in the future, they will be likely to attempt to increase their rate of purchase of the item in order to stock up before the price rise. Similarly if people expect their future incomes to be larger than their present incomes, we can expect them to buy more at the present than if they expected hard times ahead. The opposite would be true, of course, for expected lower prices or incomes in the future.

4. Changes in tastes and preferences. Sometimes people will step up their purchases of an item if they suddenly take a liking to it. For example, the demand for motorcycles and women's pant suits seems to have increased in recent years. On the other hand, yo-yos, bobby-sox, and double-breasted suits for men no longer are "in".

5. Changes in number of consumers. The total market demand for an item will be greater as the number of consumers in the market is greater. Nationwide, the demand for most goods and services has been shifting to the right because of population growth. Of course, in places where population has declined, mainly rural areas and small towns, the demand for many goods and services has declined.

SUPPLY SHIFTERS

1. Changes in the prices of resources. A decrease in the price of resources (hence a decrease in production costs) has the effect of increasing the supply of the item produced, i.e., shifting its supply to the right. As costs decline, producers can sell an item for a lower price and still retain their previous profit margins. (Bear in mind that an increase in supply also means that producers are willing to supply a given quantity for a lower price.) Of course, an increase in resource prices has the opposite affect, namely to decrease supply or shift it to the left.

2. Changes in prices of alternative items that may be produced. If prices of other goods or services that require about the same kinds of resources to produce decline, then we can expect the supply of the item in question to increase. For example, a firm that is producing both footballs and basketballs will be likely to increase its supply of footballs if the market price of basketballs declines. On the other hand, an increase in the price of an item can be expected to decrease the supply of alternative goods or services.

3. Changes in expectations of producers regarding future prices. If producers expect the price of their product to decrease in the future, they may sell off part of their inventory, thereby increasing present supply, in order to take advantage of favorable prices at the present. Accordingly, if producers expect higher prices in the future, they may decrease present supply in order to have more to sell when price is expected to be higher.

4. Changes in technology. A change in technology always has the effect of increasing supply because it has the effect of lowering production costs. Unless the new technology lowered production costs, producers would have no incentive to adopt it.

5. Changes in number of producers. The total market supply of an item will increase if the number of producers increases, assuming the average size of the producers remains constant. Finally, the supply of a good or service will decline or shift to the left with a decrease in the number of producers, again assuming no change in the average size of producers.

Public versus private goods

In the previous section we argued that market prices are determined by the forces of demand and supply and that the output mix of goods and services is in turn determined by market prices. We ought to mention at this point that the allocation of resources by market prices applies mainly to the private sector of the economy, where the output decisions are largely in the hands of private firms. However, we know that a significant share of the nation's output of goods and services (over 22 percent at the present) is distributed by the various agencies of the federal, state, and local governments.[7] Some of the major items that fall in this category are military goods and services, police and fire protection, highway and street systems, postal service, public schools, public parks, and various welfare programs.

The task faced by society in deciding on the amount and mix of these so-called public goods and services is exceedingly complex and

---

[7] The 22 percent does not include sales of goods and services by the government.

difficult. As opposed to the impersonal and more or less "automatic" allocation of resources by demand and supply in the private sector, the allocation of resources in the public sector has to be done "by hand," so to speak. That is, elected or appointed officials of the government must make the day-to-day decisions regarding what public goods and how much of each are to be provided. Of course, in a democracy these officials serve at the discretion of the electorate, so in this sense the ultimate, long-run decisions rest in the hands of the general public.

As a general rule we can say that the mix of public and private goods should be that which maximizes the welfare of society. The problem is that no one really knows what this particular mix is. Moreover, the optimum mix is likely to be different for different people. For example, the more politically conservative members of society tend to prefer a smaller proportion of total output devoted to public goods than their more liberal counterparts. Hence the actual mix of public and private goods turns out to be a compromise between the wishes of different groups in society.

Given the public's political persuasion, it is reasonable to believe also that the price or cost of a public good will influence their choices. Even though some public goods and services (such as the services of the military, and public schools) do not carry "price tags," they nevertheless have to be paid for by somebody, namely taxpayers. If taxpayers feel the cost of a public good is low in relation to its benefits, people will probably voice a desire for more of it. On the other hand, if taxpayers feel that a certain public good is not a "good buy" in relation to other public and private goods available, public officials will probably feel a pressure to reduce the output of such a good. In this sense, there is a demand for public goods and services just as there is for private goods and services. In other words, we would expect people to want to buy more of a public good when its price (or cost) is relatively low than when it is high-priced.

Lastly, we should point out that in the United States most public goods are produced by the private sector under contract to the government. For example, military and space hardware, police cars, and fire engines all are produced by private firms. In contrast, most public services are provided by people directly employed by the government, such as postal service employees, public school teachers, and military personnel.

A preview of things to come

We are now ready to embark on our study of macroeconomics. First, we will become somewhat better acquainted with the two basic problems at hand: unemployment and inflation. Then in Chapter 3 we will look at some measures of national output, particularly at GNP (gross national product). Here we will be especially concerned with the biases of GNP when it is used as a measure of economic well-being. From here we move on to the development of what we call the Keynesian model without money—the simplest model of the overall economy. With this model we will be able to shed some light on the causes of unemployment and inflation and what can be done to avoid these problems.

Although the simple model without money provides a useful starting point for the study of the economy, it is somewhat incomplete in that it does not explicitly incorporate the effects of changes in the quantity of money on the economy. Thus we turn next to a study of money, first looking at the factors that influence peoples' decisions to hold part of their wealth in the form of money—the demand for money. Then we will move on to a discussion of the supply of money, looking mainly at the banking system.

After making our acquaintance with money, we will in Chapter 7 incorporate money into the Keynesian model to develop a more complete model of the economy. Then in the chapters on fiscal and monetary policy, we will use these models to analyze the effect of government action on the economy, particularly how government policy influences the level of unemployment and inflation. In the remaining three chapters we will cover some related topics, starting with the problems of poverty and the distribution of income. We end up on the international scene, first discussing international trade and finance, then economic growth and development.

Main points of Chapter 1

1. Economics has evolved into two major subdisciplines: micro and macro economics. Macroeconomics, the topic of this book,

is concerned mainly with economic aggregates, or the economy as a whole. The problems of unemployment and inflation constitute the major part of the subject matter of macro-economics.

2. Because macroeconomics deals to a large degree with the actions of government, political considerations become important, which helps explain why economics is sometimes called the study of political economy.

3. Positive economics is concerned with "what is" while normative economics emphasizes "what should be."

4. When studying economics, especially macroeconomics, it is important to recognize that what might be true for the individual need not be true for groups of people or for society as a whole.

5. The fact that two events may occur in proximity to each other does not necessarily mean that one is the cause of the other. Both might be caused by some third event.

6. People undertaking the study of economics often bring with them preconceived ideas of how the economy functions. Unfortunately some of these ideas are erroneous or only partly true and therefore should be discarded or unlearned.

7. Economic models or theories provide a framework for thinking and as such they are useful to explain past events and help to predict future events. The words "models," "theories," and "principles" all have about the same meaning.

8. In every society human wants far outstrip the goods and services that can be produced to satisfy these wants.

9. The production possibilities curve reflects the idea that the output of a nation is limited and an increase in the output of one good or service must result in a decrease in another good or service, provided the economy is operating on the surface of the curve.

10. If all resources are not fully employed or utilized in the most efficient manner, the output of a nation will be smaller than it need be. This is illustrated by a point below the surface of the production possibilities curve.

11. Demand is defined as an inverse relationship between price and quantity; people buy more of an item when its price is low, and vice versa.

12. Supply is defined as a positive relationship between price and quantity; producers supply more of an item when its price is high, and vice versa.

13. Equilibrium price occurs at the point where buyers are willing to buy the exact amount that sellers are willing to sell. This corresponds to the intersection of the demand and supply curves.

14. If price is higher than the equilibrium, the quantity supplied will be greater than the quantity demanded, resulting in a surplus and downward pressure on price. If price is lower than the equilibrium, the quantity supplied will be less than the quantity demanded, resulting in a shortage and upward pressure on price.

15. An increase in price can be the result of an increase in demand or a decrease in supply. An increase in demand occurs if buyers become willing to purchase a larger quantity at any given price. A decrease in supply occurs if sellers offer less on the market at any given price.

16. A decrease in price can be the result of a decrease in demand or an increase in supply. A decrease in demand occurs if buyers buy less of an item at any given price. An increase in supply occurs if sellers offer a greater quantity at any given price.

17. The quantities of the various goods and services produced in the private sector are determined by the forces of demand and supply. Changes in quantities also come about because of changes or shifts in demand and supply.

18. A shift in the demand for a good or service can occur as the result of changes in: (1) prices of related goods, (2) consumer incomes, (3) expectations of future prices and incomes, (4) tastes and preferences, and (5) number of consumers.

19. A shift in the supply of a good or service can occur as the result of changes in: (1) prices of resources, (2) prices of alternative goods or services that could be produced, (3) producer expectations of future prices, (4) technology, and (5) number of producers.

20. In contrast to the impersonal and largely "automatic" allocation of resources by demand and supply in the private sector, the allocation of resources in the public sector has to be car-

ried out by government officials, who in a democracy serve at the discretion of the electorate.

Questions for thought and discussion

1. Scan an edition of your daily newspaper and try to identify all the news stories that have some economic content.
2. Try to classify each of the news stories referred to above according to whether the economic content would be primarily macro or micro.
3. Try to classify the news stories in Question 1 according to whether they would be considered statements of a positive or normative nature.
4. Try to remember from your experience two events which happened within a very close time span but which were both caused by a third event or circumstance.
5. Would you classify yourself as a liberal or a conservative? On what basis?
6. List some of your currently held ideas or opinions in the area of macroeconomics. Where did you acquire these ideas? Are you convinced they're correct?
7. What are some economic realities or "facts of life" that can be illustrated by a production possibilities curve?
8. In recent years some people have been arguing that U.S. military expenditures are too high and that we should reallocate more resources to nonmilitary goods and services. Illustrate their proposal on a production possibilities curve.
9. Draw a demand-supply diagram and denote equilibrium price and quantity. Explain what happens if price happens to be above the equilibrium. Also explain what happens if price is below the equilibrium.
10. On four separate demand-supply diagrams illustrate an increase and a decrease in demand, and do the same for supply. Also denote what happens to equilibrium price and quantity in each case.
11. Briefly explain the economic meaning of the shifts in demand and supply illustrated in Question 10 above.

12. List the factors that could cause an increase in demand for beefsteak. What effect will these factors have on the price of beef? Illustrate with a demand-supply diagram.
13. List the factors that could cause a decrease in the supply of beef. What effect will these factors have on the price of beef? Illustrate with a demand-supply diagram.
14. In certain situations it is possible to observe an increase in both the market price and the quantity exchanged of an item. In other cases, it is possible to observe a decrease in price but an increase in quantity exchanged. Using demand-supply diagrams, explain how these situations could arise.

2

Unemployment and inflation

Unemployment defined

Although we all have a general idea of what unemployment is, it will be useful, nevertheless, to look a bit more closely at its meaning. Perhaps the best way to begin our discussion is to define what is meant by the absence of unemployment, i.e., full employment. Full employment is defined as a situation where everyone who is willing and able to work at the prevailing wage rate can find a job in the line of work for which he is qualified.

There are several points that are worth noting in this definition. First, full employment, or unemployment, as used in the context of macroeconomics generally refers to people rather than machines, buildings, land, or other forms of capital. As a rule society has not been as concerned with the unemployment of nonhuman inputs as with the unemployment of human beings. It is not difficult to understand why. Machines or buildings do not become hungry or cold if their income stops nor do they suffer from the psychological ills of being idle. Yet we should not dismiss the problem of unemployed capital entirely. For one thing, the employment of human beings is often tied to the employment of capital. This is illustrated by the problems brought on by the closing of a factory or mine, especially in a small or medium-sized community. We should also bear in mind that all capital is owned by human beings. Hence a reduction in the earnings of capital means a reduction in the earnings of the owners of capital. Thirdly, we should not lose sight of the fact that capital as well as labor contributes to the total output of society. Thus if some capital is unemployed, the total output that is available to society will be less than it need be.

A second point to note about the definition of full employment is that at full employment not every adult need be gainfully employed. For example, full-time college students, housewives who choose not to work outside the home, and most retired people would not be considered employed. Of course, this is not to say that these people are idle or "non-productive." It is just that they are not considered part of the labor force. Also there are a few people who have decided that work is too distasteful and have removed themselves from the labor force.

To be sure, it is an enormous task just to determine those who are included in the labor force as well as to determine those who are the unemployed. Figures on labor force participation and unemployment in the United States are gathered each month by the Bureau of Labor Statistics by means of a sample survey of about 50,000 households. Employed persons include all those who during the survey week did any work at all as paid employees, worked in their own business or profession, or worked 15 hours or more as an "unpaid" member of a family enterprise. Also included are those who did not work during the survey week but who had jobs from which they were temporarily absent.

The unemployed include those who had not worked during the survey week but had made specific efforts to find a job within the past four weeks (of the survey) and were available for work during the survey week. The total labor force, then, is defined as the employed plus the unemployed. During the latter part of 1972, the U.S. labor force consisted of about 82 million people, of which 4.8 million were considered unemployed.

The extent of the overall unemployment in the country at a given time generally is given by a percentage figure—the percent of the labor force that is unemployed. Of course, we should not lose sight of the fact that even a rather modest percentage figure implies a large absolute figure from the standpoint of people unemployed. For example, the 5.6 percent unemployment rate in 1972 meant that on the average over 4.8 million people were out of work at any given time during the year. Add to this figure the dependents of the unemployed and we gain an appreciation for the total number of lives affected.[1] Of course, as the labor force grows because of population growth or a higher labor force participation rate, a given unemployment rate represents a growing number of people who are unemployed. Also, when we are dealing with a labor force of over 80 million men and women, a 1 to 2 percent increase in the unemployment rate affects people numbering into the millions. For example, the increase in the unemployment rate from 3.5 percent in 1969 to 4.9 percent in 1970 resulted in an increase in the total number of unemployed from 2.8 million in 1969 to 4.1 million in 1970. The further increase in the 1971 unemployment rate to 5.9 percent resulted in a total of nearly 5 million people unemployed on the average during that year.

A third subtle but fairly important point in the definition of full employment relates to the willingness of people to take jobs that are available. For example, consider the case of a $200 per week construction worker who is laid off. If no other construction jobs are available in his area, he files for unemployment insurance and is considered unemployed.

The fact that he is unemployed, however, does not mean he is unemployable. There may be other comparable jobs available that he would be qualified for such as janitor, factory worker, etc., but which he chooses not to accept. Rather than work in a different occupation, he chooses to be unemployed.

This is not intended to be a criticism of the construction worker or anyone who decides on this line of action. For the individual it can be the most rational thing to do. If he expects to be back at work again in a week or two he may not wish to seek another job. Or if a person's unemployment compensation approaches the take-home pay of another lower paying job, there isn't much incentive to take such a job. Of course, if a person is unemployed for a prolonged period of time so that his unemployment payments run out, then he might be more willing to accept a comparable or even a less desirable job. The main point is that a certain amount of unemployment may refer to unemployment from a specific job or line of work rather than not being able to find any job at all.

---

[1] This is not to say that all unemployed persons are the principal breadwinners of families. Between 50 and 60 percent of the unemployed during 1972 were "secondary" family labor force participants, namely working wives and teenagers.

We should also be aware that some unemployed people probably would be willing to work at their previous jobs for a lower wage rather than being out of work altogether. For example, the construction worker may be willing to work for $175 or $150 per week rather than being forced to accept, say, $50 to $60 per week unemployment compensation or even a $150 per week alternative job.

Unfortunately for the unemployed, wage rates tend to be rather inflexible on the down side. If a choice is to be made between an across-the-board wage cut and a laying off of the most recently hired people, both employers and labor unions tend to favor the latter alternative. A reduction in wages affects all employees of a firm or industry and needless to say does not make them very happy. And both employers and labor unions are reluctant to antagonize the rank and file of the labor force. No firm with disgruntled employees can prosper nor can a labor union be a very effective bargaining agent if its members have the feeling of being "sold out."

The other alternative, laying off the youngest and least skilled workers, affects only a small part of the labor force. Once they have left, they no longer are disgruntled employees who can cause disruptions in production. Nor do these people have much power within labor unions; some are not even members.

The main point to remember here is that there is somewhat of a built-in incentive for both employers and labor unions to choose unemployment over lower wages. At least some unemployed people would probably choose to work at their old jobs at less than the prevailing wage rather than be unemployed, but they seldom have the opportunity to make this choice.

U.S. unemployment record

It will be useful to look briefly at the long-run record of unemployment in the United States. Looking at the past 44-year period, 1929 through 1972, we can observe a substantial amount of variation in the overall U.S. unemployment rate. As shown in Figure 2–1, 1929, with an unemployment rate of 3.2 percent, was a year of relatively full employment. Then came the crash. Just four years later, in 1933, the United States reached the depth of the Great Depression suffering from an astronomical unemployment rate of

FIGURE 2–1
U.S. unemployment rate, 1929–72

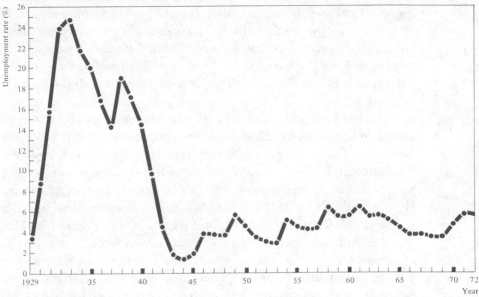

Source: *Economic Report of the President, 1970,* p. 202 and *1973*, p. 223.

24.9 percent. We will have much more to say about the Great Depression in later chapters.

The Great Depression was no overnight sensation, however. In fact it lasted all the way through the 1930s. In 1940, just before the U.S. entry into World War II, unemployment still was at a high 14.6 percent. Then at the height of World War II, 1944, unemployment fell to an almost unbelievable low of 1.2 percent. The drain of manpower into the military and the strong demand for labor undoubtedly contributed to this low figure.

The return to a peacetime economy was accompanied by a rise in unemployment, reaching 5.9 percent in 1949. During the Korean conflict the rate again declined, reaching a low of 2.9 percent in 1953. Toward the end of the 1950s, the country found itself in the "1958 recession" with an unemployment rate of 6.8 percent.[2] Un-

---

2 The question is sometimes asked, what is the difference between a recession and a depression? It has been said that it is a recession when your neighbor is out of work and a depression when you yourself are out of work; i.e., a depression is worse than a recession.

employment tended to drift downward during the 1960s, particularly during the Vietnam buildup toward the latter part of the decade. However, coinciding with the U.S. troop withdrawals from Vietnam and the Nixon administration attempts to reduce inflation, the U.S. unemployment rate exhibited a sharp upswing during the early 1970s, rising to 4.9 percent in 1970 and peaking (hopefully) at 5.9 percent in 1971. The 1972 rate declined slightly, to 5.6 percent.

It is fairly evident from these figures that war and low rates of unemployment tend to be positively correlated. During this 44-year period the United States was involved in World War II, Korea, and Vietnam. In all three cases the onset of hostilities was followed by a decrease in unemployment while the return to a peacetime situation, both after World War II and Korea, was accompanied by a rise in unemployment. In the case of Vietnam, the reduction in U.S. involvement coincided with a rise in unemployment.

Is war, therefore a necessary condition for full employment? We will be better able to answer this question in later chapters. For now, about all we can say is that government policies during wars no doubt were conducive to full employment. But we should not conclude that it is necessary to have war in order to implement policies that promote full employment. We shall return to this subject in later chapters.

Frictional unemployment

From our discussion thus far it might appear that any unemployment at all is undesirable and that we should not be satisfied until we attain a goal of zero unemployment. Would such a goal be reasonable, or even desirable? Probably not. We should bear in mind that the economy is continually changing and adapting to new opportunities. Very few business activities continue to remain unchanged month after month, much less year after year. As a result we may observe a temporary loss of work for certain employees because of short-term fluctuations in business activity, changes in employment opportunities, or a voluntary termination of work because of a desire to change jobs. Economists sometimes refer to the loss of work in these situations as "frictional" unemployment.

We know that many occupations experience busy and slack seasons during the year. Construction work, for example, typically has experienced a seasonal decline during the winter season. People who work in this industry expect temporary layoffs, and their salary during the busy season generally compensates them for this. Another example occurs in the auto industry, where a company may lay off part of its labor force for a week or two in order to bring its inventory back to a desired level.

It is a common occurrence as well in a dynamic, growing economy for employment opportunities to change. Because of changes in consumer demand, some firms or industries tend to decline and fade away only to be replaced by others. Workers who find themselves in declining industries or firms must relocate to other growing industries. Even though there may be other comparable jobs available, most people prefer to take some time to search out the best.

Related to this is the frictional unemployment brought about by employees who quit their jobs in order to search out more desirable ones. In many cases people cannot take time off to interview, etc., while holding down a full-time job. Anyone who has gone through the job searching process knows that it can be very time consuming. Sometimes a new job requires travel, buying and selling a house, or finding a different apartment. Probably most people who quit a job for one reason or another are reasonably certain of finding another. And in most cases they succeed within a few weeks or a month. Their earnings may have been temporarily interrupted, but in the long run they are able to make up the loss in their new and better jobs.

The amount of frictional unemployment that might normally be expected to prevail is not a universally agreed upon figure. During the early 1970s in the United States, the most frequently quoted figure tended to be in the range of 3 to 4 percent unemployment. Because of the persistent unemployment rate in the 5 percent range in 1971 and 1972, some economists have suggested that the normal amount of frictional unemployment for this time might well be above a 4 percent unemployment rate. Indeed it might be expected that the amount of frictional unemployment would vary according to business conditions. If the economy is sluggish and jobs are hard to find, we would expect the time it takes a person to relocate in a new job after being laid off from a declining business or voluntarily leaving a former job to be longer than when the economy is booming and the labor market is tight. For example, during World War II, the U.S. unemployment rate dipped to between 1 and 2 percent.

At any rate, the main point to be drawn from this section is that a small fraction of the labor force, normally around 3 to 4 percent, can be expected to be temporarily out of work because of movement between jobs. For purposes of economic policy, the economy can be considered at or near full employment if experiencing unemployment at this order of magnitude. Our main interest in the discussion relating to unemployment in this chapter will be with situations where the total economy experiences a slowdown in economic activity and the overall unemployment rate rises above the 3 to 4 percent range.

Duration of unemployment

So far we have been concerned mainly with the total amount of unemployment in the economy. But we should also consider how long the unemployed are out of work. It is one thing to be out of work for a week or two but quite another to lose one's main income for several months. The first case might result in a strained budget, but the second could mean the loss of home or car, or even hunger for the family. Thus we should be concerned about the duration of the unemployment existing at any point in time as well as about the total number of people unemployed.

In Table 2–1, we present the average duration of those unemployed during 1969 and 1971. We chose these years for comparison because 1969 was a year of relatively low unemployment, 3.5 percent, whereas 1971 was one of fairly high unemployment, 5.9 percent. Notice first that even in 1969, when the unemployment was within the "acceptable" range, 133,000 people had been unemployed for 27 weeks or longer. On the brighter side, we should point out that the bulk of the unemployed during 1969, 57 percent, had been out of work five weeks or less.

Looking at the figures for 1971 we see that as the overall rate of unemployment increases, there is a tendency also for the duration

TABLE 2–1
Duration of unemployment, 1969 and 1971

Duration of unemployment	1969		1971	
	Number of people (1,000)	*Percent of unemployed*	*Number of people (1,000)*	*Percent of unemployed*
Total	2,831	100	4,993	100
Less than 5 weeks	1,629	57	2,234	45
5–14 weeks	829	29	1,578	32
15–26 weeks	242	9	665	13
27 weeks or over	133	5	517	10

Source: *Economic Report of the President, 1972*, p. 224.

of the unemployment to increase. Notice that for 1971 the five weeks or less category is less than the 1969 figure, but that the remaining three categories, especially the last two, are substantially higher. We might expect this to be the case, since the more depressed the state of economic activity the more difficult it is for people to find suitable jobs to replace the ones lost.

We should bear in mind too that it is likely that even at fairly low levels of unemployment, such as 2 to 2.5 percent, some people will have been out of work for long periods of time. These might include people from depressed areas or those with few skills to offer in the job market. Unfortunately, it is not likely that government policies or programs to stimulate the entire economy can do much for these people. Instead, programs are needed to improve employment opportunities in specific geographic areas or to help people relocate to areas where jobs are available. Many of the long-term unemployed lack the skills demanded in the job market. Job training programs to increase marketable skills can be of some help to these people.

Disguised unemployment

We should also be aware that employment figures may disguise a certain amount of unemployment. Consider the case of an aeronautical engineer who is laid off and accepts employment as a parking lot attendant, which for the sake of argument is his best alternative at least for the immediate time. Although he is no longer unemployed, his income and his contribution to society's output is considerably less than it might otherwise be. When people have no choice but to work in jobs that do not fully utilize their capabilities, they are in part unemployed, or underemployed as economists might say. Thus a reduction in unemployment accomplished by the taking of less desirable jobs may in fact overstate the true reduction that takes place.

The manner in which unemployment statistics are collected also may result in a downward bias to the true unemployment figure. Recall that for a person to be unemployed, he must have made specific efforts to find employment in the past four weeks. For a person who has been out of work for months and has been turned down repeatedly in his quest for work there will likely come a time when he gives up looking, at least until some concrete opportunity presents itself. A person who has given up trying to find a job would according to the unemployment survey not be included in the labor force and hence would not be considered unemployed. However, he still would not be working. This kind of situation probably would be most prevalent among minority groups and among those with the fewest skills, i.e., the poor.

Who are the unemployed?

Although average unemployment figures such as 4 or 5 percent are useful in providing an indication of the seriousness of the unemployment problem, they do not tell us anything about the differences in employment among individuals or groups in society. As you might expect, not all employees face an equal chance of being laid off or finding a new job.

As shown in Table 2–2, unemployment is more prevalent among the young, among minority groups, and among the least skilled. Note that in 1969 when the overall unemployment rate in the United States averaged 3.5 percent of the labor force, young people between the ages of 16 and 19 experienced an unemployment rate of 12.2 percent. Part of this group came from high school dropouts and part from the 1969 high school graduates who were not able to find a job after graduation.

Notice also that in 1969 women had a somewhat higher unem-

TABLE 2–2
Unemployment rates by groups, 1969 and 1971 (percent)

	1969	1971
All workers	3.5	5.9
Both sexes, 16 to 19 years	12.2	16.9
Men 20 years and over	2.1	4.4
Women 20 years and over	3.7	5.7
White	3.1	5.4
Negro and other minority groups	6.4	9.9
Experienced wage and salary workers	3.3	5.7
Married men	1.5	3.2
Full-time workers	3.1	5.5
Blue-collar workers	3.9	7.4

Source: *Economic Report of the President, 1972*, p. 223.

ployment rate than men. We see too that blacks and other minority groups tend to have about twice the unemployment rate of white workers. We do not know how much of this increased unemployment is due to discrimination and how much is due to a lower level of education and skills among minority groups.

In general, the more skills a person has the less chance he has of being laid off. We would expect employers to be reluctant to lay off a person who cannot be easily replaced. The employer who lays off a skilled person runs the risk of not getting him back when business conditions improve. If he doesn't come back, then the firm must run the expense of finding a suitable replacement and retraining or breaking him in. For this reason firms may actually choose to lose money on a skilled person for a few months rather than lay him off. The unskilled person, however, is more easily replaced, so there is a greater tendency on the part of employers to let him go as soon as he is not producing the value of his wage.

It is interesting to observe the relatively low level of unemployment among married men as opposed to other groups. Part of the explanation, no doubt, is the longer seniority on the job, since married men as a group are older than single men. In addition, married men with families to support are likely to look harder for another job when laid off and also be more willing to accept other less desirable employment on a temporary basis.

Perhaps most noticeable is the exceedingly high unemployment rate of teenagers, more than triple the overall average rate in 1969. A large proportion of this group consists of current-year high school graduates and dropouts looking for their first full-time jobs. No doubt it also includes many former college students who have become disenchanted with the classroom. The reasons for the abnormally high unemployment rate of teenagers still are not fully understood. Many of these people may be reluctant to accept a job that is not up to their expectations. There is reason to believe also that minimum wage laws are at least partly to blame for this problem by fixing the hourly wage of new, inexperienced employees higher than their contributions to output. Hence, employers have little incentive to hire these people.[3]

As the overall unemployment rate increases, all groups tend to experience increased jobless rates, as shown for 1971. The greatest proportionate increase in the unemployment rate appears to occur in the groups with the lowest absolute rate of unemployment. For example, the unemployment rate for married men more than doubled between 1969 and 1971. Full-time workers and blue-collar workers also experienced above-average increases in jobless rates. Perhaps with more widespread unemployment, layoffs affect people with longer seniority. Also, there is less chance of finding a temporary job at lower pay.

Costs of unemployment

From the standpoint of the individual, the economic cost of unemployment is, of course, the loss or reduction in income from being out of work. Granted, a large share of U.S. workers now are eligible for unemployment compensation, which eases the problem somewhat. However, during 1972 the average weekly unemployment check was $57. For a family accustomed to a $150 or $175 per week check, this reduction in income comes as a severe shock to the family budget.

We must leave to the psychologists and sociologists the identification and measure of the mental and social problems that result from unemployment. In spite of how much we dislike trudging off to work or school on Monday mornings, most people find a life of

---

[3] See the Labor Market chapter of the micro text for further discussion of this problem.

idleness even more distasteful, especially when they have little or no income to buy recreation. Living off the "dole" may keep one alive, but it doesn't lead to a very enjoyable or interesting life.

It is necessary as well to look at the economic costs of unemployment from the standpoint of the total economy or society. Unemployment means that the economy is producing a smaller amount of real output of goods and services than it could otherwise enjoy. For this reason, nearly everyone loses from unemployment, because there is a smaller output to be distributed among the members of society. The President's Council of Economic Advisors has estimated that a 5 percent unemployment rate reduces the annual output of goods and services by almost $50 billion from what it would be if unemployment were 3.8 percent. Dividing this $50 billion loss by 209 million people, the approximate U.S. population, we obtain a per capita loss in real output of about $240 per year.

Payment of unemployment compensation to the unemployed, of course, does not reduce the loss in total output. However, it is a method of redistributing the claims to society's output. Essentially, society by introducing unemployment compensation is saying that employed people are willing to give up a part of their claims on the output of the economy and share it with their less fortunate neighbors who are out of work.

Measures of inflation

Inflation, the second major problem area of macroeconomics, is defined as a sustained rise in the general price level. The most commonly used measure of prices in the United States is the Consumer Price Index (CPI). This index is constructed by the U.S. Department of Labor, Bureau of Labor Statistics, and is intended to reflect the prices of goods and services purchased by consumers.

We will not go into a detailed study of the CPI or its construction; these topics are covered in more depth in intermediate statistics courses. However, in order to better understand the meaning of the CPI and its uses, it will be helpful if we construct one from a very simple example. Let us consider just three items: a loaf of bread, a jug of wine, and a theater ticket—the cost of eating, drinking, and being merry.

What we want to do is construct a number that will tell us how much, if at all, the prices of these items have changed over a period of time. Essentially we will represent three prices by just one number. The official CPI, of course, represents the prices of thousands of items with just one number, but the technique of construction is still the same. Assume that the time period we are interested in is from 1960 to 1972. Let 1960 be the so-called base year, the year we use for comparison. The average prices of the three items for 1960 and 1972 are shown below:

Item	1960 price	1972 price	1960 quantity
Loaf of bread	$0.25	$0.30	50
Jug of wine	1.75	2.25	10
Theater ticket	1.85	3.00	20

The next thing we must determine is quantity of each item that is consumed. If we just add raw prices, then the theater ticket, for example, carries 10 times as much weight as the loaf of bread in 1972. This could be misleading if the person did not go to the theater very often. Therefore, in constructing a price index, we have to assign a quantity to each item so that it reflects its importance in the budget.

The Department of Labor CPI uses base-year quantities; let us do the same. Some plausible quantities of these items that might be consumed by an average person during 1960 are shown in the right-hand column of the above table.

The next step is to multiply price times quantity of each item for each year. The results are shown below:

Item	1960: $P \times Q$	1972: $P \times Q$
Bread	$12.50	$15.00
Wine	17.50	22.50
Tickets	37.00	60.00
Total	$67.00	$97.50

These figures tell us that the same bundle of goods and services that cost $67 in 1960 sells for $97.50 in 1972. We can represent this change as an index by dividing the 1972 cost by the 1960 cost and multiplying by 100. We obtain:

$$1972 \text{ index} = \frac{97.50}{67.00} \times 100 = 146$$

The 1972 index of 146 tells us that the price of this bundle of goods and services increased 46 percent from 1960 to 1972. Thus the price index allows us to combine the movement of many prices into a single number.

The general formula for constructing this index is as follows:

$$I_p = \frac{\Sigma_i \, Q_{0i} \, P_{1i}}{\Sigma_i \, Q_{0i} \, P_{0i}}$$

where Q_{0i} and P_{0i} represent base-year quantity and price of the ith good or service, and P_{1i} represents the current-year price of the ith good or service. The Σ_i instructs us to sum all the $P \times Q$'s as we did above. This formula is essentially the one used by the Department of Labor to construct the CPI for each year. The formula is sometimes known as the Laspeyres formula, after the man who popularized it.

When using the CPI to measure the change in the general level of prices, we should be aware of some possible biases that tend to creep in. Perhaps most important is the bias caused by improvements in quality of goods and services over time. In constructing the CPI, the Department of Labor attempts to hold quality as constant as possible. For example, in comparing automobile prices, it chooses prices of comparably equipped cars. It would not be meaningful to take the price of a car with a standard transmission in 1960 and compare it with the price of one with an automatic transmission in 1972, for example.

However, there are certain quality changes that are difficult to hold constant. The 1972 engine may run 100,000 miles while the 1960 engine may only stand up for 75,000 miles before a major overhaul. This type of quality change cannot easily be taken account of. Because most durable goods have undergone some quality improvements over the years, many of which are difficult to measure, the CPI probably overstates the true rise in prices that can be attributed purely to inflation. In other words, part of any price rise might be attributed to better quality and part to pure inflation.

Another bias can stem from a change in the relative prices of items purchased. Notice in the above example that the price of theater tickets increased relatively more than the price of bread or wine. When the price of a good or service rises more than other prices, there is a tendency on the part of consumers to economize on the higher priced items, substituting more of the cheaper items for it. In our example, the consumer may substitute wine in place of attending the theater.

But in our construction of the 1972 price index we assumed that the consumer bought the same relative amounts of the items in 1972 as he did in 1960. If in fact the consumer had bought fewer theater tickets and more wine, as we might reasonably expect him to do, then the 1972 cost, $97.50 in our example, will overstate the true cost of the bundle of goods that the consumer actually bought. This second bias, often called the "old index number problem" by statisticians and economists, also tends to make the CPI overstate the "true" rise in prices.

A second commonly used index to measure the change in the general price level is the Wholesale Price Index (WPI). This index, also constructed by the Department of Labor, is the same type of index as the CPI except that it reflects prices at the wholesale level of both consumer goods and industrial products. Also the WPI excludes prices of personal services. Because prices of services have risen faster than prices of goods in recent years, the WPI has not risen quite as much as the CPI.

U.S. inflation record

Although we are all aware that prices have been rising in recent years, it will be useful in later chapters to have a general idea of the extent of U.S. inflation and the periods in recent history in which inflation has been most prevalent. In Figure 2–2 we present the United States CPI for the period 1929 to 1972. In this case 1967 is used as the base year, i.e., the CPI for this year equals 100.

A quick glance at Figure 2–2 reveals a long-run upward trend in prices over the past 40 years. During the early to middle 1930s the CPI fluctuated in the range of 38 to 42 (1967 = 100). In 1972 it registered 125.3. Thus prices have more than tripled over the past four decades.

Looking first at the 1930s, we observe a pronounced decline in the CPI during the early years of the decade. Between 1929 and

FIGURE 2–2
U.S. Consumer Price Index, 1929–72 (1967 = 100)

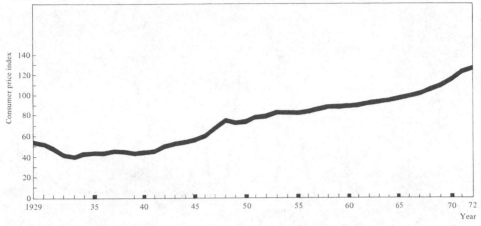

Source: *Economic Report of the President, 1970*, p. 229, and *1973*, p. 244.

1933, prices fell about 24 percent; it is difficult for us who have grown used to inflation to envison such a drastic decline in prices. As you would expect, the severe decline in the general price level is closely related to the large unemployment during that time. We will study this relationship more thoroughly in later chapters.

Although the CPI increased somewhat during World War II, its greatest rise came during the immediate postwar years. (We will consider the reason for this a little later.) Indeed, during the four-year period 1945–48 the price level increased over 33 percent. After a period of relative price stability during the 1950s and early 1960s, the CPI began to climb noticeably again during the late 1960s and early 1970s. Although prices continued to increase throughout 1971 and 1972, the rate of increase of prices was somewhat less during these two years than during the preceding two years.

In the study of inflation it is important also to know the *rate* at which prices are changing. For example, even though prices increased during 1971 and 1972, it is noteworthy that the rate of increase had declined from the previous two years. This tells us that some headway was made in the fight against inflation during these years. To facilitate the study of changes in the rate of inflation, it is helpful to look at the year-to-year percentage changes in the CPI as shown by Figure 2–3. Zero on the vertical axis indicates no

FIGURE 2–3
Annual percentage change in U.S. Consumer Price Index, 1929–72

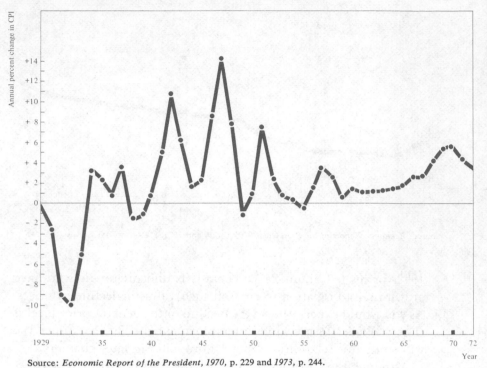

Source: *Economic Report of the President, 1970,* p. 229 and *1973,* p. 244.

change in the CPI during a given year, whereas the plus and minus values represent price increases and decreases, respectively.

Now it is a bit easier to see the fluctuations that have taken place in the rate of inflation (or deflation) over the past four decades. The sharp decline in prices during the Great Depression is reflected in the negative values of the graph at the beginning of the period. The two peaks of the graph correspond to the beginning and end of World War II.

One may question why the rate of inflation declined to a modest 2 to 3 percent during the height of World War II. The dip in the *measured* rate of inflation was caused by the imposition of rigid price controls during that time. The resumption of inflation after the war, over 14 percent in 1947, reflects the lifting of price controls and the return to free market prices. We should not conclude, however, that price controls prevent inflation. About all we can say is that price controls can prevent, at least temporarily, a rise in the measured price index. But the underlying causes of inflation and the accompanying pressure for prices to rise are likely to remain. If the pressure for price increases continues to build, black market prices become more prevalent, and sooner or later the controlled or "legal" prices have little meaning as buyers find it necessary to pay black market prices in order to obtain what they want. As a result price controls have a tendency to eventually break down. We will present a more thorough explanation of this phenomenon in Chapter 9.

Moving on into the post–World War II period we observe considerably more price stability than was experienced during the 1930s and 1940s. With the exception of the near 8 percent rise in prices during 1951, the height of the Korean conflict, inflation crept along at about a 1 to 3 percent rate during the 1950s and early 1960s. But as the country became more deeply involved in Vietnam, inflation began to gallop—or at least trot—once again.

It is fairly evident, then, that war and inflation go hand in hand. We should not conclude from this relationship, however, that war per se is a cause of inflation. We will see in later chapters that war necessitates certain government policies that result in inflation. These same policies, if carried out during peacetime, will then also result in inflation.

Several of the South American countries provide good examples of peacetime inflation. For example, during 1972, Argentina experienced a 78 percent rise in the general price level. Indeed, during January of 1972 alone the Argentine price level increased about 12 percent.[4] Although the 5 to 6 percent *annual* inflation rate during 1969 and 1970 in the United States may have seemed high to us, our South American neighbors would have considered this virtual price stability.

Demand-pull versus cost-push inflation

Although we cannot at this point present a rigorous explanation for inflation, we can present a somewhat intuitive idea of its causes.

---

[4] As a resident of Argentina during this time, it was interesting to observe that many grocery store items were marked up in price two or three times from the time they were stocked to the time they were sold.

Economists and the news media have often referred to price increases as demand-pull or cost-push inflation. Evidently these phrases are intended to explain why inflation takes place.

Demand-pull inflation is said to take place if demanders or buyers of goods and services wish to purchase a greater quantity than the economy can produce. Traditionally, demanders have been divided into three groups: consumers, investors, and the government. If the composite demand of these three groups or sectors increases more than the supply of goods and services, then prices begin to rise.

The federal government is unique among these three groups because it has the power to regulate the quantity of money in the economy. At times, particularly during wars, governments have financed a part of their increased expenditure by newly created money. Although we will study the impact of changes in the quantity of money in more detail in later chapters, at this point it will be useful to present at least an intuitive explanation of its importance.

Let us consider as a very simple example an economy that produces only 1,000 bushels of wheat per year. Let us assume also that this economy has 1,000 pieces of paper in existence that it calls money. Also suppose that each piece of paper, call it a dollar if you wish, is spent once each year for a bushel of wheat. In this particular case, each bushel of wheat is exchanged for one piece of paper. In other words, the price of a bushel of wheat is one dollar.

Now suppose we double the number of pieces of paper called money to 2,000. Again, if each piece of paper is exchanged once a year for wheat and there is no change in the quantity of wheat produced, each bushel of wheat now will be exchanged for two pieces of paper. In other words, the price of wheat now increases to two dollars. This must be true if all of the money is spent for wheat and all the money changes hands (from buyer to seller) just once during the year. The relationship between prices and the quantity of money in this example is summarized below:

Quantity of money	Quantity of wheat	Price of wheat
$1,000	1,000	$1
2,000	1,000	2

We will present a more sophisticated explanation of the effect of the quantity of money on prices in later chapters but we will see then that the same general principle holds true. For a given level of output, the larger the quantity of money (other things being equal), the higher the level of prices. Price, after all, is just a measure of how many pieces of paper (or coins) are to be exchanged for a unit of real output.

Cost-push inflation, on the other hand, is said to occur as labor unions and big business demand and obtain successive increases in wages and prices. The process of wage-price hikes allegedly can begin either with labor or business. For example, suppose labor unions demand and obtain a wage increase. Businessmen then point out that costs have gone up so they are forced in turn to increase their prices. Labor unions then point out that the cost of living has gone up so they in turn ask for another wage increase. And so the wage-price spiral goes up and up, with each party accusing the other of causing inflation.

The importance, indeed even the existence, of such a thing as cost-push inflation has been a matter of some controversy among economists. Many economists argue that there is no such thing as cost-push inflation, at least in the sense of an underlying cause of inflation. They argue that in raising prices or wages business firms and labor unions are reacting to events outside their control. For example, during inflation business firms will point out that they have little choice but to ask for higher prices on the items they sell because the prices (costs) of the inputs they must purchase to carry on business have increased. Firms which did not raise prices of their products would soon begin to suffer losses and eventually go out of business. Labor leaders voice a similar argument. They point out that the prices of things that workers buy (housing, food, clothing, etc.) are rising, hence they must ask for higher wages just to maintain their former standard of living. Since neither the business firm nor the union member has much if any control over the prices each must pay (if they could control these prices they would want to pay less not more) it is argued that neither should be blamed for inflation.

Economists who argue this line instead place the major responsibility for inflation on the shoulders of government. They point out that down through history all the major inflations in the world have coincided with large increases in the quantity of money in circulation. And national governments, at least in modern times, have the power to control the quantity of money in circulation. Indeed the issuance and control of the monetary standard is one of the more important functions of every national government. We will discuss this topic much more fully in Chapters 6 and 9.

The economic effects of inflation

We stated that the two main problems we will be concerned with in this book are unemployment and inflation. It is not difficult to see why unemployment is a problem; people out of work suffer a loss in income and society suffers a loss in real output. But why should we be concerned with an increase in the general level of prices? Is the price level of the 1930s any more desirable than the price level of the 1970s?

Inflation constitutes a problem mainly because the rate of inflation cannot be predicted with certainty and consequently its economic effects cannot be fully anticipated by the general public. As a result some people are penalized and some are rewarded, usually in a very arbitrary manner. If everyone knew what the rate of inflation was going to be in the future, no one need suffer unexpected losses or reap windfall gains. Let us briefly consider how inflation gives rise to economic gains and losses.

One important effect of inflation is that it reduces the real value of assets that do not increase in money value with the general price level. Money (cash or checking account money) probably is the most important asset in this category. If one holds cash, say $100, during a period when the price level increases, the purchasing power of this money declines. For example, if the price level should double, as it did between 1945 and 1972, the $100 would buy only half of the quantity of goods and services at the end of the period that it would in the beginning. Thus inflation "eats up" the purchasing power of money. It is as if someone had taken $50 from you under a stable price level. Indeed, inflation amounts to a tax on the holders of cash balances.

Other assets that retain a fixed money value during inflation include bonds, such as government savings bonds, and life insurance policies. During inflation these assets are purchased with dollars of relatively high purchasing power but return dollars of relatively low real value when they mature. Institutions or firms that issue these securities gain during an unexpected inflation at the expense of those who hold these assets during the time prices rise.

Inflation also penalizes people whose wages do not increase as fast as the general price level. For example, long-term union contracts negotiated before an unexpected spurt of inflation may hold wages down so that workers actually suffer a reduction in real wages (a reduction in purchasing power) during the latter stage of the contract. As a result, unions sometimes insist on a "cost of living" clause in their contracts which provides for an increase in wages in proportion to any increase in the price level.

Retired people living on pensions of fixed monetary value tend to be penalized by inflation because of the long time period between the date the money is earned and the date it is spent. People who are reaching retirement age today began their working lives 40 to 45 years ago, in the 1920s and early 1930s. In those days a pension of $80 to $100 per month looked quite good. During the intervening 40 years these people contributed money of relatively high purchasing power to pension funds in anticipation of living on this level of money income when they retired. But, as you are well aware, a $100 per month income today hardly provides a comfortable standard of living. Indeed, property taxes on one's dwelling may require almost this amount alone, especially if one has "prudently" invested a large share of his income in a house. At any rate, contributors into pension funds suffer losses, while those who invested these funds in real assets enjoy windfall gains from unexpected inflation.

Inflation also has an important impact on the borrowing and lending of money. A simple example will illustrate this point. Suppose you lend someone $100 to be paid back one year from now. Also suppose that during the year prices increase by 6 percent. The $100 in cash that you are paid back after the year is up will buy only $94 worth of goods and services at the inflated prices. In other words, the borrower obtains from you dollars with relatively high purchasing power but pays you back in "cheap" dollars. He gains, you lose.

Now, of course, you would receive some interest from the borrower. Suppose it is 6 percent. Thus you might be paid back $106 for the $100 loan. But with the price rise, the $106 is equivalent in purchasing power to the original $100 you lent. Taking into account the interest payment, we see that you obtain the same amount of purchasing power at the end of the year as your money was worth at the beginning of the year. In other words, the borrower was able to use your money free of charge.

If prices had in fact risen 10 percent, it would take $110 to buy what the $100 would have bought before you lent it. If you still received $106, the repayment would be worth $4 less than the amount you lent. As a result, borrowers tend to benefit from unexpected inflation while lenders generally suffer losses or realize gains much lower than anticipated. We will come back to this point in the following section, where we discuss the money rate and the real rate of interest.

Throughout our discussion of the effects of inflation, it has become evident that inflation takes wealth away from some and provides others with windfall gains, mainly because it was not anticipated—something like a thief in the night. If everyone could know for certain what the rate of inflation would be in the future, much could be done to alleviate its undesirable effects.

For one thing, an expected high rate of inflation would lead people to reduce their holdings of cash in order to reduce the "tax" on this asset. (We will discuss this topic more fully in Chapter 5.) Other assets, such as bonds and life insurance policies, could incorporate cost of living clauses, or their purchase prices could be lowered to reflect their lowered real value at maturity. People could invest more heavily in assets that normally increase in money value with the general price level, such as stocks, real estate, and precious stones, which could be converted into cash when needed. Pension plans and wages could be tied to the price level to avoid the losses mentioned in this regard. Lenders could charge a higher rate of interest to compensate for the loss in purchasing power of their money.

Of course, inflation cannot be predicted with certainty. As a result, inflation is likely to continue to take income and wealth away from certain people in a very arbitrary manner, while rewarding others in a similar fashion. Society would prefer an economy where prices remain relatively stable to one where inflation is present, especially a "stop and go" kind of inflation. Part of our task in the chapters to follow is to find out how inflation can be avoided.

The money rate versus the real rate of interest

The only way lenders can protect themselves in times of inflation is to charge a higher rate of interest. Of course borrowers also are willing to pay a higher rate of interest if they believe the item purchased with the loan will go up in value with the general price level. In borrowing or lending money; it is important to consider the "real" rate of interest. The real rate is equal to the money rate minus the percentage change in the general price level. Expressing this relationship in terms of a simple formula, we obtain:

$$r = i - \%\Delta P$$

where r is the real rate, i is the money rate, and $\%\Delta P$ is the annual percentage change in the general price level.

Because no one is able to predict with certainty future changes in the general price level, the real rate of interest may turn out to be different than the expected real rate. In fact, the real rate may turn out to be zero or negative. For example, if you expected a 4 percent increase in prices when lending money at a 6 percent money rate of interest, you would expect a 2 percent real rate. But if in fact prices went up 6 percent during the year, the real rate would turn out to be zero. Or if prices increased by 8 percent, the real rate of interest on the loan would be a minus 2 percent, indicating that the purchasing power of your money was less after you lent it than before. Of course if you had not made the loan and kept your money in the form of cash, it would have depreciated even more.

As yet we know relatively little about how people form expectations. In part they reflect recent experience. For example, if prices have been rising 6 percent per year for the past several years, most people would expect prices to continue rising in the coming year. However, expectations also reflect current action. For example, if the government is taking action to slow down inflation, people also take this into account and may expect only a 4 or 5 percent rate of inflation in the coming year. No one knows the real rate until the year is past.

Generally it takes time for people to reformulate their expectations. For this reason the money rate of interest tends to lag behind changes in the general price level. When prices are falling the real rate tends to be high, whereas in the early phases of inflation the real rate tends to be relatively low or even negative before it catches up. This is illustrated in Table 2–3.

TABLE 2–3
Money rates and real rates of interest in the United States, selected years

Year	Money rate*	Change in price level	Real rate
1929	5.85%	− 0.2%	+ 6.0%
1932	2.73	−10.2	+12.9
1942	0.66	10.7	−10.0
1947	1.03	14.4	−13.4
1959	3.97	0.8	+ 3.2
1969	7.83	5.4	+ 2.4
1972	4.69	3.3	+ 1.4

* Interest rate on prime commercial paper, four to six months duration.
Source: *Economic Report of the President, 1973*, p. 260.

In the early years of the Great Depression the money rate fell, but not fast enough to account for all of the decline in prices. (Note from the formula that a decrease in prices must be added to the money rate to obtain the real rate.) Thus the real rate of interest increased from 1929 to 1933 even though the money rate decreased. In part, at least, this might explain why businessmen were so reluctant to borrow and invest during this period.

During the World War II era prices began to rise. The money rate of interest also began to rise, but again the change was not enough to compensate for the change in prices. Hence the real rate on low-risk, four- to six-month prime commercial loans actually became negative. It was a splendid time for businessmen to borrow and invest.

The late 1960s became known as a time of high interest rates, but this was true only from the standpoint of the money rate of interest. The 7.83 percent in 1969 on prime commercial loans was the highest of the 40-year period. But the real rate during 1969 was only 2.4

percent. Again, this presented a fairly good opportunity for people to borrow and invest.

It is somewhat ironic, then, that during 1932 when the government wanted the business community to invest, there was little incentive to do so because of the high real rate of interest. Then in 1969 when the government wanted to discourage new investment in order to dampen inflationary pressure, the real rate of interest was relatively low, thus encouraging investment. A consideration of the real rate of interest helps explain why businessmen and consumers sometimes act contrary to the way the government would like them to act.

During times of extreme inflation the money rate of interest can reach legal upper limits for certain types of loans because of usury laws. If the inflation rate then continues to increase, the inevitable result is a continued decline in the real rate of interest. And as the real rate declines, there is an increased incentive for people to borrow and buy even more, which in turn adds more fuel to the fires of inflation.

If the money rate of interest reaches an upper legal limit, then the interest rate no longer can serve as a rationing and allocating device for loanable funds. When the demand for loanable funds becomes greater than the supply, lenders must resort to other means of rationing the available funds. They might lend, for example, on the basis of friendship, first-come first-served, or some other criteria.

During these times the people most likely to obtain loans are the very large commercial and institutional borrowers. Because of lower lending costs on larger loans, lenders often prefer to do business with a few large borrowers rather than many small accounts. Thus the people who suffer the most from usury laws during times of extreme inflation tend to be small borrowers such as small farmers, small businessmen, or prospective home buyers who are unable to obtain loans.

If the rate of inflation far outstrips the legal money rate of interest, so that the real rate becomes negative, there is a strong incentive to "pay under the table," i.e., bribe, to obtain loans. Indeed such practice is not uncommon in some developing nations where high rates of inflation prevail. Again the loans go out to large, wealthy borrowers who may be relatives of the bankers or know them on a personal basis. Borrowing money at a negative real rate of interest is a relatively easy way to get rich or richer. Of course, in order to have prolonged periods of negative real rates, the rate of inflation probably will have to be large or growing, while money rates of interest are held down by usury laws.

The unemployment-inflation dilemma

You might have noticed in our discussion of the U.S. unemployment and inflation record that when the rate of inflation declined, the rate of unemployment increased. Conversely when unemployment decreased, the rate of inflation increased. The 1930s saw falling prices but high rates of unemployment. Except for the last two years of the decade, the 1940s brought full employment but a high rate of inflation. In the 1950s and 1960s, if inflation leveled off, unemployment seemed to increase. This phenomenon was especially noticeable during the early 1970s. As the rate of inflation in the United States declined from 5.9 percent in 1970 to 4.3 percent in 1971, the average annual unemployment rate increased from 4.9 percent in 1970 to 5.9 percent in 1971.

The conventional explanation for this phenomenon utilizes what might be called the "bottleneck theory." As full employment of labor is approached, shortages occur for certain types of labor or other resources, causing prices (and wages) to increase in their respective markets. It is, of course, reasonable to believe that the economy does not run out of all its resources at the same time. As the economy approaches capacity, or full employment, those resources that are most scarce will exhibit price increases and as a result will contribute to an overall increase in the price level.

In recent years economists have focused considerable attention on the apparent unemployment-inflation dilemma. The basic question is whether or not the two goals of full employment and reasonably stable prices are in fact compatible.

The Phillips curve

The relationship between price level changes and the rate of unemployment is commonly associated with the work of A. W. Phillips, an English economist, although Phillips' work dealt mainly with the relationship between unemployment and the rate of change of money wage rates.[5] Professor Phillips hypothesized that when the demand for labor is high and relatively few people are unemployed, employers will bid wage rates up quite rapidly in an attempt to hire more workers. On the other hand, he argued that when the demand for labor is low, workers will be reluctant to take wage cuts. Thus the relationship between wages and unemployment is likely to be nonlinear, i.e., to be different when the demand for labor is high than when it is low.

By plotting a scatter diagram of the annual rate of change of money wage rates (on the vertical axis) against the unemployment rate (on the horizontal axis) for the United Kingdom, Phillips obtained what has come to be known as the Phillips curve. Basically the Phillips curve shows the amount of unemployment associated with various rates of change of the money wage rate.

In order to better understand the Phillips curve, it will be useful to plot this relationship using U.S. data. We will also be able to test Professor Phillips' hypothesis for the United States. Because of the extreme fluctuations in the 1930s and the price and wage restraints during World War II and the Korean conflict, we will limit our observations to the post–World War II years 1947 through 1972, omitting 1952 and 1953. For money wage rates we will utilize hourly wages in manufacturing. The relationship between percentage changes in money wage rates and unemployment in the United States is presented in Figure 2–4.

It is interesting to note that the scatter diagram from the U.S. data approximates a curved downward-sloping line similar to that which Phillips observed for the United Kingdom. It appears that the curve is highly nonlinear, as Phillips argued it should be. At annual wage increases below the 5 percent level, a reduction in the rate of wage increase is associated with a relatively large increase in unemployment. On the other hand, during the years when wages increase more than 5 percent, the reduction in unemployment is relatively small.

5 A. W. Phillips, "The Relation between Unemployment and the Rate of Change of Money Wage Rates in the United Kingdom, 1861–1957," *Economica*, 1958, pp. 283–300.

FIGURE 2–4
Relationship between annual percentage change in money wage rates in
manufacturing and the rate of unemployment in the United States, 1947–72*

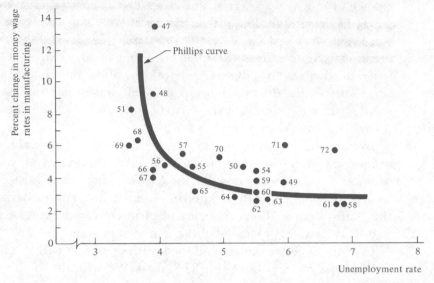

* Years 1952 and 1953 omitted.

In general it appears that a 5 to 6 percent annual increase in the money wage rate in the United States has been associated with an unemployment rate in the range of 3.75 to 4.25 percent. In other words, during the years when we have been close to full employment, wage rates have risen about 5 to 6 percent.

It is necessary to bear in mind, however, that an annual increase in money wage rates of 5 to 6 percent does not necessarily imply that the general price level is increasing by a like amount. If productivity of workers is increasing, they should be able to enjoy wage increases without the higher wages adding to the cost of the goods they produce. Indeed in order for the real income of workers to increase, money wages must be rising relative to the general level of goods and services prices.

Most of our discussion in the previous section concerned the relationship between unemployment and inflation, rather than between unemployment and money wage rates. It will be instructive, therefore, to plot the unemployment-inflation relationship on a diagram similar to Figure 2–4. Indeed, in recent years the Phillips curve has been used in large part to denote the relationship between rates of change of the general price level and the unemployment rate. Thus in Figure 2–5 we present the relationship between the annual percentage change in the Consumer Price Index and the unemployment rate. The observations are for the same years as shown in Figure 2–4.

FIGURE 2–5
Relationship between annual percentage change in the Consumer Price Index and the rate of unemployment, United States, 1947–72*

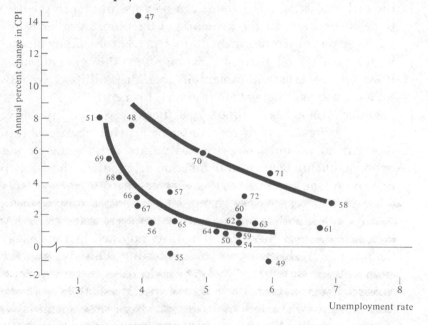

* Years 1952 and 1953 omitted.

Although the scatter diagram in Figure 2–5 is not as "tight" as in Figure 2–4, it is evident that lower rates of unemployment have been associated with higher rates of inflation and vice versa. Some economists have expressed concern, too, that the curve might have shifted to the right in recent years. Notice that the observations for the 1970s seem to be on a curve further to the right than most other years with the exception of 1947, 1948, 1958, and 1961. Concern also has been expressed that the curve may have "straightened out" in recent years. In other words, moderate rates of inflation, say 2 to 3 percent, may now be associated with higher rates of un-employment. From the curved line, it appears that a 3.5 to 4 per-cent unemployment range is associated with about a 4 to 5 percent inflation rate.

The economic rationale underlying the observed Phillips curve is not fully agreed upon and as a result the conclusions that can be drawn from the curve have been subject to considerable contro-versy in the economics profession. Some economists believe that the curve is a relatively stable function, except for the apparent shift in the early 1970s, and as a result can be a useful tool to predict the trade-off between unemployment and inflation. In other words, if we insist on full employment (3 to 4 percent unemployment), we must accept a 4 to 5 percent inflation rate as the curve implies. Or, if we find this inflation intolerable, then the Phillips curve tells us we must accept a higher rate of unemployment.

Other economists maintain that the observed Phillips curve as shown by Figure 2–5 is something of a hybrid between various short-run curves and a long-run curve, and that if there is a trade-off between unemployment and inflation it is only a short-run phe-nomenon. One argument is that if prices increase unexpectedly, it takes time for wages to catch up. Union contracts must run their course, collective bargaining must take place, and so on. In the meantime the real wages (money wages adjusted by the change in the price level) that workers receive decline. This gives employers an incentive to hire more workers, i.e. decrease unemployment, be-cause real wage costs are lower. However, it doesn't take unions very long to realize that the purchasing power of their members' pay-checks has declined because of inflation. As a result, new union con-tracts build in a margin for expected inflation, thereby raising real wages up to or beyond their former levels and pushing unemploy-ment back to its former level.

The argument is illustrated by Figure 2–6. Let us begin at point *a* on short-run curve C_0. As the rate of inflation unexpectedly in-creases from 4 to 6 percent, unemployment is reduced from 4.5 to 3.5 percent,[6] point *b* on short-run curve C_0. But as people come to

---

[6] The rates of unemployment coinciding with the rates of inflation are meant to be illustrative rather than suggesting the exact combinations that actually would occur. However, they probably are not too far removed from reality.

FIGURE 2–6
Illustrating long-run and short-run Phillips curves

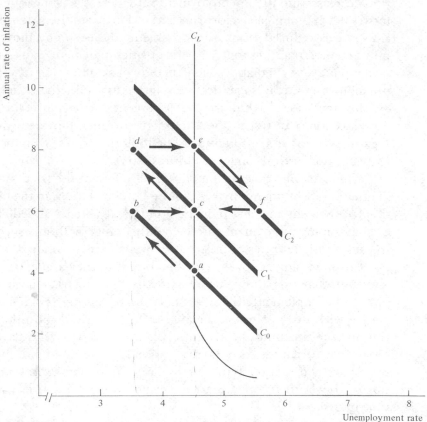

expect the 6 percent rate of inflation, the short-run Phillips curve shifts up to C_1. (Progressively higher short-run curves correspond to progressively higher expected rates of inflation.) If the rate of inflation continues at 6 percent per year, the unemployment rate eases back up to 4.5 percent as money wages catch up to the rise in prices. Another unexpected spurt of inflation up to 8 percent per year moves the economy up along short-run curve C_1 to again obtain a 3.5 percent unemployment rate (point d). But again expectations are revised, money wages catch up, and the unemployment rate increases to 4.5 percent (point e). Thus the economy proceeds to jack itself up to higher and higher rates of inflation without a sustained reduction in unemployment.

The process, of course, could be reversed so that the rate of inflation decreases and the unemployment rate increases as the economy moves down along each short-run curve. For example, if the inflation rate is reduced from 8 to 6 percent, the economy moves to point *f,* corresponding to a 5.5 percent unemployment rate. As expectations are revised and wage demands slack off due to increased unemployment, real wages decline relative to productivity and unemployment eases back down to 4.5 percent once again. Thus the economy comes to rest in the 4 to 5 percent unemployment range regardless of the rate of inflation. The long-run equilibrium points trace out the vertical long-run Phillips curve.

Economists who take such a position argue that the frictional or "natural" rate of unemployment in the United States is in the range of 4 to 5 percent and that monetary and fiscal policies aimed at reducing the unemployment rate below this range will only succeed in causing higher rates of inflation. If we expect to obtain a 3 to 4 percent unemployment rate over the long run, they argue, policies aimed at changing the conditions in the labor market itself will have to be implemented. These might be retraining programs for people with little or no marketable skills, improved job information for the unemployed, relocation help for people who have to move long distances, etc. It is also pointed out that minimum wage laws and monopoly power by large unions may be keeping wages above their free market levels, which in turn causes unemployment.[7]

Some economists take a somewhat in-between view of the two positions we have just discussed. They concede that in the long run, expansionary monetary and fiscal policies probably will only succeed in driving up the rate of inflation without being able to bring the long-term unemployment rate much below the 4 to 5 percent range. On the other hand, if these policies are unduly restrictive, say designed to bring the inflation rate down to 1 to 2 percent, we will be likely to have increased unemployment as illustrated by the downward-sloping portion of the C_L line.

---

[7] The impact of unions and minimum wage laws are discussed in the Labor Market chapter of the micro text.

Main points of Chapter 2

1. Full employment is defined as a situation where everyone who is willing and able to work at the prevailing wage rate can find a job in the line of work for which he is qualified.

2. Many people who are unemployed choose to remain so rather than accept a less desirable or lower paying job. In reality these people are unemployed but not necessarily unemployable.

3. Both employees and labor unions tend to have a built-in incentive to prefer the alternative of laying off employees to an across-the-board wage cut. Layoffs tend to affect only a small proportion of all employees, particularly the young, the new with little seniority, and the unskilled. Hence the repercussions of a layoff tend to be less severe than a wage cut.

4. Frictional unemployment refers to a temporary loss of work because of seasonal fluctuations in economic activity, contraction of certain firms or industries, and the voluntary termination of a job to look for a better one.

5. Although the rate of frictional unemployment is not a universally agreed-upon figure, it has been frequently pegged within the 3 to 4 percent range in the United States in recent years. The rate of frictional unemployment is expected to vary with conditions in the labor market, rising when the market is sluggish and falling when jobs are relatively easy to find.

6. Fortunately in recent years the largest share of all unemployment has been of relatively short duration.

7. Unemployment is most prevalent among the young, minority groups, and people with the fewest skills.

8. The United States has experienced a large amount of variation in its overall unemployment rate, ranging from 24.9 percent in 1933 to 1.2 percent in 1944. In 1972 unemployment averaged 5.6 percent of the labor force during the year.

9. Although war has been conducive to a low rate of unemployment, it does not follow that war is a necessary prerequisite for full employment. Government policies that result in full employment could as well be carried out during peacetime.

10. In addition to the loss of income to unemployed individuals, the cost of unemployment also includes a reduction in the total amount of goods and services available to society.

11. The most commonly used measure of the general price level is the Consumer Price Index (CPI). This index combines the prices of many goods and services into one number, allowing us to compare the average prices of these items between years. The formula for constructing the CPI is $(\Sigma_i\ Q_{0i}P_{1i}/\Sigma_i\ Q_{0i}P_{0i}) \times 100$.

12. Most U.S. inflation in recent times has occurred during war years because war necessitates certain government policies that result in inflation. These same policies can result in inflation during peacetime as well.

13. Demand-pull inflation refers to a situation where the aggregate demand of consumers, investors, and government is greater than the productive capacity of the economy.

14. The federal government is unique among the three groups of demanders because it can create additional money to finance purchases of goods and services. Other things being equal, the larger the quantity of money, the higher the price level.

15. Inflation constitutes a problem mainly because the rate of inflation cannot be predicted with certainty and consequently its economic effects cannot be fully anticipated by the general public.

16. Unexpected inflation harms people who hold assets of a fixed monetary value, those on fixed incomes, and lenders.

17. Inflation can be viewed as a tax on cash balances.

18. When lending or borrowing it is important to consider the real rate of interest. This is equal to the money rate minus the percentage change in the price level.

19. Because it takes time for people to change expectations, changes in the money rate of interest tend to lag behind changes in the price level. Thus the real rate of interest tends to be high during periods of falling prices and low or negative during the early years of inflation.

20. In the United States, as in the United Kingdom, high rates of unemployment have been associated with falling prices or falling rates of inflation. During periods of full employment, there has been a tendency for prices to rise.

21. The Phillips curve shows the amount of unemployment associated with various rates of change of money wages (or prices).
22. Considerable controversy surrounds the Phillips curve, at least as an indicator of the trade-off between inflation and unemployment. Some economists argue that the curve provides a good indication of a trade-off between unemployment and inflation. Others argue the observed Phillips curve is something of a hybrid of short-run and long-run curves and that there is little if any trade-off in the long run. Still others argue that there is likely to be a trade-off as inflation approaches the 1 to 2 percent range.

Questions for thought and discussion

1. Suppose you worked for a construction company (either in the office or at the building site) and a period of slack activity came along so you were laid off. Would you search out another job? What factors would you consider in making this decision?
2. Suppose you were the owner of the construction firm referred to in Question 1. Would you prefer to cut the wages of your employees by 25 percent during the slack period or lay off 25 percent of employees? Why?
3. As an employee of this firm would you rather be laid off or take a 25 percent cut in pay? Explain.
4. In what way does the official unemployment figure understate the "true" unemployment? In what way is the "true" unemployment overstated?
5. What is full employment?
6. During World War II the official unemployment rate in the United States dipped to between 1 and 2 percent of the labor force. Yet at the present we talk of a frictional level of unemployment in the range of 3 to 4 percent. In view of our World War II experience, why shouldn't we strive for no more than a 2 percent unemployment rate?
7. Construct a Consumer Price Index from the following figures for the year 1972 using 1960 as the base year.

Item	1960 price	1972 price	1960 quantity
Dormitory room	$800.00	$1,000.00	1
Cafteria meal	1.25	2.00	600
Books	5.00	10.00	20

8. What if any bias might you expect in the index in Question 7 as a reflector of the cost of going to college?

9. During 1969 the rate of inflation in the United States was about 6 percent. What is the real rate of interest that people earned on money in savings accounts that yielded 5 percent during that year?

10. Many states have usury laws setting the maximum rate of interest that can be charged. Such laws generally are defended on the basis of protecting the small borrower. But how might such laws be detrimental to small or high-risk borrowers?

11. It is likely that most people believe inflation is bad. Why is it bad?

12. It has been said that inflation is in effect a tax on cash balances held by people and institutions. In what way is this true?

13. Make a list of the different groups of people harmed by inflation and explain how and why each is harmed. Does anyone gain from inflation? Explain.

14. What is the unemployment rate and the annual percentage rate of change of money wages in manufacturing for the current year? Insert this point in Figure 2–4. What is the rate of inflation for the current year? Insert the corresponding point in Figure 2–5.

3

Measures of national output

Throughout our study of macroeconomics we will utilize several measures of national output. Some of these measures, such as GNP, have become well known to the public through magazines, newspapers, and the like. But the meaning of these measures and how they are derived are less well known or sometimes misunderstood.

Gross national product

Gross national product (GNP) is defined as the total market value of all final goods and services produced in the economy during some period of time. There are several points worth noting in this definition. First, GNP is a dollar figure. Because of the thousands of diverse goods and services that are produced in the economy it is necessary when combining them to utilize some kind of common denominator. As we learned in the first grade, we cannot add together unlike items such as apples and oranges or bobby pins and battleships.

However, if we assign a monetary value to each item, we are able to use the dollar, or any other kind of monetary unit, as a common denominator. The next question is, what money value should each item be assigned? Two possibilities come to mind: (1) market value and (2) cost of production. As the definition of GNP indicates, the Department of Commerce in measuring GNP has decided upon market value whenever possible. The decision to use this criterion is not completely arbitrary, however. The market value of a good or service is an indication of how much the item adds to the well-being or satisfaction of society. If a packet of bobby pins sells for 30 cents and a new pair of shoes sells for $30, we can infer that the pair of shoes contributes about 100 times more satisfaction to society than the bobby pins, else people would not be willing to pay 100 times more for the shoes.

One major problem of using market price as a measure of satisfaction is that not everything that is produced is bought and sold through the market. Military expenditure is one important category. In this situation, the Department of Commerce in computing GNP is forced to use cost of production rather than market price. If a missile system costs $500 million to produce, it is implicitly assumed in the GNP computations that the missiles contribute $500 million worth of satisfaction to society. Of course, some people would disagree with this assumption. To some, assigning $500 million to missiles is much like assigning $30 to a packet of bobby pins, i.e., cost of production may be an irrelevant figure as a measure of satisfaction.

Another major nonmarket item included in GNP is the rental value of owner-occupied housing. Even though an owner doesn't pay rent he receives satisfaction from his dwelling. However, it is somewhat easier to impute the rental value of a house than that of a missile system. Because there is an established rental market for homes and apartments, the Department of Commerce does utilize these figures in estimating their worth to society. A third major nonmarket item that is included in GNP is food produced and consumed on farms. Here again these prices are estimated from comparable items in grocery stores.

The second point to note about GNP is that it is the market value of all *final* goods and services. Thus GNP excludes the value of goods and services produced for resale or further processing. We might inquire, why doesn't the Department of Commerce include these items? Surely the steel that goes into an automobile or the leather that goes into a pair of shoes contributes to the well-being of society. The reason for excluding these so-called intermediate goods and services is that they are included in the market price of the final product.

A simple example will help make this clear. Consider the various stages in the manufacture of a pair of shoes. The raw material, i.e. the hide, is produced by a farmer. To simplify the example we assume the farmer is completely self-sufficient, so that the sale price of the hide on the animal is equal to the value added by the farmer. Let this be $2.

In the second step, the packing plant buys the hide for $2, separates it from the animal, and sells it to the tannery for $3. But this $3 selling price must include the $2 paid to the farmer. In other words, in order to stay in business, the packing plant must be reimbursed for the original raw material it bought plus something extra for the services it carried out. And so it is for each step in the production process. The series of steps in the production of a pair of shoes are illustrated and summarized in the following table.

Stage of production	Value of sales	Value added
Farmer	$ 2	$ 2
Packing plant	3	1
Tannery	5	2
Shoe manufacturer	10	5
Wholesaler	11	1
Retailer	15	4
	$46	$15

Notice that the value of the final product, the $15 pair of shoes sold by the retailer, is exactly equal to the sum of all the "value added" figures in column two. This is not just a coincidence. Each of the various steps in the production process contributed something to the finished product. Thus the selling price of the finished or final product is just an accumulation of the value added in these stages.

Gross national product, therefore, is in reality a value-added figure. Rather than attempting to decide which products are final products and which are intermediate, the Department of Commerce estimates the value added by each industry. This is accomplished by subtracting the purchases of each industry from the value of its sales, just as we did in the example above.

A reasonable question to ask at this point is why make such a big thing out of the value-added figure as opposed to simply using total sales of each industry in the country? Granted GNP would be considerably larger if gross sales were used, but as long as we know why it was larger why should it make any difference? The reason for using value added instead of gross sales is to avoid a bias that would occur through merger or consolidation of firms.

Suppose, in the above example, that the packing plant and the tannery merged to become one firm. Now the $3 sale of the hide from the packing plant to the tannery would be eliminated, reducing the sum of the sales column from $46 to $43. Consequently, if GNP were measured by gross sales, it could be changed simply by a change in the number of firms even though output (or value added) remained the same. Notice that the sum of the value-added column does not change with a change in the number of steps in the production process.

A third point to note about GNP is that it excludes "pure exchange" transactions. These include such things as the purchase and sale of securities, gifts, and secondhand sales. These transactions are omitted from GNP because nothing new is produced. If you buy a $100 stock certificate, for example, the person who sells it to you gains the $100 and you gain the certificate. From the standpoint of the total economy nothing has changed. It must be admitted, though, that after the transaction both you and the seller should be better off than before it; if not there would be no sense in carrying out the transaction.

About the same reasoning applies to donations and gifts. Here also nothing new is produced or created, so these should not enter GNP computations. Of course, one could argue here as well that both the giver and receiver are better off after a gift is made than before, else it would not be made. But it is difficult if not impossible to measure this kind of satisfaction, so it is simplest to leave it out of GNP.

A fourth and final point to note about GNP is that it is a "flow" figure as opposed to a "stock." Flows are always given per unit of time, whereas a stock has no time dimension. As a rule GNP is given in billions of dollars per year. It is virtually impossible, though, to imagine the magnitude of a billion dollars. If you were a billionaire, for example, and invested your money in a 5 percent savings account, you would draw $50 million per year just in interest.

GNP *as a measure of economic well-being*

An important use of the GNP figure is to compare the standard of living or economic well-being of people within a nation over a period of time or between nations at a point in time. The presumption is that the higher the GNP (the greater the output of goods and services), the better off people are. In recent years, however, more people have begun to question whether people really are better off with more goods and services. Is the modern dweller living in the noise, congestion, and pollution of the big city "better off" than his forefather who lived on a small farm in peaceful surroundings?

It is up to the individual person, of course, to answer this question for himself. We might, however, point out that modern man has the opportunity to choose among more alternatives than his forefathers. If the high-income city dweller becomes disenchanted with his life of affluence, he is free to reject it and move to a place in the country where he can lead the life of a 19th-century small farmer if he wishes.

As soon as we consider the cost of this alternative, however, it becomes clear why so few people choose it. For rejecting modern life also means rejecting the multitude of modern conveniences that go with it. It means, for example, getting up in the early morning in a small, cold, dark house without indoor plumbing as opposed to central heating, an automatic thermostat, lights that respond to a flick of our finger, etc. It means a continual struggle with nature to provide food and clothing as opposed to a leisurely walk down the aisle of a clean, modern supermarket with a choice of thousands of items at our finger tips. It means spending one's life within a few miles of home, spending evenings in the rocking chair, playing checkers, as opposed to the opportunity of worldwide travel, the theater, the symphony, big league sports, etc.

It is not necessary to elaborate further. When thinking of years gone by we tend to forget the bad things and remember the good. It is only when faced with the stark reality of the "simple" life that we appreciate the conveniences of modern society. Of course, with still higher output and incomes, more and more people will be able to buy the best of both lives. The second home is one example of this, where people can "rough it" in luxury on weekends or holidays.

Also in recent years, many high and upper middle-income people have decided that a cleaner environment is worth the cost of obtaining it. It is not surprising, either, that we don't see the push for a cleaner environment coming from the ghettos or the lower middle-income, working-class people who in fact have to contend with the most polluted surroundings. It is not that these people have no desire for a clean environment, but there are other things that they prefer to buy first.

The main point of this discussion is that a rich, high-output society has many more opportunities or choices than a poor, low-output society. The rich always have the choice of becoming poor if they choose. But the poor don't have this choice.

Biases in GNP

When using GNP to compare the economic well-being of a society over time, or between two societies, a number of biases can creep in. The first is a change in the general price level. As we know, GNP is a monetary figure. Thus with the inflationary spiral that has taken place in the United States over the past 30 years, it is clear that a dollar of GNP today is not the same in terms of real output as a dollar of GNP 30 or 40 years ago.

As an example, let us compare the years 1929 and 1972 in the United States. Gross national product as measured in the prices of each respective year was $103 and $1,152 billion, respectively. Because of the rise in the general price level, we cannot conclude that the real output of goods and services was over 10 times greater in 1972 than in 1929. In other words, inflation biases the 1972 figure upward, making it appear that people were better off in 1972, as compared to 1929, than they actually were.

It is evident, therefore, that we need to adjust or "deflate" the GNP figures so that both reflect the same general price level. We can do this with the Consumer Price Index (CPI) that we studied in Chapter 2. For example, the CPI for 1972 was 244 with 1929 as the base year (1929 = 100). In other words, prices of comparable items were 2.44 times greater in 1972 than in 1929.

If we choose we can adjust, or deflate, the 1972 GNP to 1929 prices simply by dividing by the 1972 CPI (1929 = 100) and multiplying by 100. The computations follow:

Deflating 1972 GNP to 1929 prices:

$$\frac{1972 \text{ GNP}}{1972 \text{ CPI } (1929 = 100)} \times 100 = \frac{\$1,152}{244} \times 100 = \$472$$

Here we see that if the same price level prevailed as in 1929, the 1972 GNP would have been only $472 billion.

If we wished we could adjust or "inflate" the 1929 GNP into 1972 prices. It is sometimes easier to visualize what happened in years past if we make things more comparable to our current situation. The first thing we have to do is change the CPI so that 1972 becomes the base year, i.e., 1972 = 100. To accomplish this, we divide the original 1929 = 100 CPI figures for each year by the 1972 CPI figure and multiply by 100. The computations follow:

Converting 1929 = 100 CPI to 1972 = 100 CPI:

$$\frac{1972 \text{ CPI}}{1972 \text{ CPI}} \times 100 = \frac{244}{244} \times 100 = 100$$

$$\frac{1929 \text{ CPI}}{1972 \text{ CPI}} \times 100 = \frac{100}{244} \times 100 = 41$$

These figures tell us that prices in 1929 were 41 percent as high as in 1972. Now we can inflate the 1929 GNP to 1972 prices by the same procedure we used to deflate 1972 GNP to 1929 prices.

Inflating 1929 GNP to 1972 prices:

$$\frac{1929 \text{ GNP}}{1929 \text{ CPI } (1972 = 100)} \times 100 = \frac{103}{41} \times 100 = 251$$

Here we see that if the same price level prevailed in 1929 as in 1972, the 1929 GNP would have been $251 billion. Of course, we could have used any other year as the base year to deflate GNP. Most publications use a base year or period of years that is fairly recent, so as years go by the base year tends to change. For example, in quoting the CPI during the 1950s, the years 1947–49 were generally used as the base period. During the 1960s, the 1957–59 period became the most frequently used base. Now, in the 1970s, we can expect to see 1967–69 as a common base. Using a three-year average period mitigates the problem of abnormalities of a single year coming in to distort the long-run trend. The computational procedure for deflating or inflating, of course, remains the same regardless of the base year or period used. The base period or year tells us what year's or period's prices are being used to inflate or deflate.

Although deflating GNP by the CPI removes the major part of the bias or distortion in GNP caused by changes in the general price level, we should remember that the CPI itself can be biased. As mentioned in the previous chapter it is difficult if not impossible to hold quality of items constant when comparing prices over time. If, as is likely, the quality of most items has increased over time, the measured rise in the CPI is likely to overstate the "true" increase.[1] Thus when we deflate and compare current year GNP to GNP in years past, we in effect understate current year GNP in relation to GNP long ago. A similar bias creeps in to the extent that changes in relative prices bring about changes in the mix of goods and services purchased. As explained in Chapter 2, this "index number problem" tends to make the measured CPI overstate the true rise in prices. Again the effect is to bias the growth in real GNP downward.

Secondly, we can obtain a biased impression of improvement in the economic well-being of people if we only look at the aggregate GNP of the entire economy. Taking into account the change in the general price level, we see that the U.S. GNP increased about 4.5 times during the 1929–72 period. Does this mean that the average American was able to enjoy four and a half times as many goods and services in 1972 as in 1929? No.

We must consider also the growth in the population. Even though the size of the pie (GNP) is growing, there are more people around to claim a slice of it. If the 450 percent increase in real GNP were accompanied by a comparable increase in population, there would, of course, be no increase in the economic well-being of the individual. A more relevant figure, therefore, is GNP per capita. It turns out in the United States that population did not increase as much as GNP between 1929 and 1972, so GNP per capita increased about 2.7 times, as shown below:

---

[1] If you doubt that quality has increased, look through a Wards or Sears catalogue from the 1930s, 1940s, or 1950s.

Year	Real GNP (billions) (1972 prices)	U.S. population (millions)	GNP per capita
1929	$ 251	122	$2,057
1972	1,152	209	5,512

In many developing nations, however, the picture is quite different. In the post–World War II era most have been able to increase their total real GNP. Unfortunately, for many, population growth has kept pace with, or in some cases outrun, GNP growth so the average individual is no better off than before. This is not to say, though, that accomplishing an increase in GNP has been a wasted effort. For without an increase, the relentless growth in population would have resulted in an actual decline in the output of goods and services per capita.

Governments, of course, still are interested in the aggregate GNP of nations because of its military significance. A nation with a small GNP, even though it may have a very high GNP per capita, doesn't stand much of a chance against a nation with a GNP several times its size even though the large nation may have a low GNP per capita. History has shown that total productive capacity of a nation is a more important factor in waging war than the number of people in the military. Of course, a nation with both a large population and a large productive capacity is an even more formidable opponent in war. The United States and the Soviet Union fall into this category.

So far we have adjusted GNP for (1) a change in the general price level and (2) a change in population. In the United States the unadjusted, aggregate GNP figures suggest a 10-fold increase in the output of goods and services between 1929 and 1972. Adjusting these figures for a change in the price level reduces the increase to 4.5 times. Further adjustment for population growth results in about a 2.7-fold increase in GNP per capita. Without these adjustments in the GNP, the economic well-being of people in recent years compared to years gone by is made to look better than it really is.

A third source of bias comes in because GNP does not include many nonmarket activities in the economy. In a previous section we alluded to the fact that the government in estimating GNP attempts to impute a value to food produced and consumed on farms and to owner-occupied housing. There are, however, other things that people value which are not in GNP.

A major item is leisure time. As we know, most people now work fewer hours per week than people did 40 to 50 years ago. For example, the average workweek in manufacturing in 1929 was 44.2 hours compared to 40.6 hours in 1972—a reduction of 3.6 hours per week. There can be no doubt that the average manufacturing worker places some value on this extra time that he has to himself, but this value is not included in GNP.

Or if we wish, we can look at it another way. If workers in manufacturing were forced to work 44.2 hours per week, the measured GNP would be higher than it now is. This would not mean, however, that society would be better off with the higher GNP. The fact that people voluntarily shorten their workweek is an indication that they prefer a bit more leisure to a larger paycheck. The wages that they willingly forgo are an indication of the value of the extra leisure to them.

We should not be led to believe, however, that the United States will soon become one large leisure class, working perhaps 20 to 25 hours per week. Some people have been predicting that this will happen for some time now. But the facts do not correspond to their predictions. With the exception of the period following the World War II years, when people worked long hours, the major reduction in the workweek of manufacturing workers came during the 1930s. In fact their workweek in 1972 was exactly the same length as in 1941—40.6 hours.

It appears, therefore, that the bias in GNP due to increased leisure only becomes important when comparing current year GNP with a year in the 1930s or before. Although, when comparing U.S. GNP with that of other countries, it is still a good idea to determine the length of their workweek.

Related to the leisure bias is the bias caused by the entry of women into the labor force. With the coming of laborsaving devices in the home and increased job opportunities for women, a larger proportion of the nation's females now hold down full or part-time jobs than was true 30 to 40 years ago. For example, in 1947 about 32 percent of all women in the United States participated in the labor force, whereas in 1972 this figure increased to 43.6 percent. Instead of making clothes, baking bread, minding children, and washing dishes, more women nowadays are using part of their salary to purchase these services in the market. The purchases of ready-to-wear clothing, convenience foods, restaurant meals, child care services, appliances for cleaning and food preparation, and so on, are caught by the GNP measure. When the tasks performed by these purchases were done by hand by housewives in the home they were not reflected in the GNP measure. Some offset to this bias occurs because of the decrease in employment of maids, housekeepers, and gardeners over the past 40 years. The services of these people were a part of GNP. At any rate, it would appear that the "liberation" of women from the home to factories and offices has caused our current GNP to look better than it really is in comparison to GNP 30 to 40 years ago.

The bias caused by leaving out nonmarket activities also becomes important when a society changes from a rural, self-sufficient economy to an urban, market-oriented economy. Years ago rural people were much more self-sufficient than either rural or urban people are today. They built and repaired their own utensils and tools, wove cloth, sewed their own clothes, built some of their own furniture, grew their own fuel for transportation (feed for horses), etc. Even though many of these goods and services never came through the market and hence were not caught by GNP, the people living in those days nevertheless benefited from their use.

The effect on GNP of the transformation from a self-sufficient, rural economy to a monetized, market-oriented economy is especially important for the developing nations. By catching a growing proportion of daily activities in the GNP measure, a nation can exhibit an impressive rate of economic growth that is more apparent than real.

To summarize briefly, we have mentioned three possible biases that can affect GNP because of the fact that it excludes many non-market activities. These include (1) the increase in leisure time, particularly in comparison with the 1930s and before; (2) the entry of women into the labor force; and (3) the decreased self-sufficiency, or increased market orientation, of our modern society. The increase in leisure makes the recent GNP figures look worse than they really are in comparison with the 1929 GNP figure. The second and third biases have the opposite effect of making recent year GNP figures look better than they are in comparison to years back.

The inclusion of military expenditures together with police and fire protection costs in GNP represents a fourth source of bias when using it to measure economic well-being. In the Vietnam War, for example, the federal government was forced to devote a larger share of the nation's resources to the production of military goods than would otherwise be true. As a result the nation's production of nonmilitary goods and services was smaller than otherwise would have been the case.

Even though total GNP may not have been changed by the war, the goods and services available for consumption or investment were decreased. The World War II years provide an even better example. During this war military output cut much deeper into the output of nonmilitary goods and services. Here GNP increased markedly, but the economic well-being of society certainly did not increase. Thus in times of war, or large military spending, the GNP will overstate the economic welfare of society.

The same reasoning applies to expenses for police and fire protection, although the resulting bias is not as severe. Suppose the nation is plagued with an increase in lawlessness, riots, and burnings. As a result society decides to devote a larger share of its resources to police and fire protection at the expense of other goods and services. Again GNP does not change, but clearly society is worse off from an economic point of view because it is enjoying fewer goods and services than it otherwise could if the riots, and so on, had not come about. Hence it would be of some help if the nation's expenditure on the military, police, and other "unproductive" activities were taken out of the GNP figure and presented separately. We would then be given a better measure of the goods and services that people are able to enjoy. Later in the chapter we will present GNP per capita excluding the military portion of GNP.

A fifth and last source of bias that we should be aware of is a difference in the distribution of the GNP. When we computed per capita GNP, we simply divided total GNP by the number of people in the country. We obtain the same figure regardless of how GNP is distributed. But most people probably feel that society as a whole is better off if everyone is able to share somewhat equally in the nation's output as opposed to the case where the nation's income and wealth is concentrated in the hands of a few very rich and powerful families. The oil-rich kingdoms of the Middle East provide a good example of the latter case.

We will study in more detail in Chapter 10 some of the major problems and issues in the areas of poverty and income distribution. For now, it is sufficient that we become aware that the GNP per capita figure does not tell us anything about how the GNP is distributed. We might say, however, that this problem is less severe in the United States than in many other countries of the world. Although U.S. output is not by any means shared equally, neither is it concentrated in the hands of a select few. Also, the United States has not experienced a drastic change in income distribution during its history.

Expenditure components of GNP

In order to gain a better understanding of the makeup of GNP, it will be useful to look at its components in a bit more detail. In the chapters to follow we will be particularly interested in those broad categories of expenditures on final goods and services that together comprise the major portion of GNP. These include:

1. Personal consumption expenditures. As the name implies, this category includes the expenditures of individuals and households on all so-called consumer items. It is common to further divide this category into *(a)* consumer durables such as automobiles, refrigerators, TV sets, etc.; and *(b)* consumer nondurables which include both goods (meat, bread, clothes, beverages, cosmetics, etc.) and services (medical and dental care, barber and beauty shop services, repair services, etc.).

One large item that is perhaps conspicuous by its absence is the purchase of newly constructed residential housing. For reasons to be explained shortly, this item is included in the investment category. However, the Commerce Department does compute the annual rental value of owner-occupied housing and adds this amount to consumer expenditures, along with actual rental payments on apartments and houses. Also, as mentioned, the purchases of second-hand items are not included, mainly because they represent a transfer of assets rather than a net addition to output.

2. Gross private domestic investment. Investment as used in this context refers to the expenditures on construction of physical capital or facilities, mainly buildings, machines, and tools. It does not include purchase of stocks or bonds, or money placed in a savings account. We sometimes refer to the purchase of these items as an "investment." But this does not constitute investment as defined in the national accounts, mainly because it involves a mere transfer of assets from one party to another and not an addition to the nation's stock of physical capital or productive capacity.

The distinguishing feature of investment goods as defined in the national accounts is that they yield a stream of services or returns over a long period of time. This is in contrast to consumer goods, which tend to be used up over a shorter period. One might argue that consumer durables such as automobiles and appliances yield their services over a long period too. But the line between consumer durables and investment goods had to be drawn somewhere. Recall, however, that the construction of residential housing is included as an investment good.

In addition to machines, tools, and buildings, the investment component of GNP also includes any change in inventories held by business firms. In order for GNP to accurately reflect the nation's output for a given year or time period, it is necessary to add any net *increase* in inventories that had taken place. In this case, the output or production of goods and services is greater than sales. Of course a large part of the nation's inventories are consumer goods, but the main thing is that they are included somewhere. By the same token, a net *decrease* or drawing down of inventories is subtracted from the investment figure to reflect the fact that sales of final goods and services exceeded their production.

Some explanation is in order in reference to the modifiers "Gross private domestic" in the heading of this subsection. "Gross" refers to the total new investment during a given year. It does not contain any deduction for the amount of capital that has been used up or depreciated during the year. Hence gross investment will overstate the true increase in the nation's capital. A bit later we will discuss the measure of output when depreciation of capital has been deducted. "Private" denotes investment by the so-called private sector as opposed to government investment. Finally, "domestic" refers to investment in the United States as opposed to investment in other nations. In future discussion we will refer only to gross or net investment, with the understanding that the "private domestic" adjectives also apply.

3. Government purchases of goods and services. This category of expenditures includes the purchases of goods and services by all levels of government—federal, state, and local. Included are such items as expenditures on military hardware and personnel, police and fire protection, public school operation, roads, public parks, etc. However it does not include so-called transfer payments. Basically these are gifts from various levels of government to individuals. As such these payments do not represent a net addition to output, hence they are not counted in GNP. Of course, the expenditure of these funds by the recipients on either consumption or investment goods is reflected in GNP.

To summarize briefly, we have identified the three major components of GNP from the standpoint of expenditures on final goods and services: (1) consumption, (2) investment (gross), and (3) government spending. Traditionally these components have been identified as C, I_g, and G, respectively. Thus an easy way to remember the makeup of GNP is to call to mind the simple formula:

$$\text{GNP} = C + I_g + G$$

Income components of GNP

Although we will mainly be concerned with the three expenditure components of GNP in later chapters, it should be mentioned that GNP also can be viewed from the income side. In other words, instead of measuring the expenditures on final goods and services, we can measure the income derived from the production of these goods and services. It is a bit easier to grasp this dual measure of GNP if we remember that every dollar which is spent on a final good or service is income to somebody; i.e., for every dollar of expenditure there is a dollar of income. Thus if we measure income we should obtain exactly the same total figure as when we measure expenditure.

Traditionally the Department of Commerce has divided the nation's income into four categories: (1) wages, (2) interest, (3) rents, and (4) profits. The first category, wages, represents the income of wage and salary workers, i.e., labor. Interest and rents represent the income earned by capital (machines, buildings, land, etc.), which in turn is claimed by the owners of capital. The fourth category, profits, is a residual representing what is left over for producers after paying the wages, interest, and rents. One can view this income as a reward for risk taking in initiating and carrying on production. Of course, there is no guarantee that profits will always be positive, particularly for the individual firm.

Measuring GNP in terms of income is useful in that it tells us how much of the nation's output is enjoyed by each category of resource owner. The division between wages and the other three categories is of particular interest in that it provides an indication of labor's share of the national output in relation to capital's share, although these days many workers also are owners of capital.

Dividing income into the above four categories is often referred to as the "functional distribution" of income. As the name implies, this distribution categorizes income by the function of its recipients —workers, owners of capital, and management. Income also can be categorized according to its personal distribution. With this scheme, income is divided up according to the level of income of its recipients. It tells us, for example, what share of the nation's income flows to the upper 10 percent of the nation's income recipients, what share flows to the next 10 percent, etc. We will study measures of income distribution in more detail in Chapter 10, where we discuss poverty and the distribution of income.

United States GNP, 1929–72

We now have a better idea of what GNP is and the biases that can distort it as a reflector of economic well-being. Next let us review briefly the actual GNP figures for the United States for selected years during the past four decades. The years selected represent milestones in economic activity and coincide with the years selected in Chapter 2 with regard to the discussion of unemployment and inflation. To illustrate the difference between GNP in current-year prices (unadjusted for changes in the general price level), GNP in constant prices, and GNP per capita, all three measures are presented in Table 3–1.

TABLE 3–1
United States GNP, 1929–72, selected years

Year	GNP (billions), current-year prices	GNP (billions),* 1972 prices	GNP per capita,* 1972 prices
1929	$ 103	$ 252	$2,068
1933	56	181	1,441
1940	100	299	2,263
1944	210	499	3,605
1949	256	449	3,009
1953	364	570	3,558
1958	447	647	3,999
1969	932	1,064	5,249
1972	1,152	1,152	5,517

* Adjusted by Consumer Price Index, 1972 = 100.
Source: *Economic Report of the President, 1973*, pp. 193, 219.

Although in recent years the United States has enjoyed continued growth in GNP, this has not always been the case. Both the total and per capita measures of GNP in constant 1972 prices declined during the Great Depression of the 1930s and again during the period of adjustment following World War II. The biases that we discussed in a preceding section also become more vivid when we consider the actual GNP figures. Note that there is considerable more fluctuation in GNP when it is measured in current-year prices than when changes in the general price level are taken into account. Also, as we pointed out earlier, the long-run growth in GNP is much less when measured in constant prices and is reduced even more when measured in GNP per capita.

Nonmilitary GNP

If we are using GNP as a measure of the economic well-being of people, then we ought to look also at the bias caused by military goods and services. As we pointed out, GNP may increase during war, but this does not mean that people have more nonmilitary goods and services to enjoy. We present in Table 3–2 figures on U.S. expenditures for national defense, along with the resulting GNP figures when military expenditures are excluded.

As shown in Table 3–2, the record of United States GNP after the 1930s is changed considerably when military expenditures are ex-

TABLE 3-2
United States military expenditures and nonmilitary GNP,
selected years, 1972 prices

Year	Military expenditures* Total (billions)	Per capita	Nonmilitary GNP Total (billions)	Per capita
1929	$ 2	$ 16	$ 250	$2,052
1933	6	48	175	1,393
1940	6	45	293	2,218
1944	207	1,495	292	2,110
1949	23	154	426	2,855
1953	77	481	493	3,077
1958	67	383	580	3,316
1969	90	444	974	4,805
1972	76	364	1,076	5,153

* Net of military sales.
Source: *Economic Report of the President, 1973*, p. 193.

cluded. Notice that on a per capita basis the 1944 GNP is smaller than the 1940 figure and is not greatly different than the 1929 per capita GNP. Also note that the 1949 GNP per capita now exhibits an increase over the World War II years instead of the decline shown in Table 3-1.

We should be aware as well that the growth in real GNP per capita from 1949 to 1972 is smaller when the military is excluded. The growth in real GNP per capita during this period is $2,508 when the military is included in GNP, but this figure is reduced to $2,298 when the military is excluded.

This is not to argue, of course, that the United States or other nations could abandon all expenditures on the military. Most nations find it necessary to protect the life and property of their people from outside aggression or internal insurrection. Rather, the main point is to show that the more peaceful the world can be, the more goods and services there will be for people to enjoy.

Government as a separate sector

As you are now aware, the traditional breakdown of GNP from the standpoint of expenditures includes government purchases of goods and services as a separate item or sector. Although the three-way division of GNP into consumption, investment, and government spending turns out to be useful in future discussion, one should guard against a complete separation of government from the rest of the economy. By treating government as separate entity, it is easy to regard the goods and services purchased by the government as neither consumption nor investment goods, and as such not available to the general public. But, of course, this is not true.

With the possible exception of purchases for the military and possibly police and fire protection, all goods and services purchased by the government can be classified as either consumption or investment goods. For example, expenditures on public parks and school lunches could be considered consumption goods. Government expenditures on roads and flood control projects would be considered investment goods. The main point is that the public benefits from government consumption and investment expenditures as they do from private expenditures on these two kinds of goods. Even though we will follow the convention of separating government from private sector expenditures in the remainder of this book, we should not be led to believe that government goods and services are lost or not available to the people. Aside from the cost of running the government bureaucracy, it does not "consume" any goods or services; the people do.

Net exports in GNP

Although the three expenditure items, consumption, investment, and government spending, comprise the major share of GNP, to be strictly correct we should include a fourth item—net exports. Net exports are defined as total exports minus total imports. For example, if the country sells $50 billion worth of goods and services to foreign countries and buys $48 billion in return, net exports are $2 billion.

Again it is somewhat unfortunate that foreign trade enters GNP in this manner, particularly if we wish to use GNP as a measure of economic well-being. For it implies that the more we can sell to foreign countries and the less we buy from them the better off we are. But, again, this is not true. Goods and services we use that are produced abroad benefit us as much as things produced in this country.

The effect of subtracting imports from GNP is reduced to an absurdity if we use an extreme example. Suppose we (the United States) were able to sell everything we produced to other countries but did not buy anything in return, i.e., zero imports. In this case we would not be able to enjoy any of the fruits of our labor because we would have sold it all abroad. Granted we might have a high GNP and would obtain a lot of foreign currency or gold bars in exchange for real goods and services, but not many people receive much satisfaction from the gold buried at Fort Knox. Those who would have us believe that exports are "good" and imports are "bad" must then argue that gold or foreign currencies are to be preferred over real goods and services such as automobiles, crude oil, natural gas, food, steel, radios, television sets and the host of other items that are produced in other nations but consumed in the United States.

The goal of increasing exports and limiting imports would seem to reflect a producer-oriented trade philosophy. Naturally most business firms are anxious to expand their markets, and exports provide a source of this expansion. Similarly foreign goods coming into the country represent added competition for domestic firms that is not exactly welcomed by them. But if we accept the idea that production is carried on for the benefit of consumers rather than for its own sake, then it is hard to argue that society is better off the more that can be exported and the less that is imported.[2]

If GNP is to be used as a measure of the economic well-being of society, it would make more sense to add imports and subtract exports. At any rate, exports and imports tend to balance out, so GNP is not affected very much by net exports. In 1972, for example, net exports were only —$6.8 billion out of a total GNP of $1,152 billion.[3]

---

[2] This point was made very clearly in the early 1970s with the added exports of lumber to Japan and wheat to the Soviet Union, which increased the demand for and the prices of these items in the domestic market. We shall cover this topic more thoroughly in Chapter 11.

[3] The negative value shown here means that merchandise imports were larger than exports.

Net national product

In addition to gross national product, the Department of Commerce computes a number of other measures of national output or income. A second measure is net national product (NNP). Net national product differs from GNP in that the depreciation of capital is subtracted. Depreciation of capital is often referred to as "capital consumption allowances." In a sense it is the capital that is worn out or used up during the year in the production of goods and services.

As we stated in a previous section, GNP is referred to as the total expenditure on final goods and services by consumers, investors, and government agencies. These expenditures generally are abbreviated by $C + I_g + G$, where I_g stands for gross investment.[4] Net national product, on the other hand, generally is denoted by $C + I_n + G$, where I_n represents net investment. Net investment, therefore, is equal to gross investment minus depreciation. We can summarize these relationships as follows:

$$GNP = C + I_g + G$$
$$NNP = C + I_n + G$$
$$I_n = I_g - D$$

In most years gross investment is larger than depreciation, so that there is a net addition to the productive capacity of the economy. Two periods in which this was not the case, however, occurred during the Great Depression of the 1930s and again during the World War II years. In both of these periods, depreciation was greater than gross investment, resulting in a negative I_n or a drawing down of the productive capacity of the economy.

The main use of the NNP measure, as compared to GNP, is that it should be a somewhat more accurate reflector of the net output or income of the economy. The rationale for deducting depreciation from GNP is similar to the reason it is deducted from the net output or value added of the business firm. Depreciation represents a cost of production in that it represents the capital used up in the production process. Thus we overstate the net output of the economy if this cost is not taken into account.

---

4 We delete net exports to simplify the discussion.

National income

National income (NI) is equal to NNP minus "indirect business taxes" (T_{IB}). By and large these are the sales, excise, and property taxes. National income is supposed to be a more accurate measure of income to labor and owners of capital because these taxes, of course, are siphoned off by the government. We must remember, however, that the national income measure became institutionalized before the income tax was very important or was deducted from paychecks, so years ago it was a fairly accurate indicator of incomes to resource owners.

Personal income

Personal income (PI) is defined as the income received by households before personal income taxes. It is computed by subtracting social security taxes (T_{ss}), corporate income taxes (T_{CI}), and corporate savings (S_c) from NI and adding transfer payments (T_R) to this figure. Transfer payments represent income payments from government to individuals other than for services rendered, i.e., gifts. Because personal income requires four adjustments to national income, it will be useful to summarize what we have done.

$$PI = NI - T_{ss} - T_{CI} - S_c + T_R$$

Disposable income

Disposable income (DI) is equal to PI minus personal income taxes (T_{PI}). This measure represents the income that people have to spend or save. In other words, there are only two things that people can do with their disposable income; they can spend it or they can save it. The Department of Commerce separates these two components of DI as well and publishes the annual expenditure on consumption and personal saving.

Summary of output or income measures

We have in this chapter derived five different measures of output or income. These tend to be a bit confusing and difficult to remember, but a brief summary might be helpful. Also we present the 1972 U.S. figure of each measure.

			1972 measure (billions)
1.	Gross national product		$1,152
	Less: Depreciation	$104	
2.	Net national product		1,048
	Less: Indirect business taxes	113	
3.	National income		935
	Less: Social security taxes	74	
	Corporate income taxes	61	
	Corporate saving	26	
	Plus: Transfer payments	162	
4.	Personal income		936
	Less: Personal income taxes	141	
5.	Disposable income		795
	Consumer expenditures	740	
	Personal saving	55	

Source: *Economic Report of The President, 1973*, pp. 209–12.

Main points of Chapter 3

1. Gross national product (GNP) is defined as the market value of all final goods and services produced in an economy over some period of time.

2. The market value of an item is an indication of how much the item adds to the satisfaction of society. Thus GNP is an indicator of the economic well-being of society.

3. Gross national product is the measure of value added by each industry in the economy. This is equivalent to measuring the value of final goods or services.

4. The main advantage of measuring value added is that GNP is not changed simply by a change in the number of firms in the economy or the number of steps in the production process.

5. Although more goods and services may not necessarily lead to happiness and contentment, the members of a high GNP economy have many more choices open to them than people in a poor economy. Most people, if they have the choice, choose to be rich rather than poor in spite of the costs involved.

6. Because GNP is a monetary figure, it is biased by any change in the general price level. To avoid this bias, GNP can be adjusted (inflated or deflated) for a change in prices by a price index such as the CPI.

7. To assess the economic well-being of the individual, it is necessary to look at GNP per capita.

8. Gross national product as a measure of economic well-being can also be biased because it excludes many nonmarket activities that people nevertheless value. Among these are included: (1) the value of increased leisure time, (2) the effect of increased labor force participation by women, and (3) the change from a more self-sufficient rural economy to a market-oriented, urban society. The first item makes the recent year GNP look worse than it is compared to years ago, while the other two have the opposite effect.

9. The three major expenditure components of GNP are (1) personal consumption expenditure, (2) gross private domestic investment, and (3) government spending on goods and services.

10. The four major income components of GNP are (1) wages, (2) interest, (3) rents, and (4) profits.

11. Although total GNP has grown steadily in recent years, this is by no means true for the entire period since 1929. Adjusting for the increase in the general price level and for the increase in population reduces GNP growth from a 10-fold increase to a 2.7-fold increase between 1929 and 1972.

12. Subtracting the military component from GNP reduces the attractiveness of the World War II years, Korea, and the Vietnam era from the standpoint of a high GNP per capita.

13. The practice of separating government expenditures from private consumption and investment gives the impression that government expenditures are somehow lost or not available to the general public which, of course, is not the case.

14. The practice of adding exports and subtracting imports from
     GNP implies that the country is better off the more it sells
     and the less it buys from foreign countries. From this logic
     we are forced to conclude that gold bars buried in Fort Knox
     are to be desired over real goods and services.
15. Other measures of national output or income include net na-
     tional product, national income, personal income, and dis-
     posable income.

Questions for thought and discussion

1. "Gross national product is equivalent to the total sales in the
    economy during a given year." Comment.
2. What difference, if any, is there in the way a new automobile
    is measured in GNP and the way new military hardware is
    measured?
3. "If all the husbands in the United States divorced their wives
    and hired them as housekeepers, the nation's GNP would in-
    crease substantially." Comment.
4. From 1929 to 1972 the GNP of the United States increased
    from $103 billion to $1,152 billion. From this we can conclude
    that the average person was over 10 times better off in 1972
    than in 1929. True or false? Explain why.
5. Explain how each of the following events biases (if it does)
    GNP as a measure of economic well-being for the current year
    in relation to GNP as a measure of well-being 40 years ago.
    a) An increase in the general price level.
    b) An increase in population.
    c) An increase in leisure time.
    d) An increase in welfare payments.
    e) An increase in restaurant meals relative to meals prepared
         and eaten in the home.
    f) An increase in stock market transactions.
    g) A decrease in the employment of maids and housekeepers.
    h) An increase in the proportion of women in the labor force.
    i) An increase in military expenditures.
    j) An increase in expenditures on the police because of an
         increase in crime.

6. From the following information, convert the 1965 GNP into GNP that reflects the 1972 price level:

GNP (current-year prices)	CPI (1972 = 100)
1965 .... $ 504	75
1972 1,152	100

Next convert 1972 GNP into 1965 prices.

7. "Exports are added to GNP whereas imports are subtracted from GNP. We should, therefore, strive to increase exports and decrease imports because in so doing we increase GNP and the economic well-being of society." Comment.

8. Explain how each of the following measures of national output or income differs from GNP: (a) net national product, (b) national income, (c) personal income, and (d) disposable income.

4

The Keynesian model without money

When undertaking the study of anything new, especially something as complex as an entire economy, it is usually desirable to begin at the simplest level possible. Then as we progress towards a basic understanding of the material we can probe a bit deeper for more detail. This essentially is what we will attempt to do in the following four chapters. In this chapter we begin with a simple "flow chart" of an economy and then briefly present an early view of how an economy might adjust to an unemployment situation. The major part of this chapter will develop what has come to be known as the simplest Keynesian model, or the Keynesian model without money. In Chapter 5 we will study the role of money in an economy, and in Chapter 6 we will take a brief look at the banking system in the United States. Then in Chapter 7 we integrate money into the simple Keynesian model to obtain a somewhat more detailed picture of a market economy.

An economic flow chart

Figure 4–1 is intended to present a very simplified picture of an economy. Here we see that the economy consists of two main sectors, the household sector and the business sector; and that two types of goods are produced: consumption goods and investment goods. Some of these goods, of course, can be purchased and distributed by the government, but this does not alter the fact that these items are part of the output of the economy.

FIGURE 4–1
Illustrating the flow of income and output in an economy

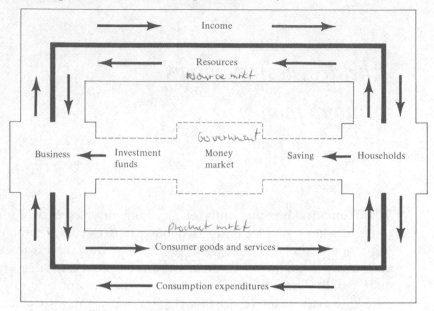

We should not be led to believe from Figure 4–1, however, that there are two separate groups in the economy, one producing and the other consuming. Certainly everyone must be a consumer to stay alive, but at the same time almost every adult is also a producer. Some, those who are part of the labor force, produce goods and services in business places; others, such as housewives, produce goods and services for themselves and their families at home.

Notice in Figure 4–1 that there are two sets of circular flows. The clockwise or outer flow represents money income and expenditures. The counterclockwise or inner flow represents real resources and consumer goods and services, As shown in the upper part of the diagram, households provide resources (labor, capital, and management) and in return receive income in the form of wages, interest, rents, and profits. The lower part of the diagram illustrates the fact that households in turn spend their income for consumer goods and services.

Of course we know that people, with the possible exception of students, do not as a rule spend all of their income; part is saved. This is illustrated in Figure 4–1 by the small saving flow coming out of the household sector. The two flows coming out of the household sector represent the idea that people can do only two things with their income: They can spend it or they can save it.

The fact that people do not as a rule spend all of their income on consumption goods and services (i.e., part is saved) frees part of the nation's resources for the production of investment goods— buildings, factories, machines, roads, etc. If society insisted on spending every dollar of its income on consumption goods, no resources would be available to produce investment goods. Thus saving is very necessary if an economy wants to grow and become more productive in the future.

The flow of saving that comes out of the household sector is funneled into a so-called money market, where it becomes available to business firms to use for the purchase of resources to produce investment goods. In passing, we should note that business firms also generate part of the saving in the economy by retaining part of their earnings to plow back into the firms. But this does not alter the basic idea that saving provides the wherewithal to invest.

To summarize briefly, the income that is generated by the production of consumption and investment flows into the household sector, where part is used by households for the purchase of consumption goods and part (the saving) is available to be used by business firms for the construction of investment goods. We should stress the word "available" in the preceding sentence. There is no guarantee that business firms will always desire to invest just the exact amount households desire to save.

Let us consider the case where desired investment is less than desired saving. This might occur if businessmen become pessimistic about the future and decide to cut back on their investment. The result is that there is a reduction in the demand for total goods and services because of the reduction in business demand for investment goods. This results in a reduced demand for resources by business firms, so that they begin to lay off employees.

This reduction in business activity might have been avoided if households at the time investment declined would have increased their consumption expenditures, i.e., decreased their rate of saving. Generally the opposite happens, however. When people expect a period of increased unemployment they generally tighten their belts and try to increase their rate of saving. This, of course, just throws more cold water on the economy as consumption expenditures decline along with investment.

The classical economists

The problem of unemployment in the economy has long occupied the attention of economists. However it is by no means true that economists have always agreed on what should be done to avoid or mitigate unemployment. In the early years of the economics profession, the predominate views of how an economy functioned seemed to be held by the so-called classical economists, a name coined by Karl Marx.[1] Of course there were divergent points of view even at that time, such as those of Karl Marx.

How did the classical economists view the economy? To put it very simply, they believed that a market economy, if left alone (little or no government intervention), was capable of generating and maintaining full employment over the long run. Although the classicists admitted the possibilities of a short-run or temporary lull in business activity and a resulting rise in unemployment, they at the same time argued that such conditions would not be likely to persist. In their view a market economy contained two adjustment mechanisms that would eventually restore it to a state of full employment. These were (1) flexible interest rates and (2) flexible wages and prices.

Regarding interest rates, the classicists argued that a decline in investment and the resulting excess of saving over investment would bring forth a glut of funds in the money market and this in turn would drive interest rates down. The reduction in interest rates would have two effects: (1) it would serve as an incentive for businessmen to increase investment spending, and (2) it would serve as a disincentive for households to save. Thus they reasoned that the decrease in saving or increase in consumption, together with greater investment spending, would stimulate the economy and as a result the economy would move back up towards the full-employment level.

The classical economists used similar reasoning with regard to flexible wages and prices. If unemployment reared its ugly head in the labor market, there would be a tendency for wages to fall as

---

[1] Three of the better known classical economists include F. Y. Edgeworth, J. S. Mill, and David Ricardo.

workers competed against each other to get the available jobs. The reduction in wages would in turn serve as an incentive for employers to hire more labor and for some people to remove themselves from the labor market. The market for consumer goods and services would behave similarly. If merchandise was produced that was not sold there would be a downward pressure on prices. And falling prices serve to maintain the purchasing power of people during periods of falling wages.

Thus the classical economists argued that the economy if left alone would return to a state of full employment in the event of temporary downturns in economic activity. In the main, the classical economists did not seem to be nearly as concerned about unemployment as they were with the level of prices. We will return briefly to the classical economists in the next chapter, where we present a simple mechanism they used to explain or predict changes in the price level.

Introduction to John Maynard Keynes

Until the early 1930s, the classical economist's view of an automatically adjusting economy appeared to be the predominate view held by economists. But then came the Great Depression. Astronomical unemployment rates of 15 to 20 percent persisted year after year in the United States. The depression dragged on towards the mid 1930s, and the economy did not seem able to adjust to regain full employment. Granted, money rates of interest declined and prices and wages fell, but still severe unemployment persisted.

Needless to say many economists began to voice some disenchantment with the classical theory. One in particular, John Maynard Keynes, an English economist, was especially influential. In 1936 Keynes came out with a book entitled *The General Theory of Employment, Interest and Money,* which has since become a classic and which greatly influenced economic thinking in the 20th century. The magnitude of the book's influence is illustrated by such terms as the "Keynesian revolution" or the "new economics."

Basically Keynes argued that there was no guarantee of full employment in a free market, "capitalistic" economy. Essentially he argued that in such an economy there is always the possibility that the "effective" demand for consumer and investment goods might not be sufficient to take off the market the entire supply that would be forthcoming from a full-employment economy.

The implication of Keynes' theory, then, is that a free market economy can find itself in a sort of equilibrium in which the level of aggregate demand for consumer and investment goods is not sufficient to generate full employment of the labor force. Keynes argued, therefore, that the government may be needed to influence or augment the level of aggregate demand so as to insure full employment.

You will note, therefore, a basic difference between the classical economists and Keynes. The classicists argued that a free market economy, even though it might experience short-term unemployment, would through flexible interest rates, wages, and prices return to a state of full employment without government intervention. Keynes put less faith in market forces and argued instead for more direct government intervention.

In order to understand Keynes' arguments, it is necessary to construct what has come to be known as the "Keynesian model" of the economy. As we said, we will begin with the model in its simplest form and then expand it a bit in Chapter 7.

Consumption and saving

The heart of the Keynesian model is aggregate demand. In the traditional method of constructing the Keynesian model, aggregate demand is assumed to consist of consumption, investment, and government spending. Let us look first at consumption.

Keynes argued that consumption was determined mainly by income. This is a fairly plausible argument. People with a $20,000 per year income can be expected to consume more goods and services than a $10,000 per year family, on the average. In addition Keynes argued that as a family's income increased its consumption increased, but not quite as much as the growth in income.

Again this is a fairly plausible argument. In order to maintain a bare minimum of food, clothing, and shelter, low-income people may have to spend their entire income and then some. College students are a good example. In fact most students probably consume more than their income, with the difference made up by gifts or borrowing. However, as incomes rise to the $8,000 to $10,000 per year figure and beyond, families can satisfy their basic needs and in addition put something away for a rainy day.

It will be helpful to represent this relationship between income and consumption in terms of a diagram. As we proceed we will utilize diagrams a great deal to illustrate ideas or concepts. In a sense, a diagram is a picture of an idea. If a "picture is worth a thousand words" then a diagram is a relatively efficient and concise method of expressing a thought.

In Figure 4–2 (A) we represent the two ideas or hypotheses that Keynes put forth regarding the relationship between income and consumption. First, the upward sloping line tells us that if disposable income increases, then consumption also increases. For example, if disposable income is $2,000 per year, the consumption line tells us that consumption is about $2,750 per year. Then as we move out along the income axis, say to $8,000 per year, consumption increases to $7,250 per year.

Keynes' second hypothesis, namely that consumption does not increase as much as income, is represented by the fact that the consumption line does not rise as rapidly as the 45-degree line. (This line is so named because it bisects the 90-degree angle made by the diagram.) Notice that anywhere on the 45-degree line, income always equals consumption. Thus if consumption increased dollar for dollar with income, the consumption line would be the same as the 45-degree line. The idea that consumption increases less rapidly than disposable income is reflected by a consumption line that is somewhat "flatter" than the 45-degree line.

The relationship between income and consumption also tells us what kind of relationship exists between income and saving. As we noted earlier, there are only two things a person can do with his disposable income: spend it or save it. Hence if we know income and consumption, we can easily derive saving. This is illustrated in Figure 4–2 (B), where the distance between the consumption line and the 45-degree line represents the amount saved at that particular level of income. We can, as we have done in Figure 4–2 (B), represent the distance between the 45-degree line and consumption on a separate diagram. The resulting line, call it the saving line, tells us how much is saved at a given level of income.

FIGURE 4–2
Relationship between income, consumption, and saving

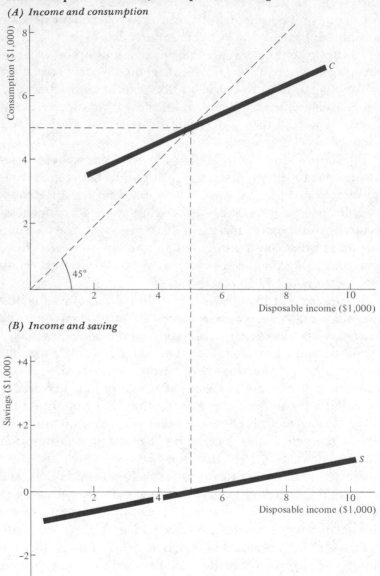

(A) Income and consumption

(B) Income and saving

Also notice the relationship between diagrams (A) and (B) in
Figure 4–2. At the point where the consumption line intersects the
45-degree line in diagram (A), consumption is equal to income, i.e.,
people spend all they take in. Saving, therefore, is equal to zero at

this level of income, and this is shown in diagram (B) where the saving line intersects the horizontal axis. In this particular example saving equals zero, or C equals DI, at the $5,000 income level. To the left of this intersection, consumption is greater than income, i.e., saving is negative. And to the right of the intersection, consumption is less than income, so saving is positive.

Propensities to consume

We can further our understanding of the relationship between consumption and income by developing the concepts of the average propensity to consume (APC) and marginal propensity to consume (MPC). The average propensity to consume is defined as the proportion of disposable income spent on current consumption of goods and services. It is computed as follows:

$$APC = \frac{C}{DI}$$

If we wish, we could multiply the resulting answer by 100 and express it as a percentage figure—the percent of DI that is spent on consumption goods and services.

One interesting thing to note about APC is that it becomes smaller and smaller the farther we move out along the consumption line as shown in Figure 4–2 (A). In the region to the left of the intersection of the consumption and 45-degree lines, APC is greater than one. In other words, consumption is greater than DI. At the intersection APC equals one and to the right, APC becomes progressively smaller than one.

Since the figures to compute APC (consumption expenditures and disposable income) are readily available, let us carry out the simple computation. The results are shown in Table 4–1. With the exception of the Great Depression and World War II, two highly atypical periods, the APC in the United States has been in the range of 0.90 to 0.95, i.e., people have been spending about 90 to 95 percent of their incomes and saving 5 to 10 percent. Notice also that there does not appear to be a discernible trend in the size of the APC over this period.

You might reasonably ask at this point, if disposable income in

TABLE 4-1
Average propensity to consume in the United States, five-year intervals, 1929-72*

Year	APC	Year	APC
1929	0.93	1954	0.91
1934	0.98	1959	0.92
1939	0.95	1964	0.92
1944	0.80	1969	0.91
1949	0.93	1972	0.93

* Computed by dividing consumption expenditures by personal disposable income.
Source: *Economic Report of the President, 1973*, p. 212.

the United States has been increasing over the years, is it not logical to expect that we would be moving out along the consumption line, so that APC should be steadily declining? Yet in Table 4-1 we see that APC has remained relatively constant during a time when incomes have grown substantially.

First it should be pointed out that the consumption line we are dealing with in the Keynesian model reflects *short-run* changes in consumer spending in response to short-run fluctuations in disposable income. Empirical evidence suggests, and it is reasonable to expect, that people do not change their spending habits in direct proportion to short-run changes in income. For example, if a family breadwinner is unemployed for six months and his annual income declines, say 40 percent, he probably will not subject his family to a 40 percent reduction in consumer goods and services during that year. The family may reduce consumer spending by 10 to 20 percent by reducing purchases of items they find least essential (restaurant meals, travel, entertainment, postponement of dental work, etc.) but not the full 40 percent. The deficit may come out of savings or possibly even from borrowing. The family doesn't cut back by the full 40 percent because it doesn't expect the reduction in income to be permanent. By the same token, a family that experiences a large increase in income during a given year, say because of an above average amount of overtime or an inheritance, will probably increase its spending some during that year but not by the full amount of the extra income, because they probably expect to be back to their former level of income the following year.

Of course, if people expect the change in income to be permanent, we can expect them to change their spending habits in accordance with their change in income. When you graduate from college and obtain a full-time job, you will likely increase your rate of spending over the present because you expect your long-run, or permanent, income to remain at this higher level. The idea that people regulate their long-run spending habits in accordance with long-run expected income was advanced by Professor Milton Friedman of the University of Chicago.[2] It has come to be known as the "permanent income hypothesis." Indeed Friedman argues that the average propensity to consume out of so-called permanent income remains virtually constant across families of various income levels at a point in time, and over succeeding generations of people with higher and higher incomes. This could explain, then, why the average propensity to consume in the United States has remained fairly constant in spite of increasing per capita incomes.

An alternative explanation for the long-run increase in consumption in proportion to the increase in income is provided by the "relative income hypothesis" which in the recent past has come to be associated with the work of Professor James Duesenberry of Harvard.[3] The idea here is that people base their consumption decisions on the relative size of their income as much as its absolute size. In other words, as people see their neighbors consuming more, they in turn also wish to consume more. Thus the consumption line shifts upward as per capita incomes increase.

Thus it is possible to explain the long-run increase in consumption expenditures in proportion to the long-run increase in income by the permanent income or the relative income hypothesis. At any rate, in the discussion that follows we will be dealing with the consequences of short-run changes in spending. Thus we can view the consumption line as being in a particular place at a point in time, as illustrated in Figure 4–3. Here we illustrate what the consumption line might have looked like in 1930, 1950, and 1972 for the U.S. economy. The dot on each line represents about where the country was on the line in each of these three years.

---

2 Milton Friedman, *A Theory of the Consumption Function* (Princeton, N.J.: Princeton University Press, 1957).

3 James S. Duesenberry, *Income, Saving, and The Theory of Consumer Behavior* (Cambridge, Mass.: Harvard University Press, 1952).

FIGURE 4-3
Upward shifts in the U.S. consumption line

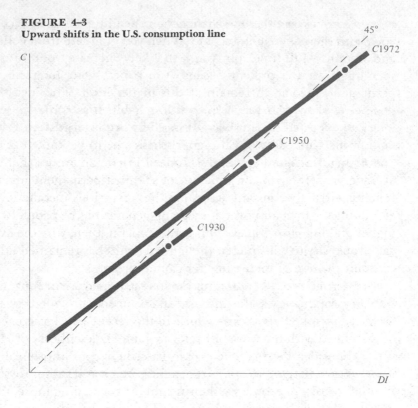

The second propensity relating to consumption, marginal propensity to consume (MPC), is defined as the proportion of *extra*
income spent on current consumption. For example, if your disposable income increases by $1 and you increase your consumption
by 75 cents, your MPC would be 0.75. Again, we can express this as
a percentage figure by multiplying the figure by 100. Of course, it
is difficult to imagine just a $1 incremental increase in income.
Most people when they receive a raise in pay enjoy something more
than this. For this reason economists utilize a simple formula for
computing MPC that provides an average MPC over a small range
of increase in income. The formula is:

$$\text{MPC} = \frac{\Delta C}{\Delta DI}$$

where the Δ symbol denotes "a change in."

We should also point out that MPC is equal to the slope of the
consumption line. Recall from your geometry or algebra that the

slope of a line is determined by dividing the vertical change by the horizontal change for a given movement along the line. This is illustrated by the consumption line in Figure 4–4. In this example, the vertical change is equal to ΔC and the horizontal change is ΔDI. An easy way to remember how to compute the slope of a line is by the simple formula:

$$\text{Slope} = \frac{\text{Rise}}{\text{Run}}$$

In other words, the "rise" of a line is equal to the vertical change ΔC in the consumption line, and the "run" is equal to the horizontal change, or ΔDI here. But notice that the formula for the slope of the consumption line is none other than the formula for MPC. Thus the slope of the consumption line is equal to MPC.

Unfortunately it is not nearly as easy to obtain estimates of the actual MPC for the country as it was to estimate APC. What we need is information on how people react to fairly small changes in disposable income. A number of studies, most using fairly sophisticated statistical techniques, have been done to estimate the actual MPC in the country.[4] However, the results vary considerably according to the data used and the specification of the statistical model. Most estimates of the nation's MPC appear to fall in the range of 0.60 to 0.90. Studies relating changes in consumption to changes in GNP generally provide estimates in the lower part of the range, while those using disposable income usually obtain estimates in the upper part of the range. We can expect these results because disposable income generally does not increase as much as GNP (or NNP). Part of the increase in GNP is siphoned off by increased taxes and business saving. Thus the change in the denominator of the MPC formula is larger using ΔGNP than using ΔDI. Therefore $\Delta C / \Delta DI$ is greater than $\Delta C / \Delta GNP$. For example, suppose GNP increases by \$1,000 and that taxes and business saving increase by \$200. In this case DI increases by \$800. If con-

---

4 See, for example, H. S. Houthakker and L. D. Taylor, *Consumer Demand in The United States* (New York: Cambridge University Press, 1966); N. Liviatan, "Estimates of Distributed Lag Consumption Functions from Cross Section Data," *Review of Economics and Statistics*, Vol. 47, February 1965, pp. 44–53; C. Y. Yang, "An International Comparison of Consumption Functions," *Review of Economics and Statistics*, Vol. 46, August 1964, pp. 279–86; and A. Zellner, "The Short Run Consumption Function," *Econometrica*, Vol. 25, 1957, pp. 552–67.

sumption increases by $600, MPC out of *DI* ($\Delta C/\Delta DI$) is equal to 0.75, while MPC out of GNP ($\Delta C/\Delta GNP$) is 0.60.

FIGURE 4–4
The slope of the consumption line

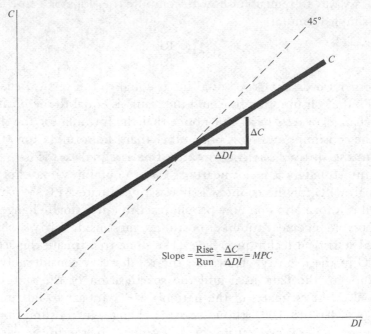

Propensities to save

Now that we know about the propensities to consume, it is a fairly simple matter to apply these same concepts to saving. In a parallel fashion we can talk about the average propensity to save (APS) and the marginal propensity to save (MPS). As you would expect from the preceding section, APS is the proportion of total disposable income that is saved, and MPS is the proportion of a change in income that is saved. The formulas for computing APS and MPS are:

$$\text{APS} = \frac{S}{DI} \qquad \text{MPS} = \frac{\Delta S}{\Delta DI}$$

The fact that people can do only two things with their disposable income, spend it or save it, means that APS and MPS bear a direct relationship to APC and MPC. The proportion that is saved (APS) plus the proportion that is spent (APC) must equal one. Moreover, the proportion of any change in income that is saved (MPS) plus the corresponding proportion that is spent (MPC) must also equal one. Thus we have:

$$APC + APS = 1 \quad \text{or} \quad 1 - APC = APS$$
$$MPC + MPS = 1 \quad \text{or} \quad 1 - MPC = MPS$$

Also the slope of the saving line, as in Figure 4–2 (B), is equal to the MPS.

Investment

The second major component of the simplest Keynesian model is investment. We will continue to define investment as it is defined in the national income accounts, i.e., the physical construction of buildings (including housing), machines, tools, etc., together with any change in inventories. As we will see a bit later, inventory change will play an important role in the model.

In the interest of preserving simplicity we will assume, in developing the simplest Keynesian model, that investment in the economy is a set or given amount, i.e., does not change at least over a modest range of income. The term "autonomous investment" is often used to describe this investment figure—a figure that is assumed or imposed on the model. We can represent autonomous investment by a straight horizontal line as in Figure 4–5 (A). Such an investment line tells us that the level of investment remains constant over the range of income shown.

It would be a bit more realistic to assume, of course, that investment would become a larger figure, the larger the income or output of the economy. This would be represented by the upward sloping line in Figure 4–5 (B). Although we will develop the model under the assumption of a fixed investment figure, later on we will point out how the model is affected by assuming that investment rises with income. At any rate, our major concern will be with changes or shifts in the entire investment line, and not so much

FIGURE 4–5
Investment and income

(A) Investment as a fixed amount   *(B) Investment increases with income*

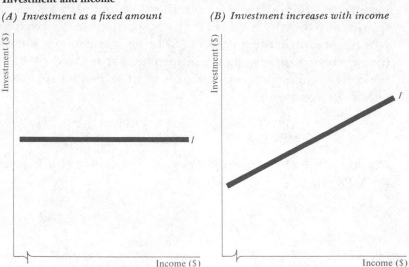

with its slope. Also, to simplify the model, we will assume that saving, which provides the wherewithal to invest, is provided entirely by households.

Government spending

The third major component of the simple Keynesian model without money is government spending. As we pointed out in the preceding chapter, we should not think of the goods and services purchased by the government as somehow being "lost" to the private sector. With the exception of the goods and services necessary to run the government bureaucracy, everything the government purchases goes back to the people in the form of either consumption goods, investment goods, or some combination of the two. Granted, the economic well-being of the population may not be enhanced by certain types of government expenditure such as expenditure on the military, but it is nevertheless part of the total output of the economy.

Again to simplify our discussion, we will assume that government spending also is a fixed or set amount, i.e., does not change over a range of income or output. We know, of course, that government purchases of goods and services tend to grow with the rest of the economy. However for relatively small changes in income or output, which we are mainly interested in, it is not too unrealistic to assume a fixed government spending figure.

Along with a fixed level of government spending, we will assume also that total taxes are a fixed or set amount, i.e., do not change at different levels of NNP. These often are referred to as lump-sum taxes. Again it would be more realistic to allow tax receipts to increase along with NNP, as would occur under an income tax. However this also would make the model more complex and, as we shall see a bit later, the directions of change predicted by the model using a fixed or lump-sum tax is the same as when we employ an income tax, although the magnitude of the change will be different.

In terms of a diagram we could represent government spending in exactly the same way we represented investment in Figure 4–5 (A)—by a straight horizontal line. Instead of drawing a separate diagram for government spending we can visualize it to be the same as the investment diagram, only in this case the horizontal line would be labeled G instead of I.

Aggregate demand

We now have developed the three main components of the simplest Keynesian model—consumption, investment, and government spending. The next task is to combine them to form what is called "aggregate demand." To obtain aggregate demand, we must add these three components together. The procedure is illustrated by Figure 4–6. Let us begin with the consumption line. This line tells us the amount that consumers desire to spend at various levels of income. The amount of consumer spending is shown on the vertical axis and the amount of income on the horizontal axis.

As a measure of total income we will utilize net national product (NNP). Recall that this is similar to GNP except that depreciation of capital has been deducted. As a result NNP should be a somewhat more accurate indicator of the net output of the economy, although we could use GNP without any change in the model

FIGURE 4-6
Deriving aggregate demand

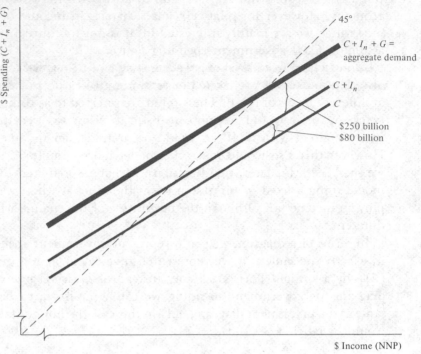

or in the analysis to follow. Most texts use NNP or the symbol Y to denote some measure of national income.

Recall that the marginal propensity to consume (MPC) defines the relationship between consumption and income. In our earlier discussion we related consumption to disposable income, since this is what consumers have available to spend or to save. However, note in Figure 4–6 that NNP is represented on the horizontal axis rather than DI. This is all right as long as we keep in mind that for every level of NNP there is a corresponding level of DI and that consumer spending depends on DI rather than on NNP.[5]

---

[5] If we assume that all saving is done by households (none by business) and taxes are fixed (the lump-sum variety), DI equals NNP minus the fixed tax. Hence changes in NNP equal changes in DI. Thus the slope of the consumption line (MPC) is the same regardless of whether we use ΔDI or ΔNNP in the denominator in calculating MPC in this case. In the case where some saving is done by business firms and taxes increase with NNP, which conforms more closely to the real world, DI does not increase as rapidly as NNP. Thus for a given ΔC, MPC will be lower using ΔNNP in the denominator than using ΔDI.

To provide some concrete figures to work with, let us assume from now on that MPC is 0.75. Thus the slope of the consumption line is assumed to be 0.75. We will not be particularly concerned with the initial level of the consumption line in our construction of the model because we will be mainly interested in studying the effects of relatively small changes or shifts in the consumption line and not in explaining its level at a point in time.

Also, to keep the example somewhat comparable to actual levels of I_n and G, we will assume that i_n equals \$80 billion and G equals \$250 billion at all levels of NNP. The addition of the \$80 billion investment to the consumption line gives us a $C + I_n$ line that is \$80 billion higher than the C line. Similarly the addition of the \$250 billion government spending component provides a $C + I_n + G$ line that is \$250 billion higher than the $C + I_n$ line shown in Figure 4–6. The resulting $C + I_n + G$ line has come to be known as aggregate demand. Essentially it tells how much consumers, investors, and government wish to spend at the various levels of income or NNP.

It is important to realize that in constructing aggregate demand simply by adding G to the $C + I_n$ line, as we have done in Figure 4–6, we have implicitly taken account of the effect of government spending on private consumption and investment. As we would expect, if the government did not provide any consumption or investment goods to the people, private purchase of consumption and investment goods would be higher than is the case with the government included. Or looking at it another way, the taxes imposed upon the people to pay for government-purchased goods and services have the effect of reducing private purchases of goods and services, because taxes reduce the purchasing power of the private sector. We must keep in mind, then, that the levels of C and I_n are influenced by the level of G. And in Figure 4–6, we have implicitly assumed that the downward shifts in C and I_n caused by the existence of G have already been taken into account.

Aggregate supply

Now that we have combined the basic components of the simplest Keynesian model and derived aggregate demand, the next step is to develop the concept of aggregate supply. In the context of the simple Keynesian model, aggregate supply can be thought of as denoting the various possible levels of output that the business sector is willing and able to produce. With this model it is assumed that the business sector will desire to produce that value of output which they expect to be able to sell. For example, if they expect to sell $1,000 billion worth of output they will want to produce $1,000 billion worth.

Because a given level of income implies the same level of spending, the line relating spending to income or output, i.e., aggregate supply, turns out to be a 45-degree line when superimposed on the aggregate demand diagram, as in Figure 4–7. This requires, of course, that the same number scale be used on both axes of the diagram. In other words, when we graph the points that correspond to equal values on each axis, we obtain a line that exactly bisects the 90-degree angle.

Equilibrium income

It is important to recognize, however, that the business sector may not be able to exactly anticipate the desired level of spending by consumers, investors, and the government as reflected by aggregate demand for any given year. For example, the business sector may expect aggregate demand to be greater than it in fact turns out to be. In this case, more goods and services might be produced than can be sold. This situation is illustrated in Figure 4–7 by the $1,200 level of income or output of the economy. Notice in this case that desired spending as reflected by the aggregate demand line is $1,150 at the $1,200 level of output.

The inevitable result of this situation is that $50 billion worth of goods remains unsold, which means that inventories rise by $50 billion. The business community, seeing this unintended rise in inventories, cuts back on production in the following year. And they will continue to reduce output, or NNP, until they reach the point where they are able to sell all they produce. This point is $1,000 billion in Figure 4–7.

Just the opposite occurs, of course, if NNP happens to be less than the point of intersection between aggregate supply and aggregate demand. Here people (including government) wish to buy more than is being produced. Inventories are drawn down unin-

FIGURE 4–7
Deriving equilibrium income

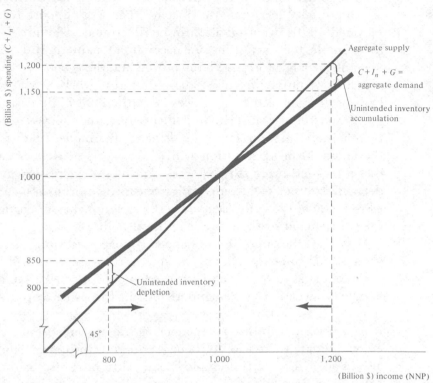

tentionally, and the business community begins to step up production, which in turn results in an increase in NNP.

As you no doubt recognize by now, there is only one point where the amount of goods and services that people wish to buy is exactly equal to the amount produced. This occurs at the intersection of the aggregate supply and aggregate demand lines. The level of NNP that corresponds to this intersection $1,000 billion in our example, is referred to as equilibrium income. At this intersection there are no forces existing to either reduce or increase the level of income or output in the economy.

Equilibrium versus full-employment income

Keynes and his followers argued that there is no reason why the equilibrium level of income in an economy must also turn out to be the full-employment level of income. In other words, they were concerned that an economy can come to rest at an equilibrium that is substantially less than the income that will support full employment. This situation also can be illustrated in Figure 4–7. If, for example, the level of income necessary to maintain full employment of the labor force is $1,100 billion and the economy comes to rest at the equilibrium of $1,000 billion, the workers who would have been employed to produce the extra $100 billion worth of goods and services instead find themselves unemployed. And, if there is no change in aggregate demand, the model predicts that the unemployment situation will tend to persist. Keynes argued that the government may have to take steps to increase aggregate demand in order to bring equilibrium income up to full-employment income. We will discuss how the government can change aggregate demand in the chapter on fiscal policy.

Of course, the opposite can happen if the equilibrium income is greater than full-employment income. In this case there will be an excess demand for goods and services which will give rise to an inflationary situation as demanders bid up the price of the scarce items.

As a third possibility, an economy could at some point in time enjoy the happy situation of being at an equilibrium income that also happened to be full employment. This, of course, is the best of all possible worlds, since everyone who wishes to work is employed and there is no tendency for inflation to occur. But would this situation persist for all time to come, or even for several years? Probably not. For during the passage of time, any economy is likely to experience changes that will have the effect of shifting aggregate demand either up or down. Let us now look at some of these changes.

Shifts in aggregate demand

Recall that aggregate demand is made up of three components: consumption, investment, and government spending. A change in the level of any of these three components will have the effect of changing aggregate demand.

1. Consumption shifts. From the standpoint of the long-run trend in the entire economy, we can view the consumption line as gradually and continually shifting upwards over time. The permanent income and relative income hypotheses discussed in a previous section provide possible explanations for this long-run upward trend in consumption in relation to income. Of course, since we are dealing with the entire economy, we would expect the growth in population also to push the aggregate consumption line to higher and higher levels. Although the continued long-run growth in consumption is important from the standpoint of maintaining a high level of aggregate demand, our major concern in the discussion to follow will be with short-term fluctuations or shifts in the consumption line.

Most economists probably would agree that a prime factor changing the level of consumption is a change in expectations of consumers. For example, suppose people suddenly become pessimistic about the future, thinking perhaps that they might be laid off. As a result they might decide to tighten their belts and reduce their rate of consumption purchases. This is illustrated by consumption C_0 in Figure 4–8 (A). Here it is shown that people wish to reduce their consumption by $10 billion at all possible income levels, which leads to a $10 billion downward shift in the aggregate demand line. The opposite might occur if people become more optimistic about the future. An increase in consumption as illustrated by C_2 in Figure 4–8 (A) would have the result of shifting aggregate demand upwards.

The expectation of the availability of goods and services in the future also tends to influence consumption during a particular period. For example, if people expect war to break out in the near future and as a result expect shortages to occur, some may increase their rate of purchase in order to stock up on items that they anticipate will be in short supply or rationed. The periods preceding World War II and the Korean conflict provide examples of this behavior. This can be illustrated by an increase in consumption from C_1 to C_2 in Figure 4–8 (A). Moreover an expectation of higher prices in the future, as commonly occurs during a war, tends to result in an increased rate of present consumption, also illustrated by C_2.

A third factor that is generally considered an important determinant of consumption is the availability of credit. As you might

FIGURE 4–8
The effect of changes in *C, I,* or *G* on aggregate demand

(A) Consumption shifts

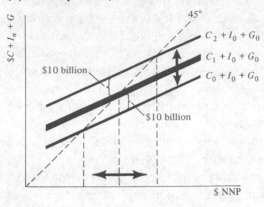

(B) Investment shifts

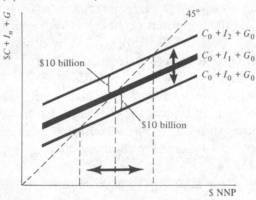

(C) Government spending shifts

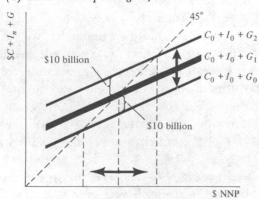

expect, this would mainly affect the purchase of consumer durables such as appliances and automobiles. If loans become difficult to obtain, consumers tend to reduce their purchases of these items as illustrated by C_0 in Figure 4–8 (A). Conversely if credit becomes easier to obtain, we might expect consumers to respond by stepping up their purchase of items bought on time.

A factor related to the availability of credit is the size of the interest rate, particularly the real rate of interest. An increase in the rate of interest increases the overall cost of an item purchased on time. If people respond to higher prices by reducing their purchases of these items, there may be a reduction in consumption, again as illustrated by C_0 in Figure 4–8 (A).

A less obvious effect of an interest rate change on present consumption is its impact on the decision to spend or to save. For example, a higher rate of interest means that a dollar of consumption given up at the present and saved will earn a higher return and will buy more in the future. In other words, the higher the rate of interest, the more a dollar saved at the present will buy in the future. Thus a rise in interest rates increases the price of present consumption vis-à-vis future consumption because it means giving up more in the future.

Changes in the stock of goods in the hands of consumers also may affect current consumption expenditures. For example, during World War II the stock of consumer durables was depleted because of the need to devote resources to war materials production. As a result, during the immediate postwar period consumer expenditures on these items probably were substantially higher than would have been true had there been no war. Even during more normal times, there might be random fluctuations in the stock of durable items that influence consumer expenditures.

2. Investment shifts. Because the ultimate aim of investment is to increase the future output of consumer goods and services, we would expect total investment also to exhibit a long-run upward trend in line with a growing economy. However, as in the case of consumption, there is also the possibility of short-run fluctuations in investment spending by the business community.

As in our discussion of consumer spending, we would have to say that expectations by businessmen play a key role in the determination of investment. Because investment by definition is something that pays off in the future, it is reasonable to expect that decisions to invest or not to invest depend a great deal on what investors expect the future to bring as far as business conditions are concerned. For example, if investors expect a strong future demand for consumer goods and services, i.e., a high level of employment and spending, it is more likely they will decide to step up current investment spending, as illustrated by I_2 in Figure 4–8 (B). Or if they expect a period of depressed business activity and high unemployment, investors tend to reduce investment spending, as illustrated by I_0 in Figure 4–8 (B). In this example we illustrate a $10 billion change in investment spending.

A second factor influencing the level of investment is the rate of interest. The interest rate is important to investment because a change in the rate of interest changes the *discounted present value* of the expected future returns of the investment. As long as the interest rate is greater than zero, a dollar forthcoming sometime in the future is worth less than a dollar in hand today. If we had the dollar in hand today, we could always lend it out with interest and obtain something more than one dollar in the future. For example, suppose we would be indifferent between having $1 now and $1.10 one year from now if we could lend the dollar out at a 10 percent rate of interest. In other words, it would take $1.10 of income one year from now to compensate us for giving up $1 of income today at an interest rate of 10 percent. Since it takes more than a dollar in the future to compensate for the dollar in hand at the present, income in the future is worth less than income at the present.

In general, businessmen will invest in buildings, machinery, and the like only if the discounted present value of the sum of the expected income stream is at least as large as the cost of the investment. A reduction in the present value of future returns, due to an increase in the interest rate, will cause businessmen to reject some investment projects that they might have accepted under lower rates of interest.

The formula for determining the discounted present value of one dollar forthcoming in the future is $1/(1 + r)^n$ where r is the rate of interest and n represents the number of years in the future that the dollar is forthcoming. To illustrate the effect of an increase in the rate of interest, let us compute the present value of the returns from an investment that pays off at the rate of $1,000 per year over a five-year period, using both a 5 percent and a 10 percent rate of interest. The results are presented in Table 4–2. At the 5 percent

TABLE 4–2
The effect of a change in the interest rate on the discounted present value of an income stream

Interest rate	Year 1	2	3	4	5	Present value
5 percent	$\dfrac{\$1,000}{1.05}$ +	$\dfrac{\$1,000}{(1.05)^2}$ +	$\dfrac{\$1,000}{(1.05)^3}$ +	$\dfrac{\$1,000}{(1.05)^4}$ +	$\dfrac{\$1,000}{(1.05)^5}$ =	$4,324
10 percent	$\dfrac{\$1,000}{1.10}$	$\dfrac{\$1,000}{(1.10)^2}$	$\dfrac{\$1,000}{(1.10)^3}$	$\dfrac{\$1,000}{(1.10)^4}$	$\dfrac{\$1,000}{(1.10)^5}$ =	$3,793

interest rate the discounted present value of the income stream of this investment is $531 greater ($4,324 − $3,793) than it is when the interest rate is 10 percent. If the cost of the investment were $4,000, it would have been profitable if the interest rate had been 5 percent but unprofitable under the 10 percent rate of interest.[6]

Thus we can expect the investment line to shift upward with a decrease in the rate of interest and downward with an increase in the interest rate. For example, I_1 in Figure 4–8 (B) might correspond to an 8 percent rate of interest while I_2 and I_0 correspond to interest rates of 6 and 10 percent, respectively. In other words, for a given level of income, the rate of investment can be expected to increase when the rate of interest declines, and vice versa.[7]

3. Government spending shifts. Since government spending is included as a separate component of aggregate demand, any decision to change the level of government spending will, of course, change the level of aggregate demand, at least in the short run. Abrupt increases in government spending have come about mainly in wartime, as illustrated by G_2 in Figure 4–8 (C). Then after the end of hostilities, government spending is reduced and G shifts downward, as shown by G_0.

In the context of the Keynesian model, the government spending component of aggregate demand takes on special significance be-

---

[6] For further discussion on investment decisions see Chapter 10 (The Capital Market) in the companion micro text.

[7] This assumes no change in the expected rate of inflation. If the price level is rising, it is important to consider the real rate of interest.

cause it can be changed by deliberate government edict to offset any changes in consumption or investment. For example, if investors become pessimistic and reduce investment by $10 billion, the government can offset this by increasing its expenditure by $10 billion, perhaps on new public works projects and the like. We will consider this topic in more detail in the upcoming chapter on fiscal policy.

The multiplier

By now it should be clear that a shift in any one or all of the components of aggregate demand will in turn change the level of equilibrium income. An increase in C, I_n, or G, for example, increases equilibrium income and vice versa. The next question we will consider is, How much does equilibrium income change for a given change in aggregate demand? A glance at the diagrams in Figure 4–8 will tell us that the change along the horizontal axis, i.e., the change in equilibrium income, is greater than the vertical shift in aggregate demand. That this must be so is purely a phenomenon of geometry. The closer the slope of the aggregate demand line is to the slope of the 45-degree line, the greater will be the change in equilibrium income for a given shift in aggregate demand.

This phenomenon is illustrated in Figure 4–9. If the aggregate demand line were horizontal, as D_0, then the change along the horizontal axis corresponding to the new intersection would exactly equal the upward shift of the line. This must be true because the slope of the 45-degree line is one, meaning that the horizontal change just equals the vertical change.

But if we increase the slope of the aggregate demand line, as in D_0', the new intersection of the two lines moves farther to the right than the upward shift of aggregate demand. In fact, as the slope of the aggregate demand line approaches the slope of the 45-degree line, a small upward shift in aggregate demand gives rise to an almost infinite increase in equilibrium income. When and if the two lines become one, there is no intersection or equilibrium—the system "blows up" so to speak. It will be easier to understand this phenomenon if you draw some aggregate demand lines of your own,

FIGURE 4-9
Illustrating the effect of the slope of aggregate demand on the change
in equilibrium income

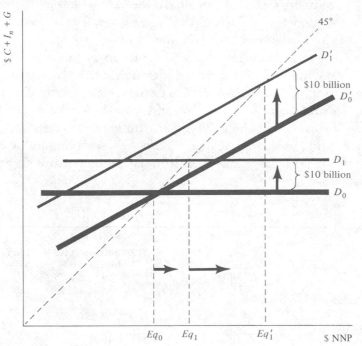

with progressively steeper slopes, and observe what happens to
equilibrium income when aggregate demand is shifted.

Recall that the upward slope of aggregate demand in this simple
model is due entirely to the upward sloping characteristic of the
consumption line. Thus the steeper the consumption line, the
steeper is aggregate demand and the greater is the change in equilibrium income. However, recall that we could have also drawn the
investment line with an upward slope as in Figure 4–5 (B). If we
had done so, this would have added to the slope of the aggregate demand line (making it steeper) and caused an even greater change in
equilibrium income for a given shift in aggregate demand.

Fortunately there is an economic rationale for the large change
in equilibrium income relative to the shift in aggregate demand—
it is called the multiplier effect. To illustrate the multiplier, let us
take as an example a $10 billion increase in consumption expendi-

tures—i.e., a $10 billion upward shift in the consumption line. The extra $10 billion spent for consumption goods and services (appliances, automobiles, clothes, housing, travel) represents extra income for the people who produce and sell these goods and services. If the MPC of these people is, say, 0.75, they will in turn spend $7.5 billion and save $2.5 billion. This $7.5 billion of new spending in turn represents $7.5 billion added income for the people who produce and sell the goods and services to the second group. The third group in turn spends $5.6 billion and saves $1.9 billion. And the process keeps rolling along. These first three rounds of new spending have added a total of $23.1 billion of new spending in the economy ($10 + 7.5 + 5.6 = 23.1$). We summarize the multiplier process in Table 4–3.

TABLE 4-3

Round	Added income	Added spending
One	—	$10.0 billion $= 1 \times \$10$ billion
Two	$10.0 billion	7.5 billion $= 0.75 \times 10$ billion
Three	7.5 billion	5.6 billion $= (0.75)^2 \times \$10$ billion
Four	5.6 billion	4.2 billion $= (4.75)^3 \times \$10$ billion
•	•	•
•	•	•
To infinity	•	• $= (0.75)^n \times \$10$ billion
	$40.0 billion	$40.0 billion

If we repeated this process round after round for an infinite number of times (a task that we do not quite have time for), we would find that the added spending column would sum to $40 billion. You might ask, at this point, how do we know that the added spending sums to $40 billion? Surely no one in his right mind, not even an economist, would carry this process out for millions and millions of rounds and add up the total.

Fortunately we can employ a convenient mathematical formula that gives the sum of an infinite convergent series. The formula is:

$$1 + x + x^2 + x^3 + \ldots x^n = \frac{1}{1 - x}$$

where x is less than one. Notice the similarity between this formula and the right-hand column in Table 4–3. In the first round the value of added spending is equal to $1 \times \$10$ billion; in the second round it is $0.75 \times \$10$ billion; in the third round it is $(0.75)^2 \times \$10$ billion, etc. If we let x in the formula equal the MPC, 0.75 in our example, the sum of the x's plus 1 equals $1/1 - x$. In our example this would equal $1/1 - 0.75$, or $1/0.25$ or 4. Thus the formula tells us that if MPC is 0.75, the total amount of new spending that will occur after the multiplier process has worked itself out is equal to $1/1 - $ MPC times the initial increase in spending. Of course we must realize that an infinite number of rounds would never take place. This is not regarded as serious criticism of the multiplier, however, because the major increase in spending comes in the first few rounds. The rounds can occur simultaneously as people anticipate changes in business activity and future income.

In this example we considered a $10 billion increase in consumer spending which led to a fourfold increase in total spending in the economy. In other words, equilibrium income would have increased by about $40 billion because of this $10 billion upward shift in the consumption line. Of course, the multiplier process also works in reverse. A $10 billion downward shift in the consumption line would have decreased equilibrium income by about $40 billion if MPC is 0.75.

We could go through the same procedure for a shift in the investment line. The reasoning would be exactly the same. A $10 billion increase, or upward shift, in the investment line would give rise to round after round of spending and respending, again resulting in a $40 billion increase in equilibrium income as shown by the Keynesian model in this chapter. Similarly a $10 billion decrease in the desire to invest leads to a fourfold decrease in equilibrium income assuming an MPC of 0.75.

We can summarize the effect of a shift in the consumption or investment lines by the following formulas:

$$\text{Change in equilibrium income} = \frac{1}{1 - \text{MPC}} \times \text{change in consumption}$$

$$\text{Change in equilibrium income} = \frac{1}{1 - \text{MPC}} \times \text{change in investment}$$

Notice that the size of the multiplier in this simple model, $1/1 - $ MPC, depends only on the size of the nation's MPC. The larger the MPC, the larger the multiplier, and vice versa. For example, if MPC is 0.80 the multiplier is 5, if MPC is 0.90 the multiplier is 10, etc. From an economic point of view the relationship between the multiplier and MPC is reasonable. The higher the MPC, the more people will spend of an incremental increase in income, hence the larger is the amount of income received by the people in the next round, etc. And according to the formula, as MPC approaches one, a small increase in income to any one person or group will give rise to an infinitely large increase in equilibrium income. Of course, this is not likely to happen, as we shall see in later chapters.

A change or shift in government spending, the third component of aggregate demand, also can give rise to a multiple increase or decrease in equilibrium income. In this case the multiplier will depend upon how the government spending is financed and the effect of government spending on private consumption and investment. If there is a surplus of funds in the treasury, say from some past year, and there is no change in C or I_n, an increase in government spending will increase equilibrium income by $1/1 - $ MPC times the increase in G. Similarly, a decrease in G decreases equilibrium by $1/1 - $ MPC times the decrease. The effect of a change in government spending becomes more complex when we consider accompanying changes in taxation, government borrowing, or changes in the money supply. We will consider these complications in more detail in the chapter on fiscal policy (Chapter 8).

Of course, in order for there to be a multiple increase or decrease in the real output of society, it must be assumed that there are idle resources available. For example, if the economy is already at full-employment income and there is an increase in aggregate demand, there will tend to be an increase in prices, i.e., demand-pull inflation, and an increase in money income, but relatively little increase in the real income or output of society. Similarly if equilibrium is greater than full employment and aggregate demand declines, the model suggests that real output should not decline appreciably until the equilibrium falls below full employment.

Main points of Chapter 4

1. The fact that people do not spend all of their income on consumer goods and services allows some of the nation's resources

to be devoted to the production of investment goods and services. In other words, saving provides the wherewithal to invest.

2. The dominant views on macroeconomics during the formative years of the discipline were put forth by the classical economists. They believed that a free market economy was capable of generating and maintaining full employment over the long run without government intervention.

3. The classical economists granted the possibility of temporary slowdowns in economic activity and resulting increases in unemployment. But they argued that a market economy contains two adjustment mechanisms that would restore the economy to full employment. These are (1) flexible interest rates and (2) flexible wages and prices.

4. According to the classical economists, an excess of desired saving over desired investment and the resulting increase in unemployment will result in a glut of funds in the money market, which in turn will drive down interest rates. A reduction in interest rates will in turn make businessmen more willing to invest and people less willing to save. This in turn will have the effect of increasing both investment and consumption spending, which stimulates the economy back to its former state of full employment.

5. The classical economists also argued that unemployment serves to drive down wages. This provides an incentive for business to hire more people while at the same time stimulating some people to leave the labor force. Both effects serve to equalize the number of people who are working with the number who are willing to work at the prevailing wage rate. Full employment occurs when the two figures are equal.

6. The excess of goods and services in the market during periods of unemployment also results in downward pressure on prices. And falling prices maintain the purchasing power of consumers during periods of falling wages.

7. In contrast to the classical economists, John Maynard Keynes argued that a free market economy could experience prolonged periods of unemployment, as the United States did in the 1930s, because of insufficient demand for consumer and investment goods. Thus he argued there may be a need for

the government to intervene in the economy, either to augment or influence the demand for goods and services.

8. The heart of the simple Keynesian model is aggregate demand, which has been traditionally defined to include (1)
consumption, (2) investment, and (3) government spending.
Government spending encompasses both consumption and
investment goods and services.

9. Keynes argued that consumption is determined mainly by
income, although an increase in income does not bring forth
as large an increase in consumption.

10. Average propensity to consume (APC) is defined as the proportion of disposable income that is spent on consumer goods
and services. $APC = C/DI$. Marginal propensity to consume
(MPC) is defined as the proportion of *extra* income that is
spent on current consumption. $MPC = \Delta C/\Delta DI$. MPC is also
equal to the slope of the consumption line.

11. The average propensity to consume in the United States has
remained fairly constant, fluctuating in the narrow range of
0.90 to 0.95 during most of the past 44 years in spite of the
more than doubling of real disposable income. This has come
about because of the upward shift of the short run consumption line over time.

12. Statistical estimates of the actual MPC for the United States
tend to fall in the range of 0.60 to 0.90.

13. The average propensity to save (APS) and the marginal propensity to save (MPS) are exactly analogous to APC and MPC
except that they relate to saving rather than consumption.

14. For the purpose of constructing the simple Keynesian model
it is assumed that investment and government spending do
not change within at least a small range of income, i.e., they
can be represented by horizontal lines on the spending and
income diagram.

15. Aggregate demand is constructed by adding investment and
government spending to the consumption line. With this procedure it is implicitly assumed that the impact of taxation and
government spending on private consumption and investment
is already taken into account.

16. Equilibrium income occurs at the point of intersection of aggregate demand and aggregate supply. At points to the right
of this intersection, aggregate supply is greater than aggregate

demand, i.e., more goods and services are produced than are sold. This results in an unintended inventory accumulation, which in turn results in a reduction in output, income, and employment as the economy moves back to the equilibrium point.

17. At points to the left of this intersection, aggregate demand is greater than aggregate supply, i.e., more is sold than is produced, inventories are drawn down unintentionally, businessmen step up production, and as a result the level of output, income, and employment is increased until the equilibrium is achieved.

18. Keynes and his followers expressed concern that the equilibrium level of income might not be great enough to correspond to full employment of the labor force. Hence there might be a need for government to increase aggregate demand in order for equilibrium income to correspond to full-employment income.

19. Changes in equilibrium income occur because of changes or shifts in aggregate demand. And changes or shifts in aggregate demand are caused by changes or shifts in the level of consumption, investment, or government spending.

20. The fact that equilibrium income changes by a multiple of the initial change in spending is a result of the multiplier effect. The multiplier effect occurs because each additional dollar of spending by one person or group is additional income to another person or group. In each successive round of the multiplier process part of the added income is spent and part is saved. The part that is spent represents added income to its recipients. The multiplier for a shift in consumption or investment in the simple Keynesian model is $1/1 - MPC$.

Questions for thought and discussion

1. "From the standpoint of total society, saving is bad because it represents a leakage out of the stream of income and spending." Comment.

2. According to the classical economists, how would a free

market economy eventually return to a state of full employment after temporary downturns in economic activity? Explain the effect of flexible interest rates and wages and prices.

3. Explain, as you would to a friend who has had no economics, the meaning of average propensity to consume and marginal propensity to consume.

4. For this past year, estimate your APC. If you earned an extra $1,000 next year, what would your MPC probably be? Explain why you think so.

5. Is it possible for a person's APC to be greater than one but his MPC to be less than one? Explain why or why not.

6. Show why the slope of the consumption line is equal to MPC. Does MPC change at different points along a straight, upward sloping consumption line? Does APC change along this same consumption line? Explain.

7. Using a diagram, construct an aggregate demand line assuming that MPC is 0.80, I_n equals $100 billion, and G equals $300 billion. (Do not be concerned about the level of the consumption line.) What crucial assumption has to be made regarding the level of C and I_n if G is simply added on to these two magnitudes?

8. Using the aggregate demand–aggregate supply diagram, explain what happens if an economy is not at equilibrium income.

9. "In the Keynesian model, equilibrium income is always full-employment income." Comment.

10. Once an economy settles down at an equilibrium income, what can cause the equilibrium to change?

11. By means of a diagram, illustrate why a shift in aggregate demand brings forth a relatively large change in equilibrium income. What is this phenomenon called? What is its economic rationale?

5

The demand for money

Let us now turn our attention to the role of money in an economy. At first glance it may appear a bit strange to talk about the demand for money. After all, you might say, money is one item that everyone could use a little more of. Most of us dream about the things we would buy or the places we would go if we just had a little more money. Can we not simply say, then, that the demand for money by most people is for some amount greater than they now have?

Although most of us would like a bit more money than we now have, our discussion of the demand for money will take on a substantially different meaning. Instead we will be interested in the fraction of a person's total wealth or assets that he wishes to hold as cash balances. Although no one has complete control over the value of his assets, we are to a certain extent free to decide how much of our assets we wish to hold as money and how much we wish to hold as earning assets, such as stocks or bonds, or durables, such as automobiles, houses, clothes, or appliances.

Before we turn to this topic, however, it will be useful to take a brief look at some of the characteristics and functions of money.

Characteristics of money

Perhaps the first thought that comes to our minds when we consider money is the image of currency and coins in our billfolds or purses. Further reflection might bring to mind the money in our checking and savings accounts at the bank. Of course, from our knowledge of history, we know that man has utilized a variety of objects as money. What was used depended mainly on the resources and technology available at the time. Primitive tribes that "lived off the land" generally utilized certain bones of agreed upon animals, stones, beads, or other objects that were not overly abundant in nature.

With the coming of animal domestication and agriculture, we read of animals such as cattle or goats, or crops such as wheat, being used as money. Then the precious metals, particularly gold and silver, came into use as money. These examples by no means exhaust the list. It is interesting to note, for example, that even cigarettes were used as money in some prisoner of war camps during World War II.

One desirable characteristic of money is that it be made out of material that is relatively cheap to produce. The more resources a society must employ to produce money, the less there are available to produce the real goods and services that sustain life and make it more interesting and enjoyable. For example, if the people of the world insisted on using a costly material such as gold as the only legal form of money, a significant share of the world's population might find it individually profitable to spend their time and effort producing money, i.e., mining. But from society's standpoint the efforts of these people would be for nought. The world would lose the goods and services that these people and their capital resources could have produced instead.

Of course, some gold will always be demanded for industrial purposes and for jewelry. But as we will see in later chapters the main demand for gold at the present still comes from governments as a backing for their currency and as a means of settling debts between countries. Gold would probably be much cheaper today were it not for this demand.

Considering the relatively high cost of mining and processing gold, or any other metal, for money, it is fortunate that paper money has come into such widespread use. The cost in terms of resources used for the paper and printing may add up to only a few dollars for millions of dollars produced. If a society decided that the face value of its money should be equal to its value as a commodity, then producers of the money (for example, miners) would have an incentive to spend up to a dollar's worth of resources to obtain an extra dollar of the money. Of course, the main motivation for adopting paper money probably came more from a desire for greater convenience than to reduce costs to society.

Going further, modern societies have devised other ways to cheapen the resource cost of money and increase its convenience of use. Checking account money is a good example. Of course, like paper money, the coming of checking accounts probably was motivated more by the increased convenience to the individual than by a decreased resource cost to society. As a result of a desire for still greater convenience, money as we know it today may someday become obsolete. We will return to this topic in a following section.

Another desirable characteristic of money is that it be reasonably durable, yet easy to carry around. No material, of course, is perfect in this regard. Cast iron may be durable but makes for a weighty change purse. Gold fares rather badly on both counts. Being a rather soft metal, it is not extremely durable, and the fact that it is a metal makes it heavy to carry around. In this regard paper would have to rank ahead of gold as a desirable form of money.

Although money should be cheap and easy to manufacture, it should at the same time be very difficult to duplicate or counterfeit. Gold ranks high on this point, which probably explains its popularity in medieval times. An ounce of gold is an ounce of gold. Of course, when gold coins came into use, the possibility of "sweating" was introduced. People soon found out that small particles of gold could be removed from gold coins simply by shaking them in a bag. And by melting the particles together, one might obtain, for example, 51 coins out of a bag of 50. This same problem occurred in prisoner of war camps where cigarettes were used as money.[1] Here the men found that by rolling a cigarette between thumb and forefinger some tobacco could be extracted without noticeably altering the form of it. Thus, some could smoke their money and have it too.

---

[1] For an interesting article on the use of cigarettes as money in a World War II P.O.W. camp, see R. A. Radford, "The Economic Organization of a P.O.W. Camp," *Economica*, November 1945, pp. 189–201. It is also interesting to note how prices varied directly with the supply of cigarettes.

Functions of money

The fact that money has existed as long as man has populated the earth ought to tell us that money is useful. The word "useful" in this case does not refer to the goods and services that money "buys." Rather it refers to the fundamental reasons for a society to utilize something called money. Money is useful for three basic reasons: it serves as (1) medium of exchange, (2) a standard or measure of value, and (3) a store of value.

Regarding the first use, if it were not for the concept of money we would have to operate under a barter system. In other words, each person would have to exchange the goods or services he produces directly with another person for the goods or services he desires. A little reflection will impress upon us how incredibly inefficient a barter system would be. For example, an economics professor would have to exchange lectures for food, clothing, etc. Not a very easy task if owners of food or clothing did not want to listen to economics lectures. The example becomes even more absurd when we consider what the producers of airplanes or ABM's would exchange for the things they desire. The lesson is clear: were it not for money people would have to spend much of their time shopping rather than producing and as a result society's output would be reduced drastically. Thus, if money did not exist, someone would have to invent it.

Money is useful also to measure the value or price of things. With a barter economy we would have to remember the price of each good or service in terms of every other good or service. For example, one economics textbook might be exchanged for a pair of gloves; three textbooks for a pair of shoes, and so on. Thus each good or service would in fact have thousands of prices, i.e., the amount of every other good or service that is worth the same as the good or service in question. It doesn't take long to realize that even in a relatively primitive society the task of determining prices would be next to impossible without a common denominator— money. With money, each good or service only has one price, i.e., its price in terms of the monetary unit.

Most people like to put away part of the fruits of their labor for future use. Thus money is useful as a store of value. Without money we would have to save material objects. But what would these objects be? Obviously they could not be things that deteriorated or depreciated with time, or else time would erase our savings. Also they should not be items that are costly to guard and store, or else a major part of our efforts would be devoted to guarding our savings rather than producing and enjoying life. Money, of course, is a convenient object to save; it doesn't deteriorate with reasonable care, and it is relatively costless to store.

What gives money purchasing power?

We know, of course, that paper money and coins are worth only a small fraction of their face value as a commodity. A ten-dollar bill, for instance, is worth only a fraction of a cent in the used paper market. But take it to a store and it can be exchanged for a good deal more than that even at today's inflated prices. The same is true of coins.

In fact, it would not be desirable for the commodity value of money to approach or exceed its face value. This happened in the early 1960s with respect to silver nickels. Shortages of silver drove its price up in the market until the value of the metal in a nickel coin was about seven cents. It soon became apparent to some enterprising people that a profit could be earned by melting down nickels and selling the metal in the market, perhaps even back to the government. Thus money that is worth more than its face value tends to disappear from circulation.

Also as mentioned earlier, if the commodity value of money approaches its face value, it is an indication that the money is far too costly to produce. If a nickel is worth seven cents, this is an indication that society is devoting seven cents worth of resources to produce each nickel—not a very good buy for society.

But we are still faced with the question, why can paper money, which has virtually no value in itself, be used to purchase valuable goods and services? We might be tempted to say that the gold in Fort Knox provides a backing hence provides a value to our paper money. But we should realize that the nation's gold reserves amount to only a small fraction of the nation's money supply. In December 1972, for example, the nation's currency, demand deposits, and time deposits totaled $514.5 billion, while the value of gold owned by the government amounted to only $10.5 billion. Thus each dollar of money was backed by only about two cents worth of gold at that time. Although the nation's gold may provide a certain confidence in the value of the dollar, its relatively small amount cannot provide each paper dollar with a dollar's worth of value.

Confidence by the people in the government that issues the paper money takes us part of the way towards the answer we are searching for. If people do not expect the government to exist in the future, it is likely that they will become somewhat reluctant to accept its paper money in payment for real goods and services. However, the basic reason for the fact that paper money has value seems to come down to the confidence of the people in the money itself. In other words, each of us accepts each unit of paper money as having a specified value as long as it is accepted by almost everyone else in society. Thus paper money seems to have value because people accept it as having value. If most people in the United States suddenly decided that they would no longer accept paper money as a medium of exchange, this form of money no longer could be used as such.

Of course, this is not to say that paper money always retains a certain fixed value in the purchase of real goods and services. As we will more adequately explain in later sections, the quantity of money in relation to the real output of goods and services in a country can be expected to have an important bearing on its value or purchasing power.

A cashless society

As we noted, money has taken many different forms throughout history. Even within fairly recent times we have seen a gradual transition from the use of currency to demand deposits or checking account money. And within the last 5 to 10 years, the credit card has become a convenient tool for making small purchases. However, the use of credit cards does not rule out the use of checks or currency. It is just a means of paying for several purchases with one check or cash payment.

A truely cashless society would be one step removed from the credit card society of today. Each person might have to present the equivalent of a credit card or some form of identification when making a purchase. But instead of billing the customer at a later date, the procedure would be to deduct the amount of the purchase from the buyer's account in his bank at the moment of purchase. In this situation there would be little need to carry cash or to have a checking account. Bills would be paid by a simple subtraction of numbers. Similarly people would receive their income when employers or buyers of services credited or added the appropriate amount to a person's account.

Although such a procedure would characterize a cashless society, it would not imply a moneyless society. The numbers that would be added to or subtracted from accounts would still be given in terms of dollars. But the dollars would not be green pieces of paper or coins. Instead they would be just numbers in people's accounts, and these accounts would be found in the memory cores of computers employed by financial institutions. Thus the concept of money would still be used, although its form would change from tangible objects, i.e., paper and metal, to intangible numbers in people's accounts.

Whether we will experience a cashless society in our lifetime will depend upon the cost and convenience of such a monetary system. If some technical problems can be solved, particularly the problem of identifying people, we may see a gradual transition to this kind of monetary system. The reason for this change is really no different than for changes in the past. The printing press made it possible for paper money to come into existence. A highly organized and coordinated banking system makes checking account money possible. And the computer may bring forth a cashless society. Of course, the use of coins and currency may still prove to be the best way to handle small day-to-day purchases made through vending machines, drugstores, etc.

Alternative measures of the quantity of money

Throughout the remainder of this chapter and the next several chapters we will refer often to the "quantity of money" in the economy. It is necessary, therefore, to define what is included in this quantity. In the context of macroeconomics there are two widely used definitions of the quantity of money. One, often called the narrow definition, includes currency and demand deposits. The other, known as the broad definition, includes currency, demand deposits, and savings or time deposits.

Which of these two definitions of money one wishes to use depends largely on personal preference. If you believe that people view their money in savings accounts in essentially the same light as their cash and demand deposits, i.e., as being currently available for spending on goods and services, then you would be more likely to include time deposits as part of the total money supply. On the other hand, if you believe that people view money in their savings accounts differently from cash and demand deposits, in that it represents money set aside for spending in the distant future, then you would be likely to exclude time deposits from the money supply. In large part, the choice of definition depends on how closely people view money in a savings account as a substitute for cash or demand deposits.

In Figure 5–1 we present the quantity of money in the United

FIGURE 5–1
Quantity of money in the United States, 1929–72

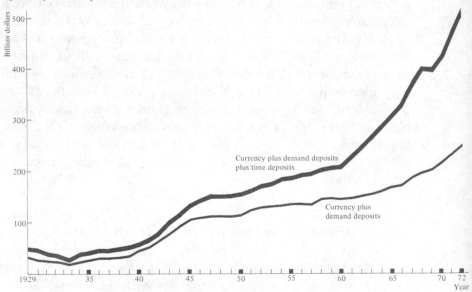

Source: 1929–47, Milton Friedman and Anna J. Schwartz, *A Monetary History of the United States, 1897–1960* (Princeton, N.J.: Princeton University Press 1963), Table A-1; 1948–72, *Economic Report of the President, 1970,* p. 236, and *1973,* p. 254.

States from 1929 to 1972 inclusive, in terms of both the narrow and broad definitions. Although we observe a long-run upward trend in the quantity of money under both definitions, there have been rather noticeable fluctuations in this trend. Perhaps most significant is the absolute decline in the quantity of money during the early 1930s. Notice also the rapid increase during the World War II years, the modest growth during the 1950s, and the speeding up of the growth during the 1960s and early 1970s. In terms of the broad definition, the quantity of money in the United States just about doubled between 1962 and 1972. The substantial increase in money held in savings accounts explains a major share of this growth.

In the United States, currency (paper money plus coins) makes up a rather small share of the total quantity of money. Using the narrow definition (currency plus demand deposits), currency accounted for about 23 percent of the total money as of December 1972. Under the broad definition, currency made up about 11 percent of the money stock at this time.

We should point out too that the currency figure includes only dollars outside of banks, that is, dollars held by individuals and business firms. If dollars held by banks were included, we would be double-counting bank deposits. For example, if currency inside banks were counted as part of the quantity of money, a $100 deposit of cash in a person's checking account would be counted once as demand deposits and secondly as the $100 in cash held by the bank. This is not to say that banks keep a dollar of cash on hand for each dollar of demand deposits. We will come back to this point in the following chapter.

Velocity of money

The velocity of money is a concept long used by economists; in fact it dates back to the 15th century. We tend to think of velocity as a measure of speed or motion. A similar meaning can be applied to the velocity of money. Here we are interested in the frequency or the number of times an average dollar changes hands during the period of a year. We know, of course, that most people do not hold all the dollars they receive as income for an entire year before spending this money. In fact, most of what we receive each month is spent within a short time for day-to-day purchases, rent, clothes, and the like.

Two different ways of defining or measuring velocity have evolved.[2] One is known as transactions velocity, the other as income velocity. Transactions velocity is obtained by dividing the total value of all transactions or sales during a period of time (usually a year) by the quantity of money, as shown by formula (1):

$$V = \frac{P \times T}{M} \tag{1}$$

where V is velocity, P represents price or value of each transaction, T the number of transactions, and M the quantity of money in the economy. If for example, the value of annual transactions, i.e., $P \times T$, totaled \$2,000 billion and there were \$400 billion in circulation, the formula tells us that on the average each dollar changed hands five times during the year.

Income velocity is obtained by dividing a measure of national income or output such as GNP or NNP by the quantity of money, as shown by formula (2):

$$V = \frac{P \times Y}{M} \tag{2}$$

where P again represents prices and Y represents a measure of the physical output of final goods and services. The expression $P \times Y$, therefore, represents the money value of GNP, if this is the income measure being used.

Since measures of national income and the money stock are readily available, we can compute the income velocity for the United States. Of course, the velocity figure will be slightly larger using the narrow definition of money, because the denominator is smaller. In Figure 5–2 we present the income velocity for the United States for each year, 1929 through 1972, under both definitions of the money stock. We will be better able to analyze the trends and fluctuations in the velocity figures a bit later in this chapter.

---

2 See Irving Fisher, *The Purchasing Power of Money* (New York: Macmillan Co., 1913), Chap. 2.

FIGURE 5–2
Income velocity of money in the United States, 1929–72

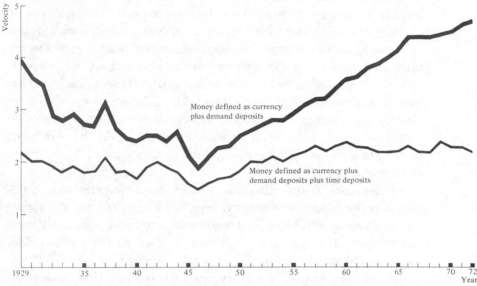

Source: Calculated from the data for Figure 5–1, using GNP as the measure of income.

Quantity equation of exchange

From the formula defining velocity, it is an easy step to derive the so-called quantity equation of exchange. Multiplying both sides of the velocity formulas by M we obtain:

$$M \times V = P \times T \qquad (1)$$
$$M \times V = P \times Y \qquad (2)$$

The first expression is known as the transaction form of the equation of exchange and the second is known as the income form. We will be mainly concerned with the income form because it utilizes figures that are readily available.

The first thing to note about the equation of exchange is that it is purely a definitional concept, i.e., it is always true. This occurs because V always takes on the value that satisfies the equation. For example, if $M = 300$, $P = 1$, and $Y = 900$, then the velocity formula tells us that $V = 900/300 = 3$. Inserting the 3 into the equation of exchange, we have $300 \times 3 = 1 \times 900$.

The quantity equation of exchange was utilized quite extensively by the classical economists. Since they were primarily interested in explaining or predicting the level of prices, the equation of exchange proved to be a convenient tool. Assuming as they did that velocity remains constant, an increase in the quantity of money must correspond to an increase in prices, real income (or output), or both. Presumably if the economy is at or near full employment, most of an increase on the right-hand side of the equation will be reflected in an increase in prices. If there is slack in the economy, both prices and real output may increase. However, there is nothing in the equation which tells us how much each can be expected to increase.

By the same token, the quantity equation implies that a decrease in the quantity of money, velocity being constant, will bring forth a decline in money income by a reduction in prices, real output, or both. If wages are rather inflexible on the downward side, as we argued earlier, then most of the decline will be in real output. In reality the quantity of money is not likely to decline in an absolute amount. This has occurred only rarely in the past four and a half decades, with the largest decline during the Great Depression. During "normal" times the government generally increases the quantity of money along with the growth of the economy. Indeed, even a slowing down in the growth of the money supply is noteworthy. We will have more to say about the relationship between money, prices, and output in Chapter 9.

Since the coming of Keynes, or Keynesian economics, the quantity equation has become a seldom-used museum piece in the economist's bag of tools. One of the major criticisms of the quantity equation as an analytical device is the assumption of a stable velocity. For example, if velocity happens to decrease as the quantity of money increases, there need not be any change in the total income or output of the economy.

Nowadays few if any economists argue that velocity is stable. But a number of economists argue that even though velocity is not stable, it is a stable function of a limited number of variables. In other words, they argue that it is possible to explain and predict changes in velocity because such changes are caused by identifiable changes in the economy. These economists, led perhaps by Professor Milton Friedman, are sometimes called the "new quantity theorists" as opposed to the old quantity theorists who took velocity as a constant.[3]

The new quantity theory of money

Basically the new quantity theory of money is a theory of the demand for money in that it attempts to explain and predict changes in velocity. The old quantity equation of exchange provides a useful starting point for our discussion. Recall that:

$$M \times V = P \times Y$$

Dividing both sides of the equation by V, we obtain:

$$M = 1/V \times P \times Y$$

If we let $1/V = K$, then we have

$$M = K \times P \times Y$$

where K is just the fraction of the nation's money income (or GNP) held as cash balances. For example, if $P \times Y$ is \$1,000 billion and M is \$250 billion, we see that K must be $1/4$. In other words, people hold one fourth of the annual value of the nation's output as cash. Or we could say that people hold the equivalent of three months' income as cash. Keep in mind too that K is just the reciprocal of velocity. For example, if K is $1/4$, velocity must be 4.

Notice also that if K increases, i.e., if people hold a larger amount of money in relation to their income, velocity decreases. Thus if we can identify the major factors that influence the amount of money people wish to hold in relation to their income, we have at the same time identified the factors that influence velocity. With this in mind, let us turn to a discussion of the motives for holding money.

Motives for holding cash balances

First, it is reasonable to expect that one motive for holding money is to make future purchases. By holding money people can

---

[3] See for example, Milton Friedman, "The Quantity Theory of Money: A Restatement," in Milton Friedman (ed.), *Studies in the Quantity Theory of Money* (Chicago: University of Chicago Press, 1956).

spread their purchases out over a period of time from the date of their income. Naturally it would not be very convenient for people to make all of their purchases at one point in time, say right after payday. Instead most of us prefer to spread our purchases out over a period of time, and as a result we need to hold some cash in order to have money for these purchases.

A second major reason for holding cash is to have a reserve against future contingencies. We never know, for example, when a sudden toothache will necessitate an unplanned trip to the dentist or a flat tire on the car will require an unforeseen purchase at a service station. Hence, most of us like to have a few dollars set aside to avoid financial embarrassment in case of unforeseen situations. Also, it is desirable to have some money on hand to take advantage of exceptional bargains. If we knew in advance just how much we would spend in the coming year we would not have to hold as much in reserve.

Business firms also hold a certain amount of money either in the form of cash in their vaults or deposits in banks. From the standpoint of business firms, money or cash balances can be looked upon as a factor of production that saves on other services, particularly labor. For example, without a cash reserve, each payday someone in each firm would have to take the time to sell enough of the firm's assets, such as stocks or bonds, in order to acquire the necessary cash to pay its employees. Thus holding part of the firm's assets in cash or money also proves to be convenient for the business firm and increases its productivity. Also firms, like individuals, may desire to have ready cash available either as a reserve against contingencies or to take advantage of exceptional bargains that come along.

Cost of holding cash balances

So far we have seen that individuals and business firms hold a certain amount of their wealth or income in the form of money for two main reasons: (1) as a means of spreading out purchases or expenditures between their receipts of income, and (2) as a reserve against unforeseen future expenditures. Next let us consider a major factor that determines what proportion of existing income people wish to hold in the form of money—the cost of holding money.

Offhand one might say that the cost of holding money is negligible, because banks are willing to guard our money for a minor cost. But it is necessary to take into consideration how much monetary assets could earn if they were converted into so-called earning assets, such as stocks, bonds, or consumer durables. Consider, for example, the option of holding $1,000 in cash or in your checking account versus holding the $1,000 in bonds. The cash or checking account money earns no interest. But the same amount of assets held in the form of bonds can be expected to earn interest, say 7 percent per year. In this example, the bonds would earn $70 per year in interest income. Hence the cost to the individual of holding wealth or assets in the form of money instead of earning assets is the interest income that could be earned on these assets. The higher the interest on earning assets, the more costly it becomes to hold money. Granted, time deposits earn a certain amount of interest. However, the interest return on time deposits may be lower than the interest return on other assets. If so, the cost of holding assets in the form of time deposits is the difference between their return and the return on other assets such as stocks or bonds.

The existence of inflationary pressure in the economy also adds to the cost of holding money. For example, if the price level is rising at the rate of 6 percent per year, the purchasing power of each dollar held in the form of cash decreases by the same amount. Because inflation erodes the purchasing power of money, people may respond by decreasing their cash holdings during this period. In fact, during extreme inflations money becomes something of a "hot potato." For example, during the German hyperinflation of the early 1920s, people began to insist on being paid every day or even twice a day. Indeed, if one's wage depreciates by 10 to 20 percent from morning to evening, it pays to demand payment at noon in order to buy something that increases in value with the price level. If inflation continues to increase, the economy tends to revert to a barter system. In this case the government may have to scrap the old money and introduce a new monetary unit.

Of course, during an inflation the money rate of interest tends to rise, and so to a certain extent the interest rate takes the cost of inflation into account. However, during extreme inflations the money rate of interest generally does not rise fast enough, or cannot rise enough because of usury laws, to fully compensate for the inflation. Hence inflation generally adds to the cost of holding cash over and above the increase in interest forgone.

The opposite would be true if the economy is experiencing a decrease in prices such as occurred in the United States during the Great Depression. Now money becomes more attractive to hold because its purchasing power is increasing as the price of goods and services decline. The probable decrease in the money rate of interest during such a period may reflect in part the decreased cost of holding cash.

A demand curve for money

Economists have found it useful to summarize the relationship between the rate of interest and the amount of money people wish to hold by means of a "demand" curve, sometimes called a "liquidity preference" curve. In a financial context, liquid assets are assets consisting of cash or assets that can be readily converted into cash. Therefore, the liquidity preference curve, or demand curve, represents the desire of people to hold liquid assets, i.e., monetary assets, in relation to the cost of holding these assets as reflected by the interest rate.

As shown in Figure 5–3, the money demand curve is represented by a downward sloping line. At high rates of interest the interest income of earning assets is high, which means that the cost of holding monetary assets is relatively high. As a result it is assumed that people prefer to hold a smaller amount of money, other things being equal. Similarly, at lower rates of interest, the cost of holding money declines, hence people prefer to hold a larger proportion of their wealth as cash or monetary assets.

More specifically, if the money rate of interest should rise from i_1 to i_2, the people in the country desire to decrease their holdings of money from M_1 to M_0. Similarly a decrease in interest to i_0 prompts people to increase their holding of money to M_2. We will discuss the determination of the interest rate and the reasons why it changes in Chapter 7.

FIGURE 5–3
A demand curve for money

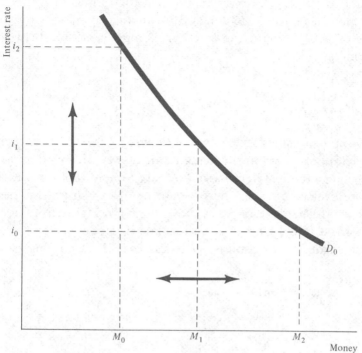

At the present time there is considerable disagreement among economists regarding the degree of responsiveness of money holders to changes in the rate of interest. Some economists maintain that people are relatively unresponsive to changes in the interest rate, i.e., that the money demand curve is relatively steep, at least in the normal range of interest rates, say from 3 to 10 percent. Other economists believe that changes in the rate of interest prompt people to change their cash holdings to a significant degree. This latter group would be especially prone to argue that the money demand becomes horizontal or close to horizontal at very low rates of interests, perhaps at 1 percent or less. We will see after we develop the more complete Keynesian model that the degree of responsiveness of money demand to interest rate changes has important implications for monetary policy.

The various quantities of money represented on the horizontal axis of Figure 5–3 are absolute amounts, which we can then relate either to a person's (or an economy's) total assets or to his money income. In relating the demand for money to velocity, our major interest will be with the fraction of money income held as cash balances.

Shifts in the demand for money

Most economists probably would agree, however, that there can be significant shifts in the demand for money. If, for example, people change their preferences and desire to hold more money at any given level of interest, there would be a shift upward and to the right of the demand curve as shown by D_2 in Figure 5–4. Note that at a given interest rate, i_0, the increase in money demand from D_1 to D_2 means that people wish to increase their holding of mone-

FIGURE 5–4
Shifts in the demand curve for money

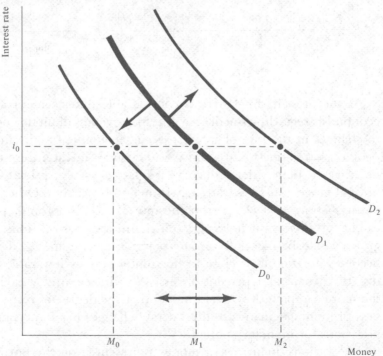

tary assets from M_1 to M_2. Similarly a decrease or shift to the left of the liquidity preference curve reflects a decreased desire of people for monetary assets vis-à-vis earning assets. This is illustrated by D_0 in Figure 5–4. Thus at any given interest rate, say i_0, money demand curve D_0 tells us that people desire to decrease their holding of money from M_1 to M_0.

Factors shifting the demand for money

Perhaps the main factor shifting the money demand curve is a change in money income. In general, as incomes rise people tend to increase their holdings of money or monetary assets. From our own personal experience we know that as children our holdings of monetary assets were relatively small because our money income and expenditures were small. As children we may have held only a few dollars in a piggy bank, mainly for use as spending money or to save up for some special purchase or occasion. Then as young adults attending high school and college, perhaps holding a part-time job, our income and expenditures increased somewhat. Along with this increase in income, most of us increased the amount of monetary assets we held. Much the same is true for income growth of the entire economy. As expected, when operating on a larger scale with higher incomes, people find it convenient to hold a larger amount of money for the purposes of spacing purchases or keeping something in reserve for contingencies. Thus D_2 in Figure 5–4 would correspond to a higher level of money income than D_1. By the same token D_1 would correspond to a higher income than D_0.

In addition, the money demand curve can shift because of expected changes in future economic conditions. For example, suppose people expect a recession in the near future. Because of the increased possibility of being laid off, it is reasonable to expect that many people will attempt to set aside a bit more money to tide them over the recessionary period. This situation also would correspond to the shift from D_1 to D_2 in Figure 5–4. Of course, just the opposite might occur if people expect a high level of economic activity for several years to come. With less concern over the future, the money demand curve for the economy then might shift to the left as people try to convert monetary assets into nonmonetary types.

Relationship between velocity and the demand for money

In our discussion of the quantity equation of exchange, we pointed out that velocity is not likely to be a fixed number. Proceeding to the new quantity theory, we saw that $1/V$ is simply the proportion of income held as cash balances. In our discussion of the demand for money, we considered three major factors influencing the desired amount of monetary assets held by people. These are (1) the cost of holding money as reflected mainly by the interest rate, (2) the level of money income, and (3) the expected future economic conditions of the economy. The first is reflected in the downward sloping nature of the curve; the other two are reflected by shifts in the curve.

A change in the demand for money, either because of a movement along the curve or because of a shift in the curve that is greater than a change in income, implies that people desire to hold a different amount of money in relation to their income, i.e., that there is a change in K. But recall that $K = 1/V$. Thus a change in K also implies a change in velocity. More specifically, a movement from i_1 to i_0 as illustrated in Figure 5–3 and the accompanying increase in the desired holdings of cash balances from M_1 to M_2 means that people wish to increase the proportion of their money income held as cash balances (either broadly or narrowly defined). This in turn means that K is increased and velocity is decreased. The opposite, of course, holds true if the interest rate increases from i_0 to i_2. Here the desired holdings of money decrease from M_1 to M_0, resulting in a lower K and a higher velocity. A shift in the demand for money for a given money income has a similar effect. As illustrated in Figure 5–4, a shift from D_1 to D_2 increases desired holdings of money from M_1 to M_2, thereby increasing K and decreasing velocity. A decrease in the demand for money as illustrated by D_0 in Figure 5–4 gives rise to a decrease in K and an increase in velocity.

We might ask at this point, How does a change in the desired stock of money affect the velocity of money? It is important, first of all, to distinguish between the individual and society. If the individual wishes to increase his holdings of cash balances, he can sell part of his other assets or reduce spending in order to build up his cash reserves. But when we consider all individuals as a group, i.e., the entire society, we must remember that when one person increases his cash holdings someone else must decrease his, assuming that the total stock of money in society does not change. In other words, as a group it is impossible for society to increase its actual nominal cash balances even though it might desire to do so.

Nevertheless, the desire to increase cash balances can have an effect on the economy and on velocity. If nearly everyone attempts to increase his cash balances by selling assets or decreasing spending, there will be a tendency for prices and output to decline, which is to say that the money value of GNP declines. Hence if we divide the same nominal stock of money into a reduced level of money GNP, velocity will decrease.

We should also point out that even though the actual nominal stock of money may remain unchanged, people are able to satisfy their desire for increased real cash holdings because of the decline in the price level. That is, the reduction in prices makes every dollar worth more, so in the final analysis people are able to achieve their goal of increasing the value of the cash they hold. Economists would refer to this as an increase in the *real* cash balances held by the public.

A similar line of reasoning can be employed to explain what happens when people try to decrease their holdings of cash balances. In this case people attempt to buy assets in exchange for cash or increase their rate of spending in order to draw down their cash balances. This increased spending might then lead to inflationary pressure, which in turn would give rise to a higher money value of GNP. When we divide the same nominal amount of money into a higher money GNP, we obtain an increase in velocity. By the same token, it is argued that when prices increase, the desire for decreased cash balances is satisfied because the real value of society's nominal cash balance has been decreased.

We should point out, too, that many economists argue that the major disturbances in the monetary sector have come mainly on the supply side. In other words, they believe that the demand for cash balances is rather stable, except for a gradual shifting to the right over time in response to a rise in income. However, they point to rather excessive year-to-year fluctuations in the growth of the supply of money. We shall study this contention in more detail in the chapter on monetary policy.

Changes in velocity

Now that we have some idea of the relationship between the demand for money and velocity, we are in a better position to at least speculate on the reasons for the observed changes in velocity over the past four decades as shown in Figure 5–2. We should caution, however, that this is an area of considerable controversy in economics and that much remains to be learned regarding the factors that influence velocity as well as the manner in which velocity is influenced.

Looking first at the early 1930s, the era of the Great Depression, we observe in Figure 5–2 a rather sharp decline in velocity, particularly in reference to the narrow definition of money. Most economists probably would agree that the depressed state of economic activity contributed to the increased desire to hold cash balances and so to the decrease in velocity. With unemployment growing, many people undoubtedly wished to build up their cash reserves in case they might be laid off. Indeed, there is a good possibility that an attempt to increase cash balances itself contributed to the depression, as people reduced their spending in order to build up their cash reserves. Thus it can be argued that there was something of a snowball effect in operation. The initial increase in unemployment probably contributed to expectations that led to a decrease in velocity, which in turn contributed to more unemployment.

Of course, most economists probably would attribute more importance to the drastic reduction in the supply of money during this time than to the increased desire to hold cash balances. We will be better able to assess this argument after we have developed the more complete Keynesian model in Chapter 7.

It is interesting to note that velocity continued to decline during the World War II years. But as we know, this period was just opposite in character to the Great Depression—rising prices and full employment instead of deflation and high unemployment. On the surface, at least, it might appear that we must look to other reasons for the increased desire to hold cash balances during World War II.

It has been argued by some economists, however, that the same basic reason that brought forth a decrease in velocity during the 1930s, continued to affect peoples' behavior during the 1940s—namely, economic instability. It must be admitted that during World War II many people expected the economy to hit bottom again once hostilities ceased. Consequently it seems reasonable to believe that there might have been a continued attempt to increase the amount of cash held by people relative to their incomes. Also, there wasn't much for consumers to spend their money on during World War II.

The post–World War II years brought a reversal to the downward trend in velocity and in fact brought rather a sharp increase in velocity at least from the standpoint of the narrow definition of money. Several explanations have been offered for this phenomenon. First it is pointed out that in spite of the Korean War, the 1958 recession, and Vietnam, the United States has enjoyed a certain amount of economic stability, at least in comparison to the Great Depression and World War II. When people feel somewhat more secure economically, they may wish to reduce their cash balances in relation to their income. Also, people desired to build up the depleted stock of consumer durables after World War II.

It has been suggested, too, that the upward trend in interest rates since World War II, especially during the 1960s, has made it more expensive to hold cash relative to other assets. As a result there would be somewhat of an incentive to economize on holding cash. It is not at all certain, however, whether interest rates have risen enough to noticeably affect peoples' decisions to hold cash vis-à-vis other assets. At the same time, we do observe that people have been holding more and more of their money (broadly defined) in the form of time deposits, particularly during the 1960s. It is tempting to argue that recent increases in the interest rates paid on time deposits may have had something to do with this.

Another possible explanation for the recent increase in velocity is the increased use of the credit card. By being able to charge a greater share of our purchases, it may be possible to reduce our cash balances. In other words, we can make our outflow of cash more nearly coincide with paydays. Then in between paydays we need not hold as much cash on hand for day-to-day purchases.

Main points of Chapter 5

1. The demand for money in the context of this chapter refers to the amount of money people wish to hold in relation to their income or wealth.

2. Throughout history man has utilized a variety of different objects as money. What was used depended mainly on the technology and resources available at the time. Money should be relatively cheap to produce, reasonably durable, and hard to duplicate.

3. From the standpoint of total society, money has three main functions: it serves as (1) a medium of exchange, (2) a standard of value, and (3) a store of value. Money can be thought of as a tool that enhances the total output of society. Without money people would be required to spend a large share of their time shopping rather than producing.

4. Even though paper money has no value as a commodity, it can be used as a medium of exchange if the majority of people in society are willing to accept it in payment for goods and services.

5. In years to come we may experience a trend towards a cashless society where income and expenditures will be characterized by bookkeeping entries rather than an exchange of paper or metal. This does not mean, however, that we will have a moneyless society. The monetary unit will continue to be used but will change in form from tangible paper or metal to intangible numbers in the memory cores of computers.

6. Narrowly defined, the quantity of money includes currency plus demand deposits. Under the broad definition, the quantity of money includes currency, demand deposits, and time deposits.

7. The velocity of circulation of money is a measure of how many times a year the average dollar changes hands. Transactions velocity is obtained by dividing the value of all transactions during the year by the quantity of money. Income velocity is obtained by dividing some measure of net income or value added (such as GNP) by the quantity of money.

8. By multiplying both sides of the velocity formula by M, we obtain the quantity equation of exchange. The transactions form is equal to $M \times V = P \times T$. The income form is equal to $M \times V = P \times Y$.

9. According to the quantity equation, an increase in the quantity of money must result in an increase in prices unless offset by a proportionate decline in velocity or increase in real output. Similarly a decrease in the quantity of money must result in a fall in prices or output, unless offset by an increase in velocity.

10. A major criticism of the simple quantity equation of exchange is that velocity is continually changing, so that predictions based on a constant velocity may prove erroneous.

11. The proponents of the new quantity theory of money argue that although velocity may not remain constant from year to year, it is possible to explain or predict changes in velocity by a limited number of other factors.

12. By dividing both sides of the quantity equation of exchange by V we obtain the equation $M = 1/V \times P \times Y$ or $M = K \times P \times Y$ where K is equal to $1/V$. Another way to interpret K is that it is the fraction of money income held as cash balances. The new quantity theory is concerned with explaining and predicting changes in K or velocity.

13. Individuals desire to hold a certain fraction of their assets in the form of cash in order to make purchases at times other than at the receipt of income. Also people desire to hold a certain amount of cash for unforeseen purchases.

14. The cost of holding money is the income or services forgone by not holding this wealth in the form of earning assets.

15. The demand curve for money represents the relationship between the cost of holding money, denoted by the money rate of interest, and the amount that people wish to hold. It is a downward sloping line, implying that as the cost of holding cash diminishes people will be willing to hold larger quantities relative to their total wealth or income.

16. Shifts in the demand for money may occur as the result of changes in income or changes in expected economic conditions. For example, as incomes rise, the money demand curve tends to shift to the right, meaning that people wish to hold

a larger amount of money at a given interest rate. If people expect hard times in the future they tend to increase their holdings of money in anticipation of reduced future income.

17. A movement down along the demand curve for money because of a lower interest rate results in an increase in the desired holdings of money and a corresponding increase in K and decrease in V. The opposite occurs with an increase in interest; the desired holdings of M decrease and as a result K decreases and V increases.

18. A shift to the right (increase) in the demand for money for a given money income increases desired M and as a result K increases and V decreases. A shift to the left (decrease) in the demand for money decreases desired M and thus there is a decrease in K and an increase in V.

Questions for thought and discussion

1. Suppose you find yourself as a Peace Corps worker among a primitive Indian tribe in the Amazon region. Assume that the tribe has virtually no contact with the outside world. Also suppose that all exchange transactions between the members of the tribe take place by barter, i.e., the tribe has never used money.
   a) If you wished to persuade the tribe to adopt the use of money, what arguments could you use? Would it be sufficient just to convince the tribal leaders?
   b) What objects would you suggest as a possible money? Why?
   c) Would there be a need for different denominations?
   d) Who, if anyone, should control the quantity to be used? Why should it be controlled?

2. Explain the difference between a cashless society and a moneyless society.

3. How does the use of money increase the productivity of society?

4. Do you view money in a savings account differently than you view cash or demand deposits? Why? What does your answer imply about the definition (broad or narrow) of money you prefer to use?

5. Explain the meaning of velocity of circulation. Also explain the difference between transactions velocity and income velocity.

6. What is the relationship between the velocity formula and the quantity equation of exchange?

7. According to the equation of exchange, what happens in an economy if the quantity of money is increased more rapidly than the growth in real output? What assumptions did you make about the components of the equation of exchange to make this prediction? Is there any evidence in U.S. history to support this prediction?

8. What happens in an economy if the quantity of money is reduced in absolute terms? What must you assume about the quantity equation to make this prediction? Is there any evidence in recent history to support this prediction?

9. "The quantity equation can be criticized because the two sides of the equation may not always be equal." Comment.

10. What was your annual money income last year? How much money on the average did you hold as currency, demand deposits, and time deposits? What was your income velocity? How does this compare to the overall U.S. average?

11. Have you increased the average amount of cash balances you hold since you graduated from high school? Is your present income velocity different from what it was during your high school years? If so can you explain why?

12. *a)* What does the money demand curve show?
    b) What is the meaning of a shift in this curve?
    c) What factors tend to shift the curve?

13. Explain the relationship between movements along the demand curve for money and changes in velocity.

14. Explain the relationship between shifts in the money demand curve and changes in velocity.

6

The supply of money

In Chapter 5 we were concerned mainly with the amount of money people wish to hold given certain conditions such as prevailing interest rates, incomes, and expectations of future economic activity. In this chapter we will be concerned mainly with the actual supply of money in the economy and how this supply is changed. We will see that the commercial banking system is the primary vehicle for changing the quantity of money. And we will see also that the Federal Reserve System has the power to influence the actions of commercial banks.

Because commercial banks and the Federal Reserve System play such vital roles in determining the money supply, it will be useful to become better acquainted with their structures and functions. However, in our study of the banking system we will utilize the balance sheet a great deal. So before we undertake our discussion of banking let us first review this important accounting tool.

The balance sheet

Basically the balance sheet itemizes the assets, liabilities, and net worth of a person, firm, or institution as of a particular point in time. Assets can be defined as anything of value. A person's assets typically would include clothes, car, real estate, appliances, cash, stocks, bonds, etc. A business firm's balance sheet would include mainly the real estate and capital equipment that the firm has under its control, together with its monetary assets such as cash and bank deposits. A commercial bank's assets include many of the same items found in an ordinary business firm. There are some special items among a bank's assets, however, that will come to our attention later.

We should be aware, though, that the asset value of a particular item does not tell us anything about who has ultimate claim on the item. For example, if you "own" a $1,000 automobile but have $500 yet to pay on it, you have a $500 claim on the auto and the lender has a $500 claim. The balance sheet would carry the auto as a $1,000 asset regardless of how much you still owed on it. For this reason it is necessary to know the amount of liabilities and net worth also.

The liability figures in a balance sheet indicate the amount owed to creditors. Sometimes the balance sheet will separate short-term from long-term liabilities to indicate how soon the debts will have to be paid. For our purposes it will be sufficient to know just that liabilities are debts that will have to be paid sometime in the future. Net worth represents the assets owned free and clear by the individuals controlling the assets. Essentially we can view liabilities as the creditors' claim to the assets in a balance sheet and net worth as the owners' claim to these assets.

As its name implies the balance sheet must always balance, that is, the total value of assets must always equal the total claim on these assets. We are assured that assets always equal liabilities plus net worth because the net worth figure is obtained as a residual by subtracting liabilities from assets. These relationships are summarized below:

$$\text{Assets} = \text{Liabilities} + \text{Net worth}$$
$$\text{Net Worth} = \text{Assets} - \text{Liabilities}$$

A convenient method of presenting the balance sheet is in the form of a T account. With this format assets are listed on the left side of the vertical line and liabilities and net worth on the right side. The following example illustrates the format of a T account balance sheet and some typical entries for a college student. Notice that the balance sheet is drawn up at a particular point in time. Typically business firms or institutions compute their balances at the end of the calendar year or fiscal year. The asset figures should reflect the current market value of the items listed, $1,500 in this example. The unpaid balances of two loans outstanding represent the liabilities of the student, $500 in this example. The $1,000 net worth figure is found by subtracting the $500 in liabilities from the $1,500 assets total.

**Balance sheet of a college student
as of a point in time**

Assets		*Liabilities + Net worth*	
Automobile	$1,000	Bank loan	$ 300
Typewriter	100	Loan from parents	200
Clothes	400	Net worth	1,000
	$1,500		$1,500

Evolution of banking

Equipped with this knowledge of the balance sheet, we now are ready to take a closer look at banks and banking. Of course, banks, like most of our institutions, did not suddenly appear in their present form. Therefore, let us consider briefly how the early banks probably came into existence.

During the early period of civilization, gold and silver were the predominate forms of money. Those who were fortunate enough to accumulate a sizable amount of these metals were confronted with the problem of keeping it safe from those who were bent on redistributing the wealth of the land, i.e., thieves and robbers. It should not be surprising then that the ancient goldsmith emerged as the person best able to store money for safekeeping. Since the basic raw material used in his business had to be closely guarded anyway, the goldsmith, no doubt, found it profitable to take in other people's gold for safekeeping in return for a fee. Of course, at the time of deposit the customer was given a receipt indicating the date and amount of deposit. Understandably this receipt had to be presented when the depositor wished to reclaim his gold.

In providing a storage service the goldsmith's place of business became, in effect, a warehouse for gold. It also became the forerunner of the modern bank. The goldsmiths accepted deposits of money and paid it out again on demand. But this describes in large part the activities of a modern bank. However, present-day banks also make loans. Let us see how this activity might have emerged.

It probably didn't take long for the more perceptive goldsmiths to discover that during any one day the gold withdrawn was in large part offset by the gold deposited. During some days withdrawals may have exceeded deposits by a small amount, or vice versa. But on any given day, the goldsmith was not likely to have all his gold withdrawn, unless his reputation suddenly became suspect. We know too that gold is a completely homogenous commodity, that is, an ounce of gold is an ounce of gold no matter who deposits it. Hence the actual gold that was withdrawn during any one day probably was the same gold that had come in through deposits on that very day or the day before. After all, because gold is homogeneous there would be no need for the goldsmith to dig to the bottom or to the back of his vault to locate gold deposited months or years before. At any rate, the perceptive goldsmith undoubtedly noticed that a relatively large share of his gold deposits was lying in his vault gathering dust.

Let us say, for example, that only about 20 percent of his gold was actively used to pay withdrawals on days when deposits were unusually low. For all practical purposes the remaining 80 percent of the gold was never used. In fact it no doubt was considered a hindrance, since it required more space and provided a greater temptation for would-be robbers.

There always have been people who were in need of loans for various and sundry purposes. Without people or institutions that specialized in making loans, borrowers had to prevail upon friends or relatives. For the very poor who had only poor friends and poor relatives, there wasn't much chance of obtaining credit. It took people awhile to get used to the idea of paying interest, however. And without interest to compensate for waiting and for the risk involved, there isn't much incentive to lend money.

Once the payment of interest, in one form or another, became socially acceptable, the goldsmiths discovered a grand opportunity to benefit both themselves and their customers. By lending out some of this unused gold they provided a source of credit for people who wanted to make a fairly large purchase, such as a house or a cart. These people were certainly helped because the loans, no doubt, enabled many of them to purchase resources that increased their earning power and standard of living, just as is true today. The goldsmith benefited because of the interest income that he earned from his loans. Finally, his depositors benefited because they could now be paid for depositing gold rather than having to pay for the storage service.

So far we have followed the evolution of banking through two steps. First, institutions evolved to satisfy the demand for storage services by people who had accumulated money. Second, these institutions, goldsmiths in the main, discovered that daily deposits and withdrawals normally came close to canceling each other out. Thus goldsmiths could lend out part of their deposits, keeping only a part on reserve. Today we refer to this procedure as fractional reserve banking.

It will be helpful to represent each of these steps on a balance sheet. To simplify the procedure we will ignore the items not directly connected with the transactions we are interested in, such as the assets representing physical facilities and net worth. The balance sheet on the left below represents the deposit of $1,000 in gold. (In ancient times, of course, the dollar had not been conceived, but we will use it in our example because it is the monetary unit most familiar to us.) The physical commodity gold becomes an asset to the goldsmith because it is now under his control. On the right side of the T account we must represent the claims to this gold. Since the gold was owned entirely by the depositors, the entire claim to the gold is represented by the receipts given out by the goldsmith. These receipts, therefore, were liabilities to the goldsmith because he eventually was called upon to pay out this amount in gold.

The right-hand balance sheet illustrates the lending out of part of the gold on deposit. In this example we show a $500 loan. The IOU, promissory note, or whatever the borrower gave the goldsmith at the time the loan was made, becomes an asset to the goldsmith. This is offset on the asset side by a $500 reduction in the gold item because it is taken out by the borrower. Note that total assets remain unchanged at $1,000; only the form is changed. The liabilities side remains unchanged in both form and total.

Deposit of $1,000 in gold				Lending $500 of the original $1,000 deposit			
Assets		*Liabilities + Net worth*		*Assets*		*Liabilities + Net worth*	
Gold	$1,000	Receipts	$1,000	Gold	$ 500	Receipts	$1,000
				IOUs	500		
					$1,000		$1,000

An additional step towards banking as we know it today was taken when depositors began to use their deposit receipts as money. It is fairly easy to see how this practice came into being. Visualize yourself as living in that time with, say, $50 of gold on deposit at the local goldsmith. Suppose that you decided to trade in your old chariot for the latest model. Suppose also that the new chariot cost you $50 in gold plus your trade-in. You could, of course, make a trip to the goldsmith to draw out your $50 in gold. But the chariot dealer would just have to return to the goldsmith the same day with the same gold for redeposit. Both you and the chariot dealer could save a trip to the goldsmith if you just endorsed your deposit receipt over to the chariot dealer, instructing the goldsmith to pay him the $50 on demand.

The practice of exchanging deposit receipts instead of gold resembles a well-known practice in use today—namely, that of exchanging checks instead of the actual currency on deposit in banks. Thus the deposit receipt was the forerunner of the present-day check. Of course, the check is a bit more convenient because it can be made out in any denomination. Eventually people discovered this, and as a result deposit receipts were made more flexible. With more widespread use, receipts or checks became a widely accepted form of money.

So far we have taken the goldsmith analogy to the point where it is just one step removed from the modern bank. The evolutionary process became complete when goldsmiths began to give out deposit receipts instead of gold when making loans. It is easy to visualize how this practice got started. Suppose, in the $500 loan example, that the people who took out these loans turned around and immediately redeposited the gold in the goldsmith's vault. The goldsmith then would have to give these people deposit receipts. After all we would not expect borrowers to want to carry gold around any more than the people who originally deposited it. Moreover, as deposit receipts became a commonly accepted form of money, it would be foolish to risk losing the gold that had been borrowed when pieces of paper would serve the same purpose.

Of course, for borrowers who did not want to take the gold with them, it was natural that the physical removal and immediate rede-posit of gold at the time loans were transacted should be eliminated. Now all the goldsmith had to do was fill out a deposit receipt that borrowers could take with them. Notice, however, that this pro-cedure results in a somewhat different balance sheet than resulted from the more primitive loan transaction shown earlier, where the borrower took the gold with him. The following balance sheet illustrates the case where $500 of the original $1,000 deposit was loaned out, but instead of physically removing the gold borrowers accepted deposit receipts.

**Lending out $500 of the original $1,000 deposit
and issuing deposit receipts to the borrowers**

Assets		*Liabilities + Net worth*	
Gold	$1,000	Receipts to depositors	$1,000
IOUs	500	Receipts to borrowers	500
	$1,500		$1,500

Notice here that if receipts to borrowers are considered money, then the goldsmith, or lending institution, in fact creates money by making loans and issuing these receipts. We will discuss this phe-nomenon in more detail just a bit later when we look at the trans-actions of a modern commercial bank.

We have now taken the goldsmith to the point where he was doing essentially the same things as the modern commercial bank. First, he took in deposits; second, he made loans; and third, he issued and honored deposit receipts that in effect became money. Let us now take a brief look at the commercial banking system as it exists today in the United States.

Commercial banks

By commercial banks we have in mind those institutions that among other things offer checking account services. This category does not include savings and loan associations and mutual savings banks. Although these institutions also accept deposits and make loans, they do not offer checking account services. As we will see a bit later, this characteristic in conjunction with the fractional reserve requirement has an important bearing on the money supply.

As of December 31, 1971, there were 13,783 commercial banks in the United States. Those that received their charter from the federal government are called national banks, and those operating under a state charter are known as state banks. At the end of 1971 there were 4,599 national banks and 9,184 state banks in the United States. All of the national banks are required to hold membership in the Federal Reserve System, that is, they must buy stock in the system. Each state bank is free to choose whether or not it wishes to be a member of the Federal Reserve System. Of the 9,184 state banks, only 1,128 were members. At the same time, we should point out that most of the larger state banks are members, so the major share of the deposits in the country come under the jurisdiction of the Federal Reserve System.

All member banks are required to hold a certain fraction of their deposit liabilities on reserve as cash in their vaults or on reserve in the Federal Reserve bank in their district. This fraction, often called the reserve ratio, varies between demand and time deposits and also between large city banks and small "country" banks, as shown in Table 6–1.

TABLE 6–1
Required reserve ratios for member banks as of January 1973

	Demand deposits	Time deposits
Reserve city banks	17.5%	5%
"Country" banks	13.0%	5%

The 17.5 percent figure, for example, means that reserve city banks must maintain at least $17.50 on reserve either in their own vaults or in their Federal Reserve banks for each $100 of demand deposits on their books. The other figures have a similar meaning. The Federal Reserve Board of Governors has the authority to change these reserve ratios over a fairly broad range, although this power is seldom used. We should point out, too, that nonmember state banks must maintain reserves against their deposits. These

reserves are kept in the reserve city banks which tend to be located in the financial districts of large cities. In a sense, these large reserve city banks act as Federal Reserve banks for the smaller "country" banks.

It is probably assumed by many people that legal reserve requirements were set up to protect depositors. No doubt they have this effect. But an equally valid reason for having legal reserve requirements is to provide a means for the Federal Reserve System to have some control over the maximum amount of bank loans and thus over the maximum quantity of money in the economy. We will see shortly that in the process of making loans, commercial banks actually create money.

Before we can discuss commercial bank transactions, it is necessary that we have some understanding of the Federal Reserve System. We will see that many commercial banks' transactions directly affect one or more Federal Reserve banks.

The Federal Reserve system

Throughout the 19th and early 20th centuries the United States economy suffered from rather large and frequent ups and downs in economic activity. Following the panic of 1907, Congress became convinced that a major cause of the country's financial woes came from the country's decentralized banking system. At the time the banking system was comprised of thousands of private commercial banks, each operating as a business seeking to make a profit.

It became evident that the rational, profit-maximizing behavior of each commercial bank operating on its own was not conducive to the stability of the total economy. For example, during expansionary periods banks faced a strong demand for their loans. As a result banks obliged by increasing loans. But as we will see shortly, this action increased the money supply, which augmented the boom and ensuing inflation. On the other hand, during recessionary periods, banks along with businessmen became pessimistic about the future, and as a result reduced their loans outstanding. This in turn reduced the money supply, which contributed to a still further reduction in economic activity.

During certain periods within the year the banking community experienced shortages and surpluses of money. For example, during the Christmas shopping season the volume of business activity tends to rise substantially. Recall from the preceding chapter that an increase in income of GNP shifts the demand for money to the right, reflecting the increased volume of transactions. Unless there is a corresponding increase in its supply, money becomes "scarce" and interest rates rise. As a result there may be an unnecessary curtailment of economic activity. Similarly during slack periods of the year, mainly during the first quarter, the supply of money that would fulfill the demand without a rise in interest rates during the peak season would be too large, resulting in unnecessary instability in the money market.

Because of these seasonal fluctuations in the demand for money, it became clear that the country also needed an agency that could provide an "elastic" currency, that is, a money supply that could expand and contract with the seasonal fluctuations in the economy. Thus the need for a central bank became evident because of the "perverse elasticity" of money that accentuated booms and recessions, and also because of the need for a greater elasticity of the money supply during peak and slack periods within the year.

Thus on December 23, 1913, President Woodrow Wilson signed the Federal Reserve Act, which brought into being the Federal Reserve System. Understandably there was a great deal of reluctance on the part of bankers to create a strong, centralized banking authority located in Washington or New York. Yet the inadequacy of a completely decentralized banking system was evident. As a result the Federal Reserve System was set up as somewhat of a compromise between a powerful government bank such as the Bank of England or Bank of France and a totally private banking system.[1]

To maintain some form of decentralization, the country was divided into 12 Federal Reserve districts, each having a Federal Reserve Bank. Several of the Federal Reserve banks have one or more branches located in other cities of the district. The Federal Reserve System is supervised by a seven-member Board of Governors located in Washington, D.C. The Board of Governors is assisted by a

---

[1] For a detailed description of the Federal Reserve System and its functions, see Board of Governors of the Federal Reserve System, *The Federal Reserve System: Purposes and Functions.*

Federal Advisory Council and a Federal Open Market Committee. As the name implies, the Advisory Council advises the Board of Governors on monetary policy. The Open Market Committee buys and sells securities, which as we will see later in the chapter affects the quantity of money in the economy.

Federal Reserve banks are sometimes called quasi-public banks because they are owned by private commercial interests but controlled by the Board of Governors. The Board of Governors is really a government agency, because the members are appointed by the President of the United States.

Federal Reserve banks also have been called "banker's banks" because they perform essentially the same functions for commercial banks as commercial banks do for private individuals. You and I, for example, cannot walk into a Federal Reserve Bank and make a deposit or negotiate a loan. But these services are available to commercial banks who happen to be members of the Federal Reserve System. We will see later why a commercial bank might be in need of a loan. The United States Treasury also maintains a deposit in the Federal Reserve System, so in a sense the Fed, as it is often called, serves as the bank for the federal government.

We can obtain a better idea of the economic characteristics of the Federal Reserve System by looking at the balance sheet for the entire system, as shown below:

Consolidated balance sheet of the Federal Reserve System as of December 31, 1972 (billions)

Assets		Liabilities and net worth	
Cash	$ 0.3	Reserves of member banks	$25.5
Gold certificates	10.3	Treasury deposits	1.9
Securities	69.9	Federal reserve notes	58.8
Loans to banks	2.0	Other liabilities and net worth	8.4
Other assets	12.1		
Total Assets	$94.6	Total Liabilities and Net Worth	$94.6

Source: *Federal Reserve Bulletin*, January 1973.

On the asset side, the largest item is securities. Mainly these are U.S. Government Bonds issued by the Treasury. The Open Market Committee is continually buying and selling securities, which we will see has an important bearing on the quantity of money in the economy. Gold certificates represent the stock of gold held by the

U.S. government. The loans item represents short-term credit extended to commercial banks that are members of the Federal Reserve System for the purpose of bolstering their reserves.

On the right side of the balance sheet the three items listed all represent liabilities of the Federal Reserve. Commercial banks that are members of the Federal Reserve System are required to keep a certain fraction of their deposit liabilities on reserve, either in their respective Federal Reserve banks or as vault cash in their respective banks. Member bank reserves represent liabilities of the Federal Reserve System because these funds are in a sense held in trust for the commercial banks and may be relinquished at any time. Treasury deposits represent the checking account money that the federal government has on deposit for the purpose of paying its bills. Federal reserve notes, the largest single liability item, is the official name of the paper currency in use today in the United States.

Commercial bank transactions

In order to understand how the banking system can alter the quantity of money in the economy, it is first necessary to understand the nature of transactions that take place within the banking community. We already have caught a glimpse of the banking world in our discussion of the goldsmith at the beginning of the chapter. As we proceed, you will probably note a strong resemblance between the modern commercial bank and the ancient goldsmith. It will be easier to understand banking transactions if we start with the most basic, the deposit of cash by a customer, and then move on from there.

1. *Deposit of $10,000 cash by a customer.* Suppose, to make the example more meaningful, that you decide to open up a bank. After receiving your charter you rent some facilities and obtain some of the basic equipment used by a bank, which among other things might include a vault and some conservative clothing. On your first day of operation a local businessman brings in $10,000 in cash and wishes to establish a checking account in your bank.

Our main interest at this point is how this transaction affects your balance sheet. The $10,000 in cash that has come under your control becomes an asset of your bank. In the balance sheet below we refer to this cash deposit as total reserves. Of course, we know a balance sheet must balance, so at the same time there is a corresponding increase on the liabilities side. This is accomplished by increasing the demand deposit item by $10,000. Bear in mind that demand deposits represent a liability to you because you may be required to pay this amount to your customer at any time. To simplify the arithmetic, assume the required reserve ratio is 0.20, or 20 percent, so that along with the $10,000 increase in demand deposits your required reserves increase by $2,000 (0.20 × $10,000). Thus out of the $10,000 deposit of cash, $2,000 is taken up by required reserves and the remaining $8,000 is excess reserves. In the balance sheets to follow we show only the changes that take place, in order to concentrate on the particular transaction at hand.

Deposit of $10,000 in cash by a customer

Assets	*Liabilities + Net worth*
Total reserves (cash) + $10,000 Required reserves +2,000 Excess reserves +8,000	Demand deposits + $10,000

Notice in this transaction that you have not yet created any money. The cash that has come into your bank is now removed from the money supply (recall that only cash outside of banks is considered part of the quantity of money) but this has been offset by the increase in demand deposits. The quantity of money in the economy has changed in composition, from cash to demand deposits, but not in total amount.

2. *Deposit of required reserves in Federal Reserve bank.* Assume you are a member of the Federal Reserve System and decide to deposit the entire amount of required reserves in the Federal Reserve bank in your district. In this transaction only the Federal Reserve balance sheet is affected, because your reserves remain the same. You still have $10,000 in total reserves: $2,000 in the Federal Reserve bank and $8,000 in your vault.

**Federal Reserve balance sheet
deposit of $2,000 required reserves
in the Federal Reserve bank**

Assets	*Liabilities + Net worth*
Cash + $2,000	Member bank reserves + $2,000

3. A $1,000 check is drawn on your bank.   It is reasonable to suppose that your depositor will begin to write checks against his account. Suppose he buys $1,000 worth of supplies and pays for the purchase by writing a check. Naturally the supplier will soon after deposit this check in his account, which we will assume is in some other bank, call it Bank B. We will see that this transaction affects the balance sheets of three banks: your bank (call it Bank A), the Federal Reserve, and Bank B.

Your depositor, of course, must have his checking account balance reduced by the amount of the check. But how will you know he has written a check? The procedure followed is for Bank B to first add $1,000 to the supplier's checking account and to offset this by adding $1,000 to the reserve entry in his balance sheet. Then the check goes to the Federal Reserve bank, which adds to or credits Bank B's reserves by $1,000 and subtracts from or debits your reserves (Bank A) by a like amount. This service that the Fed provides for its members is often referred to as a "clearing house" function. The Federal Reserve bank then sends the canceled check back to you, which informs you that your depositor should have his checking account reduced by $1,000 and that your reserves in the Federal Reserve are reduced by the same amount. Lastly you send the canceled check back to your depositor, so he knows his account has been reduced. The entire transaction is summarized by the balance sheets below:

Effects of a $1,000 check drawn on Bank A

Bank A

Assets		Liabilities + Net worth	
Reserves	−$1,000	Demand deposits	−$1,000

Federal Reserve

Assets		Liabilities + Net worth	
		Bank A reserves	−$1,000
		Bank B reserves	+$1,000

Bank B

Assets		Liabilities + Net worth	
Reserves	+$1,000	Demand deposits	+$1,000

Note that all three balance sheets continue to balance after the transaction is complete. In fact it is always a good idea to represent commercial bank transactions by balance sheets because they provide a good check on one's accuracy. If the balance sheets do not balance after working through the transaction, you can be sure you have made an error. Unfortunately the converse is not true; erroneous balance sheets can still balance.

Assuming that the original $10,000 depositor is the only person who has put money into your bank, the $1,000 check has reduced your total demand deposits and reserves to $9,000. With a 20 percent reserve ratio, this means that your required reserves drop slightly, to $1,800, and that your excess reserves are reduced to $7,200 ($9,000 − $1,800). Of course, it is reasonable to believe that before long your depositor also would bring checks into your bank that were drawn on other banks. These checks would tend to replenish your reserves at the Fed and increase your bank's demand deposits.

So far we have not created any new money. The practice of writing checks just transfers demand deposits from one bank to another. In the above example, your bank lost $1,000 in demand deposits but Bank B gained a like amount.

Money creation

Being a banker, naturally you are eager to make loans, because the interest return on money lent out is a prime source of income for most banks. The first question is how much you can loan out. Let us suppose that checks coming into your bank have offset checks going out. Thus, your balance sheet shows $10,000 in demand deposit liabilities and $10,000 in total reserves as illustrated in the top balance sheet below. The required reserve ratio of 0.20 tells you that 20 percent, or $2,000, of the $10,000 demand deposits must be kept on reserve either in your vault or at the Federal Reserve bank. Thus, the remaining 80 percent, or $8,000, represents the value of new loans that can be made to the public.

Consider next what happens when a likely prospect comes along in need of an $8,000 loan, say to build an addition to his home. He signs a promissory note agreeing to pay you certain specified interest and payments on the principal. In return you set up a checking account for him. The moment you set up this checking account, you, in effect, create $8,000 in additional money. After all, demand deposits are money. Thus, banks create money by making loans.

So far you have added $8,000 to the demand deposit item in your balance sheet. Now you have a total of $18,000 in demand deposits in your bank, backed up by $10,000 in reserves. This situation is depicted in the middle balance sheet below. But notice that at this point you still have excess reserves. Under the 0.20 reserve ratio you are required to have only $3,600 in reserves, but you still have $10,000. What happened? Did we make a mistake?

The answer is no, because as soon as this $8,000 loan is spent (checks are written against it) you must expect that these checks will be deposited in some other bank. And you recall from the check-writing transaction of the previous section, a check drawn against your bank reduces your reserves at the Fed by the amount of the check. Suppose, then, that the entire loan is spent by writing a single check, say in payment to a contractor. If the contractor deposits this check in his bank, say Bank B, the Fed reduces your reserves by $8,000 (you had better be sure you have $8,000 at the Fed) and increases the reserves of Bank B. The end result as it affects your bank is shown on the bottom balance sheet.

The process of making a loan; balance sheet of Bank A

Initial situation

Assets			Liabilities + Net worth	
Reserves		$10,000	Demand deposits	$10,000
Required reserves	$2,000			
Excess reserves	8,000			

Loan is made

Assets			Liabilities + Net worth	
Reserves		$10,000	Demand deposits	$18,000
Required reserves	$3,600			
Excess reserves	6,400			
Note		8,000		
		$18,000		$18,000

Loan is spent

Assets			Liabilities + Net worth	
Reserves		$ 2,000	Demand deposits	$10,000
Required reserves	$2,000			
Excess reserves	–0–			
Note		8,000		
		$10,000		$10,000

In this example, we assumed that the demand deposits were created at the time of the loan. We could have assumed instead that the borrower took his money in cash, say 80 crisp $100 bills. You still would have created $8,000 in additional money, because cash inside banks is not considered part of the money supply whereas cash outside banks is a part of the money supply. Eventually, of course, the contractor who received the $8,000 would take it to his bank for deposit, thus exchanging cash for demand deposits. So we end up at the same place regardless of whether we assume the loan goes out as a check or as cash.

Multiple expansion

The story of your loan doesn't end when the $8,000 check is cleared against your bank. Let us now go to Bank B, the contractor's bank. When the check has cleared, the Fed increases Bank B's reserves by $8,000 and at the same time Bank B's demand deposit item is increased by the same amount. But if Bank B receives $8,000 in new demand deposits and reserves, we know part of this $8,000 will be excess reserves. Operating under a reserve ratio of 0.20, 20 percent of the $8,000 or $1,600 represents required reserves. The remainder, $6,400 in this example, is excess reserves available to be loaned out.

In order to focus entirely on the $6,400 loan that Bank B can make, let us omit the other items on its balance sheet. The top balance sheet below represents the influx of new reserves into Bank B because of the $8,000 check. The middle balance sheet shows the immediate effect of making the loan, and the one on the bottom shows the end result after the loan is spent. Notice in this case that Bank B has created $6,400 in new demand deposits by making the loan.

So far, in these first two rounds of the multiple expansion process, a total of $14,400 in new money has been created—$8,000 with your original loan and $6,400 with Bank B's loan. There is no reason why the multiple expansion process has to stop here. We could carry it on to Bank C and then round after round to infinity. But by now you probably see what is going on. When a loan check comes into a bank, the bank acquires some excess reserves which

Second round of the multiple expansion process; balance sheet of Bank B

Receipt of $8,000 check

Assets			*Liabilities + Net worth*	
Reserves		$ 8,000	Demand deposits	$ 8,000
Required reserves	$1,600			
Excess reserves	6,400			
		$ 8,000		$ 8,000

Loan is made

Assets			*Liabilities + Net worth*	
Reserves		$ 8,000	Demand deposits	$14,400
Required reserves	$2,880			
Excess reserves	5,120			
Note		6,400		
		$14,400		$14,400

Loan is spent

Assets			*Liabilities + Net worth*	
Reserves		$ 1,600	Demand deposits	$ 8,000
Required reserves	$1,600			
Excess reserves	–0–			
Note		6,400		
		$ 8,000		$ 8,000

enable it to increase its loans. Of course, the amount of the loan and the demand deposits created become smaller and smaller the further the process is carried. The multiple expansion process is summarized in Table 6–2.

TABLE 6–2
Summary of the multiple expansion process

New total reserves		*Excess reserves, loans made, dollars created*		
Bank A	$10,000	$ 8,000 = 1 ×	$8,000	
Bank B	8,000	6,400 = 0.80 ×	8,000	
Bank C	6,400	5,120 = (0.80)² ×	8,000	
	•	•		
	•	•		
	•	•		
To infinity	•	•		
		$40,000		

You probably noticed a similarity between the multiple expansion process and the multiplier discussed in Chapter 4. Rather than carrying the process out to infinity, which becomes a bit tedious before long, we can employ a simple formula to determine how much the money supply will eventually increase. Recall from Chapter 4 the following expression:

$$1 + x + x^2 + x^3 + \cdots + x^n = 1/1 - x$$

In this case

$$x = 1 - \text{the reserve ratio}$$

Thus

$$1/1 - x = 1/1 - (1 - R)$$

where R is the reserve ratio. But

$$1/1 - (1 - R) = 1/1 - 1 + R = 1/R$$

because the ones cancel out.

Therefore, to find the ultimate expansion of the money supply stemming from an influx of new excess reserves, we multiply the original increase in excess reserves by 1/reserve ratio. In our example $R = 0.20$, so the "money multiplier" is $1/0.20$ or 5. Thus the sum of the right-hand column in Table 6–2 is equal to $1/0.20 \times \$8,000$ or $\$40,000$.

We should at the same time remember that the multiple expansion process can work in reverse, that is, a decrease in excess reserves can bring about a multiple contraction of the money supply. For example, suppose the contractor (no pun intended) pays back the $8,000 loan. You decrease his checking account by $8,000 and tear up his note. Now you have "destroyed" $8,000. If you do not relend the $8,000, the total money supply in the country will decline by $1/R \times \$8,000$. This happens because Banks B, C, D, etc., lose reserves as checks are drawn against them for payment to your contractor friend. In the process they lose reserves and must contract their loans outstanding also. Lest you receive the impression, however, that the entire banking system revolves around your bank, remember that any commercial bank in the country has the same option of renewing or not renewing loans.

It is necessary to mention also that the full multiple expansion or contraction takes place only if the participating banks are "fully loaned up" at all times, that is, they keep no excess reserves. In reality, though, most banks try to retain some excess reserves rather than operating right at the margin, so to speak. Generally if banks face a strong demand for loans and high interest rates can be obtained, they tend to operate with less excess reserves than when the loan business is sluggish and interest rates are low. If a bank happens to find itself with less than the legal reserves, it can in an emergency borrow from its Federal Reserve bank, although the Fed tends to discourage habitual borrowers.

Bear in mind that the multiple expansion or contraction process is not likely to approach an infinite number of rounds. However, the major change in the money supply comes during the first few rounds. In the example above the first three rounds alone created $19,520 or almost half of the ultimate expansion. At any rate, the multiplier of $1/R$ provides an upper bound to how much the money supply will expand or contract for a given change in excess reserves.

Bond purchases

A commercial bank with excess reserves on its books may choose to purchase bonds rather than make direct loans to individuals or businessmen. Most banks in fact like to diversify their portfolios and purchase a variety of earning assets with their excess reserves. Government bonds, either federal, state, or municipal, are a popular investment for banks. The bonds may be purchased directly from the issuing agency or from a second party who happens to be holding them. Either way, the purchase of a bond by a bank has the same effect as making a loan, that is, it creates money.

This will be easiest to see if we go back to our original example before your bank made the $8,000 loan. Instead suppose you had purchased $8,000 in bonds held by a wealthy widow who wanted to use the money for a new Cadillac. Once you have the bonds, you either pay her the cash, give her a certified check, or create a checking account in her name. In any case, you have created $8,000 in new money. As soon as the lady spends the $8,000, another bank is likely to experience an increase in its deposits and excess reserves and off we go again on the same multiple expansion process.

An implication of fractional reserve banking

By now you probably realize that a bank does not hold in cold storage, so to speak, all the money that has been brought in for deposit. A certain fraction, the required reserves, must be held; but the remainder, or excess reserves, can be used to make loans or purchase bonds. As we pointed out at the beginning of the chapter, a bank is able to operate with fractional reserves because on any one day deposits and withdrawals tend to cancel out. During a normal day the difference between deposits and withdrawals may not exceed 2 or 3 percent of a bank's total deposits. Hence, if a bank has 15 to 20 percent of its deposits on reserve there generally is no danger of running out of cash.

There have been times, however, when depositors became fearful that their banks would close and they would lose their hard-earned cash. In the early 1930s, for example, when a rumor would start in town that the bank was about to close, depositors rushed in to draw their money out. When this happened it was inevitable that the bank should close. If enough of a bank's depositors became convinced that a bank was going to fail, it failed.

After the financial crisis of the early 1930s the Federal Deposit Insurance Corporation (FDIC) was set up. Nowadays all deposits are insured up to $15,000, so there is no need for most people to fear losing their deposits. From time to time we still hear of people keeping their money in a mattress or some such hiding place because they distrust banks. No doubt a good share of this distrust was built up during the Great Depression.

Federal Reserve transactions

In our discussion of the Federal Reserve System we noted that the Open Market Committee is continually buying and selling securities in the market. We will now see that these transactions are an important determinant of the supply of money in the economy.

First let us consider the sale of a $1,000 bond to an individual. To pay for the bond the person writes out a $1,000 check against his account in a commercial bank. When the check clears, the Fed deducts $1,000 from the bank's reserve account and in turn the bank deducts this amount from the person's checking account. The initial transaction is illustrated below:

Initial result of a Federal Reserve sale of a $1,000 bond to an individual

Commercial bank		Federal Reserve bank	
Assets	Liabilities + Net worth	Assets	Liabilities + Net worth
Reserves —$1,000	Demand deposits —$1,000	Securities —$1,000	Bank reserves —$1,000

Notice first that the bond sale by the Fed immediately reduces the money supply by $1,000, that is, demand deposits are reduced by this amount. But we should be aware that commercial bank reserves also are reduced. If the reserve ratio is 0.20, required reserves decline by $200 and excess reserves go down by $800. From our discussion of the multiple expansion and contraction process, we know that this $800 decline in excess reserves will result in an ultimate contraction of $1/0.20 \times \$800$ or $4,000 in the economy, in addition to the initial $1,000 decline, making a total decrease in money of $5,000.

The opposite happens, of course, when the Fed purchases bonds in the open market. Here a $1,000 purchase immediately increases commercial bank reserves and demand deposits by $1,000. After the multiple expansion process has run its course, the initial $800 increase in excess reserves allows the money supply to increase by another $4,000, making a total increase of $5,000.

The Fed also buys bonds from and sells bonds to commercial banks. The final outcomes of these transactions are the same as those where the Fed dealt directly with an individual, although the initial effect is slightly different. A bond sale by the Fed to a commercial bank will be paid for by subtracting commercial bank reserves on the Fed's balance sheet. Hence there is no immediate decline in demand deposits, but the $1,000 reduction in excess reserves eventually can result in a $1/0.20 \times \$1,000 = \$5,000$ reduction in the money supply. The same reasoning applies to a bond purchase from a commercial bank by the Fed, except that now there would be a multiple expansion of money.

The main point to keep in mind here is that a Federal Reserve sale of a bond reduces the money supply and a purchase tends to increase money. Intuitively these transactions make sense. An open-market sale injects bonds into the private economy but in exchange pulls money and reserves out. Conversely an open-market purchase pulls bonds out and in exchange injects money or reserves into the economy.

Whether or not the full multiple expansion or contraction process takes place depends a great deal on the action of banks and the general public. This is especially true on the expansion side. For example, suppose the Fed wants to increase the money supply through an open-market purchase. But if banks are reluctant to make loans or if people are reluctant to borrow, the money supply may expand relatively little. Yet experience has shown that open-market operations do in fact change the money supply in the desired direction.

Main points of Chapter 6

1. The balance sheet itemizes the assets, liabilities, and net worth of a person, firm, or institution. Assets include anything of value. Liabilities represent the claims of creditors against the assets, and net worth represents the owner's claim to the assets. Assets always equal liabilities plus net worth because net worth is computed as the difference between assets and liabilities. Thus Assets = Liabilities + Net Worth because Net Worth = Assets − Liabilities.

2. Goldsmiths who provided places of safekeeping for money emerged as the forerunners of modern banks. Because deposits came close to offsetting withdrawals on any given day and because gold or money is a homogeneous commodity, only a small fraction of the total gold deposits actually changed hands during a day's business. Hence, goldsmiths found that part of their gold deposits could be loaned out. This was the beginning of fractional reserve banking.

3. To avoid carrying gold, people soon began to exchange de-

posit receipts in place of gold. This was the beginning of checking account money or demand deposits.

4. We can identify three steps in the evolution of banking: first, the deposit of money or gold for safekeeping with people called goldsmiths; second, the lending out of gold because only a small fraction was actively in use; and third, the gradual acceptance of deposit receipts as money.

5. As of December 31, 1971, there were 13,783 commercial banks in the United States. Of this total, 9,184 were state banks. Although a majority of the state banks are not members of the Federal Reserve System, the largest ones do belong, so the largest share of the deposits in the country is under the jurisdiction of the Fed.

6. Each commercial bank is required to hold a certain percentage of its deposits on reserve as cash in its own vault, in the Federal Reserve Bank of its district, or in a reserve city bank. The percentage of deposits that must be held as reserves is known as the reserve ratio. These reserves are intended to protect depositers, but perhaps more important they provide a control for the Fed over the maximum amount of loans that can be made by commercial banks.

7. The Federal Reserve System was established in 1913 to prevent unwanted expansions and contractions of money and credit during boom and recession periods, respectively, and also to provide for an "elastic" currency because of seasonal fluctuations in business activity within the year.

8. The Federal Reserve System consists of 12 Federal Reserve banks, one in each of the 12 districts, and a number of branch banks. The system is controlled by the seven-member Board of Governors appointed by the President of the United States.

9. A deposit of cash by a customer in exchange for demand deposits does not change the total quantity of money in the economy; it only changes the form in which money is held from cash to demand deposits.

10. When a check is drawn on Bank A and deposited in Bank B, the demand deposits and total reserves in Bank A are drawn down by the amount of the check, but these items are increased by the same amount in Bank B. Thus there is no

change in total bank reserves or in demand deposits outstanding.

11. Commercial banks create money by making loans because the borrower receives demand deposits or cash that he can later spend. When the loan is spent and deposited in another bank, this amount adds to the second bank's deposits and total reserves. Part of these reserves become excess reserves on which the second bank can make loans, etc. The maximum multiple expansion that can take place is equal to $1/R$ times the initial increase in excess reserves. The same formula applies to a multiple contraction brought on by a reduction in excess reserves.

12. The purchase of a bond by a bank has the same effect as making a loan. Money is created in exchange for the bond. The same multiple expansion process takes place.

13. One implication of fractional reserve banking is that only a small proportion of a bank's total deposits are available for withdrawal on a given day.

14. The sale of bonds by the Federal Reserve to individuals or commercial banks has the effect of pulling money out of the private economy and reducing reserves. Hence there is a multiple contraction of the money supply. On the other hand the purchase of bonds by the Federal Reserve (either from banks or individuals) serves to inject additional money and reserves into the economy, thereby allowing a multiple expansion of the money supply.

Questions for thought and discussion

1. Construct a balance sheet for yourself showing only your major assets and liabilities along with your net worth.

2. Commercial banks sometimes have been called "warehouses for money." In what ways are commercial banks similar to conventional warehouses, such as places to store fur coats? In what ways do banks differ from ordinary warehouses? What is the main difference in the commodity stored?

3. Explain why banks are able to loan out a substantial share of the money they receive as deposits.
4. Trace out the major steps that took place in the evolution of the banking system.
5. Explain what happens in the banking system when you write a check in payment for your tuition. Use balance sheets.
6. Suppose you are discussing banking with a friend who works in a bank. You point out that banks actually create money. But your friend says nonsense, the bank only lends out a fraction of its deposits. Thus how can it create money? How would you explain what happens?
7. Your banker friend in Question 6 really "breaks up" when you say that banks can create $5 in new money for every dollar of new cash that comes into the banking system. Try to explain this.
8. It has been said that checks are nothing more than warehouse receipts. Is there an element of truth to this statement? Explain.
9. How is a bond purchase by a commercial bank similar to a loan by the bank?
10. What would happen to the bank you have your checking or savings account in if every depositor wanted his money on the same day?
11. "If the Federal Reserve wants to increase the money supply it should purchase government bonds." True or false? Explain.
12. Will your answer to Question 11 be different if the Fed buys bonds from banks or from individuals? Explain.

7

The Keynesian model with money

In Chapter 4 we developed the simplest Keynesian model of an economy. Then in Chapters 5 and 6 we turned our attention to money, looking first at the demand for cash balances and secondly at the banking system. Our task in this chapter is to integrate money into the simple Keynesian model in order to build a somewhat more complete model of the economy. With this more complete model, which we shall call the Keynesian model with money, we will be better able to explain the causes of unemployment and inflation and to analyze policies that might be taken to ease these problems.

Equilibrium in the goods and services sector

The equilibrium NNP that we obtained in the Keynesian model without money presented in Chapter 4 can be thought of as an equilibrium of the goods and services sector of the economy. Recall that equilibrium NNP in the context of this model occurs where aggregate demand is equal to aggregate supply. At this point the desired aggregate demand of consumers, investors, and the government is equal to the desired output of goods and services by the business community. Thus at equilibrium there is neither an unintended accumulation or drawing down of inventories. And as a result there is no "pressure" on the economy for a change in output or income. To refresh your memory, the simple Keynesian model without money is shown in Figure 7–1.

FIGURE 7–1
The Keynesian model without money illustrating equilibrium NNP

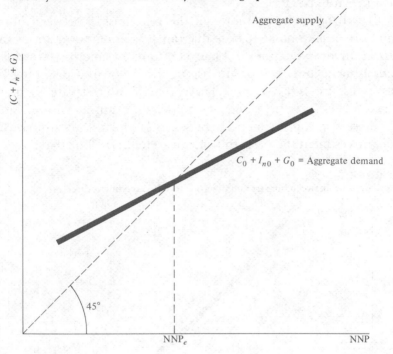

Interest and investment

In our discussion of the investment component of aggregate demand, the interest rate was a major determinant of the level of annual investment. When the interest rate rises, the level of investment tends to decline because the higher interest rate reduces the expected level of profits. Also with a high interest rate and a "tight" credit situation, loans tend to be more difficult to obtain, which also discourages investment. The opposite is true, of course, for a decline in the rate of interest, which tends to stimulate investment. Of course, any change in interest which changes the investment component of aggregate demand will in turn change the level of aggregate demand. Hence a rise in the interest rate tends to shift the aggregate demand line downward and reduce equilibrium NNP. By the same token, a lower rate of interest is associated with a higher aggregate demand line and a high level of equilibrium NNP.

It will be useful to represent the relationship between interest and investment on a separate diagram. Economists would say there is an inverse relationship between interest and investment. In graphing such a relationship we obtain a downward sloping line, as in Figure 7–2. At the relatively high interest rate i_2, the annual level of net investment is equal to I_0. But at a lower rate of interest, say i_1, investment increases to I_1, and at the still lower rate of i_0 investment increases to I_2. Let us refer to the line that traces out

FIGURE 7–2
Relationship between interest and investment—the investment line

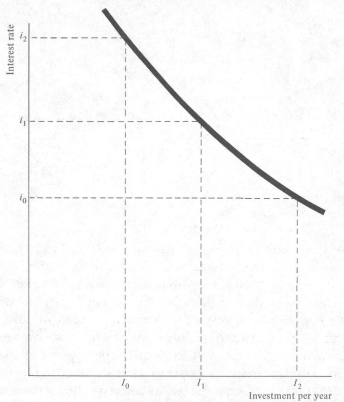

the relationship between interest and investment as the investment line.

At this point it will not be necessary to concern ourselves with the exact relationship between interest and investment, that is, we will not specify whether investment changes a great deal for a 1 percentage point change in interest or whether there is only a slight change in investment. Later on in the chapter we will see, however, that the responsiveness of investment to the interest rate is of considerable importance. Bear in mind too that we have no way of determining from our discussion so far what rate of interest and investment will prevail in an economy. All we have done is to trace out a relationship between the two.

Interest and equilibrium NNP

If we pull together the discussion so far, it becomes apparent that the interest rate has an important bearing on the equilibrium level of NNP. The chain of causation can be summarized as follows:

Interest $\rightarrow$ Investment $\rightarrow$ Aggregate demand $\rightarrow$ Equilibrium NNP

Thus if we choose an interest rate such as i_1, in Figure 7–2, we can determine from the investment line that the annual level of net investment will be I_1. If we add this amount of investment to consumption and government expenditures, we can determine the aggregate demand line. And once we know aggregate demand we can immediately determine equilibrium NNP, or equilibrium in the goods and services sector, as economists sometimes refer to it.

We present in Figure 7–3 the three aggregate demand lines that correspond to the three rates of interest and investment shown in Figure 7–2. Note that aggregate demand is held down by a high rate of interest because investment is relatively small. Then as the interest rate declines, investment increases and aggregate demand also increases. Furthermore, the upward shifts in aggregate demand give rise to higher equilibrium levels of NNP. The interest rate in the parentheses after each aggregate demand line correspond to those in Figure 7–2 and serve as a reminder that each aggregate

FIGURE 7–3
Relationship between the interest rate and aggregate demand

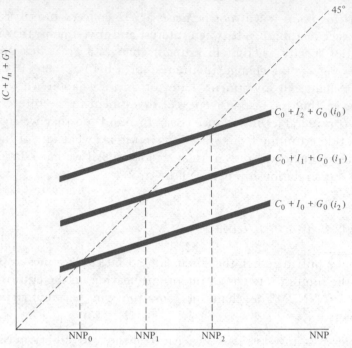
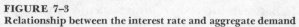

demand line corresponds to a particular level of interest and investment.

The IS curve

Economists have found it convenient to summarize the relationship between the interest rate and equilibrium NNP by a line, much as we did in Figure 7–2 for the relationship between interest and investment. Again in this case we observe an inverse relationship between the two variables. At high rates of interest equilibrium NNP is relatively low, but as interest declines and aggregate demand shifts up the equilibrium level of NNP increases.

The three combinations of interest and equilibrium NNP presented in Figure 7–4 correspond to those shown in Figure 7–3. All

FIGURE 7–4
Relationship between the interest rate and equilibrium NNP—
the *IS* curve

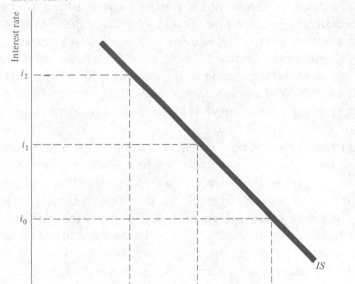

we have done is to rearrange the diagram somewhat, placing the interest rate on the vertical axis but keeping NNP on the horizontal axis. To simplify the presentation, we have utilized only three different interest rates and equilibrium levels of NNP. There is no reason, of course, why we could not have chosen hundreds of arbitrarily small changes in interest and then plotted the hundreds of corresponding equilibrium NNP levels. But three combinations are sufficient to convey the idea that a relationship exists between the interest rate and equilibrium NNP.

The line traced out in Figure 7–4 is commonly referred to as the *IS* curve. Its name is derived from the fact that at every level of equilibrium NNP (the corresponding intersections of aggregate demand and aggregate supply) the desired level of saving is equal to the desired level of investment.[1] Hence the investment equals saving characteristic is often abbreviated by $I = S$, or just IS for short. The IS curve also is known as the EE curve, where EE stands for expenditures equilibrium. This label reflects the idea that the curve represents alternative equilibrium levels of expenditure in the goods and services sector of the economy. Because the IS label is the older and more common of the two, we will use it from now on. But regardless of the label, the main thing to keep in mind is that every point on the curve represents an equilibrium level of NNP for a given interest rate.

If you reflect back for a moment to Chapter 4, you may remember that the model we developed then implied there was only one equilibrium level in the goods and services sector. But now we see that there is an entire range of possible equilibrium points, as shown by the IS curve in Figure 7–4. However, the information that we have at our disposal at this point does not allow us to determine which of these many possible equilibrium values of NNP will actually prevail in an economy, mainly because we do not know what interest rate will prevail. All we have done so far is to trace out a relationship between many possible interest rates and their corresponding levels of equilibrium NNP.

So far, all we know about the IS curve is that it is downward sloping in nature, i.e., there is an inverse relationship between the interest rate and equilibrium NNP. But we will see in the next two chapters that the exact slope of the IS curve will be an important determinant of the appropriate government policies to reduce unemployment or inflation. Thus it is necessary to understand what determines the slope of the IS curve. That is, what will make the line slope downward very steeply or what will cause it to have a very gentle slope?

An important factor affecting the IS line slope is the slope of the investment line. If the investment line is very steep, as I in Figure 7–5 (A), then the corresponding IS curve will also be very steep as shown by IS in Figure 7–5 (B). A very steep investment line reflects the idea that investment is not very responsive to changes

---

[1] A proof of this relationship is provided in Thomas F. Dernburg and Duncan M. McDougal, *Macroeconomics* (4th ed.; New York: McGraw-Hill Book Co., 1972), pp. 99–119.

FIGURE 7–5
Relationship between the slope of the investment line and the *IS* curve

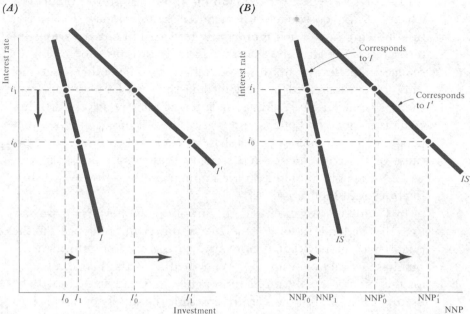

in the interest rate. For example, an interest rate decline from i_1 to i_0 in Figure 7–5 (A) does not bring forth much of an increase in investment. As a result there is a relatively small upward shift in the aggregate demand line, which in turn means that equilibrium NNP will not change by very much. On the other hand, an investment line that is relatively flat, like I' in Figure 7–5 (A), implies that investment changes a relatively large amount for a given change in interest. And the large change in investment brings forth a relatively large change in aggregate demand and NNP.

Equilibrium in the monetary sector

In constructing the *IS* curve, we have shown that many possible equilibrium levels of NNP are possible in the so-called goods and services sector of the economy. But we have no way of determining at this time which equilibrium level of NNP will actually prevail at a point in time. This can be done only after we have determined equilibrium in the so-called monetary sector.

To determine equilibrium in the monetary sector we must utilize the concepts of the demand for and the supply of money. In Chapter 5 we constructed a demand curve for money. This was a line showing how much money people wish to hold at various interest rates. We assumed that at high interest rates people tend to reduce their desired holdings of cash in favor of other assets because of the increased interest income that can be obtained from the nonmoney assets. And at low interest rates relatively little income is forgone by holding assets as cash, so it may be argued that people choose to hold a larger share of their assets in this form because of the convenience and security that money provides. The wishes of people to hold cash are summarized by a downward sloping line, as in Figure 7–6 (A).

In Chapter 6 we discussed the supply of money. Here we saw that the Federal Reserve can have a powerful influence on the quantity of money that is put out into the economy through the purchase or sale of securities. We will discuss the Fed's influence on the money supply more thoroughly in Chapter 9. It will be useful at this point, however, to represent the supply of money by a line, much as we did for the demand for money. Only in this case the line will be nearly vertical or at least will be steeply upward sloping when graphed against the interest rate. A vertical supply of money line means that the quantity of money in the economy remains constant at various levels of the interest rate. An upward sloping line means that the quantity of money increases at higher levels of the interest rate. The latter situation would seem to depict reality a bit more closely, since commercial banks are likely to increase their loans outstanding and consequently increase the quantity of money when the demand for loans is relatively large and the interest rate is high. In this situation we can expect that commercial banks will be closer to being "fully loaned up" than when the demand for loans is relatively small and the interest rate is low. Thus in our future discussion of the supply of money, we will represent it by a steeply upward sloping line, as in Figure 7–6 (B). Our main concern however, will be with shifts in the supply of money line rather than with its slope. These shifts, as we will explain in Chapter 9, come about because of changes in Federal Reserve policy and action.

Our next task is to combine the demand and supply diagrams

FIGURE 7–6
Representing the demand for and supply of money

(A) Demand for money

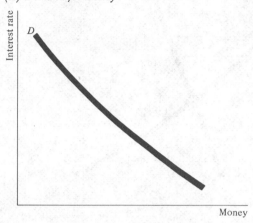

(B) Supply of money

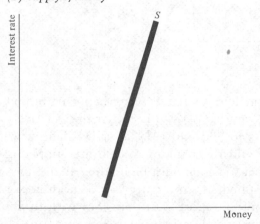

of Figure 7–6 into one to determine equilibrium in the monetary sector. Notice that both diagrams have interest on the vertical axis and money on the horizontal axis. Thus we can just superimpose one diagram on the other to obtain Figure 7–7. This diagram will allow us to determine the so-called equilibrium in the monetary sector.

Perhaps the easiest way to explain the meaning of equilibrium in the monetary sector is to begin at an interest rate that does not

FIGURE 7–7
Equilibrium in the monetary sector

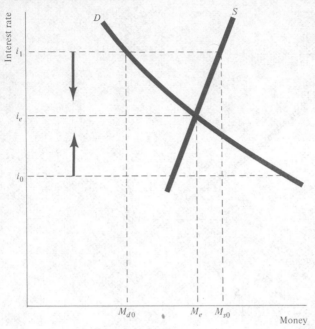

represent equilibrium and then see what happens. Suppose by accident the interest rate happens to be i_1. At this relatively high rate the public wishes to hold only M_{d0} as cash balances, whereas the Federal Reserve and the banking system are supplying M_{s0}. Keep in mind now that someone must be holding at all times all of the money that is supplied, M_{s0} in Figure 7–7. So at interest rate i_1 people are actually holding more cash than they wish to hold. As you might expect, then, people might try to loan out some of their "excess" money and as a result additional funds appear on the loan market. With the additional funds available, borrowers are able to press for lower interest loans. Soon competition in the loan market drives the interest rate down.

On the other hand, if the interest rate happens to be relatively low, say at i_0, people desire to hold more cash than is being supplied to the economy. Then as people try to sell earning assets such as stocks and bonds in exchange for cash, there is a reduction of funds in the money market which serves to drive the interest rate upwards.

Notice that in both of these disequilibrium situations the change in the interest rate, either a rise or a fall, changes the preference of people for holding their assets as cash. As the interest rate declines, the amount of money people wish to hold comes closer and closer to the amount actually supplied. Similarly as the interest rate increases, people desire to hold less and less of their wealth as cash until the amount they desire to hold exactly coincides with the amount actually supplied. Thus the interest rate serves as the mechanism for equilibrating the desired holdings of cash (money demand) with the actual holdings of cash (money supply).

By now you probably recognize that unless the interest rate corresponds to the intersection of the demand and supply curves for money, there will always be a pressure on it to change. Thus the interest rate that corresponds to this intersection, such as i_e in Figure 7–7, is referred to as the equilibrium rate of interest in the monetary sector.

The LM curve

Perhaps you recall from Chapter 5 that a major factor shifting the demand for money is the income or output of the economy. As the income of people increases, they tend to hold larger amounts of money for any given interest rate. Thus it is necessary to bear in mind that any time we see a demand curve for money, such as shown in Figure 7–7, we must also remember that it is drawn for a given income level of society. A higher income level would imply a higher demand for money, that is, a demand that lies farther to the right than the one shown in Figure 7–7.

So far, then, we have just derived one possible equilibrium rate of interest for the economy. But as soon as we speak of many possible equilibrium levels of NNP, as shown by the expenditures equilibrium line, we must also speak of many possible equilibrium rates of interest. We can follow a procedure very similar to that used in constructing the *IS* curve and construct a line showing the relationship between various levels of equilibrium NNP and the corresponding equilibrium rate of interest. In this case we will choose various possible levels of equilibrium NNP to obtain a series of possible equilibrium levels of the interest rate as determined in the monetary sector of the economy.

In constructing this relationship we will assume a constant (non-shifting) supply of money. (Later on we will see what happens when the supply of money does shift.) Each of the demand curves for money shown in Figure 7–8 (A) corresponds to a given level of

FIGURE 7–8
Relationship between NNP and the equilibrium rate of interest—the *LM* curve

(A)   *(B)*

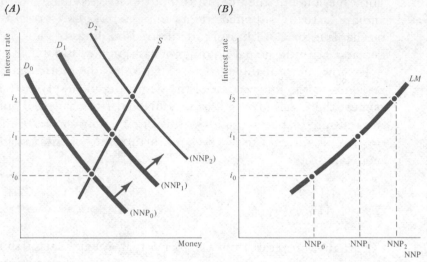

NNP, as denoted in the brackets. At a relatively low level of NNP, such as NNP_0, the demand for money will be low, as illustrated by D_0, and as a result the equilibrium interest rate will be low. As we choose higher levels of NNP, denoted by NNP_1 and NNP_2, the corresponding demand for money increases to D_1 and D_2 and the resulting interest rate increases to i_1 and i_2, respectively.

If we plot the equilibrium rates of interest shown on the vertical axis of Figure 7–8 (A) against the corresponding levels of NNP, we obtain an upward sloping line as illustrated by Figure 7–8 (B). This line or relationship is commonly referred to as the *LM* curve. It is so named because every point on the curve represents an equilibrium between the demand for money (sometimes called the "liquidity preference" curve or *L* for short) and the supply of money (or *M* for short). Thus it has come to be known as the *L* = *M* curve, or just *LM*. The curve also has been labeled *ME* to denote equilibrium in the monetary sector of the economy, i.e., monetary equilibrium. Since the *LM* label is somewhat more common, we will utilize it from now on. But regardless of the label, the main thing to keep in mind here is that the curve traces out a series of many possible equilibrium rates of interest for many possible levels of equilibrium NNP. The upward sloping nature of the line reflects the idea that higher levels of NNP result in higher rates of interest, given the supply of money.

So far all we know about the *LM* curve is that it slopes upward. But it will become important in the following two chapters to know what affects the slope of this curve. The slope of the *LM* curve depends to a large extent on the slope of the demand curve for money.[2] If the demand curve for money is relatively flat, as in Figure 7–9 (A), meaning that people are quite responsive to the interest rate in deciding how much they wish to hold, then the *LM* curve also will be relatively flat. In this case, a given increase (shift to the right) in the demand for money because of an increase in NNP raises the interest rate only a relatively small amount, as illustrated by Figure 7–9 (A). Thus the *LM* curve does not rise very much at higher levels of NNP, meaning that the curve is relatively flat.

On the other hand, if the demand for money is relatively steep, as in Figure 7–9 (B), reflecting the idea that changes in the interest rate have little effect on the amount of money people wish to hold, the resulting *LM* curve also will be steep. Here you will note that a given shift to the right of the demand for money because of an increase in NNP raises the interest rate a large amount, as shown by Figure 7–9 (B). Thus the *LM* curve rises relatively fast as we move out to progressively larger levels of NNP, meaning that the *LM* curve is relatively steep.

It will be useful to prove to yourself the relationship between the slope of the demand curve for money and the slope of the *LM* curve by deriving the *LM* curves that go along with Figures 7–9 (A) and (B). Be careful to draw the *horizontal* shift in the demand curves the same in both cases, as they are shown in Figure 7–9 (A) and (B).

To summarize briefly, so far in this chapter we have derived the *IS* and *LM* curves. The former was obtained by choosing alterna-

---

2 To be strictly correct we should state that the slope of the money supply curve also influences the slope of the *LM* curve; the steeper the supply of money curve, the steeper is *LM*, given the demand for money. However, the available evidence suggests that although the money supply curve slopes upward, it is relatively close to vertical. See William E. Gibson, "Demand and Supply Functions for Money in the United States: Theory and Measurement," *Econometrica*, Vol. 40, No. 2, March 1972, pp. 361–70.

FIGURE 7–9
**Relationship between the slope of the demand for money and the
slope of the *LM* curve**

(A) Results in a flat LM curve

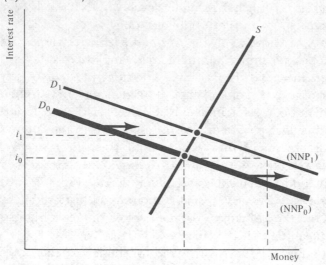

(B) Results in a steep LM curve

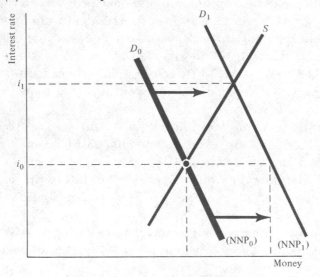

tive rates of interest and observing what happens to the equilibrium
NNP. We found that with lower rates of interest, investment increases, which shifts the aggregate demand line upward, giving us a

higher equilibrium NNP. The relationship between the interest rate and the resulting equilibrium level of NNP is summarized by the *IS* curve. The *IS* curve slopes downward because lower rates of interest correspond to higher levels of equilibrium NNP. Also the slope of the *IS* curve depends on the responsiveness of investment to changes in the rate of interest.

The *LM* curve was obtained by choosing alternative levels of NNP and observing what happens to the equilibrium interest rate in the economy. At higher levels of NNP, the demand for money increases, which results in a higher equilibrium rate of interest. The relationship between the level of NNP and the interest rate is summarized by the *LM* curve. The *LM* curve slopes upward because higher levels of NNP result in higher equilibrium interest rates. Also the slope of the *LM* curve depends on the responsiveness of the demand for money to changes in the interest rate.

Overall equilibrium

We know now that there are many possible equilibrium levels of NNP and many possible equilibrium levels of the interest rate in the economy, as shown by the *IS* and *LM* curves. Our next step, then, is to determine which of these possible equilibriums will actually prevail. Suppose we pick an interest rate and find its corresponding level of NNP from the *IS* curve. But if this interest rate is either too high or too low to be the equilibrium rate in the monetary sector for this level of NNP, pressures will exist in the money market to change the interest rate. As soon as the interest rate changes, there is a change in the equilibrium level of NNP, which forces us to start the entire trial-and-error process over again. It is easy to see how this little game would soon drive an ordinary person up the wall; perhaps even an economist would find it frustrating.

A much easier way of determining overall equilibrium in the economy is to superimpose the *IS* and *LM* curves on the same diagram and observe where they intersect. This is shown in Figure 7–10. Notice here that there is one interest rate and one level of NNP, i_e, and NNP_e, respectively, that result in a simultaneous equilibrium in both the expenditures and monetary sectors of the

FIGURE 7–10
Overall equilibrium

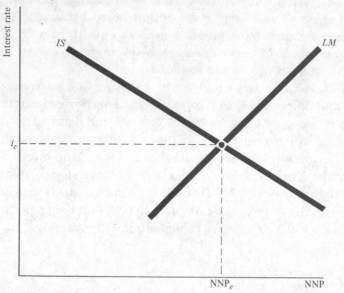

economy. By choosing i_e we find that the corresponding equilibrium level of NNP in the expenditures sector is NNP_e. But it also turns out that NNP_e is the level of income that results in an equilibrium interest rate of i_e in the monetary sector. Now the economy is in a complete or overall equilibrium. There are no pressures in either sector to cause a change in either the interest rate or NNP.

Although Keynes presented all the ingredients and the rationale for this more complete model in his book, another English economist, J. R. Hicks (a recent Nobel prize winner), should be credited with formulating the *IS* and *LM* curves.[3] Alvin Hansen, an American economist, also was influential in making these relationships explicit.

Shifts in the IS curve

Now that we have developed the more complete model and determined equilibrium NNP, our next task is to investigate how

---

[3] J. R. Hicks, "Mr. Keynes and the 'Classics': A Suggested Interpretation," *Econometrica*, Vol. 5 (1937), pp. 147–59.

changes can take place in the equilibrium level of income or NNP. Basically these changes can occur because of shifts in the *IS* curve, the *LM* curve, or both. Let us consider the *IS* curve first.

Recall that the *IS* curve is derived from the aggregate demand–aggregate supply diagram. As the interest rate declines, investment increases and aggregate demand shifts up, resulting in a higher level of equilibrium NNP. The *IS* curve then traces out the relationship between the interest rate and equilibrium NNP as derived by the aggregate demand–aggregate supply diagram.

A shift in the *IS* curve will take place if there is a shift in one or more of the three components of aggregate demand (consumption, investment, and government spending) that is not related to changes in the interest rate.[4] For example, an increase in aggregate demand will occur if consumers decide to increase their spending at any given level of income. Perhaps the easiest way to see the effect of such an increase in aggregate demand on the curve is to construct the *IS* curve before and after the shift in aggregate demand. This is illustrated in Figure 7–11 (A) and (B). To conserve space, aggregate demand is labeled D and NNP is denoted by Y in the diagrams to follow. The lines labeled D_{i_1} and D_{i_0}, in diagram (A) represent higher levels of aggregate demand stemming from lower levels of the interest rate (i_0 is less than i_1). The corresponding shift of the *IS* curve is shown below in diagram (B).

Now suppose we have an upward shift (increase) in aggregate demand that is unrelated to any change in the interest rate. Each of these aggregate demand lines, denoted by D' in diagram (A), lies above the original lines, at a given interest rate. Note, therefore, that equilibrium income, denoted by Y, is higher at each interest rate level. As a result, the corresponding *IS* curve, labeled IS', lies to the right of the original curve. Hence an upward shift in aggregate demand results in a shift to the right (an increase) in the *IS* curve. As you might expect, a decrease in aggregate demand will result in a shift to the left (a decrease) in the *IS* curve. You might verify this on your own.

---

4 We assume here that the interest rate only affects investment. Also keep in mind that any shift in investment due to interest rate is already incorporated into the *IS* curve.

FIGURE 7–11
**Illustrating the effect of an increase in aggregate demand on the
IS curve**

(A) Increase in aggregate demand

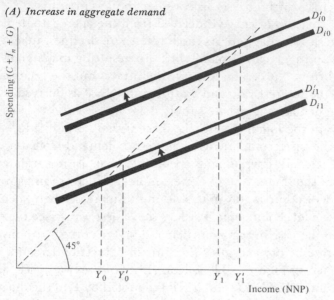

(B) Resulting increase in the IS curve

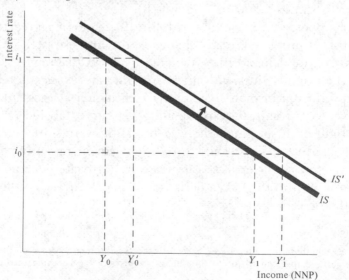

Shifts in the LM curve

Recall that the *LM* curve is derived from the demand for and supply of money diagram. At higher levels of NNP, there is a greater demand for money and as a result the equilibrium rate of interest increases as NNP increases, given a fixed supply of money. The *LM* curve traces out the relationship between different levels of NNP and the corresponding levels of the equilibrium interest rate.

A shift in the *LM* curve will occur if there is a shift in either the demand for money (at any given level of income), the supply of money, or both. Let us consider the demand side first. Suppose, for example, people decide to increase their demand for cash balances at any given income level. This is illustrated in Figure 7–12 (A) by the demand lines labeled D_0' and D_1'. Notice in this case that the equilibrium rate of interest is higher for each level of NNP. The resulting effect on the *LM* curve is to shift it up and to the left, i.e., to decrease it. This is considered a decrease because each interest rate now corresponds to a lower level of income. We will see in the following section that this also leads to a decrease in equilibrium NNP. Of course, the opposite holds true for a decrease in the demand for money. Here the *LM* curve will increase, i.e., shift to the right.

The *LM* curve also will shift if there is a shift in the supply of money. Let us consider the case where the Federal Reserve makes an open-market purchase of securities, thereby increasing the supply of money (shifting the money supply line to the right). This is illustrated in Figure 7–13 (A). Here we see that for each level of income and corresponding demand for money, there is a lower equilibrium rate of interest. By plotting these interest rates against their respective income levels in diagram (B), we obtain a shift to the right in the *LM* curve, denoted by *LM'*.

To summarize this section briefly, we see that an increase in the demand for money decreases (shifts to the left) the *LM* curve. An increase in the supply of money has the opposite effect, that of increasing the *LM* curve. It would be helpful to construct diagrams similar to Figures 7–12 and 7–13 showing the effects of a decrease in demand for money and in the supply of money. Your results

FIGURE 7–12
Illustrating the effect of an increase in the demand for money on the *LM* curve

(A) Increase in the demand for money

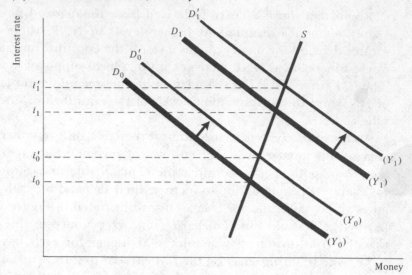

(B) Resulting decrease in the LM curve

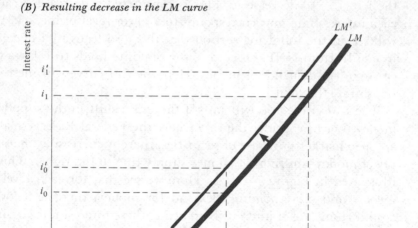

should show an increase in the *LM* curve resulting from the decrease in demand for money, and a decrease in the *LM* curve resulting from a decrease in the supply of money.

FIGURE 7–13
Illustrating the effect of an increase in the supply of money on the
***LM* curve**

(A) Increase in the supply of money

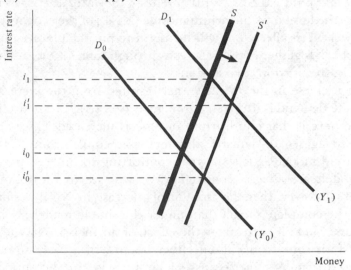

(B) Resulting increase in the LM curve

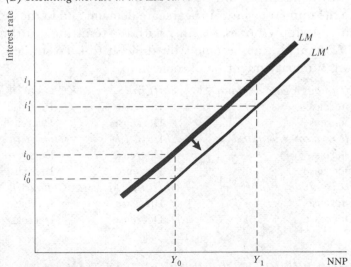

Changes in equilibrium NNP

As you would expect, a shift in either the *IS* or the *LM* curve changes the level of equilibrium income (NNP) of the economy. To see how NNP is affected, it will be useful to put the more complete model back together and briefly run through some of the shifts discussed in the previous two sections.

The increase in the *IS* curve that resulted from the increase in aggregate demand is illustrated in Figure 7–14 (A). The main thing to note here is that equilibrium income is increased. Since an increase in aggregate demand also increases equilibrium NNP in the simple model, it is somewhat comforting to observe that the two models are at least consistent. We will see in the following chapter, however, that the amount of increase in NNP is smaller under the complete model than under the simple model.

Figure 7–14 (B) illustrates the effect of an increase in the *LM* curve. This could come about either because of a decrease in the demand for money or because of an increase in the supply of money. Here again we observe an increase in equilibrium NNP. Naturally the opposite results occur with a decrease in *IS* or *LM*, and it may be useful to illustrate this with diagrams of your own.

Since the numerous shifts in aggregate demand and in the money demand and supply curves, together with the resulting shifts in the *IS* and *LM* curves, can become a bit difficult to keep straight, the following summary might be of some help.

1. *Shift in aggregate demand*	*Shift in IS*	*Change in NNP*
Increase	Increase	Increase
Decrease	Decrease	Decrease
2. *Shift in money demand*	*Shift in LM*	*Change in NNP*
Increase	Decrease	Decrease
Decrease	Increase	Increase
3. *Shift in money supply*	*Shift in LM*	*Change in NNP*
Increase	Increase	Increase
Decrease	Decrease	Decrease

The rationale for fiscal and monetary policy

Now that we have become acquainted with the mechanics of the more complete model, we are ready to put it to use. In the follow-

FIGURE 7–14
The effect of an increase in the *IS* and *LM* curves

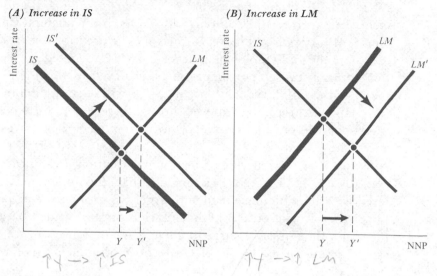

(A) Increase in IS   *(B) Increase in LM*

FIGURE 7–15
Illustrating unemployment and inflationary situations with the complete model

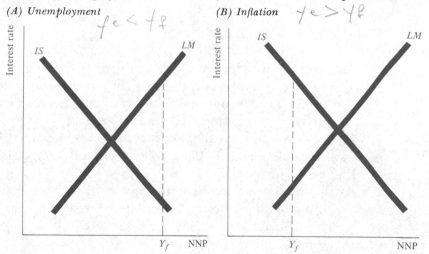

(A) Unemployment   *(B) Inflation*

ing two chapters we will utilize this model along with the simple model developed in Chapter 4 to identify the causes of unemployment and inflation and to prescribe the appropriate government policies that can lead us toward the goal of full employment without inflation.

More specifically we will see that it is possible for equilibrium NNP to be less than the level of NNP that provides full employment. In this case the economy will suffer from unemployment. This is illustrated by Figure 7–15 (A). Here equilibrium NNP is less than the full-employment level of NNP, denoted by Y_f. In this situation full employment can be achieved by shifting either the *IS* or the *LM* curve to the right. As we will see in the following two chapters, this can be achieved through government fiscal policy, which operates on the *IS* curve, or through monetary policy, which affects the *LM* curve.

Figure 7–15 (B) reflects an inflationary situation. In this case the equilibrium level of NNP is greater than the full-employment level, with the difference made up largely by an increase in prices rather than in real output. This situation can be avoided by shifting either the *IS* or *LM* curve to the left. Again, as we will see, this can be accomplished by either fiscal policy or monetary policy.

Main points of Chapter 7

1. The point of intersection between aggregate demand and aggregate supply can be thought of as equilibrium in the goods and services or expenditures sector of the economy.
2. The relationship between the interest rate and the level of annual investment in the economy can be represented by a downward sloping line. The lower the interest rate, the larger the level of investment.

3. As the interest rate declines and investment increases, there are corresponding upward shifts in the aggregate demand line, which in turn results in higher levels of equilibrium NNP in the goods and services sector.

4. The *IS* curve is obtained by plotting alternative interest rates against its corresponding level of equilibrium NNP. The *IS* curve is downward sloping because lower rates of interest correspond to higher equilibrium levels of NNP in the goods and services sector.
5. The slope of the *IS* curve is determined mainly from the slope of the investment line. If the investment line slopes down

very steeply, meaning that investment is not very responsive to changes in the interest rate, the *IS* curve also will be relatively steep.

6.   Equilibrium in the monetary sector corresponds to the intersection of the demand for and supply of money curves. At rates of interest higher than the equilibrium, people do not desire to hold as much money as the monetary authority is supplying. As people try to reduce their money holdings by attempting to lend, the rate of interest declines until the point is reached where the demand for money is equal to the supply.

7.   The *LM* curve is obtained by plotting the equilibrium interest rates that are obtained from alternative levels of NNP. At higher levels of NNP the demand for money is increased, resulting in a higher point of intersection between the demand and supply of money. Thus the *LM* curve slopes up, meaning that higher levels of NNP correspond to higher equilibrium rates of interest in the monetary sector.

8.   The slope of the *LM* curve depends upon the slope of the demand curve for money. If the money demand curve is relatively steep, the *LM* curve also will be relatively steep, and vice versa.

9.   Overall equilibrium in the economy occurs at the intersection of the *IS* and *LM* curves. At the overall equilibrium, the interest rate and NNP are perfectly matched; NNP_e corresponds to i_e in the monetary sector, and i_e corresponds to NNP_e in the goods and services sector.

10.   An increase in aggregate demand results in an increase in equilibrium NNP for a given interest rate. Thus we obtain a corresponding increase or shift to the right by the *IS* curve.

11.   An increase in the demand for money results in an increase in the interest rate for a given NNP. Thus we obtain a corresponding decrease or shift to the left by the *LM* curve.

12.   An increase in the supply of money results in a decrease in the interest rate for a given NNP. Thus we obtain a corresponding increase or shift to the right by the *LM* curve.

13.   Equilibrium NNP is increased by an increase or shift to the right by either the *IS* or the *LM* curve. The opposite holds true for a decrease or shift to the left by either curve.

14.   The objective of fiscal and monetary policy is to keep the

equilibrium level of NNP close to the level of NNP that provides full employment of resources, particularly labor.

Questions for thought and discussion

1. How can changes in the interest rate affect aggregate demand and equilibrium NNP as determined by the simple model?
2. Using diagrams, derive the *IS* curve. Why does it slope down?
3. Illustrate how the slope of the investment line influences the slope of the *IS* curve.
4. If we know the *IS* curve, can we determine the level of equilibrium NNP? Explain why or why not.
5. How do changes in NNP affect the demand for money?
6. Using diagrams, derive the *LM* curve. Why does it slope upwards?
7. If we know the *LM* curve, can we determine the level of equilibrium NNP? Why or why not?
8. Using the *IS–LM* curve diagram, denote the equilibrium interest rate and NNP.
9. In what way is the simple model developed in Chapter 4 a part of the more complete model developed in this chapter?
10. Show the effect of a decrease in aggregate demand on the *IS* curve.
11. Show the effect of a decrease in the demand for money on the *LM* curve.
12. Show the effect of a decrease in the supply of money on the *LM* curve.
13. Indicate the effect that each of the following changes would have on the complete model and on the equilibrium level of NNP. Also illustrate each with a diagram.
    a) An increase in the desire of consumers to spend at any given level of NNP.
    b) A decrease in the desire of businessmen to invest at any given level of interest and NNP.
    c) An increased desire on the part of individuals to hold money as opposed to other assets.
    d) A sale of securities by the Federal Reserve System.
    e) A cutback in government spending at the end of a war.
    f) An increase in government spending to wage war coupled with a Federal Reserve sale of securities.

8

Fiscal policy

Although "fiscal policy" has become somewhat of a household phrase, it will be useful nevertheless to define its meaning in rather precise terms. We can think of fiscal policy as the conscious attempt by government to promote full employment without inflation through its spending and taxing powers. Throughout this chapter, then, we will be primarily concerned with the effects of government spending and taxation on the level of output and employment in the economy.

Evolution of fiscal policy in the United States

In preface to our discussion of fiscal policy, we should make it clear that the deliberate attempt by government to promote full employment by its spending and taxing powers is a relatively recent phenomenon. We observe its beginning during the early years of the Franklin Delano Roosevelt administration, as evidenced by the creation of the public works programs instituted to create jobs and stimulate economic activity.

Yet a close reading of the record reveals that the idea still had a long way to go.[1] Although President Roosevelt endorsed the public

---

[1] See Herbert Stein, *The Fiscal Revolution in America* (Chicago: University of Chicago Press, 1969) for a comprehensive review of the development of fiscal policy.

works programs, he was not entirely convinced that a big public spending program was the answer to the country's unemployment problem. For example, upon seeing a list of projects under a $5 billion spending program, President Roosevelt proceeded to rip the list to pieces in the presence of his cabinet, indicating that many of the projects were impractical or useless.[2] Roosevelt agreed in May 1933 to a $3.3 billion spending program as something of a compromise between the $5 billion proposal and the $1 and $1.5 billion suggested by him.

It is also interesting to note that President Roosevelt appeared quite concerned about balancing the budget at that time. To meet the growing federal deficit, Roosevelt asked for and received tax increases in 1935 and 1936. Granted, the 1935 tax increase was directed mainly at high-income persons and large corporations in order to reduce the concentration of wealth. But the 1936 increase was more clearly sold on the basis of raising additional revenue.

The 1936 tax increase, during a time when unemployment was running 15 to 20 percent, illustrates the strong adherence to the balanced budget philosophy by the Roosevelt administration. It is inconceivable that similar action would be taken today under the same circumstances. Of course, this is not to say that Roosevelt would have adhered to the same policy had he been able to benefit from the 40 years of hindsight available to us. The main point is that we have learned a great deal since that time about how the economy operates and the appropriate policies to be undertaken. Certainly, Keynes' book, *The General Theory* (1936), must be acknowledged as making a significant contribution to our understanding. But, as will become evident as we proceed, we still have a lot to learn.

The passage of the Employment Act of 1946 represents another significant milestone towards the establishment of a deliberate and conscious set of spending and taxing policies aimed at promoting full employment without inflation. In this act Congress declared that it was the responsibility of the federal government to promote the maximum employment, production, and purchasing power of the economy. The act also established a Council of Economic Advisors to assist the President on economic policy, and a Joint

---

2 *Ibid.*, page 53.

Economic Committee of Congress to investigate economic problems of a national interest.

Since that time we have witnessed a gradual lessening of adherence to the goal of balancing the federal budget and a growing adherence to the goal of maintaining a stable and fully employed economy. For example, in the past presidential campaign, relatively little was said about balancing the budget in the years to come compared to cutting the unemployment rate and stabilizing prices. Of course, this is not to say that budget deficits are of no significance. As we will see a bit later, deficits, if financed by money creation, can result in inflationary tendencies. But at least there is less concern now than in years past that federal deficits will cause the country to "go broke," whatever that means.

Built-in stabilizers

Before we turn to a discussion of the deliberate changes in taxes and spending that can be undertaken by the government to promote full employment without inflation, it is necessary to call attention to fiscal policy measures that have been built into our economic system. These policies specify that government spending or tax changes will take place automatically in response to upturns or downturns in economic activity.

Two important automatic spending measures are unemployment compensation and the various welfare programs. These programs, you will note, are designed to stimulate the economy during recessionary periods, i.e., periods of increased unemployment. For example, as unemployment rises and family incomes fall, the influx of money through unemployment compensation prevents a more drastic decline in economic activity. Then as the economy recovers and people return to their jobs, a reduction in unemployment compensation helps to hold down inflationary pressure in the future period. Thus unemployment compensation is in effect an automatic or built-in stabilizer for the economy. Welfare programs have a similar effect, although these are perhaps more important as a means of livelihood for persons outside the labor force and the long-term unemployed.

The U.S. progressive income tax also can be thought of as somewhat of a built-in stabilizer. By a progressive income tax we mean a tax by which the rate of tax increases with higher incomes. Thus in recessionary periods the government taxes the income of the economy at a lower rate than during inflationary times. In a sense, then, the progressive income tax is a built-in stabilizer because it leaves proportionately more purchasing power in the economy during recessions and pulls proportionately more out during inflationary times.

Built-in or automatic stabilizers often are referred to as nondiscretionary fiscal policy because they operate without specific congressional edict. Granted, of course, the built-in stabilizers were originally created by an act of Congress, but once they are instituted Congress does not have to pass further legislation in order for the stabilizers to "do their thing."

Most of our discussion in this chapter will dwell on so-called discretionary fiscal policy. Here we have in mind tax or spending policies designed to deal with specific problems during specific periods of time. A good example of such a policy is an income tax surcharge. By adding an additional, temporary tax, the government pulls purchasing power out of the economy to reduce inflationary tendencies. Other examples of discretionary fiscal policies include the public works projects of the 1930s and the start of the superhighway construction program of the late 1950s. Both of these policies were aimed at stimulating business activity so as to reduce unemployment during these periods, although the highway program was sold in part at least by citing its military significance.

In our discussion of discretionary fiscal policy, we will utilize the Keynesian models that we developed in Chapters 4 and 7. Indeed the major reason for developing these models is to provide a framework for analyzing government policies.

Fiscal policy in the context of the simple Keynesian model

In discussing the simple Keynesian model in Chapter 4 and again in regard to the complete model of Chapter 7, we mentioned that

the equilibrium level of NNP may not coincide with full-employment NNP. If equilibrium occurs at a lower level of NNP than is
necessary for full employment, an unemployment situation will
develop. Conversely, if equilibrium NNP is greater than the level
that corresponds to full employment, inflation will appear.

The problems of unemployment and inflation are illustrated in
the context of the simple Keynesian model in Figure 8–1 (A) and
(B). Notice in diagram (A) that full employment can be obtained
only if there is an upward shift in aggregate demand. This can be
accomplished either through an increase in government spending,
a tax cut, or some combination of the two. As you recall from
Chapter 4, an increase in government spending adds to the aggregate demand for goods and services and as a result adds to the total
output and income of the economy.

Of course, it is necessary to assume in this case that the increase
in government spending does not result in a decrease in private
consumption or investment. For example, if the government decides to build a number of atomic powered electric generating
plants, private companies might well decide to reduce their construction of a like number of these plants. Hence the decrease in
private investment might simply cancel the increase in public investment. If the government is interested in shifting aggregate
demand upward, it should, therefore, purchase goods or services
that are not readily substituted for private goods and services.
There is less likelihood of offsetting reductions in private expenditure if the increased government spending concentrates primarily
on public goods such as highways, public parks, and yes, even on the
military or the space programs. Of course, the government should
not spend for the sake of spending, but rather should spend on
goods and services that maximize the welfare of the public.

The manner of financing the increased government spending
also is of extreme importance. If the government should happen to
have a surplus in the treasury at the time of the increased spending,
there is no problem. However, if the treasury is bare, which is most
likely to be the case if the economy is in a downturn and tax receipts
are down, the government must obtain additional funds from somewhere. A number of alternatives are available. The government
can increase taxes. But this would be a rather unwise alternative if

FIGURE 8–1
Fiscal policy in the context of the simple Keynesian model without money

(A) Unemployment policy

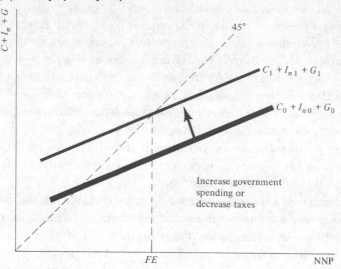

(B) Inflation policy

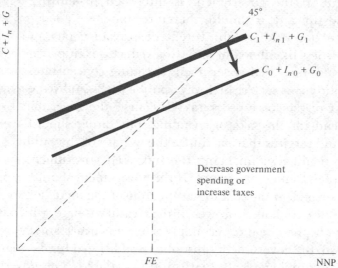

the objective is to stimulate economic activity, because higher taxes draw purchasing power out of the economy and dampen economic activity.

It is reasonable to expect, therefore, that the government most likely will engage in deficit spending during a recession. In other words, it will spend more than it receives in taxes. In this situation the government still has two alternatives: (1) it can borrow from the public by selling government bonds or (2) it can print money. We will be better able to evaluate the outcomes of these two alternatives in the following chapter on monetary policy, but an intuitive explanation at this point will call attention to the problems involved. Let us consider first the sale of government bonds. Recall from Chapter 6 that the sale of government bonds to commercial banks or the public reduces the money supply. But in reducing the money supply, the government can increase interest rates and consequently dampen economic activity. Thus, the undesired outcome of financing the increased government spending could, in this case, at least partially offset the desired effect of the increased spending. Of course, the Federal Reserve may choose to make an open-market purchase of bonds at this same time which, you recall, tends to increase the money supply.

The difference between government spending and tax revenue also can be made up by printing additional currency. In this case, the government uses newly created money to buy goods and services over and above that which it could buy with its tax funds and money obtained from borrowing. Of course, the end result is usually an increase in the money supply. We will see in the following chapter that an increase in the money supply serves as an additional stimulant to the economy. Hence the increase in government spending will not have to be as great to achieve full employment as the simple model illustrated in Figure 8–1 (A) might imply. Although, again in this case, the Federal Reserve has the power to offset the influx of newly printed cash by selling government securities in the open market.

Perhaps the main point to be made here is that the manner of financing additional government spending can have important side effects that either work to offset the impact of the additional spending or make it more potent than might be anticipated.

During a recessionary period, as depicted by Figure 8–1 (A), as an alternative to increasing its spending, the government could decrease taxes. This action also would stimulate the economy by leaving more dollars in the hands of households and business and in so doing allow the private sector to increase its spending. However, many of the same financing problems discussed above rise in regard to a tax cut. Presumably the government would not wish to decrease its spending during a recession, so the decrease in taxes again leaves the government with a budget deficit. The same alternatives we discussed in regard to an increase in government spending are available. In order to hold government spending at its previous level, the loss of revenue because of the tax cut can be made up by selling bonds to the public (borrowing), printing money, or some combination of the two. And as we saw, the resulting changes in the nation's money supply will tend to offset or augment the effect of the tax cut unless the Federal Reserve chooses to take action to hold the money supply constant.

Although the options of an increase in government spending and a tax cut have similar economic consequences, there are some other considerations that the government may wish to take into account. For one thing, it is rather difficult for the government to use the increased spending tool swiftly, because new projects or programs generally take time to conceive and set in motion. This is especially true for large investment projects such as roads, land reclamation, etc.

Political considerations are important also. An additional problem with increased government spending is that it tends to be distasteful to the more conservative members of society. For an administration that must draw on bipartisan support, as all do, the combination of high unemployment and increased government intervention in the economy may be more than a political party wants to bear. On the other hand, a tax reduction during a recessionary period can be instituted rather quickly and at the same time Congress can demonstrate to the folks back home that it is doing something about the high unemployment. Much political hay was made out of the tax cut that was instituted during the Kennedy administration. A like amount of increased government spending might have gone by largely unnoticed.

The problem of excess demand and inflationary pressure on the economy is illustrated in Figure 8–1 (B). Here the problem is just the opposite of what we have been discussing. The relatively high level of aggregate demand has pulled the equilibrium level of NNP past the point of full employment. Hence the increased money value of NNP that occurs as the economy moves past the full-employment point *(FE)* is due largely to higher prices rather than increased output. In this situation the appropriate action by the government would be to decrease or shift down the level of aggregate demand, assuming that it wants to reduce the inflationary pressure on the economy.

As you would expect from the previous discussion, in this case the government should decrease government spending, increase taxes, or perform some combination of the two. Either or both of these measures serve to draw purchasing power out of the economy and relieve the pressure of private demand against the available supply of goods and services. From the standpoint of government finance, there is much less of a problem here than we encountered in the unemployment case. The budget surplus that the government might acquire because of its reduced spending or increased taxation can easily be held until needed at some later date.

Perhaps the most troublesome problem stemming from any decrease in government spending is the rise in unemployment brought on by the loss of government contracts. Firms that produce goods and services for the government have little alternative but to lay off employees when this market dries up. Markets for new products and new jobs for these released employees do not emerge in a "twinkling of an eye." It takes time for business firms to retool to new markets and for unemployed people to search out new jobs. If the government spending cut is severe, as is generally the case following a war, the adjustment period may take several years. Hence we might expect to observe an increase in unemployment following a significant reduction in government spending. Moreover, if the inflation has built up a momentum, the immediate consequences of a government spending cut may be rising unemployment with continued inflation, as occurred during the greater part of 1970.

A tax increase, the other fiscal policy alternative open to the government during an inflation, is subject to a different kind of problem, namely that of political expedience. Few members of Congress like to go on record as favoring higher taxes especially before an upcoming election. As a result there is likely to be considerable foot-dragging and debate over tax bills that really should be enacted quickly if they are to have their desired effect. A good example of this problem occurred during the latter part of the Johnson administration, when Congress debated the proposed tax increase for about two years before passing it. We will discuss the political considerations of fiscal policy later in this chapter.

The simple Keynesian model as a predictive device

One advantage of the simple Keynesian model is that it is possible to specify to the dollar how much the government should change its spending or taxes in order to bring the economy to a full-employment equilibrium without inflation. Of course, we must specify where the full-employment equilibrium is in relation to the current NNP, and also we must know the nation's marginal propensity to consume (MPC). Assuming that this information is possible to obtain, let us see how this little predictive device works.

Recall from our discussion of the multiplier process in Chapter 4 that a dollar of new or additional spending will bring forth several additional dollars of spending. This occurs because spending by one person is income to another, and when people receive income they generally spend part of it. The fraction of an additional dollar of income that is spent is defined as the marginal propensity to consume. Also recall from Chapter 4 that the government spending multiplier is equal to $1/1 - \text{MPC}$, assuming there is not a change in the private sector which offsets a change in government spending or that the financing problems do not cause a change in the money supply. Therefore, if MPC is 0.75, as we have assumed, an additional dollar of government spending ultimately will bring forth $4 of new spending in the economy $(1/1 - 0.75 = 4)$.

Referring back to Figure 8–1 (A), suppose the economy is "stuck" in an unemployment equilibrium corresponding to the intersection of the 45-degree line and the existing level of aggregate demand $(C_0 + I_{n0} + G_0)$. To provide some plausible numbers for our problem, let us assume that the full-employment NNP is equal to $936 billion and the unemployment equilibrium is $900 billion.

Thus the economy should be nudged ahead by $36 billion to attain full employment. In terms of the diagram, we can view a $1 billion increase in government spending as shifting the aggregate demand line upwards by $1 billion. Now we know that with a multiplier of four, a $1 billion increase in government spending increases NNP by $4 billion. Thus it is not very difficult to figure out that government spending should increase by $9 billion to push the economy ahead by $36 billion. A convenient formula[3] that can be used to determine how much government spending should be changed to obtain the desired change in NNP is:

$$\Delta G = \Delta \text{NNP}/M_g$$

where ΔG is the calculated change in government spending or shift in the aggregate demand line, ΔNNP is the desired change in NNP, and M_g is the government spending multiplier.

This formula can be applied, of course, to either an upward shift in aggregate demand to remedy unemployment or a downward shift to ease inflationary pressure. If, for example, the economy is experiencing inflation, as depicted by Figure 8–1 (B), all we have to do is estimate the difference between the "overemployment equilibrium" and *FE* and then insert this number into the above formula. For example, if *FE* is $936 billion and the overemployment equilibrium is $952 billion, the desired decrease in equilibrium NNP would be $16 billion ($952 − $936). Inserting $16 billion into the above formula, we can determine that the government could remedy the inflationary situation by reducing its spending by $4 billion.

Offhand it may appear that the government could achieve the same effects through comparable changes in taxes as through the changes in spending we have just discussed. But this is not quite right. A $1 billion tax change will not have as large an impact on the economy as a $1 billion change in government spending. In other words, a $1 billion tax decrease, for example, will not shift the aggregate demand line up by the full $1 billion. Why? To understand this phenomenon, it is first necessary to be aware that people do not change their spending by the full amount of the

---

[3] From our definition of the multiplier we know that $\Delta G \times M_g = \Delta NNP$. Dividing both sides of this equation by M_g, we obtain the formula above.

tax change. The MPC tells us that. For example, if the government reduces taxes by $1 billion, the people will have an additional $1 billion that can be considered as additional disposable income. But it is not likely they will spend the entire $1 billion; they will spend part and save part. If their MPC is 0.75 the people will spend $0.75 billion and save the remaining $0.25 billion. Thus a tax decrease of $1 billion will shift the aggregate demand line upwards by only $0.75 billion if the MPC is 0.75.

The fact that people increase or decrease their saving as well as their spending in response to a tax change is the reason why the tax multiplier is less than the government spending multiplier. With just a little extra effort we can determine how much less the tax multiplier will be. Perhaps the easiest way to approach this is to compare the multiplier process of a government spending change with a comparable tax change. In Table 8–1 we compare the first

TABLE 8–1
Comparing the multiplier process of a government spending change with a tax change

$1 billion increase in government spending	*$1 billion decrease in taxes*
Round 1 .... $ 1 billion	$0.75 billion
Round 2 .... 0.75	0.56
Round 3 .... 0.56	0.42
.	.
.	.
To infinity	.
$ 4 billion	$ 3 billion

three rounds of the multiplier process for a $1 billion government spending increase with a $1 billion tax decrease. Notice that on the first round in the government spending column, the entire $1 billion is spent. But in the tax column the first round only shows $0.75 billion being spent. The remaining $0.25 billion is saved. And in all subsequent rounds the numbers in the tax column are smaller.

Using the multiplier formula developed in Chapter 4, we see that the total increase in spending in the economy will increase by $4 billion because of the $1 billion initial increase in government spending. However, in the case of the $1 billion tax decrease, total spending only increases by $3 billion. Hence the government spending multiplier is four in this case and the tax multiplier is three, or one less. The amazing thing about this is that under the assumptions of the simple model, the tax multiplier always will be one less than the government spending multiplier for a lump-sum tax such as we have assumed. If we let MPC be 0.80, for example, M_g would be five and M_t (the tax multiplier) would be four. The fact that the tax multiplier is one less than the government spending multiplier can be proven algebraically, but this is best left to the intermediate level macro course.

Now that we know that the tax multiplier is always one less than the government spending multiplier, we can modify the formula that we developed in regard to a government spending change so it can be used also to predict a tax change. Now we have:

$$\Delta T = \Delta \text{NNP}/M_t$$

where ΔT is the computed change in taxes, ΔNNP is the desired change in NNP, and M_t is the tax multiplier. Also keep in mind that $M_t = M_g - 1$.

Using this little formula, we can compute the tax changes that will bring the economy to the desired full-employment equilibrium. Faced with an unemployment situation where FE was $936 billion and the underemployment equilibrium was $900 billion, the necessary $36 billion increase in NNP could be achieved by a $12 billion tax decrease ($\Delta T = 36/3 = 12$). Or in the inflationary situation where NNP needed to be reduced from $952 to $936 billion, the job could be accomplished by a $5⅓ billion tax increase ($\Delta T = 16/3 = 5⅓$).

Keep in mind, though, that even if the needed tax changes are larger than the government spending changes, the tax changes shift aggregate demand by the same amount as the government spending changes. It just takes a larger tax change to do the same job as a given government spending change. If we want to determine how much a tax change shifts aggregate demand, we can use the formula $\Delta D = \Delta T \times \text{MPC}$, where ΔD is the vertical shift in aggregate demand and ΔT is the tax change.

The balanced budget multiplier

It is interesting to note as well that increasing government spending and taxes by a given amount will increase the equilibrium level of NNP by this very same amount. For example, suppose the government increases its spending by $1 billion and at the same time increases taxes by $1 billion so as to maintain a balanced budget, at least for this change in spending. If the MPC is 0.75, the government spending multiplier tells us that the government spending increase by itself will increase equilibrium NNP by $4 billion. But because M_t is one less than M_g, the tax increase will not completely offset the government spending increase.

Viewing this process as a sequence, the $1 billion government spending increase shifts aggregate demand upward by $1 billion and increases equilibrium NNP by $4 billion after the multiplier process has run its course. Applying the tax increase to this new, higher aggregate demand line, we know from our previous discussion that initial spending will decline by $0.75 billion, so that aggregate demand shifts down by $0.75 billion. Or we can apply the tax multiplier to the $1 billion increase in taxes to determine that equilibrium NNP declines by $3 billion. Thus the government spending increase pushes NNP up by $4 billion but the tax increase pulls it back by $3 billion, leaving a $1 billion net increase.

If we had increased government spending and taxes by $10 billion, the net increase in NNP would have been $10 billion. Moreover, this would be true regardless of the size of the MPC. It will be helpful to prove this to yourself by choosing different changes in G and T and working out the outcomes under different values of MPC. You will find that the value of MPC does not alter the fact that comparable changes in G and T always change equilibrium NNP by this exact same amount. Economists refer to this phenomenon as the balanced budget multiplier. The value of this multiplier is one, because equilibrium NNP changes by one times the initial change in G and T. Of course, in order to obtain a balanced budget multiplier of one, we have to assume that people do not reduce their expenditures on consumer goods and services in response to an increase in these items purchased and distributed by the government. If people reduce their expenditures on consumer goods and services dollar for dollar with the increase in government purchases of these items, the balanced budget multiplier will be zero.[4]

---

[4] For a summary of the various possible multipliers under varying assumptions, see Martin J. Bailey, *National Income and the Price Level* (New York: McGraw Hill Book Co., 1962), p. 79.

Implicit assumptions of the simple model

Because the simple Keynesian model seemingly gives such exact and simple answers to complex problems, it may leave the impression that we know more than we really do about combating unemployment or inflation. We ought to review, therefore, some of the basic assumptions that we have made in using the model. As we pointed out, it is assumed that changes in government spending are not offset by opposite changes in private spending. Also we have assumed that government spending changes have not affected the money supply.

In our discussion of taxes and the tax multiplier we have implicitly assumed that taxes are of a lump-sum variety. In other words, the total tax payment is assumed not to change with a change in income. Thus the tax multiplier for a progressive income tax can be expected to be somewhat different. About all we need to say here is that the tax multiplier for a progressive income tax will be somewhat smaller than the lump-sum tax multiplier we have discussed in this chapter. This is proven algebraically in more advanced macro courses, but we can at least present the economic rationale behind the difference here. Under the progressive income tax, a tax decrease, for example, means that the various tax rates are reduced. But as the economy is stimulated and NNP increases, more people are caught in the higher tax brackets, which tends to offset somewhat the initial tax reduction. Hence tax revenue does not decline as much as under a lump-sum tax, so NNP does not increase as much. Thus the tax multiplier is somewhat smaller for the income tax.

A very crucial assumption of the simple model is that either the interest rate does not change with changes in aggregate demand, or if the interest rate does change it does not affect the level of consumption or investment to a signficant degree. There is a great deal of disagreement among economists as to how important the interest rate is to consumption or investment. Those who argue that the interest rate is not very important in determining investment (i.e., the line graphing the interest rate against investment is nearly vertical) would in turn argue that the simple model is a fairly accurate predictor of the effects of fiscal policy on the economy. In other words, they would say that the multipliers discussed in this chapter provide a fairly accurate picture of the changes that would actually occur with changes in government spending or taxation.

On the other hand, those economists who maintain that the interest rate changes significantly with shifts in aggregate demand, and that these changes have a significant effect on investment and consumption, tend to place relatively less faith in the simple model as a predictive device. Given their assumptions, the economic rationale of their arguments is quite plausible. An increase in government spending, for example, and the subsequent increase in aggregate demand increase the rate of interest because of the increased demand for loans to finance much of the additional investment and consumption. The increase in the rate of interest, however, tends to dampen or hold back investment and consumption, so that equilibrium NNP does not increase as much as would be predicted by the government spending multiplier. The complete Keynesian model with money provides a better framework for analyzing this argument, however, so let us now consider fiscal policy in the context of this model.

Fiscal policy in the context of the Keynesian model with money

Fiscal policy, as you know, relates to changes in government spending and taxation to obtain full employment without inflation. We also know that changes in government spending and taxation affect aggregate demand in the context of the simple model. Thus in terms of the complete model we would have to say that fiscal policy affects the *IS* curve, because it is derived from aggregate demand.

Our first task, then, is to see how changes in government spending or taxation affect the *IS* curve. To begin, we know that an increase in the governmental spending component of aggregate demand shifts aggregate demand upward for a given interest rate. And, as shown by Figure 7–11, there will be a corresponding shift to the right by the *IS* curve. A decrease in taxes has a similar effect. Only in this case the consumption component of aggregate demand increases, because disposable income now makes up a larger share of a given NNP.

Figure 8–2 (A) represents a situation where the economy is suffering from unemployment. The equilibrium level of NNP corresponding to the intersection of the *IS* and *LM* curves is less than the level that corresponds to full employment. The appropriate fiscal policy in this case is to increase government spending, decrease taxes, or use some combination of the two. In terms of Figure 8–2 (A) the objective is to shift the *IS* curve from IS_0 to IS_1. Of course, the problems of a possible reduction in private spending when the government increases its spending or of financing a deficit without altering the money supply still confront us in this model as in the simple model.

The problem of an inflationary economy is depicted in Figure 8–2 (B). In this situation the intersection of the *IS* and *LM* curves falls to the right of full-employment NNP. Although the money value of NNP is higher at this point than at *FE,* the difference is due more to an increased price level than to greater real output. In other words, the level of NNP corresponding to the intersection of IS_1 and *LM* is inflationary. The objective, then, is to have the equilibrium level of NNP correspond to full-employment *(FE)* NNP. If the government wants to use fiscal policy to accomplish this objective, it can decrease government spending or increase taxes so as to shift the *IS* curve left until it intersects *LM* at the point that corresponds to full employment without inflation.

We should be reminded again of the problems involved in such a policy. A decrease in government spending may eventually reduce inflationary pressure, but the adjustment period when laid-off workers search for new jobs and business retools for the private market may be long and painful. As we mentioned in regard to the simple model, when the brakes are put on there will likely be a period when inflation, if it has built up momentum, keeps rolling along while unemployment is rising.

The multipliers in the context of the complete model

In our use of the simple model, we were able to predict in rather precise terms the exact amount government spending or taxes

FIGURE 8–2
Fiscal policy in the context of the complete model

(A) To correct for unemployment

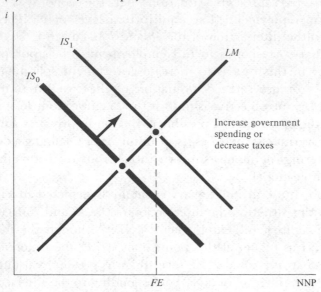

(B) To correct for inflation

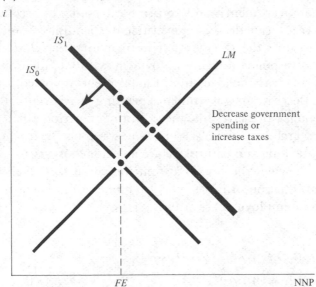

should be changed to achieve full employment without inflation. In this more complete model, however, we cannot be as precise. It is not that the complete model is less adequate; indeed it is more adequate because it takes the monetary sector into account. The reason we cannot use the multipliers to predict full-employment NNP in the model is that changes in the interest rate either hold back or augment the spending or tax changes.

Consider the unemployment situation depicted in Figure 8–3.

FIGURE 8–3
Fiscal policy and the dampening effect of a higher interest rate

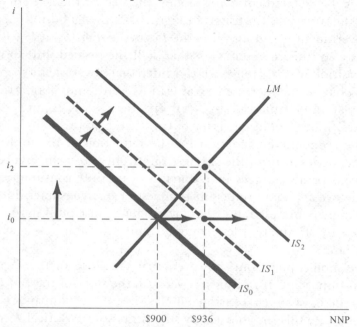

Choosing the same numbers as we used in the unemployment example for the simple model illustrated in Figure 8–1 (A), let full-employment NNP be $936 billion and the unemployment equilibrium be $900 billion. If the government spending multiplier is four, a $9 billion increase in government spending will shift the *IS* curve to the right by the horizontal distance of $36 billion. Recall that the $9 billion upward shift in aggregate demand increased equilibrium NNP by $36 billion. But you will note in

Figure 8–3 that a $36 billion horizontal shift will not be sufficient to bring the *IS* curve up to intersect *LM* at the point that corresponds to full-employment NNP. Thus the necessary government spending increase, according to this model, will have to be greater than $9 billion. How much greater will depend on the slope of the *LM* curve. The steeper the slope of *LM*, the more government spending will have to be increased (or taxes decreased) in order for the *IS* curve to intersect *LM* at the point corresponding to full-employment NNP. Thus fiscal policy is a rather ineffective device if the *LM* curve is relatively steep. Recall from Chapter 7 that the steeper the demand curve for money, the steeper the *LM* curve.

In the situation illustrated in Figure 8–3, the $9 billion increase in government spending shifts the *IS* curve from IS_0 to IS_1. But as you can see this represents less than half the needed shift to reach the position of IS_2. Hence we can infer that government spending would have to be increased by at least $18 billion to obtain the desired $36 billion increase in NNP. In other words, it appears that the multiplier would be closer to two than to four.

The economic explanation for the reduction in the multiplier is that the increase in the interest rate from i_0 to i_2 in Figure 8–3 dampens or discourages investment and possibly consumption. If people become more reluctant to invest or buy consumer durables with higher interest rates, the government must push harder and harder to stimulate the economy, and this implies a smaller multiplier.

We should point out, however, that the slope of the *IS* curve also is important. If *IS* is nearly vertical, the slope of the *LM* curve does not have much bearing on the size of the multiplier. You might verify this for yourself by superimposing a vertical *IS* curve on Figure 8–3 and observing that a $36 billion horizontal shift now brings the vertical *IS* curve over the desired distance to intersect with *LM* at the full-employment level of NNP. A vertical *IS* curve means that investment exhibits absolutely no response to changes in the rate of interest. In other words, the investment line is vertical when graphed against interest on the vertical axis.

Those economists who are "pro-fiscal-policy" will tend to argue that the investment line is nearly vertical, which implies a nearly vertical *IS* curve. Economists who are more skeptical of fiscal policy, on the other hand, stress the importance of the interest rate on investment and the resulting slope of the *IS* curve. The more responsive investment is to changes in the interest rate, the less steep the *IS* curve will be and the harder it is for fiscal policy to have much effect on the economy.

Fluctuations in economic activity

Ideally we would like to see the economy exhibit a stable growth trend in the output of goods and services, thereby avoiding excessive recessionary or inflationary tendencies. But in reality, most, if not all, growing economies experience considerable fluctuation in economic activity. Fiscal policy, as we mentioned, is one means of smoothing out these economic fluctuations.

Figures 8–4 and 8–5 might prove helpful in gauging the extent of economic instability in the United States economy over the past four decades as well as providing some insight into the possible causes of the instability. Here we present the year-to-year percentage changes of the major components of gross national product. A percentage change of a component that is above the zero axis, i.e., positive, implies growth during that particular year. The higher the line, the larger the percentage growth. Conversely, if the line falls below the zero axis into the negative region, it is an indication that the particular item declined in absolute amount during the year. We present all items in real terms, i.e., deflated by a change in the price level, to more clearly identify basic shifts in the expenditure pattern of the economy.

Perhaps the first impression received from Figure 8–4 is the relatively large fluctuations in gross investment compared to personal consumption expenditures. In the United States, at least, investment seems to be a very volatile component of GNP. Notice that investment took a number of wild swings during the 1930s, plummeting sharply during the early part of the decade, recovering briefly in the mid-30s, only to take another noticeable decline during 1938. The two sharp swings of investment during the 1940s were, of course, a result of World War II. At the outbreak of the war investment was curtailed to devote all possible resources to war production. Then after the war, investment bounced back to rebuild our aging productive capacity.

FIGURE 8–4
Annual percentage changes in U.S. personal consumption and gross private domestic investment expenditures, 1930–72 (1967 prices)

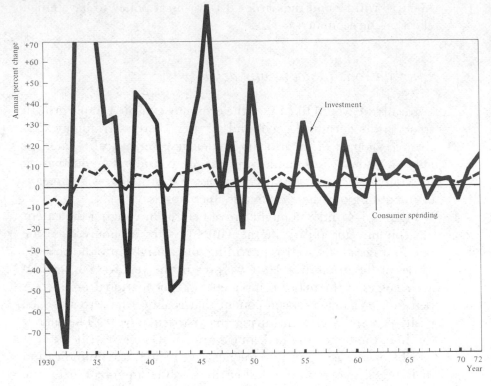

Source: *Economic Report of the President, 1973*, p. 193.

The post–World War II era brought somewhat less severe fluctuations in investment, although we can observe nine different years when it declined in absolute terms. The variation in real personal consumption expenditure has been on a much more moderate scale. Granted, consumption did decline in absolute terms during the 1930s, but not the percentage decline observed for investment. As with investment behavior, the post–World War II years also brought a moderation in consumer expenditure variation. In fact, the major portion of the 1960s brought a relative stability in consumption, at least more stability than the economy had experienced during the previous three decades.

Turning next to Figure 8–5, we observe a comparable degree of fluctuation in government spending, particularly at the federal

FIGURE 8–5
Annual percentage changes in federal, state, and local government expenditures,* 1930–72
(1967 prices)

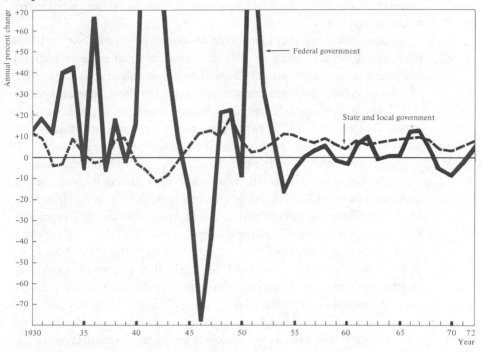

* Net of government sales.
Source: *Economic Report of the President, 1973,* p. 193.

level. This is not to imply, however, that fluctuations in government spending are necessarily undesirable. Indeed, according to our previous discussion, the government should step in during recessionary times to bolster spending in the economy, as it did during the 1930s. The increased public expenditure on public works projects and the like was designed to help pull the economy out of the depths of the Great Depression.

Of course, the major changes in federal government spending came during and immediately following war periods. The largest relative changes occurred in connection with World War II, first to mobilize the economy from a peacetime to a wartime basis, then to cut back on the huge military expenditure after the war. It is not difficult, either, to identify the Korean and Vietnam military buildups on Figure 8–5, although these were not of the relative magnitude of World War II. The expenditures of state and local governments, although exhibiting some fluctuation during the 30s and 40s, have since then been one of the more stable components of the economy.

In the context of the Keynesian model with money, we can look upon an absolute decrease in consumption or investment spending as contributing to a shift to the left in the *IS* curve. Unless offset by comparable increases in government spending, the end result is a decrease in equilibrium NNP and an increase in unemployment. By the same token, rapid increases in consumption or investment can be represented by a significant shift to the right of the *IS* curve, thereby contributing to inflationary pressure in the economy.

It should also be kept in mind that substantial fluctuations in government spending, unless to offset changes in private spending, can contribute to rather severe fluctuations in overall economic activity. Such fluctuations have come about mainly as a result of wars, either to build up the military or to reduce it. The space and military cutbacks during 1969 and 1970 provide an example of this problem. As a result there seems to be increasing concern over the destabilizing effects that the federal government can have on the economy. In view of the sizable fluctuations in federal spending, it seems that this is an area where greater stability could be achieved.

The degree of influence over the total economy by any one component of GNP will depend also on its relative size. For example, annual consumption expenditures are about 3.9 times as large as gross investment spending. Hence a given percentage change in consumption is likely to have a much larger absolute impact on the economy than an equal percentage change in investment. The figures in Table 8–2 provide an indication of the relative importance of each component of GNP and how the relative importance of each has changed over the years.

Notice that personal consumption is by far the largest component of GNP. Thus, rather small percentage changes in consumption can bring substantial absolute changes in total spending in the economy. The second major point of interest in Table 8–2 is the substantial increase in the role of the federal government in the economy. Federal spending has now become a substantially larger fish in the economic pond, and as a result sharp changes

TABLE 8–2
Relative size of the major components of U.S. gross
national product, 1929 and 1972

| | Percentage of GNP | |
Component	1929	1972
Personal consumption	69	62
Gross domestic investment	20	16
State and local government*	9	13
Federal government*	2	9

    * Net of government sales.
    Source: *Economic Report of the President, 1973*, p. 193.

in direction of federal spending can create some rather large waves
in economic activity.

Timing of fiscal policy

In our discussion of fiscal policy, we started out with the simple
Keynesian model, which provided us with simple and exact answers. But then we began to get a hint of complications when we
looked at financing problems and the effect of government spending reductions on the level of employment. Still more complications were brought in when we graduated to the more complete
model. Here we saw that the simple multipliers may not be correct
after all, so that we cannot be as precise in saying how much the
government should change its taxes or spending to correct an unemployment or inflationary situation.

Two additional problems arise in the implementation of fiscal
policy; both relate to timing. The first is the problem of when to
undertake needed changes in government spending and taxation in
order to stabilize the economy. The second is the lag between
the decision to undertake spending or tax changes and their effects
on the economy.

The first problem is really a matter of identifying when the
economy is headed for a recession or a runaway inflation. As we
saw in the previous section, the economy tends to fluctuate from
year to year in a rather uneven and unpredictable fashion. The
difficulty, then, is to decide whether an upturn or downturn is just
a minor fluctuation or whether it is the beginning of something

big. If the government takes rather drastic measures to curb a recession, for example, at the hint of a slight downturn in economic activity, the result might well be a forthcoming inflationary spiral. Theoretically, then, the government should take anti-recessionary measures (a spending increase or a tax cut) when the economy is just beginning to enter a downturn in economic activity as illustrated by time T_0 in Figure 8–6. By the same token, anti-inflationary measures should be reserved for a time such as T_1. The object is to smooth out the booms and busts, as shown by the even dashed line starting at T_0 in Figure 8–6.

FIGURE 8–6
Illustrating the problem of the correct timing of fiscal policy

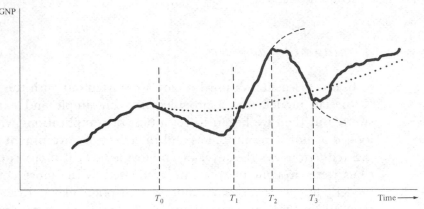

If the government is successful in identifying critical turning points in the economy, such as T_0 and T_1, there is still the question of doing something soon enough to have the desired effect. Suppose, for example, that the time span between T_0 and T_1 is three years. If it takes the government two years to push a tax cut through Congress or a similar period to decide on new government projects, the actual effect may be just the opposite of what is desired. If the anti-recessionary measures do not begin to be felt until around T_1, the result may well be to stimulate the economy in the forthcoming boom period following T_1. As a result the inflation following T_1 could be even worse than it would have been had no action been taken at all. This is illustrated by the dashed line beginning at T_2. Also, it is not very feasible to shut down government projects that have been initiated during a recession even when an inflationary period looms on the horizon. Hence these additional projects serve to accentuate the forthcoming inflation.

The same problems of timing and effect confront the government when inflation threatens, such as at T_1. Again a tax increase or a spending reduction may require one or two years to pass Congress (especially the tax increase if there is an upcoming election). As a result the antiinflationary policy may become a prorecessionary policy and pull the economy into a more severe state of unemployment, as illustrated by the downward sloping dashed line beginning at T_3.

There is also the problem of predicting when actual government spending or tax changes will have their major effect on the economy. We have implicitly assumed in our previous discussion that the desired effect of policy takes place immediately after action is taken. But this need not be the case. The major problem is that relatively little is known about the duration of lags between government action and its effect. Indeed the lag may change from one year to the next.

Another difficulty of implementing fiscal policy is that the government may have higher priorities than maintaining an economically stable economy. One of the major priorities appears to be that of waging war. Although the federal government may be fully aware of the destabilizing effects of a huge military buildup or cutback, it may still choose to implement these policies. This is not to pass judgment on the rightness or wrongness of such decisions; each instance must, of course, be evaluated separately. The main point is that the federal government may be faced with conflicting goals, and the goal of economic stability may not always come out on top.

The politics of fiscal policy

By now you probably realize that fiscal policy is not nearly as simple as it might have first appeared in the context of the simple model. The more complete model brought out some additional complexities and controversies, but even this is a crude tool when we consider the timing aspects and other goals of government.

We should emphasize that fiscal policy is not acted out in a political vacuum. The tax and spending changes we have been talking about take place only through action of Congress and the executive branch of government. Differences in viewpoint between liberals and conservatives tend to be reflected in differences in policy recommendations.

As mentioned in Chapter 1, liberals tend to favor or at least accept increased government spending on goods and services, while conservatives prefer a lesser role for government. Thus during a time of increased unemployment we would expect liberals to favor increased government spending and conservatives to argue for a tax reduction. For example, the 1964 tax cut has been described as a victory for conservative fiscal policy.

Assuming agreement can be reached on the appropriate spending increase or tax cut (in the case of increased unemployment) further decisions have to be made on where the additional spending should take place, or whose taxes should be reduced. Most senators and congressmen, regardless of political affiliation, like to obtain a "fair share" of any increase in government spending for their area or constituents. Understandably, this creates conflict, since the amount of any needed spending increase is not likely to be great enough to be spread across the entire nation.

In regard to a tax decrease, disagreement is likely to arise on who should obtain a tax break and the kind of taxes to be reduced. For example, should we have a proportionate, across-the-board tax decrease, or a tax reduction only for certain income levels such as low-income people? Or should businessmen be given a tax cut, say in the form of accelerated depreciation or investment credits, to stimulate economic activity? It is not likely that liberals and conservatives will readily agree on the answers to these questions.

The political controversy generated by a proposed government spending decrease or tax increase (as would be appropriate during inflation) is likely to be even more intense. Even if there is general agreement on the need for a spending decrease, few senators or congressmen are going to welcome it for their states or regions, particularly before an election. The people whose jobs depend on government spending, or who benefit in some way from this spending, can be very vocal in their opposition to spending cuts. At any rate it is becoming apparent that it is a good deal easier for government to increase spending than to decrease it.

A proposed tax increase involves similar problems. With the cost of living rising, probably more rapidly than wages during the early stages of inflation, few lawmakers are likely to push for higher taxes and further reduce the real take-home pay of workers. Again this is particularly true in a period immediately preceding an election. Some people have advocated giving the President power to vary income tax rates, within limits, in order to obtain more flexibility and more prompt action. However it doesn't appear that Congress will soon buy such a proposal.

The main point of all this is that there is much more to fiscal policy than just identifying the full-employment level of NNP and shifting aggregate demand or the *IS* curve to the desired point. Of course, the formal models are still valuable in determining the appropriate action—even though they cannot tell us when to take the action, or if it is politically feasible.

The national debt

A discussion of fiscal policy would not be complete without bringing in the national debt, or the public debt as it is often called. The national debt can be defined as the amount of money the government owes the people. The government borrows from the people by issuing and selling government bonds. In recent decades many people have expressed concern about the size of the national debt. We hear phrases such as "the country going bankrupt" or "fiscal irresponsibility" in relation to the government's increasing the public debt.

Is the public debt really something to be concerned about? It is important first to keep in mind that the public debt is debt which the government owes to the people. However, because the people "own" the government, it is debt which the people owe to themselves. If the government decided to pay off, say, $100 billion of the public debt, it would increase taxes by $100 billion and immediately pay this amount back to the people. As you can see, this $100 billion dollar payment would not make the nation any "poorer" because the people would still have the $100 billion. Granted, there may be some redistribution of wealth towards former bondholders, but the total wealth of the nation would remain unchanged. Of course, it is not likely the government ever would want to pay off such a large amount of the debt in a short period of time, because it would probably have a destabilizing effect on the economy.

A helpful analogy is to consider the public debt as you would consider debt owed by your right hand to your left. When the debt is paid, your right hand has less money but your left hand has more, so in net you are neither richer or poorer. The public debt would be another matter, however, if the government had borrowed from another nation. For example, if the United States owed $100 billion to the Canadian government, paying off the debt would leave the United States with $100 billion less in goods and services. But because the U.S. public debt is owed mainly to U.S. citizens, its existence should not be a cause for concern.

The figures in Table 8–3 permit us to take a brief look at the

TABLE 8–3
Public and private debt in the United States, selected years (1969 prices)

Year	Public debt (billions) Federal	State, local	Private debt (billions)	Federal debt Per person	% of GNP
1929	$ 35	$ 29	$ 346	$ 287	16%
1939	112	43	327	801	47
1945	515	27	286	3,681	119
1949	335	29	321	2,245	85
1959	304	73	665	1,710	50
1969	320	133	1,271	1,576	34
1971	331	152	1,324	1,584	32

Source: *Economic Report of the President, 1973,* p. 266; deflated by Consumer Price Index, 1969 = 100.

growth and magnitude of the public debt. In the interest of clarity, the debt of the federal government is separated from the debt of state and local governments. Also, for the sake of comparison, figures on private debt are provided. All debt figures are presented in constant 1969 prices to facilitate comparison over time.

Notice first that the debt of the federal government increased very rapidly from 1929 to 1945. During the 1930s the federal debt increased about threefold, mainly because of the Great Depression and the attempt of the federal government to stimulate the economy by increasing its spending. The public works projects of the 1930s bear evidence of this increased spending. As the country moved into the 1940s the World War II period brought even greater increases in the federal debt. During this period the cost of goods and services purchased by the federal government far exceeded its tax revenues, even though taxes were increased. The excess of government purchases over tax revenue was made up in part by borrowing from the people (selling government bonds) and in part by printing money.

In view of the large and rapid mobilization from a peacetime to a war economy, these policies probably were the most expedient that the government could have taken. Taxing for the full cost of the war, no doubt, would have dampened work incentives during a time when the country needed a 100 percent effort from all its citizens. Except for a brief period during the Korean War, the federal government has been able to decrease its debt somewhat since World War II, at least until the Vietnam War. Note, however, that the federal debt again increased during the 1960s.

The upward trend in state and local government debt followed a somewhat different pattern. There was some increase in this debt during the depression years, but not to the extent of the federal debt. And during World War II state and local government debt declined, taking into account the increase in the price level. Since the end of World War II, however, state and local debt has increased about fivefold. The "baby boom" following World War II, bringing increased demand for school facilities, no doubt is a major factor contributing to this increase. Also the highway building program of the late 1950s and 1960s necessitated further borrowing by state governments.

Except during World War II and the immediate postwar period the private debt—debt between individuals and between business firms—has been larger than the public debt. Moreover, the increase in private debt has been especially rapid during the 1960s, reflecting perhaps a general feeling of optimism on the part of consumers and businessmen.

Although many individuals and politicians have expressed concern over the growth and size of the federal debt, it must be admitted that relative to the size of the economy, the federal debt has decreased substantially since World War II. On a per capita basis, the federal debt has declined in real terms by almost one half since the end of World War II. And as a percent of GNP, the federal debt has declined by about 70 percent. It should be kept in mind that the debt figures presented in Table 8–2 have been inflated to 1969 prices to facilitate comparison over time. Thus the actual debt that prevailed in years past was substantially smaller than is shown by the table. For example, the federal debt in 1929 was only $16.5 billion in 1929 prices.

Adjusting the debt figures by the CPI does not alter the fact that debt which is incurred during inflation is paid back with inflated dollars. Thus the lenders (the people who have purchased government bonds in the case of public debt) suffer a loss because of inflation. For example, $1,000 "invested" in a 25-year government bond in 1944 was worth only about $500 in real purchasing power when the bond matured in 1969 because of the doubling of the price level over the intervening period. Thus the people who purchased war bonds during the 1940s in effect paid a "tax" that they probably didn't count on at the time the bonds were purchased.[5]

Who pays the economic cost of war?

It is evident that the major share of the federal debt existing today was incurred to finance wars, mainly World War II and to a lesser extent Korea and Vietnam. The fact that the government chose not to finance the entire cost of wars through increased taxes has prompted some people to argue that borrowing to finance part of the cost of war passes this portion of its cost on to future generations. Is this a valid argument?

Perhaps the best way to look at the economic cost of war is in terms of what is given up. During a war the people living at the time must forgo consumer goods and services in order to produce more war goods. This is true regardless of whether the government taxes, borrows, or prints money to finance the war. In taxing or

---

[5] This, of course, neglects the interest that was earned during the period. However, because the rate of inflation has been higher than the rate of interest on these bonds, their real rate of interest has been negative.

borrowing, the government removes purchasing power from the private sector. This reduces the purchase of nonmilitary goods and services by the public while increasing the wherewithal of the government to buy military goods and services.

Printing money has the same effect. The extra money is used by the government to purchase military goods and services and the resulting price increase reduces the purchasing power of money and other assets of a fixed money value such as bonds. In a sense, then, printing money is the same as levying a tax—it is a tax on people who hold assets that do not rise in value with the price level.

Young men drafted into military duty during a war, or at any other time for that matter, also bear a disproportionately high economic cost of the military. This happened because the military pay for most young men has been substantially less than what they could earn in civilian life, even taking into account the food, clothing, and lodging that is provided. We can say, therefore, that war is too "cheap" because its dollar cost does not reflect the full value of nonmilitary goods and services given up. The change to an all-volunteer army with higher wages for servicemen has the effect of shifting part of the cost of the military from the shoulders of servicemen to the taxpaying public.

We must conclude, therefore, that the economic cost of war, as well as the cost of human life, is borne by the people living during a war. The fact that future generations "inherit" the public debt does not alter this fact. Because we must also remember that the government bonds inherited by future generations are assets that offset this debt. Even the interest to service the debt, which amounts to about 6 percent of the federal budget, cannot be considered a burden, because this money goes back to the public.

There is one sense in which future generations bear the economic cost of war, and that is through the reduction of investment during wartime. For example, during the height of World War II, the relatively small amount of gross investment was not large enough to offset the depreciation of capital equipment, so there was a net decline in the nation's capital stock. As a result the nation's productive capacity is somewhat smaller today than it might have been without the war. This effect is, of course, much greater for countries that are ravaged by war.

Is the United States a war economy?

In our discussion of unemployment and inflation in Chapter 2 we noted that wars have brought decreased unemployment and prosperity, while a return to a peacetime economy has brought increased unemployment. This observation has prompted some people to argue that the United States is a war economy, meaning that war is necessary to provide full employment.

But as we mentioned, it is not reasonable to expect an economy to adjust immediately back to a peacetime economy when war is ended. The laying off of millions of people from the production of military goods and the release of millions of men from military service amounts to a drastic shock to the economy. It may take several years for the economy to completely adjust.

But after the adjustment period is over, can we expect the economy to absorb all the people who want to work? Those who argue that unemployment will always plague a peacetime free-market economy imply by their argument that society has all the goods and services it desires; everyone is in a state of being completely satiated. Of course, this is not likely to be true. Very few people, if any, can truthfully say that they have everything they desire. Hence as long as there are people who long for goods and services they do not have, which includes, by the way, a pleasant environment, there is no reason why everyone in society who wants a job at the free-market wage should not be working. Thus it is by no means clear that the existence of a large military establishment is needed to provide full employment.

Main points of Chapter 8

1. Fiscal policy can be defined as the conscious attempt by government to promote full employment without inflation through its spending and taxing powers.
2. The public works program of the Roosevelt administration represented an early attempt at influencing the level of eco-

nomic activity by government spending. The Employment Act of 1946 made it the explicit responsibility of government to maintain full employment.

3. Built-in stabilizers are fiscal policy measures that go into effect automatically in response to changes in economic activity. They are designed to counteract or smooth out cyclical changes in the economy. Some examples include unemployment compensation and the progressive income tax.

4. In the context of the simple Keynesian model, an increase in government spending or a decrease in taxes shifts aggregate demand upwards, thereby increasing equilibrium NNP and reducing unemployment. Conversely, to combat inflation the aggregate demand line can be shifted down by means of a decrease in government spending or an increase in taxes.

5. Some problems of undertaking fiscal policy as described by the simple Keynesian model include the possibility of offsetting changes in spending by the private sector and the problem of financing a deficit so as not to induce offsetting changes in aggregate demand. There is also the problem of Congress acting too slowly to obtain the desired results. In addition, a decrease in government spending during inflation will probably bring increased unemployment.

6. Knowing the nation's MPC and the desired change in NNP, it is possible to use the simple Keynesian model to predict the needed change in government spending or taxes to alleviate unemployment or inflation. The formula that can be used to specify a government spending change is $\Delta G = \Delta \text{NNP}/M_g$. The formula for specifying a needed tax change is $\Delta T = \Delta \text{NNP}/M_t$.

7. Under the assumption of a lump-sum tax, the tax multiplier in the simple model is one less than the government spending multiplier. This occurs because the entire change in government spending shows up on the first round of the multiplier process, but in the case of a tax change the first round of the multiplier process is equal to MPC times the tax change.

8. The balanced budget multiplier is one, meaning that an equal change in G and T will change equilibrium NNP by one times this change in G and T.

9. An important implicit assumption of the simple Keynesian

      model is that changes in the interest rate caused by changes in aggregate demand do not in turn cause offsetting changes in investment or consumption.

10.   In the context of the complete model with money, an increase in government spending or a decrease in taxes shifts the *IS* curve up and to the right, thereby increasing equilibrium NNP and decreasing unemployment. Conversely, to combat inflation, the *IS* curve can be shifted down and to the left by means of a decrease in government spending or an increase in taxes.

11.   The slopes of the *IS* and *LM* curves have an important bearing on the effectiveness of fiscal policy. If *IS* is downward sloping but not vertical and *LM* is upward sloping, fiscal policy is less effective than is implied by the simple Keynesian model.

12.   The most volatile component of United States GNP appears to be investment spending, although the federal government has contributed to rather large fluctuations because of wartime spending and postwar adjustments. However, some moderation in fluctuations of economic activity can be observed since World War II.

13.   Another complication of fiscal policy that plagues both the simple model and the complete model is the matter of timing. For example, anti-recessionary policy that is implemented too late or takes effect later than anticipated can contribute to future inflationary pressures and have a destabilizing effect. Similarly, anti-inflationary measures that mistakenly take effect during a recession make the recessions worse than if the government had done nothing.

14.   Political considerations become important in fiscal policy because changes in government spending and taxes must be acted upon by the Congress and the executive branch of government.

15.   The public debt is debt which the government owes to the people and is incurred by the sale of government bonds to the people. However, because the people "own" the government, it is debt which the people owe to themselves. Thus paying off the debt does not involve a loss of wealth or purchasing power to the nation as a whole.

16. The economic cost of a war is borne by the people living during the war period because they must give up consumer goods and services in order for the nation to produce more military goods. This will be true regardless of whether the government borrows from the people by selling them bonds, prints money, or taxes them for the full cost of the war.

17. Young men drafted into military service in a sense pay a "tax" to support a war because their pay has been substantially less than they could have earned in civilian life, even taking into account the food, clothing, and lodging provided.

18. The adjustment from a wartime to a peacetime economy can be expected to bring increased unemployment. However, as long as there are people who would like to consume more goods or services than they now do, there is no reason why everyone who wants to work at the prevailing wage rate should not be working. Thus the existence of a large military establishment should not be needed to provide full employment.

Questions for thought and discussion

1. Illustrate, using the simple Keynesian model, how an unemployment situation could arise. What would be the appropriate fiscal policy to combat this unemployment? Illustrate the consequences of this action on your diagram.

2. Do the same as in Question 1 for an inflationary situation.

3. Suppose in some distant future year you find yourself a member of the President's Council of Economic Advisors. Suppose also that the country is experiencing increased unemployment. The President has heard of the simple Keynesian model and wants to use it to predict necessary government policy. What cautions might you pass on to the President in using this model?

4. "In reducing unemployment, a $100 million government spending increase is equivalent to a $100 million tax decrease." Do you agree? Explain.

5. Compare the effect of the government spending multiplier as depicted by the simple model with this multiplier in the

more complete model. Will the multiplier be larger or smaller in the complete model? Specify your assumptions.

6. If full-employment NNP is $100 million greater than the current equilibrium NNP, how much should the government increase its spending to promote full employment in the context of the simple model? Assume the MPC is 0.80. Would this increase in government spending be large enough in the context of the complete model? Explain.

7. Referring back to Question 6, how much should taxes be decreased to reach full employment? Would your answer be the same for the complete model? Explain.

8. Suppose the government wants to increase spending by $10 billion because of necessary government programs. In order not to cause any inflationary pressure on the economy, how much should the government increase taxes? (Assume the simple lump-sum tax.)

9. Suppose in some distant future year you are elected a member of Congress. During an inflation, what considerations would you take into account in deciding if you are in favor of an increase in taxes or a decrease in government spending? Similarly, what factors would you consider in deciding whether you favored a spending increase or a tax cut during a period of increased unemployment?

10. How might fiscal policy have a destabilizing effect on the economy?

11. "Paying off the public debt would drive the country over the edge of bankruptcy." Do you agree? Explain.

12. "By borrowing from the people to finance a war, the government is able to pass a major portion of the cost of the war on to future generations." Do you agree? Explain.

13. Strictly from an economic standpoint, do you think that government bonds are a good investment for a person during wartime? Explain.

14. "Young men drafted into the military pay a disproportionately high economic cost of fighting a war." Do you agree? Explain.

9

Monetary policy

We now come to the second major tool of the government to promote full employment without inflation—monetary policy. We can define monetary policy as the deliberate action of the government or monetary authority to manage the supply of money and the interest rate with the goal of achieving and maintaining full employment without inflation. In the United States the monetary authority is the Board of Governors of the Federal Reserve System. An important group of people within the Federal Reserve System is the Open Market Committee. This committee, which is dominated by the Board of Governors, is responsible for deciding upon the time and magnitude of Federal Reserve purchases and sales of government securities in the securities market. As we will see shortly, this is the major tool that the Fed uses to influence the quantity of money in the economy.

Money versus the interest rate

As you might have gathered from the preceding chapters, the effect of money and the interest rate on the economy has been subject to a great deal of controversy among economists and government policymakers, extending from the Great Depression up to the present. One major point of contention has been the appropriate indicator for monetary policy. In deciding on the correct monetary policy to follow, should the major indicator be the interest rate or should it be the quantity of money? During much of the history of monetary policy in the United States, it appears that the interest rate has served as the prime guideline for action, although in recent years there seems to have been a shift in emphasis towards the money supply as the appropriate indicator for policy.

It is not difficult to understand why the interest rate has served a dominant role when we remember that the Federal Reserve Board of Governors has been comprised mainly of commercial bankers. In the world of commercial banking, the interest rate is of vital importance. Bankers, of course, are aware that a relatively high interest rate tends to reduce the amount of borrowing, while a low interest rate stimulates borrowing and spending. With this experience, it is understandable that the monetary authority should place considerable emphasis on the interest rate as a means of influencing economic activity. But undue emphasis on the interest rate creates some problems.

First, it might appear that the maintenance of a stable interest rate would promote a stable economy. The problem with this idea is that there are many factors contributing to changes in economic activity other than the interest rate. Suppose, for example, that businessmen become pessimistic about the future, expecting a slowdown in economic activity and a subsequent accumulation of unsold goods. Naturally they will tend to reduce their rate of investment at the prevailing rate of interest. In this case the decreased demand for loans will by itself tend to reduce the rate of interest somewhat. If the monetary authority wishes to restore the former rate of investment and economic activity, it should decrease the interest rate even more to offset the pessimistic attitude of businessmen. If the monetary authority attempted to keep the interest rate up at its initial level, it would just contribute to the recession, because this would reduce investment even more.

Taking another example, this one from more recent U.S. experience, suppose the government decides to increase its spending by a large amount to wage a war. If the country is at or near full employment already, the increased demand for goods and services pressing on the available supply can be expected to drive prices up unless private spending is reduced. In this case the monetary authority should drive the interest rate up even further in order to reduce private investment and to a certain extent reduce private consumption. Trying to maintain a stable interest rate in these situations would just add to the inflationary pressure in the economy.

The Fed's preoccupation with the money rate of interest has caused a great deal of confusion about the appropriate monetary policy and at times may have led to a perverse policy. During the Great Depression, for example, the monetary authority was able to point to the decline in the money rate of interest as evidence that the appropriate policy was being followed. In retrospect, it appears now that the Fed in fact followed an extremely prorecessionary policy in allowing the money supply to decline by a third from 1929 to 1933. The observed decline in the money rate of interest during this time appears to have been just a straw in the wind as far as having much effect on the economy. Indeed, some economists argue that if the Fed had even maintained the money supply at the 1929 level, the Great Depression probably would have turned out to be a mild recession, thereby making a drastic reduction in the interest rate unnecessary. Although, in the event of a continued rise in unemployment, the interest rate then should have been pushed down to lower and lower levels until spending began to pick up. Thus the maintenance of a stable interest rate in the face of recession or inflation will involve a perverse monetary policy, while allowing the interest rate to seek its own level generally implies a very weak monetary policy or no policy at all.

Confusing the interest rate, which might be considered the price of money, with ordinary prices of goods and services also leads one to erroneous policy recommendations. For example, during the inflationary spiral of the late 1960s, it was not uncommon to hear proposals coming from Congress calling for a reduction in the interest rate so that the price of money would not add to the inflation of the economy. The problem, however, is that such action would have added to the inflationary pressure in the economy rather than reducing it. Inflation tends to result in a high money rate of interest, but it does not follow that by reducing the rate of interest inflation will be curbed. Indeed, as we will see later in the chapter, just the opposite is likely to happen.

Primary tools of monetary policy

As mentioned, the Federal Reserve System is the monetary authority in the United States. Since monetary policy is largely a matter of regulating the money supply, let us explore next the tools available to the Fed to carry out this task. Essentially the Fed has three primary tools: (1) open-market operations, (2) changes in the required reserve ratio of commercial banks, and (3) changes in the discount rate that commercial banks pay to borrow from the Federal Reserve.

We already have discussed the effect of open-market operations in Chapter 6, but perhaps just a bit of review will prove helpful. Recall that the Fed is continually buying and selling government securities in the bond market. For example, an open-market purchase of a bond from a bank, institution, or individual leads to an increase in the money supply. In this case the Fed receives the bond, which is not money, and in exchange the seller receives a check (or cash) which is money. Thus the quantity of money in the economy increases as the result of the open-market purchase. In the case of purchasing a bond from a bank, the initial change occurs as an increase in bank reserves, but ultimately new money is created when the banking system makes loans against these reserves. Keep in mind too that the money supply is likely to change by some multiple of the initial bond purchase because of the multiple expansion effect. And, you recall, a similar line of reasoning applies to the open-market sale of a bond by the Fed. Here the Fed receives money, the seller receives the bond, and as a result the money supply is likely to decline by a multiple of the bond purchase. Open-market purchases and sales of bonds are the major tools that the Federal Reserve uses to change the quantity of money in the economy.

We might reasonably ask at this point, How can the Fed be sure that it will always be able to buy or sell the desired amount of bonds? After all, people are not forced to do business with the Fed. The answer is that when buying bonds, the Fed must offer a price that is competitive in the market or prospective sellers will sell to other buyers. If the bond purchase is extremely large, the Fed may have to increase its bid price in order to induce more sellers to part with their bonds. Similarly when the Fed sells bonds, it may have to reduce their price to a point that makes the offering attractive to prospective buyers.

We should point out too that the price of a bond and the interest rate are inversely related. For example, suppose the government sells a $1,000 bond and as specified on the bond agrees to pay 6 percent annual interest to the holder, or $60 per year. Even if the market price of the bond should decline to $500, the $60 annual interest still continues to be paid by the government. Only now the holder of the bond receives a 12 percent return on his money—$60 per year from $500 invested. Thus a decrease in the market price of bonds implies that their interest return rises. If bonds become cheap enough, the interest return eventually becomes attractive enough for buyers to take the bonds off the hands of the Fed. (Of course, the Fed may suffer a capital loss in the process, but it is not in business to make profits anyway. The Federal Reserve System exists to regulate the money supply and in so doing stabilize the economy at a level that represents full employment without inflation.) On the other hand, an increase in the price of bonds implies that their interest return decreases.

The second major tool that can be used by the Fed to regulate the supply of money is the legal reserve ratio. Recall from the discussion of banking in Chapter 6 that commercial banks are required to hold a certain fraction of their deposits on reserve, either as cash in their own vaults or as money in a reserve account in their Federal Reserve bank (if the bank is a member of the Federal Reserve System). By changing the legal reserve ratio, the Fed can change the amount of bank loans and thus change the amount of money in the economy. Remember that banks create money by making loans.

In our examples in Chapter 6, we assumed for convenience of computation a required reserve ratio of 0.20, meaning that commercial banks are required to keep 20 cents on reserve against each dollar of demand deposits. Thus $1,000 of total reserves in the banking system can support $5,000 in demand deposits ($1/R \times$ $1,000$), assuming the multiple expansion process has run its course and banks are fully loaned up. Now if the Fed should reduce the required reserve ratio to, say, 0.10, this same $1,000 in total reserves could support $10,000 in total deposits. Banks could in this case increase loans and thus increase demand deposits. On the other hand, an increase in the reserve ratio would require banks to contract their deposits for a given amount of reserves.

Notice, if you will, the basic difference between open-market operations and a change in the reserve ratio. The former is a device to change the total reserves in the banking system while the latter is a means of changing the amount of deposits that can be supported from a given amount of total reserves. However, the Federal Reserve seldom uses its power to change the legal reserve ratio, mainly because it is almost too powerful a tool. Even a very small change in the reserve ratio has rather drastic effects on the banking community and causes large and abrupt changes in the money supply.

The third major tool or device that the Fed can use to change the money supply is a change in the discount rate. The discount rate is the rate of interest that the Fed charges member banks when these banks obtain loans from the Fed to bolster their reserves. Occasionally a commercial bank will find itself dangerously close to the upper limit of its loans (given its reserves) or actually over the limit, especially during peak lending periods. In this situation the commercial bank can temporarily increase its reserves by borrowing reserves from the Fed.

The Fed generally changes the discount rate in conjunction with a large open-market transaction. Suppose there is inflationary pressure in the economy which prompts the Fed to make a large open-market sale in order to reduce reserves and the money supply. The resulting tight money situation and high interest rates provide banks with an incentive to borrow from the Fed in order to maintain reserves so that loans need not be reduced greatly. This is just good business. But to make it less profitable for banks to borrow for reserves, the Fed will raise the discount rate along with the open-market sale. Similarly, when the Fed wants to stimulate bank lending it can reduce the discount rate to make it more profitable for banks to borrow to obtain reserves.

Secondary tools of monetary policy

The three items discussed in the previous section are the three main tools the Federal Reserve can use to regulate the supply of money in the economy and thus to influence economic activity. The Fed also has a number of othcr means to influence economic activity that we might mention briefly. First there is the idea of moral suasion, sometimes called "jawbone control." These terms describe attempts by the Fed to influence commercial bank lending by persuasive means. For example, during inflationary times the Fed might frown on excessive borrowing by a bank that tries to expand its reserves. Similarly, during recessionary times the Fed might extol the virtues of a vigorous lending policy.on the part of banks. Perhaps the main drawback of moral suasion is that it doesn't work very well. When it comes to making a choice between bowing to the wishes of the Fed and maximizing profits, most self-respecting bankers choose the latter.

The Fed also can influence economic activity by what is known as selective credit controls. For example, the Fed regulates the length of the repayment period on installment loans. If people are required to repay a new car loan in, say 24 months as opposed to 36 months, fewer people tend to buy new cars. Another device is the regulation of margin requirements on stocks. If, for example, the margin requirement is 60 percent, a person need only pay 60 percent of the price of the stock from his own money and is allowed to borrow the remaining 40 percent.

Monetary policy in the context of the simple model

The fact that the simple model contains no information on the monetary sector of the economy limits its usefulness as a device to analyze the effects of monetary policy. However, it is possible to present an intuitive idea of how monetary policy affects the economy in the context of this model.

It is easiest to trace the effects of a change in the money supply in the simple model if we view the process as sort of a chain of causation. To begin, suppose the Fed makes a large open-market purchase. From our past discussion we know that this action increases money and bank reserves. With increased reserves banks can undertake to expand their loans. After all, banks earn a large share of their income from loans so it would be foolish to hold the extra reserves in cold storage.

However, in order for banks to induce individuals and businesses to borrow more, they will probably have to lower their interest charges. A reduction in the interest rate provides an incentive for business firms to borrow for new investment projects such as buildings, machines, equipment, etc. Lower interest rates provide an incentive for consumers to save a bit less and spend a bit more, particularly on consumer durables such as autos and appliances. In the simple model this increase in spending would be represented by an upward shift in aggregate demand.

Our knowledge of the multiplier process tells us that new spending will increase by some multiple of the initial increase in consumption and investment and give rise to an increase in equilibrium NNP. We can summarize the chain of causation as follows:

Increase in $M \rightarrow$ Decrease in $i \rightarrow$ Increase in I and $C \rightarrow$ Increase in aggregate demand $\rightarrow$ Increase in equilibrium NNP

Of course, just the opposite would be expected to occur in the case of an open-market sale of bonds. The resulting decrease in money and reserves leads to an increase in the interest rate, other things being equal. Then as investment and possibly consumption decline, aggregate demand shifts down, resulting in a decrease in equilibrium NNP.

The effect of monetary policy also can be illustrated on the familiar aggregate demand and supply diagram shown by Figure 8–1 of the previous chapter. Diagram (A) of Figure 8–1, if you check back, represents an unemployment situation. Here the appropriate monetary policy would be to increase the money supply so that the interest rate declines and shifts aggregate demand upward. In the case of the inflationary situation illustrated by Figure 8–1 (B), the appropriate monetary policy would be to reduce the supply of money, thereby increasing the interest rate, shifting aggregate demand downward, and reducing equilibrium NNP.

We cannot be as precise in predicting the ultimate effects of monetary policy, however, as we were able to be with fiscal policy. Recall that by using the multiplier, we were able to predict to the exact dollar how much of a tax or government spending change was needed to match equilibrium NNP with the full-employment level. In order to make such precise predictions for monetary policy, we would need two additional pieces of information. First we would have to know how much an open-market purchase or sale of bonds would change the interest rate. Second, information would be needed on how much investment or consumption changes in response to a given change in the interest rate.

Economists have been able to gather a little information on the response of investment to changes in the interest rate, although the general area of the relationship between interest rate changes and spending changes is still open to considerable controversy. Even less is known about the impact of an open-market purchase on the interest rate and the process that occurs in the economy when the interest rate changes.

Monetary policy in the context of the complete model

Because the more complete model explicitly includes in the *LM* curve the demand for and supply of money, it is somewhat better suited to an analysis of monetary policy than the simple model. Recall from Chapter 7 that an increase in the supply of money, as would occur during an open-market purchase of securities, results in a shift to the right by the *LM* curve. As illustrated in Figure 9–1 (A), such action would be appropriate during a period of increased unemployment. In this situation the objective is to shift the *LM* curve to the right until equilibrium NNP corresponds to the level of NNP that generates full employment, *FE* in Figure 9–1 (A).

As in the simple model, the increase in the money supply lowers the equilibrium rate of interest in the economy. With more money available in the loan market, competition for money is less intense, and borrowers can shop around for more favorable rates. As the interest rate declines, investment (and perhaps consumption) increases, thereby increasing total spending and output in the economy. In other words, the overall equilibrium level of NNP increases. It is evident, then, that should the economy find itself in an unemployment situation, the appropriate monetary policy would be an increase in the money supply.

Of course, if the economy finds itself in the midst of an inflationary situation, the model suggests that the appropriate mone-

FIGURE 9–1
Monetary policy in the context of the complete model—
corrective for unemployment and inflation

(A) Correcting for unemployment

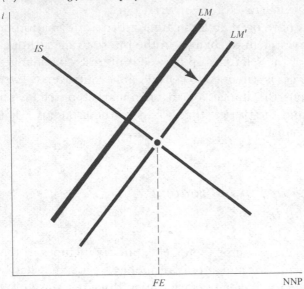

(B) Correcting for inflation

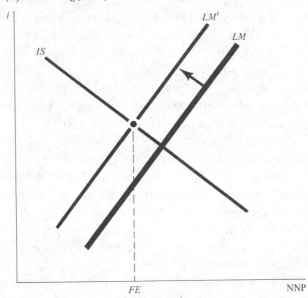

tary policy would be to decrease the money supply so as to shift the *LM* curve to the left as depicted in Figure 9–1 (B). However, as we found out in 1969 and 1970, an absolute decline in the money supply, or even a zero growth in money over a period of a year, is very strong medicine for the economy that is likely to result in undesirable side effects, namely increased unemployment. Although the *IS–LM* model provides us with the before and after equilibrium points for a policy change, it does not tell us what happens to the economy on the way from one equilibrium position to another, which can be quite important. Economists refer to this as a "comparative statics" model as opposed to a "dynamic" model that traces out the path of adjustment.

Unfortunately our understanding of the process of adjustment to changes in the money supply is quite meager. It does appear, however, that if people have come to expect continuing inflation, a reduction in the money supply has a more immediate impact on output and employment than on prices. It is true that the rate of increase in the price level would probably turn down after a short time and the price level eventually stabilize or even fall, but not without a substantial cost in terms of increased unemployment.

A more reasonable policy recommendation for the inflationary situation depicted in Figure 9–1 (B) would be to slow down the rate of increase of the money supply if it is greater than the growth in real output of the economy, rather than recommending an absolute decrease as suggested by the model. For example, if real output is growing at 5 percent per year and the money supply at a 10 percent rate, the growth of the money supply should be cut to about 5 or 6 percent. Granted, inflation probably would not slow down as much and as quickly as under an absolute decrease in the money supply, but the undesirable side effects (increased unemployment) would be less severe. If the annual growth in the money supply is stabilized at the 5 to 6 percent level and the economy continues to grow at about this rate, prices should eventually stabilize, although at a higher level than before the inflation started. Certainly no one advocates that the price level be rolled back to the level of some previous year; an antiinflation policy should be considered quite successful if it keeps the price level from rising much more than 1 or 2 percent per year into the future.

With growth in aggregate demand over time, we can think of the

IS curve as shifting to the right. With growth in the money supply, the *LM* curve also is shifting to the right. Thus we can think of equilibrium NNP as continuing to increase over time. The policy suggested in the preceding paragraph would have the *LM* curve shifting to the right at about the same rate as the *IS* curve. The task of the monetary authority, then, is to get equilibrium NNP in step with full-employment NNP without inflation, and keep it in step.

Effectiveness of monetary policy

In the preceding chapter we mentioned that the effectiveness of fiscal policy depended to a large extent on the shape of the *IS* and *LM* curves. The same is true for monetary policy. Monetary policy will be most effective if the *LM* curve is relatively steep, as in Figure 9–2 (A). Here a change in the money supply changes equilibrium NNP by almost the same amount, regardless of the shape of the *IS* curve, as long as it is downward sloping.

On the other hand, if the *LM* curve is relatively flat, a shift right or left in the curve has a relatively small effect on the level of equilibrium NNP. Hence, monetary policy is relatively weak or ineffective, as shown in Figure 9–2 (B). The diagrams are drawn so that the horizontal shift in the *LM* curves is the same in both diagrams. But note how much more equilibrium NNP increases in response to an increase in the money supply when the *LM* curve is relatively steep.

As mentioned in Chapter 7, the slope of the *LM* curve depends to a large extent on the slope of the demand curve for money. If the demand curve for money is relatively steep, the *LM* curve also will be steep and monetary policy will be quite effective, as shown in diagram (A) of Figure 9–2. On the other hand a relatively flat demand curve for money implies a relatively flat *LM* curve and a somewhat ineffective monetary policy, as shown in diagram (B).[1]

---

[1] For estimates of the slope of the actual demand curve for money in the United States, see Ronald L. Teigen, "Demand and Supply Functions for Money in the United States: Some Structural Estimates," *Econometrica*, 1964, pp. 476–509; and William E. Gibson, "Demand and Supply Functions for Money in The United States," *Econometrica*, March 1972, pp. 361–70.

FIGURE 9–2
The slope of the *LM* curve and the effectiveness of monetary policy

(A) Monetary policy effective

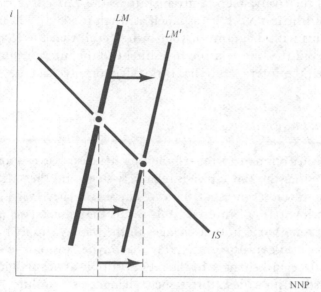

(B) Monetary policy ineffective

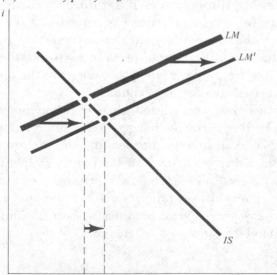

We should also be aware that the slope of the *IS* curve has an important bearing on the effectiveness of monetary policy. If the *IS* curve is relatively steep, a given shift in the *LM* curve cannot change equilibrium NNP by as much as when it is flat. You might illustrate this with diagrams of your own. Recall that the *IS* curve will be steep if the line relating investment to the interest rate also is steep; i.e., the interest rate has little effect on investment.

Monetarists versus Keynesians

It has been common to regard the "monetarists" as economists who believe that the *LM* curve is relatively steep and the "Keynesians" as those who argue that the *LM* curve is relatively flat, particularly at low rates of interest. As a result the monetarists argue that "money matters," in that changes in the money supply have a strong impact on equilibrium NNP. The Keynesians on the other hand tend to regard changes in the money supply as of smaller consequence, sometimes describing such changes as "pushing on a string," meaning that they have little bearing on total spending, at least in periods of increased unemployment.

Recently Professor Milton Friedman, regarded by many as the leading spokesman for the monetarists, has argued that the major difference between the monetarists and the Keynesians is not and never has been due to a difference of opinion regarding the slope of the *LM* curve, but lies rather in the way changes in the quantity of money are perceived to affect the economy.[2]

In the *IS–LM* model we constructed, changes in the money supply affect total spending through changes in the interest rate and the subsequent changes in investment spending and the multiplier process. In Friedman's view, changes in the money supply have a far wider and more direct influence on total spending. For example, an increase in the money supply prompts holders of money to look for ways to dispose of their excess holdings of cash (assuming no shift in the demand for money). In the process they may buy

---

[2] See Milton Friedman, "Comments on the Critics," *Journal of Political Economy*, September-October 1972, pp. 906–50.

interest-bearing securities, bidding up the price of these securities and lowering the interest rate on them.

But, according to Friedman, holders of these excess cash balances are not limited to buying securities, as is implied by our *IS–LM* model. They can as well buy automobiles, appliances, clothing, etc., in an attempt to rearrange their portfolios away from cash towards "earning" assets. If indeed this is the case, then an increase in the money supply prompts an increase in spending on the first round that is not limited to an increase in investment.

In the case of a decrease in the money supply, holders of cash will seek to replenish their cash balances by attempting to sell assets (including but not limited to securities) or by reducing their rate of purchase of real assets. At any rate, according to this view, the impact of money supply changes on total spending is greater than is implied by the *IS–LM* model. Thus the distinction between a monetarist and a Keynesian is somewhat more subtle than simply a difference of opinion over the slope of the *LM* curve.

Timing of monetary policy

In our discussion of fiscal policy we mentioned that the time the policy was put into effect was of major importance in obtaining the desired results. This is equally valid for monetary policy.

Our models tell us that in the event of rising unemployment, the appropriate monetary policy is to increase the money supply. If the money supply is already being increased from year to year, the appropriate policy would be to step up the rate of increase so as to push the *LM* curve to the right just a bit faster. Conversely, if inflation is the problem, we learned that the rate of growth of the money supply should be decreased. Keep in mind, though, that if inflation has built up a momentum, a reduction in the growth of the money supply is likely to result in increased unemployment and continued inflation, at least for a time.

Neglecting for the moment the other problems of monetary policy, the first order of business is to identify when the monetary authority should "step on the gas" and increase the money supply to combat rising unemployment or "apply the brakes" to ease inflationary pressure. As we pointed out in the previous chapter, it is not at all evident when these policies should be pursued because the economy is continually experiencing small ups and downs in economic activity. The critical problem, then, is to distinguish a small and temporary slowdown in economic activity from a full-fledged recession, or a small upturn from an inflationary spiral.

Because of the political implications of rising unemployment or inflation, there is a great deal of controversy regarding the state of the economy. At the first glimpse of rising unemployment, the political party that is not in power generally calls for a change of policies and leadership, claiming that the country is headed for a deep recession. On the other hand, the party in power is likely to argue that the economy is experiencing a temporary downturn and soon will recover to its former state of high employment. It is evident, then, that the monetary authority cannot expect to always please both political parties at once, nor should it try. From this standpoint, it is perhaps fortunate that the Federal Reserve Board of Governors is somewhat of an autonomous body, to some extent shielded from conflicting pressures of the political parties.

But the Fed is still faced with the problem of when to take action. It must be aware, too, that action at the wrong time can be worse than no action at all. For example, if the Fed steps up the rate of increase of the money supply in the mistaken belief that the economy is headed for a downturn, the result will be a needless inflation in the months and possibly years to come. Or if it sharply curtails the rate of increase of the money supply, thinking that inflation is upon us when it is not, the result may well be a needless increase in unemployment in the future. As illustrated in Figure 9–3, the correct time to undertake an expansion of the money supply or increase its rate of growth, i.e., engage in an "easy money" policy, is at time T_0. Or if the economy is headed for an inflationary spiral, such as at T_1, the models imply that the Fed should cut back on the rate of growth of the money supply, i.e., engage in a "tight money" policy. The object of these policies, of course, is to smooth out the fluctuations in the economy, as illustrated by the dashed line beginning at T_0 in Figure 9–3.

FIGURE 9–3
The timing of monetary policy

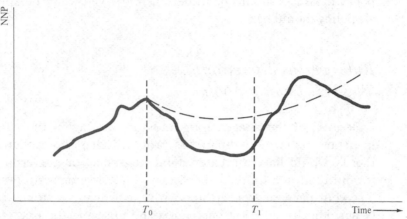

Lags in monetary policy

Assuming that the Federal Reserve is able to accurately identify the correct time to ease up or tighten up on the money supply, as the case may be, an even more difficult problem is to predict the lag between the policy action and the time when this action has its major effect on the economy. In our discussion of the Keynesian models, we have implicitly assumed that changes in the money supply have their full effect in the immediate time period. In reality, this is not likely to be the case. When we consider that both the multiple expansion process of the money supply and the spending multiplier of the goods and services sector are involved with a change in the money supply, it is not too difficult to understand why time is required for the policy action to have its full effect. Professor Friedman argues, in fact, that the lag in the effect of monetary policy is both long and variable.[3] For example, the major expansionary effect of a money supply increase may take three to four months at one time and six to eight months at another. If there is little chance of predicting the length of the lag involved in a

---

[3] Milton Friedman, "The Lag in Effect of Monetary Policy," *Journal of Political Economy*, Vol. 68 (December 1960), pp. 617–21.

policy action, there is little chance of accurately specifying when policy measures should be undertaken, or even what the appropriate policy should be.

Rules versus discretion: The Friedman proposal

Because of the alleged long and variable lag in the effects of monetary policy, Friedman has proposed that the monetary authority would have a greater stabilizing effect on the economy if it would follow a simple rule of increasing the money supply about 5 percent per year to keep step with the growing economy instead of periodically stepping on the gas and applying the brakes in response to downturns and upturns in economic activity.[4]

Notice, however, that Friedman is not saying that monetary policy is of little importance. Indeed he is saying that money is so important that large fluctuations in the money supply can cause large and damaging fluctuations in economic activity.

We can obtain a good idea of the uneven growth in the money supply that Friedman is concerned about from Figure 9–4. This graph in part shows the annual percentage change in the money supply for each year from 1930 to 1972. The positive numbers denote growth and the negative numbers denote decline in the total money supply (currency outside banks and demand deposits). Similar fluctuations can be observed using the broader definition of money.

Fluctuations in the growth of the money supply

A quick glance at Figure 9–4 reveals that there has been considerable variation in the year-to-year change in the U.S. money supply over the past four decades. As you can see the major fluctuations came during the early 1930s, the era of the Great Depression,

---

4 Milton Friedman, *A Program for Monetary Stability* (New York: Fordham University Press, 1959).

FIGURE 9–4
Annual percentage change in the U.S. money supply* and money GNP, 1930–72

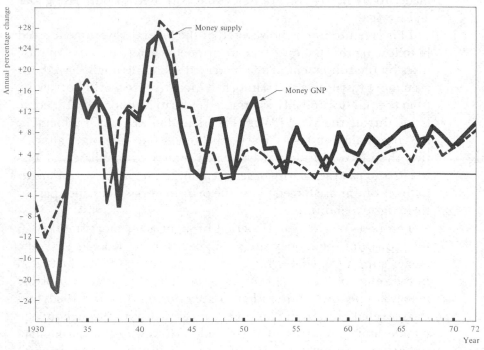

* Currency plus demand deposits.

and during the World War II years. The large number of commercial bank failures during the early 1930s is generally given as the major reason for the drastic decline in the money supply at that time. In fact, many economists argue that had the Federal Reserve stepped in quickly and made emergency loans of reserves to the banks, there would not have been this large disturbance in the monetary sector. After a period of substantial increase in the money supply during the mid-1930s, it took another rather severe drop during 1937.

The most dramatic increase in the money supply came during World War II years. The sharp increase in government spending caused by the war was not matched by equal increases in taxes. As a result, the federal government's budget ran sizable deficits during this period. Part of the deficits were made up by borrowing from the public., i.e., selling government bonds, or war bonds as they were called then. The remainder of the annual deficits was made up by newly issued money that was used to purchase goods and services.

This is not to imply, however, that the federal government erred in following this policy. As we mentioned earlier, attempts to raise taxes by the full extent of the increased spending might have been even more disruptive and dampened incentives to work. Borrowing from the public probably was pushed close to its upper limit. People living during the World War II years undoubtedly still remember the large-scale campaigns to sell war bonds. The only other alternative, then, was to issue newly created money to purchase war materials and pay the salaries of servicemen. In fact, most governments in times of war are forced to use the printing press to finance part of their war expenditures.

The post–World War II period brought a bit more stability in the growth of the money supply. Except for the Korean War, the money supply growth during the major part of the 1950s fluctuated in the range of 2 to 4 percent per year. The rate of growth of the money supply picked up rather sharply during the early 1960s and then leveled out around an 8 percent growth rate throughout the middle and latter part of the decade. However, 1969 brought a rather sharp contrast, exhibiting a decline in the rate of growth of the money supply. Essentially this reflects the tight money policy of the Nixon administration in attempting to curb the inflation that gained momentum during the latter part of the 1960s. During the early 1970s the rate of growth of the money supply again climbed up over the 8 percent mark.

The proponents of the Friedman proposal which calls for a stable year-to-year growth in the money supply equal to the annual growth in output of goods and services maintain that had such a policy been followed in the past, the economy would have enjoyed much more stability. Of course the Federal Reserve points out that it is not always that easy to maintain a stable, year-to-year growth, particularly if other objectives such as financing a war override the goal of economic stability. Also many, if not most, economists are not yet convinced that strict adherence to an inflexible rule is better than a flexible policy designed to "lean against the wind" and counteract fluctuations in economic activity.

Price and wage controls

During periods of excessive inflationary pressure, many governments have resorted to price and wage controls in an effort to stem the upward spiral of prices. In the United States, price and wage controls have been instituted generally in times of armed conflict in an effort to hold down the increase in prices. The stringent controls instituted during World War II, and the somewhat more flexible controls put into effect in August 1971, are two examples. Price and wage controls have precipitated a substantial amount of controversy among economists, political leaders, and the general public. Thus it will be useful for us to review some of the arguments in favor of controls, together with some of the problems that controls bring about.

Those who favor price and wage controls tend to place relatively little faith in the ability of traditional fiscal and monetary policies (such as reduced government spending, higher taxes, or tight money) to do the job. Some who favor controls may grant that traditional policy might eventually stem inflation but argue that the time required is too long or the unemployment effects too severe to be acceptable to the general public.

It is argued also that controls can help to break the inflation psychology that people may have acquired during a prolonged period of inflation. If antiinflationary policies such as a tax increase or a reduced rate of money creation accompany the controls, the momentum of inflation is likely to be more quickly checked. In this case unions are not likely to be as demanding in asking for future wage increases and people in general need not be as concerned about getting rid of their cash by purchasing real assets that rise in value with the price level. Thus pressure for price increases is eased somewhat in both the labor and product markets. With an ease in wage demands, employers are likely to be more willing to retain or hire employees, thus easing the unemployment problem brought on by restrictive fiscal or monetary policies.

Economists who oppose price and wage restraints will often point out that the imposition of controls does not remove the basic causes of inflation. They argue that inflation is caused basically by

either an excessive increase in spending, as represented by a substantial shift to the right in the *IS* curve, or too rapid growth of the
money supply, denoted by an excessive shift to the right of the *LM*
curve. The impostion of price and wage restraints may suppress
the symptoms of inflation but does not remove its underlying
cause.

It is argued also that unless price and wage controls are applied
universally, those prices or wages not affected will grow even more
rapidly. In other words, it would be something like squeezing a
balloon—if you push in at one place it will bulge out at another.
But if all prices and wages are frozen, then it is argued that the
economy is placed in a sort of straitjacket. That is, there is no way
for consumers to provide signals to producers through the price
system.

As pointed out in Chapter 1, resources are allocated in a market
economy mainly on the basis of market prices. If the price of one
product rises relative to others, it is a signal to producers that consumers desire more of this product relative to others. Producers, in
attempting to increase profits by producing more of the higher
priced product, at the same time satisfy the desires of consumers.
Similarly if the price of a resource increases, producers have an incentive to economize on its use by substituting lower priced resources in its place. Thus the imposition of price and wage controls
takes away the allocating function of product and resource prices.

Perhaps the most serious problem encountered with price and
wage controls is that they result in shortages in the product and
resource markets which in turn lead to rationing and blackmarket
activities. This phenomenon is discussed more thoroughly in Chapter 6 of the micro text, but it will be useful to introduce (or review) the problem at this time. The problem is more clearly seen
by means of the simple demand and supply diagram developed in
Chapter 1 and reproduced in Figure 9–5.

Recall that the demand curve shows the quantities of a good or
service that people will buy at various possible prices. It is drawn
in a downward sloping manner to reflect the idea that people tend
to buy less of a product when its price is high and vice versa. The
supply curve, on the other hand, tells us the quantities that producers (or sellers) will place on the market at various possible prices.

FIGURE 9–5
Illustrating the effect of price controls

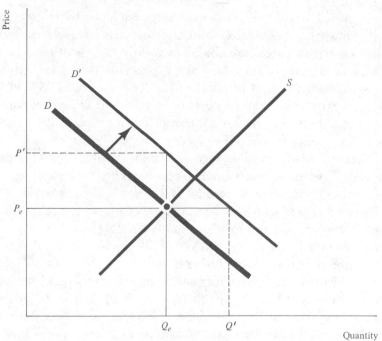

It is drawn upward sloping to represent the idea that sellers will
increase the quantity they will place on the market as price increases, and vice versa. Finally the equilibrium price is determined
by the intersection of the demand and supply curves.

Suppose we begin where the market is in equilibrium and freeze
the price at P_e. No problem is encountered as long as the demand
and supply curves remain at their original position. However, as is
characteristic of inflation, demand rises relative to supply. To
simplify the diagram, we let the supply curve remain in its original
position and represent the demand in some future period as D'.
Notice that at the controlled price P_e, suppliers continue to offer
Q_e on the market. But at the new higher level of demand, buyers
are willing to pay a higher price, denoted by P', for this quantity.
Of course, it is against the law to pay or to charge a price higher
than P_e. So suppliers continue to place only Q_e on the market,

which is less than the quantity, Q', which buyers would like to buy at this price.

As a result of this situation two things are likely to happen. First, if the difference between Q_c and Q' is substantial, the government will have to institute some kind of rationing scheme, such as issuing ration stamps to buyers that allow them to purchase a limited amount of the item. Most people who experienced the World War II years still recall rationing very well. Basically, price controls take away the rationing function of price and replace it by the use of ration stamps or coupons.

A second likely consequence of price controls is the emergence of a black market. Some buyers who have a strong desire to buy more than their ration allotment and have the money to do so will try to find sellers who will accept money "under the table" in exchange for more of the scarce good than their ration stamps allow. Usually there are sellers who will oblige such buyers. The black-market price in this case will be at P'.

As demand continues to increase relative to supply and the black-market price diverges further and further from the controlled price, blackmarket transactions are likely to become more prevalent. As a result the legal or controlled price becomes less meaningful. If the inflation continues, the system of price controls either breaks down or the legal prices are adjusted upwards closer to the true equilibrium prices. Thus price and wage controls have not enjoyed much success as a means of controlling inflation.[5]

We also should mention that price indexes such as the CPI reflect the legal prices during the period of controls. As a result the price index tends to mask or cover up the inflationary pressure in the economy. So instead of rising gradually, it remains relatively stable for a time and then spurts upward when the controls are removed or revised upward.

---

[5] For an account of the results of wage and price controls in Western European countries since the end of World War II, see Lloyd Ulman and Robert J. Flanagan, *Wage Restraint: A Study of Income Policies in Western Europe* (Berkeley: University of California Press, 1971). According to the authors, the various wage and price policies in various countries have exhibited a common characteristic: "periods of effectiveness were typically short-lived; they were frequently followed by wage and price explosions which sometimes blew up the policies themselves" (p. 223).

Main points of Chapter 9

1. In conducting monetary policy it can be argued that a more appropriate guide for action is the quantity of money rather than the interest rate. Maintenance of a stable interest rate can result in an unstable economy.

2. During a recession, the decreased demand for loans results in a decrease in the money rate of interest. In this situation the monetary authority should take action to push down even harder on the interest rate to induce increased spending by investors and consumers. A policy that attempted to hold the interest rate up at its initial level would just contribute to the recession.

3. During an inflation, the increased demand for loans tends to push the interest rate higher. To hold the interest rate down in this case just adds to the inflationary pressure. The correct policy here would be to push the interest rate even higher to reduce the incentive of the private sector to spend.

4. The three main tools that the Federal Reserve has at its disposal to change the money supply include (1) open-market operations (buying and selling government bonds), (2) changes in the required reserve ratio of commercial banks, and (3) changes in the discount rate that commercial banks pay the Fed for borrowed reserves.

5. The Fed can increase the money supply by (1) purchasing government bonds from banks, institutions, or the general public; (2) reducing the required reserve ratio; or (3) reducing the discount rate. The open-market purchase of bonds is the main method of increasing the money supply. A decrease in the money supply is accomplished by selling bonds, increasing the reserve ratio, or increasing the discount rate. The open-market sale is the primary method of decreasing the money supply.

6. The Federal Reserve can always buy the desired amount of bonds by increasing their price. An increase in the price of

bonds is equivalent to a decrease in their interest return. The Fed also can sell the desired amount of bonds by decreasing their price, which is equivalent to raising their interest return.

7. Secondary tools of monetary policy include moral suasion and various credit controls.

8. Monetary policy in the context of simple Keynesian model is accomplished by the following chain of causation: Change in $M \rightarrow$ Change in $i \rightarrow$ Change in I and $C \rightarrow$ Change in aggregate demand $\rightarrow$ Change in equilibrium NNP.

9. The ultimate effects of monetary policy appear to be more difficult to predict than the effects of fiscal policy.

10. In the context of the complete model, monetary policy shifts the *LM* curve, thereby changing the equilibrium level of NNP. An increase in the money supply shifts *LM* to the right whereas a decrease shifts it to the left.

11. In terms of the *IS–LM* model, monetary policy is most effective if the *LM* curve is relatively steep and the *IS* curve relatively flat.

12. Professor Friedman argues that the distinction between the monetarists and the Keynesians is in the way changes in the supply of money are perceived to affect the economy. According to Friedman, the monetarists view changes in the quantity of money as affecting the asset balance of people, causing them to either (*a*) try to get rid of excess cash by stepping up their purchases of goods, services, and securities (in the case of a money supply increase) or (*b*) try to increase their holdings of cash by selling or reducing their rate of purchase of these items (in the case of a money supply decrease). In the Keynesian model, a change in the money supply is perceived as affecting the interest rate in the money market, thereby affecting investment spending and other spending through the multiplier process.

13. A major problem of implementing monetary policy is its timing. There are two facets of the timing problem: (*a*) the correct time to undertake policy action and (*b*) the time when this action has its major effect on the economy. Action taken at the wrong time or having an effect at the wrong time can be more harmful than no action at all.

14. Because of these timing difficulties, Friedman has proposed

that monetary policy would be more stabilizing if the monetary authority would follow the simple rule of increasing the money supply about 5 percent per year to keep step with the growing economy.

15.   Economists who believe that "money matters," tend to argue that the fluctuations in the growth of the money supply have contributed to the economic instability that the United States has experienced during the past four decades.

16.   An argument in favor of price and wage controls is that they can dampen the inflation psychology of the general public and in so doing increase the effectiveness of antiinflation policies as well as reducing the resulting increase in unemployment. A drawback of price and wage controls is that they take away the allocating function of price, meaning that consumers have no way of indicating to producers their desire for changes in the mix of goods and services produced. Perhaps the major problem of controls is the creation of shortages, rationing, and blackmarket activities.

Questions for thought and discussion

1.   "During the Great Depression the money rate of interest declined substantially. This is an indication that the Federal Reserve followed the correct monetary policy at that time." Do you agree? Explain.

2.   "In the Keynesian models, monetary policy has its effect on the economy through changes in the interest rate. This is an indication that the Federal Reserve should try to maintain a stable interest rate if it wants to maintain a stable economy." True or false? Explain.

3.   Explain how the Federal Reserve can regulate the supply of money to the economy.

4.   "If the Fed undertakes a policy of moral suasion during an inflationary period, it is an indication that commercial banks are acting against their own self-interest." True or false? Explain.

5.   Explain how monetary policy works in the context of the sim-

ple Keynesian model without money. Use a diagram in your explanation.

6. Explain how monetary policy works in the context of the complete Keynesian model with money. Include a diagram in your explanation.

7. Does the slope of the *IS* and *LM* curves have any bearing on the effectiveness of monetary policy? Explain and illustrate.

8. *a)* If you were a Keynesian, how would you explain the effect on spending of changes in the money supply?

   b) If you were a monetarist, how would you explain the effect on spending of changes in the money supply?

9. Explain how timing is important in the implementation of monetary policy. Also discuss the problem of lags.

10. What has been the rate of growth of money supply during the past year? (See the latest *Economic Report of the President* or a Federal Reserve Bulletin.) Would you say that this rate of growth is conducive to inflation, to unemployment, or to full employment without inflation in the coming year? Explain.

11. "Friedman's proposal of following a simple rule of increasing the money supply about 5 percent per year implies that changes in the quantity of money cannot have much effect on the economy, and therefore an active or discretionary monetary policy will be of little consequence." True or false? Explain.

12. Explain why rigid price controls in a time of substantial inflation result in shortages, rationing, and blackmarket activities.

10

Poverty and the distribution of income

The economic well-being of a particular individual or group in society depends upon (1) the size of the national output or income and (2) how the output or income is distributed. Our discussion of unemployment and inflation touched on both factors. Unemployment reduces the national income or output from what it would otherwise be. It also results in the unemployed obtaining a relatively smaller share of the national output. Indeed, our concern with unemployment probably stems more from a concern over income distribution than over the size of national output.

Inflation also affects the total and the distribution of national output. Although we have not emphasized this point, a high rate of inflation creates distortions and uncertainties in the economy that are likely to reduce economic growth and thus reduce total output from its potential maximum. We will discuss the reasons for this in Chapter 12. It is evident, however, that inflation does affect the distribution of income and wealth. People whose incomes rise less rapidly than the price level or who hold assets that do not rise with the price level (money, for example) suffer a reduction, either relative or absolute, in their income or wealth.

In view of our implicit concern over income distribution in the preceding chapters, it will be instructive to cover this topic in a more explicit manner. We will be mainly interested in the people at the lower end of the income scale—the poor. First we will look briefly at some of the problems of identifying the poor and measuring the distribution of income. Then we will turn to some of the policies and programs that influence the distribution of income in the United States, particularly how these policies affect the poor.

Defining poverty

At first glance it may seem odd to be concerned with such a seemingly obvious definition. Surely, you might say, the poor are the people with little money. In general terms you would certainly be correct—additional cash in the pockets of the poor would go a long way in alleviating poverty. But how much additional cash? How low does a family's income have to be before the family is considered "poverty stricken"?

During 1973 the government considered an income of about $4,200 per year to be the "poverty line" for a family of four. A single individual living alone with an income of about half this amount would be considered to be on the edge of poverty. We should remember that the demarcation line that defines the so-called poor is used purely for the sake of convenience of definition. A family a few dollars over the line is really not much better off than a family a few dollars below, although the former is not defined as poor while the latter is.

In addition, the definition of poverty has changed over the years, partly because of inflation and partly because of general economic growth. In the early 1960s, for example, when the nation became acutely aware of the current poverty problem, a $3,000 income per year for a family of four was considered to be the cutoff point. Back in the late 1920s and early 30s, families with $3,000 per year income in today's prices would have been considered quite well off. The poverty line then was something less than $2,000 per year in current prices. If we compare the United States with other nations, even the more wealthy ones such as the Western European countries and Japan, a $4,200 per year equivalent level of purchasing power would be considered quite comfortable in these countries. And in the underdeveloped nations, the equivalent of $4,200 per year income in current U.S. purchasing power would be considered a mark of absolute affluence.

It is quite evident, then, that poverty is a relative thing. Its definition depends to a large extent on the "public conscience." As the nation's overall average income rises, so does the accepted demarcation line between the "rich" and "poor."

Even recognizing the tendency for the definition of poverty to change over the years and from country to country, the selection of a single number to represent the poverty line is, as you might suspect, a gross over-simplification. Perhaps most important is the need to recognize the variety of circumstances and environments that people find themselves in. For example, we would expect a family with young children to require more income to maintain a certain living standard than a couple.

Looking at Table 10–1, it appears, in spite of the old cliché, that

TABLE 10–1
Estimated annual budget cost for a moderate living standard, urban United States, 1972*

Single person, under 35 years old	$ 4,160
Husband and wife, under 35 years old:	
No children	5,613
One child under 6 years	6,967
Two children under 6 years	7,769
Husband and wife, 35–54 years old:	
One child, 6–15 years	9,322
Two children, older 6–15 years of age	11,231
Three children, oldest 6–15 years of age	12,918

  * Adjusted 1967 data, using the increase in the Consumer Price Index between 1967 and 1972 as adjustment factor.
  Source of 1967 data: *Statistical Abstract*, 1969, p. 349.

two cannot live as cheaply as one. However, comparing the single person with the married couple, it does appear that two living together can live more economically than two living separately, which tells us something about the economic incentive for marriage. Also, as shown in Table 10–1, families with older children have to spend considerably more than families with younger children to maintain the same standard of living.

Although the living costs quoted in Table 10–1 provide for a standard of living much above the poverty level, they do make it clear that different family circumstances require different incomes to reach a comparable living standard. For example, a single person of college age can live moderately well for about $4,160 per year. A family with three children of school age will need over three

TABLE 10–2
Comparison of annual budget costs for a four-person family in metropolitan and nonmetropolitan areas under two living standards, Spring–1970

	Lower		*Moderate*	
	Metro	*Nonmetro**	*Metro*	*Nonmetro**
Food	$1,933	$1,780	$ 2,491	$2,281
Housing	1,453	1,322	2,579	2,158
Transportation	481	610	916	894
Clothing and personal	820	753	1,153	1,065
Medical care	580	480	582	483
Other consumption	359	281	661	540
Total consumption	$5,626	$5,226	$ 8,382	$7,421
Other costs and taxes	1,435	1,286	2,551	2,179
Total cost of budget	$7,061	$6,512	$10,933	$9,600

* Places with population of 2,500 to 50,000.
Source: Department of Labor, Bureau of Labor Statistics, "Three Budgets for an Urban Family of Four Persons," Supplement to Bulletin No. 1570–5, 1972, pp. 10–11.

times this amount to attain the same living standard—a fact worth remembering when the desire to reproduce becames especially strong!

The place of residence also bears strongly on the amount of income needed to attain a given living standard. As shown in Table 10–2, it costs more to live in a large metropolitan area than in a smaller town. The largest difference appears to be in housing, although food, clothing, personal and medical care, and other items such as education and recreation cost more to buy in the larger cities. Transportation cost is the only item that is larger in the smaller towns and cities. This is not because autos or public transportation are higher priced in smaller towns; mainly it reflects the longer distances required to travel to work, shopping, etc.

Although the costs of maintaining comparable living standards for farm families are not shown in Table 10–2, we would expect these figures to be somewhat lower still, principally because of lower food costs. The Social Security Administration has estimated living costs for farm families to be about 70 percent of those for urban families, although this estimate might be a bit low. The Bureau of the Census places this figure at about 85 percent of the figure for corresponding nonfarm families.[1]

[1] U.S. Bureau of the Census, *Current Population Reports,* Series P-60, No. 68, "Poverty in the United States, 1959 to 1968" (Washington, D.C.: U.S. Government Printing Office, 1969), p. 11. For a good account of the rural poverty problem, see *The People Left Behind,* a report by the President's National Advisory Commission on Rural Poverty, 1967.

The concept of permanent income

In our discussion so far we have considered income only during a given year. If a family's income is below the poverty line for a particular year, the family is considered poor. But even taking into account the complexities mentioned in the previous section, defining poverty by a single year's income still involves some problems. We must consider, as well, variation or changes in income. Perhaps the most noticeable problem here is the year-to-year fluctuation in income. Consider two comparable families: one has a steady $4,500 year year income and the other has an income that fluctuates from, say, $3,000 per year to $9,000 per year every other year. Over a period of 10 years the $4,500 per year family is never included in the poverty group if the cutoff point is $4,200 per year. On the other hand, the second family would fall within the poverty group in 5 out of the 10 years, even though its average income over this 10-year period would have been $6,000 per year—$1,500 per year higher than the first family.

Thus, the incidence of poverty, as poverty is currently defined, can be reduced simply by reducing the variability of income. Indeed, the second family actually could suffer an absolute reduction in average income over a number of years and still be defined as "better off" simply because it escapes the every-other-year poverty classification. But it is hard to imagine that the second family would consider itself better off with a $1,500 per year smaller, although less variable, income.

This phenomenon is important to recognize because a society can be misled into thinking that its people are better off just because it succeeds in reducing the proportion of the population that falls into the poverty group in any one year. A more accurate measure would be the proportion of families that fell below the poverty line over a period of several years. In the above example, the second family would never be considered poverty stricken if income were averaged over a period of just two years at a time.

A related problem, and perhaps even more important, is the way in which a family, or person, views its long-term income potential. Most college students, for example, do not consider themselves poverty stricken even though their incomes might place them in this category. They know that in a few years, or less, they will be able to enjoy a substantial increase in income. Thus, college students tend to enjoy a much higher standard of living than, say, ghetto dwellers with comparable incomes but little or no hope of ever improving their lot. There can be little doubt, too, that the psychological effect of having a low income is much different for a college student than for a ghetto dweller. The hope of someday breaking out of one's poverty conditions makes these conditions somewhat more bearable. In a sense, poverty is a state of mind as well as the state of one's bank account.

The fact that people tend to look at their long-run earning potential in making consumption decisions probably makes current expenditures on consumption a better measure of poverty than current income. For example, if you have a current income of $2,500 per year but expect to be making $10,000 per year in two years, your current consumption per year is likely to be a great deal larger than someone who expects little or no increase in income. The idea that long-run average income, or permanent income as it is called, is an important determinant of current consumption was first brought out by Friedman in his book *The Theory of the Consumption Function*. This idea is generally referred to as the permanent income hypothesis.

Another reason for paying attention to current expenditures instead of current income as a measure of poverty is to take account of people who live off their savings. The phenomenon is particularly important for retired people. For example, it is not uncommon to observe an older person or couple selling some property or stocks to pay for medical care, buy a new car, or take a trip. Indeed people save during their lifetimes for these very purposes. This is not to say, however, that there is no need to be concerned about poverty among our older people. Many are truly poor. The point is that there is a great deal of difference between the situation where a couple has $3,000 per year income and zero savings or wealth, and the case where a couple has the same income but $100,000 in wealth. The first couple is poor; the second is not.

The distribution of income in the United States

Although mere numbers can never reflect the depression and anxiety of the poor, it will be instructive, nevertheless, to look briefly at the extent of poverty in the United States. Because of the difficulty of obtaining data, we are forced to largely gloss over the complexities and problems of measuring poverty that we have just considered.

It is necessary to bear in mind, too, that as long as the income of the nation is not divided up exactly equally, some people, by necessity, will have to be on the lower end of the income scale. Thus, in viewing figures on the distribution of income it is useful to look both at the dispersion of income between the lowest and highest income recipients and the number or percentage of people that fall into the various income levels.

In Table 10–3 we present the percentages of families that fall within six specified before-income-tax brackets for 1947, 1960, and 1970. To make the three years comparable, the 1947 and 1960 income figures were adjusted for changes in the general price level before the percentages were computed. Thus, any upward movement that is shown in family incomes is due to real economic growth rather than to inflation.

TABLE 10–3
Percentage distribution of money income of families in the United States, selected years, constant 1970 dollars

Annual income level	1947	1960	1970
Under $3,000	22.5%	15.6%	8.9%
$ 3,000 to 4,999	24.2	14.1	10.4
5,000 to 6,999	22.7	16.7	11.8
7,000 to 9,999	17.0	24.7	19.9
10,000 to 14,999 .... ⎫	13.5	19.3	26.8
15,000 and over .... ⎭		9.5	22.3
	100.0%	100.0%	100.0%
Median family income	$5,259	$7,376	$9,867

Source: U.S. Bureau of the Census, *Current Population Reports,* Series P-60, No. 80, "Income in 1970 of Families and Persons in the United States" (Washington, D.C.: U.S. Government Printing Office, 1971), p. 23.

From the figures presented in Table 10–3 we would have to conclude that the old adage "the rich get richer and the poor get poorer" does not hold true, at least for the United States. As shown, over 22 percent of all U.S. families had incomes lower than $3,000 (in 1970 prices) in 1947. (If we had computed the 1947 percentages using 1947 prices, over 49 percent of all families would have fallen in the $3,000 and under group). But in 1970, as we see, only about 9 percent of all families were included in the $3,000 and under income group. The influence of economic growth is evident, too, in the upper end of the income scale. In 1947 only 13.5 percent of all families had incomes of $10,000 or more (in 1970 prices), whereas in 1970 the percentage of families in this group increased to almost 50 percent. At any rate, the near doubling of median income from the end of World War II to the present reflects an across the board increase in incomes rather than just an increase in the incomes of the wealthy.[2]

We cannot tell from the overall upward movement of family incomes, however, whether the dispersion of incomes is becoming narrower or whether poor families are getting a relatively larger slice of the pie. The figures in Table 10–4 provide some indication

TABLE 10–4
Percentage share of total before-tax U.S. money income received by each fifth of families and top 5 percent of all families, selected years

Family group	1950	1960	1970
Lowest fifth	4.5	4.9	5.5
Second fifth	12.0	12.0	12.0
Third fifth	17.4	17.6	17.4
Fourth fifth	23.5	23.6	23.5
Highest fifth	42.6	42.0	41.6
Top 5 percent	17.0	16.8	14.4

Source: U.S. Bureau of the Census, *Current Population Reports,* Series P-60, No. 80, "Income in 1970 of Families and Persons in the United States" (Washington, D.C.: U.S. Government Printing Office, 1970), p. 22.

of the relative distribution of incomes. Here we observe that if all families are ranked by income level from the lowest to the highest, the lowest 20 percent received only 5.5 percent of the total money income in 1970. However, it is interesting to note too that the lower income groups have increased their share of total income slightly during the post–World War II years. For example, the lowest fifth of the families increased their share of the income pie from 4.5 percent in 1950 to 5.5 percent in 1970. The increasing share of the lower income families has come at the expense of the highest fifth, and particularly at the expense of the highest 5 percent of the nation's families, as shown in Table 10–4. Remember, too,

---

2 Median family income is defined as that level of income which 50 percent of the families are below and 50 percent above.

that these figures are before-tax income, so if the higher income families are taxed at higher rates, the after-tax distribution would show less dispersion than is shown in Table 10–4.

The Lorenz curve

Economists have long used a device to describe the nation's income distribution that is perhaps a bit more illustrative than numbers such as are shown in Table 10–4, a device called the Lorenz curve after the man who developed it. The Lorenz curve is obtained by plotting the cumulative percentage of the nation's income against the cumulative percentage of the nation's families or individuals receiving this income. Generally income is represented on the vertical axis of the diagram and households or individuals on the horizontal axis, as shown in Figure 10–1.

FIGURE 10–1
The Lorenz curve

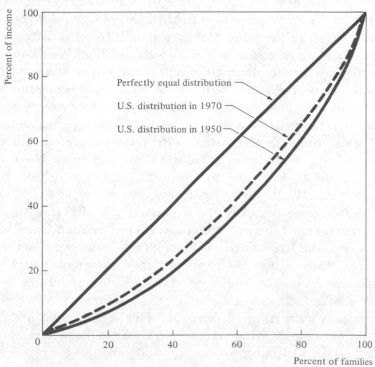

Perhaps the easiest way to understand the Lorenz curve is to ask, What would the curve look like if the nation's income were distributed in a perfectly equal manner? In other words, suppose everyone received the same income. In this case, 20 percent of the nation's families would receive 20 percent of the income, 40 percent would receive 40 percent of the income, etc. Plotting these figures on a Lorenz curve diagram would result in a straight, upward sloping line, as shown in Figure 10–1.

Of course, we know that no nation exhibits a completely equal distribution of income. The lowest 20 percent of the families generally receive substantially less than 20 percent of the income, whereas the highest 20 percent of the families receive much more than 20 percent of the income. What does the Lorenz curve look like in a situation such as this? In this case if we plot the percentage of income received by the lowest 20 percent of the families, say in the United States for 1950, we go up on the vertical axis only to 4.5 percent according to the figures in Table 10–4. Proceeding on, we see that the cumulative income of the bottom 40 percent of the families, as shown in Table 10–4 for 1950, amounts to 16.5 percent of the total income for that year. Hence in plotting this combination, we choose the point that corresponds to 40 percent on the horizontal axis and 16.5 on the vertical axis. If we continue on in this manner for the 60 and 80 percent points on the horizontal axis, we obtain points that also lie below the straight, bisecting line. And by connecting these points, we obtain the Lorenz curve. Note that this curve lies below the straight line that depicts perfect equality.

We can conclude therefore that the more unequal the distribution of income, the more curvature there will be in the Lorenz curve. Indeed if all of the income of the country were received by just one family, the curve would be a vertical line at a right angle to the horizontal axis, like the right-hand side of Figure 10–1. By the same token, if there is a trend towards a more equal distribution of income, the Lorenz curve will flatten out and move closer to the straight, bisecting line. As mentioned, there appears to have been a slight trend towards a more equal distribution of income in the United States in recent times. Thus the Lorenz curve is somewhat flatter now than 20 to 30 years ago. This is illustrated in Figure 10–1, where the 1970 Lorenz curve lies closer to the perfect equality line than the 1950 curve.

The Gini ratio

Economists often use another term to describe the distribution of income—the Gini ratio or Gini coefficient. The Gini ratio is derived from the Lorenz curve diagram and is defined as the ratio of the area between the Lorenz curve and the perfect equality line to the total area below the perfect equality line. In terms of Figure 10–2, it is the ratio of area A over the total area $A + B$, i.e., the Gini ratio is equal to $A/A + B$.

FIGURE 10–2
Deriving the Gini ratio

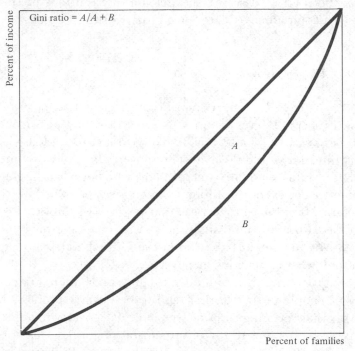

The size of the Gini ratio or coefficient can vary from zero to one. As a nation moves closer to perfect equality in its income distribution, the Gini ratio will approach zero. This occurs because area A, the numerator in the fraction, becomes smaller and smaller as the Lorenz curve becomes flatter and approaches the perfect equality line. At the extreme of perfect equality, area A disappears or becomes zero, which means that the value of the fraction becomes zero. Conversely, as a nation moves toward complete inequality of the income distribution, the Lorenz curve approaches the boundaries of the rectangle and area B grows smaller and smaller. At the extreme of complete inequality, area B disappears, so the ratio is equal to A/A or one.

Nations that have a relatively low Gini ratio have relative equality in their distribution of income. The advantage of using the Gini ratio is that it enables us to describe a nation's income distribution by a single number rather than a series of numbers such as Table 10–4 or a diagram such as Figure 10–2. Of course, the Gini ratio also can be used to describe the income distributions of smaller groups of people, such as states or municipalities.

Poverty in the United States

With a little reflection, it soon becomes clear that poverty is a relative concept. If every family in the world had an income of $4,200 per year, we would not be likely to consider $4,200 as the poverty line, nor would the concept of poverty be likely to come up. Everyone would be equally rich or poor, whichever you prefer. By the same token, even a millionaire might feel poor in a world of billionaires. It appears, therefore, that poverty will always be intimately tied up with the distribution of income. We have looked briefly at the income distribution of the United States; now let us take a somewhat closer look at poverty.

Although no one is immune from being poor, there are certain groups of people in society that tend to be poverty prone. This is not to say that certain groups of people prefer poverty to affluence; poverty is mainly the result of circumstances rather than preferences. Table 10–5 provides a partial listing of family characteristics that allow us to identify groups of people where the incidence of poverty is relatively high.

In determining the incidence of poverty shown in Table 10–5, the Department of Commerce attempted to take into account some of the varying circumstances mentioned earlier in this chapter, such as differences in number of children and place of residence. For

TABLE 10–5
Selected characteristics of families in relation to the incidence of poverty,* 1959 and 1970

Selected characteristic	Percent below poverty line 1959	1970
1. Sex and race of head:		
White—male head	13.3	6.2
White—female head	34.8	25.0
Black—male head	44.2	18.3
Black—female head	72.0	54.4
2. Residence:		
Nonfarm	16.1	9.6
Farm	44.6	18.5
3. Age of head:		
14 to 24 years	26.9	9.1
25 to 54 years	16.0	5.1
55 to 64 years	15.9	7.0
65 and over	30.0	15.7
4. Size of family:		
2 persons	19.6	10.7
3 and 4 persons	12.8	7.7
5 and 6 persons	20.2	9.7
7 persons or more	45.6	22.8
5. Occupation group of head:		
Professional and managerial	5.0	1.5
Clerical and sales	5.7	2.1
Craftsmen and foremen	7.2	3.1
Operatives and kindred workers	14.1	5.1
Service workers, including domestics	25.3	6.2
Nonfarm laborers	29.4	12.3
Farmers and farm workers	54.1	25.9

* Poverty threshold for a family of four was $2,973 in 1959 and $3,968 in 1970 (current dollars).
Source: U.S. Bureau of the Census, *Current Population Reports,* Series P-60, No. 68, "Poverty in the United States: 1959 to 1968" (Washington, D.C.: U.S. Government Printing Office, 1969), p. 4; and Series P-60, No. 81, "Characteristics of The Low Income Population: 1970" (Washington, D.C.: U.S. Government Printing Office, 1971), pp. 3–4.

example, the poverty line for a four-member nonfarm family in 1970 was set at $3,968. This figure increases to $6,426 for a seven-member or larger nonfarm family. Also the lower cost of living on farms is taken into account as reflected, for example, by the poverty line of $3,407 for a four-member farm family in 1970. The substantial reduction in the poverty line for farm families is accounted for in large part by the lower cost of food on farms. In fact, the core of the poverty definition was the cost of a nutritionally adequate food plan as determined by the U.S. Department of Agriculture. Annual revisions in the poverty line were based on price changes in this predetermined food budget.

Finally, in measuring the income of families in order to judge whether a family was above or below the poverty line, the following receipts were not counted as income: (1) receipts from the sale of property such as house, stocks, bonds or car; (2) bank withdrawals; (3) borrowed money; (4) tax refunds; (5) gifts; and (6) inheritances and insurance payments. On the basis of our previous discussion the omission of some of these items might be questioned, but at least it is important to know what is included in measured family income.

Looking first at poverty in relation to sex and race of head of family, we see that poverty is much more prevalent among fatherless families, especially among fatherless black families. Over half of this latter group fell below the poverty level in 1970. Regarding residence, we see that the incidence of poverty is almost twice as high among farm families as among their city counterparts, even taking into account the decrease in cost of living on farms.

As we might expect, poverty is more prevalent among the very youngest and very oldest families, although as we mentioned no account was made of the wealth or savings of this latter group. Again, as we might expect, poverty is more prevalent among the very largest families. Finally, we see that the occupation of the family head has an important bearing on the incidence of poverty. As expected, the higher income professional, managerial, and skilled craftsmen occupations result in the least amount of poverty. On the other end of the scale, farmers and farm laborers exhibit the most poverty, followed by service workers and nonfarm laborers.

Perhaps the most striking thing about Table 10–5 is the tremendous decline in the incidence of poverty from 1959 to 1970. All of the categories mentioned exhibited a reduction in poverty during this period. In fact, in many instances the percentage of families below the poverty line dropped by a half or more. This phenomenon clearly demonstrates the influence of general economic growth on poverty. If everyone can be made a little richer, the poor benefit as well as the rich.

Of course, as we pointed out, society's concept of what constitutes a poor family or individual generally changes with continued economic growth. As the povery line inches upward, the same families that escaped the poverty group in the 1960s may find themselves right back in during the 1970s. In large part, the income necessary to escape poverty depends on what goods and services society considers as necessities. Indoor plumbing was once considered a luxury; now it is a necessity, at least in the United States. Similarly animal protein in the diet is considered a luxury in many underdeveloped nations, while it is considered a necessity in the United States. Indeed, it is not difficult to imagine that in the years to come many present-day luxuries such as air-conditioning and convenience foods will come to be considered as necessities.

Myths about poverty

In the United States at the present time it is taken for granted by most people that poverty is an undesirable thing and that society would be better off if it were eliminated. Strangely enough, this thinking did not always prevail. Throughout history a number of long-standing myths about poverty were commonly accepted, and perhaps still are accepted by some people today.

One such myth was that every society needed to keep a certain fraction of its population poor in order to have a source of labor for the disagreeable and menial tasks that had to be done. For example, it was thought that if no one were poor, who would clean the streets, collect the garbage, or maintain the sewers? As societies have developed, however, this fear has been proven to be unfounded. The invention and adoption of machines has taken much of the drudgery out of many of these jobs and completely eliminated others. People did not realize that a freely functioning labor market would take into account the varying amount of disagreeableness in jobs and compensate the people who held undesirable jobs with higher wages. For example, the bank clerk who takes part of his salary in comfortable working conditions no doubt would be happy with the salary of the sanitary engineer (garbage man).

Another myth that might be more prevalent than we would like to admit is that poor people are inherently lazy and the only thing that keeps them working is the fear of starvation. Thus it is reasoned that these people must be kept poor in order for them to be industrious. What was often forgotten here was that relatively low wages provide poor people with very little incentive to work or to improve their lot. As an example, it is sometimes argued that some minority groups in the United States today are inherently lazy because they do not strive for more education in an attempt to improve themselves. But we must remember that discrimination in the labor market has prevented many of these people from capturing a return on their educations, and hence there was little incentive for them to invest in more education.

Still a third myth, that again is probably held by some people who are not poor, is that poor people have deliberately chosen to be poor because of the mental and physical cost involved in breaking out of the poverty class. The stereotyped hillbilly or skid row dweller is generally used as an example. Granted there will always be a few people in every society who wish to "drop out." But the mass exodus of people from the poverty level to the middle class in the United States and other developed nations provides a strong case for arguing that most people take advantage of opportunities to escape the grasp of poverty. Indeed, it is very hard to argue that the poor live a carefree and easy life. Pounding the pavement in search of even a temporary job, or worrying about where next month's rent will come from, would not be considered an easy life by most middle- or high-income people.

With the gradual abandonment of such myths, many nations have adopted policies or programs aimed at reducing poverty. Let us now turn our attention to some of these measures.

Implicit programs that help the poor

Before considering the more explicit poverty or income redistribution programs, we ought to mention that the extent of poverty is influenced a great deal by other circumstances in the economy as well. These include:

1. General economic growth. Although we do not generally consider economic growth as a program to help the poor, there can be no doubt that the across the board increase in incomes has greatly reduced the extent of poverty in the United States and in the other more highly developed nations of the world. This is clearly shown in Table 10–5, where the incidence of poverty during the 1960s has been reduced by a half or more for many groups. Remember, too, that these figures are based on a current definition of poverty. Had we used the poverty definition from the 1930s the incidence would have been even lower.

2. *A full-employment economy.* Since poor people make up a disproportionately large share of the unskilled labor force, a rise in unemployment hits poor people hardest. In our discussion of unemployment in Chapter 2, we pointed out that the unskilled tend to be the first laid off. The unemployment rate among blue-collar workers rises faster than that for all workers during a recession, in spite of the fact that the blue-collar category includes many skilled craftsmen who do not face as great a threat of layoffs. Thus during recessions the poor tend to be hurt the most.

3. *A stable price economy.* The presence of an unexpected high rate of inflation also hurts the poor; indeed it is likely to make some people poor. Those who keep a relatively large share of their assets in the form of cash, savings deposits, bonds, or life insurance policies are, of course, made relatively poorer by inflation. Contrary to popular opinion, poor people tend not to be large debtors. Because unexpected inflation helps debtors at the expense of creditors, the poor as a group tend to end up relatively worse off during inflation. Retired people living off cash savings or a relatively fixed income experience a reduction in the purchasing power of their already low incomes. In addition, upward adjustments in unemployment compensation and welfare payments, which sustain a large share of the poor, tend to lag behind increases in the general price level, particularly during the early stages of inflation.

4. *Public education.* Although we may not think of public education as a policy or program to help the poor, there can be no doubt that such has been the case. The relationship of education to poverty is very clear. If we take a cross section of poor people, we find them in many different situations. Some are white, others black. Some live in big cities, others in small towns or on farms. We find the poor in every region of the country and from divergent backgrounds. Indeed, the poor are far from a homogeneous group. If we tried to find a common characteristic that fitted most poor people, aside from a lack of money, probably the closest we could come would be their low level and poor quality of education.

The relationship between income and education is illustrated by Table 10–6. Here we see that at the lowest educational levels, median income is the lowest. This is true for both white and non-

TABLE 10-6
Relationship between income and education, United
States, 1970

Education level	Median income White families	Nonwhite families
Less than 8 years	$ 5,933	$ 4,589
8 years	7,882	5,538
1–3 years high school	9,509	6,466
4 years high school	11,054	7,894
1–3 years college	13,822	10,409
4 or more years college	15,841	13,271

Source: U.S. Bureau of the Census, *Current Population Reports,*
Series P–60, No. 80, "Income in 1970 of Families in the United
States" (Washington, D.C.: U.S. Government Printing Office,
1971), pp. 64–66.

white families. Notice, however, that for each educational level non-white families exhibit lower incomes than their white counterparts —the fruits of discrimination and possibly a lower quality education.

The mere fact that income bears a close positive relationship to education does not guarantee, of course, that large numbers of poor people can use education to escape from poverty. Education is a very costly activity and not many poor people could afford to purchase much if they had to pay the full cost. Thus, if education is to be a major means of escape from poverty, a large share of its cost must be borne by the public. In public elementary and high schools, the entire operating costs are financed by tax revenues. In public colleges and universities, student tuition generally covers a third or less of the operating costs of the institutions, with tax revenue covering the major part of the remainder.

In spite of generous public support of educational institutions in the United States, it has been argued that the poor and lower middle class still subsidize the college education of the higher income people. The argument has some validity. Low-income people pay taxes to support public colleges and universities but utilize these institutions to a much smaller extent than the higher income people. This is especially true for poor people among minority groups.

One way to make higher education much more accessible and responsive to poor people is for the government to directly support or subsidize people (students) rather than educational institutions.

One proposal is to give students vouchers that they could "spend" at the educational institution of their choice. This would have the advantage, also, of creating some competition between educational institutions, which in turn should promote greater efficiency and higher quality of services provided.

Recently a number of states have ruled it unconstitutional to finance public schools by property taxes because of the resulting inequality in educational opportunity. A high-income community will tend to have a higher tax base, and as a result more income is generated to operate the school system than in a poor community. Financing schools by means of a state or federal income tax would remove some of the inequality brought on by financing public schools through local property taxes.[3]

Indeed it can be argued that schools in poorer communities should be even better than schools in high-income communities in order to make up for some of the environmental disadvantages experienced by children in poor families and neighborhoods. It is becoming more evident that the attitude of parents toward education and the opportunities that children have for out-of-school learning are important determinants of future earning potential.

Explicit programs to help the poor

In addition to the points mentioned in the previous section, there are other programs and policies designed more or less to alter the income distribution towards more equality. These include:

1. Minimum wage laws. Since poor people tend to be on the low end of the wage scale, minimum wage laws affect the poor primarily. At first glance it may appear that minimum wage laws are a boon to poor people. After all, if a poor person cannot be paid less than $1.80 per hour, say, his income will be higher than if his wage were $1.25 per hour. What is often forgotten, however, is that the higher minimum wage can only benefit the poor person if he is working. If the market wage is lower than the minimum wage, the inevitable result will be a reduction in the employment opportuni-

---

[3] Of course, owners of real property would benefit from a reduction in property taxes because of greater reliance on income taxes.

ties for poor people. Indeed, it has been argued that a minimum wage law harms poor people more than it helps them because of the increased unemployment that it causes among the people at the low end of the wage scale.[4]

2. *Farm programs.* Since poverty has been and still is relatively prevalent on farms and in rural areas, various farm programs have been designed to bolster farm incomes. In large part these programs have taken the form of supporting the prices of various agricultural products above their free market levels. Again, it may appear reasonable to believe that such a program would benefit poor farmers. If a farmer can receive $2 per bushel for his wheat, for example, his income ought to be higher than if he received $1 per bushel. But one of the problems of such a program is that the setting of a support price higher than the market level reduces the quantity demanded of farm products (which includes foreign buyers as well). Thus the government has to set limits on how much farmers can produce in order to keep the surpluses at manageable levels. At any rate, the nation ends up using scarce resources to produce products that no one wants to buy.

An even more important problem of farm programs is that they end up helping large, high-income farmers to a much greater degree than they help poor farmers. A little simple arithmetic makes this point clear. A small farmer who produces 100 bushels of wheat for sale will gain $100 extra income if the price of wheat is raised from $1 to $2 per bushel by the support price. But the large farmer who sells, say, 10,000 bushels of wheat per year gains $10,000 in extra income from the program. It is becoming increasingly clear that present farm programs are causing a more unequal distribution of income among farmers.

The amount of government program benefits on a per farm basis for 1969 is presented in Table 10–7. Here we see that the average benefit to the smallest farms amounted to only $300 per year compared to $14,100 for the largest farms.

3. *Welfare programs.* Included under this general heading are a variety of programs specifically designed to help poor people, such as the Aid to Families with Dependent Children (AFDC), hospital

---

[4] For further discussion of the effects of minimum wage laws see Chapter 9 (The Labor Market) of the companion Micro text.

TABLE 10–7
Government program benefits to farmers in 1969 (dollars per farm)

Source of benefit	Farms with annual sales of					
	Less than $2,500	$2,500 to 4,999	$5,000 to 9,999	$10,000 to 19,999	$20,000 to 39,999	$40,000 and over
Price supports	$100	$ 300	$ 600	$1,100	$2,100	$ 9,000
Direct payments	200	700	1,100	1,700	2,500	5,100
Total per farm	$300	$1,000	$1,700	$2,800	$4,600	$14,100

Source: Charles L. Schultze, "The Distribution of Farm Subsidies: Who Gets the Benefits?" (Washington, D.C.: Brookings Institution, Staff Paper, 1971), p. 30.

and medical care for the poor, school lunches, food stamps, etc. At the end of the 1960s about $20 billion dollars per year in public funds went into these various programs, up from about $7 billion per year in 1960. Although these programs undoubtedly help the poor, they have undergone a growing amount of criticism in recent years.

It appears rather strange that the real cost of welfare has more than doubled in the United States during the past decade while the incidence of poverty (measured without welfare payments) has declined by almost one half (Table 10–5). Many middle-income taxpayers are beginning to ask embarrassing questions. Moreover many poor people complain that too much of the money is eaten up in administering the programs and as a result not enough "welfare" reaches them. The present welfare programs also give rise to a number of undesirable side effects. For example, there is the built-in incentive for breaking up families. Poor families with several children find that the income of the wife and children can be increased in many instances if the husband leaves home and the family goes on welfare. This is reflected in the substantial increase in the proportion of fatherless families among urban blacks—from 23 percent in 1960 to 29 percent in 1968. Indeed, there are more fatherless children living in New York City today than there are people of all ages in most other American cities.

Some welfare programs also have the effect of in a sense placing a 100 percent tax on additional income to the poor. For example, if the husband of a poor family finds a job that pays an after-tax wage equivalent to the AFDC payment for his wife and children and rejoins the family, the payments stop, leaving the family with the same net income with the job as without. Thus there isn't much incentive for fathers of poor families to take jobs and reunite with their families.

The present welfare program also provides a strong incentive for people to leave rural areas, particularly in the South, and migrate to the large northern cities. This occurs because of the much larger welfare payments made by northern states. For example, the maximum monthly AFDC payment for a family of four is about six times higher in New Jersey than in Mississippi. Surely, with urban congestion and pollution, it does not seem desirable to hasten migration to large cities.

4. Social security and unemployment insurance. These two programs are more straightforward and less controversial than the ones we have just discussed. Perhaps the major criticism of the social security program is that it also has elements of the 100 percent tax phenomenon. If a retired person wants to supplement his income with part-time work, he must be careful not to earn over the allowable maximum, or he loses his social security benefits. If these benefits are lost, it is equivalent to a 100 percent tax on wage income over the cutoff point.

5. Progressive income tax. Although the income tax is the major revenue source for government, the fact that the tax rates are intended to increase with income makes it also an income redistribution scheme. In fact, the government can obtain any income distribution that is desired simply by adjusting the tax rates. For example, if it wanted more equality it could increase the tax rates on high incomes and reduce them on low incomes. An income tax in its purest, unadulterated form is considered by many economists to be the fairest and least distorting tax that a government can levy.

Unfortunately the U.S. income tax is not very "pure" in that it contains a number of loopholes that allow certain people to escape the tax altogether and others to pay a greatly reduced tax. One very large loophole is the capital gains treatment. Here expenses incurred in the creation of capital gains can be written off against ordinary income while the gains are taxed at only one half the rate on ordinary income. Thus a person can reduce his tax by one half by taking his income as capital gains. Also the payment of the tax can be postponed indefinitely because capital gains are not taxed until realized.

Another unfortunate aspect of tax loopholes is that each year millions of dollars' worth of man-hours are devoted to figuring out ways to avoid paying taxes. It pays for individuals to do so, but it amounts to an absolute waste for the nation. It is also unfortunate that the ones who gain most from loopholes are the highest income people. The poor and middle-income people who have their income taxes deducted from their wages have relatively little chance to take advantage of loopholes.

Negative income tax

The negative income tax is a relatively new proposal that has received a great deal of attention of late. First proposed by Milton Friedman in his 1962 book, *Capitalism and Freedom,* the basic idea has been called a number of things including "income maintenance" or a "guaranteed annual income." The proposal is surprisingly simple. If society is really serious about helping poor people and wants to help them in the most efficient way possible, the best way is for the government to supplement their incomes by a so-called negative tax—a payment from the government to the poor.

Perhaps the easiest way to understand how the negative income tax plan might work is to look at a specific example. Suppose that under the ordinary income tax schedule, a family of four could earn up to $4,000 per year without paying any federal income tax. Next, let us consider the case of a poor family of four with a total income of $3,000 per year. This family would after the end of the year file an income tax return reporting that it had an income deficit of $1,000. Let us assume that the negative tax rate or the refund rate is 50 percent. In this case the family would receive a $500 check (0.50 × $1,000) from the government, which in a sense is a negative tax—a payment from the government to a citizen instead of vice versa. Thus the family would end up with a total income of $3,500: $3,000 from its initial income plus $500 in "negative taxes."

It is important to recognize, too, that the negative tax rate would be something less than 100 percent. In other words, the government would not make up the entire difference between a family's initial income and the zero tax income ($4,000 in our example).

For example, suppose the family had an opportunity to earn an extra $500, so that its initial before-tax income would increase to $3,500. With a $500 deficit, the government would mail a check for $250, giving the family a total income of $3,750: the initial $3,500 plus the $250 negative tax. In this second case the family's after-tax income would have increased to $3,750. If the government had made up the entire difference between the $4,000 base and the family's actual income, the total income would have been $4,000 in both cases. There would be no incentive for the family to earn additional income if it remained below $4,000. But as long as the negative tax rate is less than 100 percent, the family still has an incentive to earn money on its own. Of course, the negative tax rate and the base zero tax income can be set at any level desired as long as the rate is kept below 100 percent. The 50 percent rate and $4,000 income are just examples. Additional refinements could be built into the plan, such as allowing deductions from actual income for such things as medical expense before calculating the negative tax.

The arguments in favor of the negative tax are quite convincing. First, it would be possible to eliminate or at least reduce the variety of present programs that are overburdened with administrative expense and often treat different groups very unequally. The negative income tax would not suffer from either of these shortcomings. Second, poor people would not have to suffer the indignities and degradation that they are now subject to in the welfare schemes that label the poor in full view of their neighbors. Also, programs that dole out a few dollars for this and a few dollars for that treat the poor as if they were second-class citizens who could not be trusted with money. To be poor is bad enough, but to suffer the indignities of the present welfare setup is more than some can bear.

Of course, the negative income tax scheme does present some problems. Probably the major concern of middle- and high-income tax payers is that the assurance of a guaranteed annual income would prompt people with low-paying jobs to simply quit working and live off the taxes of employed people. However the less than 100 percent negative tax rate feature would mitigate this problem somewhat, since a family always would have a higher net income by working than by not working. Indeed the AFDC and social security programs are more open to this criticism than the negative tax scheme. Granted there are likely to be some people with low-paying second jobs who would quit such jobs if their incomes were supplemented. This would increase full- or part-time employment opportunities for teenagers and college students.

Negative tax payments might also prompt some working wives of low-income families to drop out of the labor force. The effects could be both good and bad—good if these wives could devote more time to raising their children, bad if it prompted them to have more children (assuming we are concerned with overpopulation). On the latter point, care would have to be taken not to build incentives into the negative tax scheme to increase the number of children.

The way in which people might spend the money received from negative tax payments also troubles some people. What is to stop poor people from buying booze, football tickets, and color TV sets with their extra income (i.e., from acting like middle-class Americans)? Our willingness to provide welfare for low-income people appears to be influenced by what the recipients get from the welfare. Necessities such as food, clothing, and shelter are most desired, as evidenced by the food stamp, AFDC, and public housing programs.

Yet this is a somewhat naive approach. If a poor family receives $100 worth of food stamps or subsidized housing, this leaves $100 more of its own money with which to buy such no-no's as mentioned above. Providing welfare "in kind" rather than in money is not likely to maximize the welfare of the recipients for a given budgetary cost. Items that are given free or at a reduced price will of course be accepted, but may not be what the family would have bought had they received an equivalent amount of cash. If what they would have bought is different, we can infer that the payment in kind is less desirable than the cash. For example, which would you prefer: $1,000 worth of low-income housing or $1,000 in cash? The provision of low-income housing also has a tendency to create ghettos, something that could be avoided if low-income people were given an equivalent amount of money and were free to live where they chose.

The cost of a guaranteed income scheme is regarded by some as being out of the realm of possibility. Naturally if we set the minimum income level high, the cost will be high. But this is not the question. The relevant question is whether the amount society decides to spend on welfare, say $20 billion, can be more efficiently spent by the current setup or by the negative tax scheme. There can be little doubt that the negative tax scheme would be much more efficient and equitable. We could avoid a large part of the welfare bureaucracy that has grown up over the years, giving this money directly to poor people. We could be sure that the poor would indeed receive the benefits, and in a way that would not degrade them or label them as second-class citizens.

Main points of Chapter 10

1. The definition of poverty depends to a large extent on the average income and wealth of the population. The higher the income, the higher the line of demarcation between rich and poor.

2. The family income necessary to rise above the poverty classification also depends on size of family and place of residence.

3. The extent of poverty in any one year depends upon the long-run expected income as well as current income. The idea that current consumption depends upon long-run expected income is known as the permanent income hypothesis.

4. The percentage of families under the $3,000 per year income level has fallen from 22.5 percent in 1947 to 8.9 percent in 1970 in constant 1970 dollars.

5. During the past 20 years, the before-tax income distribution in the United States has tended toward greater equality.

6. The Lorenz curve shows the percentage of total income received by a certain percentage of the population. A straight-line diagonal Lorenz curve illustrates perfect equality. The more curvature of the Lorenz curve, the more unequal the distribution of income.

7. The Gini ratio is the ratio of the area between the actual Lorenz curve and the perfect equality line to the total area under the perfect equality line. A Gini ratio of zero denotes

complete equality of income, whereas a ratio of one denotes complete inequality.

8. In the United States poverty is more prevalent among black families, farmers, families in the very youngest and very oldest age categories, larger families, and those in the unskilled occupations.

9. Because of general economic growth, the percentage of families defined as poor declined substantially in all family classifications between 1959 and 1970.

10. Some past and present myths about poverty include: (1) every society needs poor people to furnish labor for menial and undesirable tasks, (2) poor people are poor because they are lazy, and (3) the poor have deliberately chosen to be poor because of the mental and physical cost of increasing their incomes.

11. In the United States the poor do benefit greatly from programs or policies not designed specifically as poverty programs. These include: (1) general economic growth, (2) full employment, (3) stable prices, and (4) public education.

12. Other programs or policies designed to more specifically help poor people include: (1 minimum wage laws, (2) farm programs, (3) various welfare programs, (4) social security and unemployment insurance, and (5) the progressive income tax.

13. The farm program and traditional welfare programs have come under increasing criticism in recent years because of their high cost and undesirable effects both upon the poor and the rest of society.

14. A relatively new proposal put forth by Professor Milton Friedman is the negative income tax plan. Under this plan, families below a specified income level would receive a "negative tax" or payment from the government.

15. An important feature of the negative income tax plan would be a negative tax rate of less than 100 percent. This would allow families to increase their total incomes without having their negative tax payments decreased by a like amount. Hence there would still be an incentive for poor people to improve their incomes on their own.

16. A major concern of people about the negative tax scheme is its adverse effect on work incentives. Also, some raise objections

that the money will not be "wisely" spent, and that the scheme would be too costly for taxpayers.

Questions for thought and discussion

1. "A poor family in the United States also would be considered poor in India." Do you agree? Why or why not?
2. Sometimes it appears that families become poorer as they grow older even though their incomes are rising. Do you think there is any substance to this observation? Explain.
3. The high rate of poverty among aspiring artists, actors, and actresses is well known. Why do you suppose people persist in choosing these lines of work? (Hint: Also consider how poverty is measured.)
4. Consider two families, one made up of two college seniors just recently married and the other a couple in their late 50s. Both couples have incomes of $2,500 this year. Which is poorer, and why?
5. Consider two groups of people, one made up of the students in your economics class and the other of people who regularly attend concerts on campus. Which group would probably have the most unequal income distribution? Draw hypothetical Lorenz curves for each group. Which would have the highest Gini ratio?
6. Does your current income place you in the "poverty class"? If it did, would you consider yourself poor? Why or why not?
7. After college, what percentage of your annual income would you be willing to pay in the form of taxes for the purpose of giving to people with less income than yourself? Why this particular amount?
8. Some people argue that the poor have gotten that way because of an unwillingness to work hard in school in order to obtain a good-paying job, or because they refuse to work hard on the job or stick to it in order to move up the pay scale. How do you feel about this argument?
9. It has been said that society can obtain any desired distribution of income it desires by means of an income tax. Do you agree? Explain.

10. Do you think teenagers and college students are helped or harmed by the minimum wage law? Explain.
11. Set up a simple negative income tax scheme for a family of four.
12. If you were a welfare recipient, would you prefer food stamps and public housing or a negative income tax? Explain why.

11

International trade and finance

Our discussion thus far has centered mainly on the national economy and the problems of unemployment and inflation. In this chapter we will broaden our perspective somewhat and look at the international economy, specifically at the phenomenon of trade between nations.

We should bear in mind throughout the discussion that nations exist because of artificial boundaries that men have devised. Were it not for border guards, barricades, checkpoints, etc., we could travel across national boundaries without being aware that we had done so. The artificial and temporary character of nations or national boundaries is aptly illustrated by their continual formation and dissolution throughout history. For example, we now think of East and West Germany as separate countries, whereas just a few decades ago they were a single country. What was once trade between two people or two business firms now has become international trade between people located in different countries.

The main point to be made here is that international trade is just trade between two people, business firms, or groups of people who happen to find themselves enclosed within different national boundaries. Too frequently we lost sight of this simple fact and consider international trade as trade between two countries or governments. Of course, governments have a great deal to say as to whom we buy from and sell to, and at what price, as we shall see more vividly later in the chapter.

The basis for trade

Perhaps the easiest way to understand the basis of all trade is to consider why each of us as an individual engages in trade. If people did not trade with each other everyone would have to be self-sufficient. However, the extreme inefficiency of self-sufficient people is well documented throughout history, starting with the cave men. It didn't take people, even the most primitive people, long to discover that by specializing in one or a few activities, their total productivity could be increased greatly. For example, in tribal societies it is well known that certain people made the utensils, others hunted, and still others cared for the domestic animals and crops. These people knew that output of the entire tribe was increased when even a modest amount of specialization took place.

The opportunity to increase output also accounts for present-day trade between people, whether it be people in the same neighborhood or people of different regions of a country or different countries. In the United States, for example, it would be foolish for people in the northern part of the nation to attempt to grow their own citrus fruits—the output of the entire nation is increased when people in the South and West produce the nation's fruit, part of which is traded with the people of the North for items produced there. A trade barrier between North and South surely would reduce the output of the entire country, because each region would have to undertake production for which it was not well suited. The same reasoning applies to trade between countries. (In the discussion that follows we will speak of international trade as trade between two countries. But keep in mind that in reality it is trade between people living within different national boundaries.) If the United States attempted to produce its own coffee, for example, it would have to forgo the production of a relatively large amount of other products because of the resources that would have to be devoted to relatively inefficient coffee production.

The examples in the preceding paragraph illustrate what is perhaps most obvious reason for the increase in total output or productivity resulting from trade—differences in climate or natural resources. Citrus fruits and coffee require special climates, so it makes sense to produce these products in the areas that have the appropriate climate. Similarly, the extraction of minerals or petroleum can take place only where nature provides these resources. Other examples include the location of a fishing industry in a specific area because of the proximity to a large body of water, or the existence of lumbering because of abundant tree growth. It wouldn't make much sense for the Great Plains to produce lumber and the Northwest to produce corn, for example.

In addition to differences in the natural endowment, specialization and trade takes place because of the past establishment of traditions and institutions that favor a certain industry. For example, Japan has become well known for its light manufacturing industries, Germany for its machines and tools, Sweden for its high-quality steel, and Switzerland for its watches. Traditions of workmanship and knowledge are passed down from generation to generation, giving the nation or region a distinct advantage in certain kinds of production.

The existence of a particular industry often gives rise to other supporting industries and institutions. For example, trade centers or markets are established where buyers and sellers can get together. Financing institutions develop that cater to a particular industry because of the specific knowledge required. If a large share of the people are employed by an industry, it is common for the public schools to offer training that is specifically applicable to the industry. Economists refer to the increase in productivity that occurs because of the formation of other supporting industries or institutions as "external economies." In other words, an industry may become more productive as it becomes larger because of the existence of other supporting industries and institutions.

It is sometimes argued that the people of certain regions or nations have some innate ability or characteristic that makes them better suited for certain occupations. For example, the Japanese have gained a reputation for being nimble and able to assemble tiny components of their products. The Germans and Swiss, on the other hand, often are thought of as possessing a characteristic of preciseness which makes them well qualified to produce tools and instruments. It is not clear if such traits are inherent in the population or if they are learned or acquired through generations of people doing the jobs that require these traits. At any rate, if differences in skills between populations do exist, regardless if they are inherent or acquired, it is reasonable to expect that a nation or area will be better off if it accentuates the activities that it is comparatively good at.

Comparative advantage

It is fairly easy to see how specialization and trade can be beneficial to areas or nations because of special advantages in the production of certain goods or services. As mentioned, these advantages may stem from climatic conditions, natural resource endowments, human skills, etc. It is possible, however, to find areas or even nations that seem to have been shortchanged by nature and as a result do not possess special advantages vis-à-vis other areas or nations. In these cases, will there be any incentive for the more productive nations to trade with their less productive neighbors? After all, in order to have trade between two nations, or even two people, it is necessary for both to gain from the transaction. If one trader gains and the other loses, the loser will refuse to trade.

We are indebted to an early English economist named David Ricardo for first shedding some light on this question. Using the production of cloth and wine in Portugal and England as an example, Ricardo demonstrated that even though Portugal might be able to produce each unit of wine and cloth more "efficiently" than England, it still was to the advantage of Portugal to engage in trading these two commodities with England. The incentive for trade to take place in this situation is much less obvious than the examples we discussed earlier, where each country has a special advantage in one of the commodities.

The key to understanding the basis for trade in this latter situation is found in the concept known as "comparative advantage." Perhaps the easiest way to understand this concept is to construct a simple example. Let us use the United States and the United Kingdom as our two countries, and wheat and wool as our two products. If you wish you may assume that the United States is more efficient in both, or vice versa. We will see a bit later that any difference in the level of absolute efficiency between the two countries does bear upon the problem.

In Table 11–1 we present some possible levels of output for each

TABLE 11–1
Examples of production possibility schedules for wheat and wool in the
United States and the United Kingdom

Possibility	United States		United Kingdom	
	Wheat	*Wool*	*Wheat*	*Wool*
A	480	0	120	0
B	320	20	80	10
C	160	40	40	20
D	0	60	0	30

commodity in each country (in millions of bushels and bales).
Notice that when wool is increased in each country the output of
wheat declines, and similarly if more wheat is produced the quantity
of wool must decline. This tells us that each country has a limited
amount of resources and, therefore, each cannot simultaneously
increase the production of both commodities. Economists often
refer to these figures as production possibilities schedules. If these
figures were plotted on diagrams we would obtain production possibilities curves, as discussed in Chapter 1.

Using the figures in Table 11–1, we can calculate the cost of
wheat and wool in the two countries. First notice that should the
United States wish to increase its wool output from 0 to 20 million
bales it must give up 160 million bushels of wheat. In other words,
each bale of wool costs eight bushels of wheat in the United States.
In the United Kingdom we see that each additional bale of wool
costs only four bushels of wheat. Thus in comparing the two countries, we would say that wool is expensive in the United States and
cheap in the United Kingdom in terms of the wheat given up to
obtain it.

The cost of wool can be obtained in the same manner. Moving up
from the bottom of the table, we see that the United States gives up
20 million bales of wool to obtain 160 million bushels of wheat, or
0.125 bale of wool for each bushel of wheat. In the United Kingdom
the first 40 million bushels of wheat are obtained by giving up 10
million bales of wool, or 0.25 bale of wool for each bushel of wheat.
Thus we can conclude that in terms of wool, wheat is cheap in the
United States and expensive in the United Kingdom. These costs
are summarized in Table 11–2.

Because wool is relatively cheap in the United Kingdom com-

TABLE 11–2
Costs of wheat and wool

	United States	United Kingdom
Cost of wool in terms of wheat	8 bushels	4 bushels
Cost of wheat in terms of wool*	0.125 bales	0.25 bales

* Notice that the wheat costs are the reciprocals of the wool costs and vice versa.

pared to the United States, economists would say that the United Kingdom enjoys a comparative advantage in the production of wool vis-à-vis the United States. Similarly, the comparatively low cost of wheat (in terms of wool) in the United States gives the United States a comparative advantage in the production of this product. Notice that in our derivation of comparative advantage we did not say anything about the absolute efficiency of wheat and wool production in the two countries. The important distinction is the relative efficiency of producing one product versus the other. In the United States, wool production is relatively inefficient (in this example) because a relatively large amount of wheat must be given up to obtain the wool. In the United Kingdom, wheat production is relatively inefficient because much wool must be given up to obtain the wheat.

The gains from trade

So far in the example we have illustrated a situation where the United States has a comparative advantage in wheat and the United Kingdom has a comparative advantage in wool. So what? We will now show that because of comparative advantage, each country, by cutting back on the production of its high-cost product and increasing the output of its low-cost product and then trading part of its "cheap" product, can end up with more of both products. The only thing required for this little sleight-of-hand trick is that the trading price be someplace between the productions costs in both countries.

In our example, the production cost of a bale of wool is eight bushels of wheat in the United States and four bushels of wheat in the United Kingdom. Suppose the two countries could agree on a middle-ground price of, say, six bushels of wheat from the United States for each bale of wool it buys from the United Kingdom. Notice that this is a good deal for the United States, because in order to obtain more wool by producing it domestically, it would have to give up eight bushels of wheat per bale of wool. Similarly this price implies that the United Kingdom pays one sixth of a bale of wool for each bushel of wheat. This is a good deal for the United Kingdom, because by producing more wheat domestically it must give up one fourth of a bale for both countries to trade.

Let us now illustrate how both countries can end up with more of both products after trading. As an initial situation, suppose both countries are producing at possibility *B* shown by Table 11–1. In this situation, the United States is producing 320 million bushels of wheat and 20 million bales of wool, while the United Kingdom is producing 80 million bushels of wheat and 10 million bales of wool.[1] Now let us suppose the United States cuts back on its production of wool by 5 million bales. The 8 to 1 cost ratio tells us that the United States can expand its wheat output by 40 million bushels. Also suppose the United Kingdom cuts back on wheat production by 32 million bushels. The 4 to 1 cost ratio in the United Kingdom tells us that they can expand wool output by 8 million bales. (We will discuss how these changes might be initiated in the section on international markets.)

To complete the example, let us suppose the United States sells 36 million bushels of wheat to the United Kingdom in exchange for 6 million bales of wool. Recall that the agreed upon price was six bushels of wheat for a bale of wool. After the transaction is complete, note that the United States now has 324 million bushels of wheat (360 − 36) and 21 million bales of wool (15 + 6). The United Kingdom now has 84 million bushels of wheat (48+ 36) and 12 million bales of wool (18 − 6). In other words, both countries now have more wheat and more wool. This delightful phenomenon happened because each country increased the output of the product in which it had a comparative advantage and then traded part of this increased output to the other country for the

---

[1] Keep in mind that these figures only represent an example and are not intended to illustrate the actual production of these two products in the United States and the United Kingdom.

product it found expensive to produce. The results are summarized in Table 11–3.

TABLE 11–3
Illustrating the gains from trade

	United States		United Kingdom	
	Wheat	*Wool*	*Wheat*	*Wool*
Before trade	320	20	80	10
After trade:				
Domestic production	360	15	48	18
Add imports		+6	+36	
Subtract exports	−36			−6
Total	324	21	84	12

Incomplete specialization

In the preceding example, it turns out that the total output of wheat and wool in the United States and the United Kingdom is maximized if the United States specializes in wheat and the United Kingdom in wool. But in reality, complete specialization would not be likely to take place.

In order to make this example as simple as possible, we left out a number of complicating factors. Even in a simplified form, international trade examples have a tendency to become complex and confusing. One simplification is that in the production possibilities schedule shown in Table 11–1 we assumed that wheat could be transformed into wool, or vice versa, at a constant cost over the entire range of possibilities. In the United States, for example, we assumed that the cost of obtaining an additional bale of wool was eight bushels of wheat regardless of the amount of each produced. We made the same assumption for the United Kingdom, only here we assumed a constant ratio of 4 to 1.

In reality we would not expect the same cost ratio to prevail over the entire range of production possibilities. For example, in the United States there are certain parts of the country (such as mountainous or hilly areas) where wool production can be carried out without much sacrifice of wheat because wheat could not be grown on the hills anyway. Thus the first few million bales of wool could be obtained quite economically in terms of wheat given up. But then as more and more of the nation's resources are devoted to wool production, more and more of the productive wheat land is taken over by this activity. Hence at relatively large amounts of wool produced, additional wool becomes more costly because more and more wheat is given up to obtain the added wool. The same is true for expanding wheat production. Trying to grow wheat in the high mountain plateaus will reduce wool output considerably but would add relatively little to wheat output. Hence wheat becomes expensive.

In this more realistic situation of increasing costs, we would expect that beyond some point it would not pay to trade.[2] For example, the United States might continue to produce a little wool domestically because the first few million bales might be produced as cheaply (in terms of wheat) as in the United Kingdom. Similarly, the United Kingdom might continue to produce some of its own wheat because of certain areas that can produce wheat very economically.

We also should consider transportation costs. In order to move the products of one nation to another additional resources are required to provide the transportation services. With increasing costs, at some point the comparative advantage might become so small that it would not be large enough to offset the added costs of transport. This would be particularly important in the case of heavy or bulky products. We don't observe much international trade in cement blocks, for example.

The absolute size of a country and the per capita income of its inhabitants also can be expected to influence the degree of specialization. As you would expect, large nations such as the United States tend to be much more diverse in terms of climate and natural resources than smaller nations. Much of the trade between states within the United States would be international trade if the country were made up of a number of smaller countries. In addition, a small nation, even if it specializes in a particular product, may not be able to satisfy the total demand of a large high-income nation. Hence the larger country may have to produce a portion of the product domestically in addition to importing in order to satisfy the total demand for it.

---

2 The production possibilities curves drawn in Chapter 1 illustrate increasing costs. If you plotted the numbers in Table 11–1, you would obtain a straight, downward sloping line as the production possibilities curve.

The extent of a nation's trade with other countries is influenced also by political and military considerations. If the government of one nation is not on speaking terms with the government of another nation, trade between the two countries is not likely. It is unfortunate that ideological differences between the political leaders of nations are allowed to determine whether or not the people of the respective countries can trade with each other. As we saw in Table 11–3, the output available to the people of both nations can be increased because of trade.

National policies aimed at achieving "self-sufficiency" are common, particularly among developing nations. The implication is that a nation is better off if it produces most of everything it consumes. As we saw in the preceding section, this will not be true if the nation has a comparative advantage in one or more products. An obvious exception, of course, is military goods. No nation wants to rely on other nations to provide the products for its war machine —another cost of war.

Private gains and losses from trade

In our previous discussion we stressed that society as a whole gains when nations tend to concentrate their production on goods and services they are comparatively good at, and trade any excess for goods that other nations can produce more cheaply (in terms of other goods given up). However, we should point out that specific individuals or groups within an economy are likely to reap economic gains from trade, and other groups are likely to suffer losses.

It is relatively easy to see how profits can be made. Suppose some enterprising American, while reading international price quotations, notices that the price of a bale of wool in the United Kingdom is equal to four bushels of wheat but that it takes eight bushels of wheat to be worth the equivalent of a bale of wool in the U.S. market. What a splendid opportunity to make an easy buck! He can buy wool in the United Kingdom, offering a bit more than the 4 to 1 ratio. After paying the transport charges, the difference, which might be the equivalent of two or three bushels of wheat for each bale of wool, would be pure profit for the importer of wool.

Of course, the same thing could be done with wheat. The import-export firm could buy wheat relatively cheaply in the United States and sell it in the United Kingdom where it is relatively expensive. Again the difference between buying and selling price, less transport charges, would be a pure profit. Indeed this kind of activity has made millionaires out of a number of people. This is not to say that such import-export activity is harmful. On the contrary, it is very beneficial. The consumers of wool in the United States can enjoy a more abundant supply at a lower price. The same thing is true for the consumers of wheat in the United Kingdom.

There are some additional beneficiaries of opening up trade. The producers of wheat in the United States are likely to enjoy an increased price for their product because of the additional demand of consumers in the United Kingdom. Similarly, wool producers in the United Kingdom are not likely to complain about the stronger demand and rising price for their product. And with these price increases, U.S. wheat producers and U.K. wool producers both will find it profitable to increase output.

If the two governments allow free trade to take place in wheat and wool, before long the relative prices of these two products will come closer together in the two countries. In other words, as more wheat comes into the United Kingdom, the price of wheat relative to wool is likely to fall, say from four bushels of wheat per bale of wool to perhaps five and a half bushels per bale. By the same token, as wool becomes more plentiful in the United States, the wheat to wool price ratio will tend to decline from, say, 8 to 1 to perhaps 6.5 to 1. However, we would not expect the relative prices to exactly equalize in the two countries because of the transportation costs of bringing wool into the United States and wheat into the United Kingdom. Thus the pure profits of exporters and importers will tend to diminish as trade increases in volume.

However, as mentioned, there are some people who lose because of international trade, at least in the short run. In terms of our example, it is likely that U.S. wool producers and U.K. wheat producers will find the prices of their products declining because of the increased supply from abroad. As a result, people who suffer economic losses from trade may attempt to persuade their respective governments to prohibit or at least limit the import of cheap products from abroad by instituting various trade barriers, mainly import quotas and tariffs. Of course, the advocates of quotas and tariffs have used numerous arguments other than self-protection to justify the existence of trade barriers. Unfortunately many of their arguments are based on questionable economic reasoning. It will be useful to briefly explain the effects of trade barriers and analyze some of the arguments used to justify such barriers.

Quotas and tariffs

As the name implies, a quota simply limits the amount of a good that can be brought into a country. A quota may be set up to exclude a good entirely or allow the import of a certain amount per year. A tariff, on the other hand, is in effect a tax on an imported good. As a result of tariffs, the prices of imported goods to domestic consumers are increased over what they would otherwise be. And, as you would expect, the higher prices discourage domestic buyers from purchasing imported articles. Thus quotas and tariffs both have the effect of reducing trade. The following are some of the more common arguments to justify trade restrictions.

1. Tariffs as a revenue source.   Governments, of course, generally are on the lookout for sources of revenue, particularly for ways to "fleece the goose with the least amount of squawking." It might seem logical, therefore, to impose a tax on foreign producers, i.e., let foreigners help pay the country's taxes. But in reality the people of the nation imposing the tariff end up paying the equivalent of the tax anyway. This occurs because the tariff has the effect of reducing the real output of the country so the people have less goods and services to consume. The general income tax (without loopholes) is a less costly method of financing government expenditure, because it tends not to distort the economy and thereby reduce real output.

2. Tariffs to equalize for low-cost foreign labor.   A common argument for tariffs in the United States is that the wages of labor in foreign countries are but a fraction of U.S. wages, and therefore foreign products can be made more cheaply and drive U.S. products off the market. A basic flaw in this argument is that it makes no mention of why U.S. workers receive higher wages. In market economies the wage of a worker is determined ultimately by his productivity. If a person is paid $30 per day, he has to produce at least $30 per day in order for his employer to pay his wages.

Workers in other nations who happen to be paid a fraction of U.S. wages find themselves in this unhappy situation because their output is so small—a fraction of the output of U.S. workers. Mainly this stems from the fact that low-paid foreign workers have a relatively small amount of capital (machines, tools, etc.) to work with. Also their skills may be lower than U.S. workers. Both of these factors explain why foreign workers, especially those in underdeveloped countries, earn such low pay. The main point is that well-paid labor does not imply high-cost products. The important factor in determining the cost of a product is the price of labor and capital in relation to their productivities. A U.S. worker may earn three times the pay of a foreign worker, but if his contribution to output is over three times that of the foreign worker, the U.S. worker is actually the cheaper of the two. Indeed as we will see in Table 11–7, the United States sells more to the developing nations, those with the lowest paid labor, than it buys from them.

Of course, it is to be expected that the low-wage countries may have a comparative advantage vis-à-vis the United States in the production of certain items, just as the United States has a comparative advantage in other items. In these situations it pays to engage in trade. As we pointed out in a previous section, both countries gain by trading.

Carried to its logical conclusion, the low-wage argument would imply also that no trade should be allowed between nations at all. As you recall, trade takes place because of comparative advantage. If tariffs are employed to offset comparative advantage, there is no incentive to trade. The effect of this is to reduce the total output available to the countries involved and to the world as a whole.

3. The "infant industry" argument. Sometimes people attempt to justify tariffs on foreign products in order to reduce competition to a newly established domestic industry. The argument is that small industries should be given protection until they can grow large enough to take advantage of economies of scale and thus produce at a lower cost some time in the future.

The problem with this argument is that an industry should not come into existence unless it can earn a rate of return on its capital that is comparable to other nonsubsidized industries.[3] If the return on its capital is lower, the economy could enjoy a larger real output by investing in other industries. For example, if the rate of return on other additional investment in the economy is 10 percent, then the rate of return on the infant industry over the long run should also be at least 10 percent. If it takes a tariff to achieve a 10 percent return, we know that the true rate of return is less than that, indicating that the economy is misinvesting its resources. If the return is relatively high, as is often implied, then it should not need a tariff to become established. The high profits in the latter years should be great enough to compensate for any losses in its early years.

4. Tariffs for retaliation. It has been argued that although tariffs and quotas on imports are undesirable, a nation often is forced to retaliate against other nations which have set up trade restrictions of their own. But it can be argued that a government which retaliates by increasing its tariffs really does not have the economic well-being of its people in mind. For the imposition of a tariff by a nation reduces the products coming into that country, thereby reducing the total amount of goods and services available to its people. The fact that one government chooses to reduce the economic well-being of its people is not a good reason for another government to follow suit. Retaliatory tariffs are analogous to two governments trying to best each other, each saying, "I can deprive my people of more things than you can deprive yours of."

5. "Buy American." Quite frequently we see bumper stickers or advertisements urging us to buy American-made products. Apparently the objective is to keep foreign products out while providing employment for U.S. workers. However, it is necessary to keep in mind that thousands of U.S. workers are employed in industries producing for foreign markets. Unless we buy from other countries, they cannot buy from us. Without trade, some of the workers in export industries would have to find jobs in other industries. So it is not clear that workers in these other industries end up any better off in the long run.

The "buy American" slogan also is used as an argument for

---

[3] A possible exception to this rule occurs when the industry in question results in external effects on other industries, i.e., lowers their production costs.

keeping American dollars at home. Yet, as we pointed out in Chapter 5, money is just a convenient tool for exchanging goods and services. The important things are the real goods and services that are available to society, not the number of pieces of paper called money that it has. The amount of money in a society can be increased simply by the government's cranking up the printing presses.[4]

In our discussion so far we still haven't presented a convincing argument for tariffs and quotas. But we cannot deny that they are extremely popular throughout the world. Thus, there must be some reason for having them. To be perfectly honest, tariffs and quotas can result in a short-term gain for specific industries. In our wheat and wool example, the entrance of foreign wool in the United States or foreign wheat in the United Kingdom probably would have reduced the price of wool in the United States and the price of wheat in the United Kingdom, or at least kept prices lower than they would otherwise be. By placing tariffs or quotas on these products and reducing imports, U.S. wool producers and U.K. wheat producers probably would enjoy higher prices.

Thus, when advocating trade restrictions, industry spokesmen should, to be honest, admit that tariffs or quotas will help them by keeping the prices of their products higher than they would otherwise be. Efforts to increase tariffs or lower quotas often increase during downturns in economic activity, as we have observed in the late 1960s and early 1970s. The object is to keep out foreign products so as to maintain higher domestic prices. The problem, of course, with being honest about trade restrictions, at least in a democracy, is that the public may not be as willing to grant special favors to specific industries if they realize that these special favors work to the detriment of the rest of society. Thus numerous excuses or rationalizations are thought up, such as those we have just discussed, to justify trade barriers.

It should be stressed also that trade restrictions are likely to provide only short-term benefits to the industries that they are designed to help. In the long run, many of the people in the protected industries probably would have been better off to leave and enter

---

4 Keep in mind, though, that large fluctuations in the quantity of money can have important effects on the real output of an economy.

industries in which the nation has a greater comparative advantage. By doing so their incomes might be increased even more because of their greater productivity in other lines of work. Tariffs and quotas often serve to delay adjustments that eventually come about in the long run.

A more subtle, but economically justifiable, argument for a trade barrier on a particular item can be made if a country either buys or sells a large share of the world's production of the commodity in question. The underlying economic rationale for the argument is presented in more advanced international trade courses, but a brief intuitive explanation will be helpful here.

Consider first a nation that sells a relatively large share of the world's output of an item, such as Brazil in the case of coffee. By restricting exports, Brazil is able to significantly decrease the quantity of coffee exchanged on the world market and therefore drive up the price it receives for coffee. As a result Brazil as a country is able to enjoy higher total profits from its export trade.[5] Keep in mind that this is a case of placing a barrier on exports rather than on imports. Most of our previous discussion centered on the latter.

A case can be made for taxing or placing a quota on an import if the nation buys a substantial share of the world's output of the item. In this case the resulting decrease in the quantity imported depresses the world price and as a result the price paid for the item by the importing country will be lower than if free trade were allowed.[6] However, in order for such a situation to arise the country in question must consume a substantial portion of the world's consumption of the product. Since consumption patterns of nations tend to be less diverse than production patterns, it is extremely difficult to find examples where a single importer can have a significant impact on the world consumption of a product. Cer-

---

[5] For those who have had microeconomics, the objective is to equate marginal cost with marginal revenue, analogous to the behavior of an imperfectly competitive firm on the selling side (see Chapter 8 of the companion micro book). If free export is allowed by a number of firms, price and quantity will correspond to the intersection of marginal cost (supply) and demand facing the country. Profits will be increased by restricting exports to the point of intersection between marginal cost and marginal revenue.

[6] In this case, the objective is to purchase the quantity corresponding to the intersection between marginal resource cost and demand, as in the case of a monopsonist (see Chapter 9 of the micro text). If free trade is allowed, the quantity imported will correspond to the intersection of supply and demand.

tainly this argument could not be used to justify the major portion of import trade barriers that nations have set up.

We should caution, too, that in the cases of these justifiable export or import barriers, the benefit will extend only so far. By placing the barrier too high, the nation can be made worse off than it would have been with no barrier at all. It should also be kept in mind that the barriers just discussed are justifiable only from the standpoint of the country in question. Those nations that must pay a higher price for products they buy or receive a lower price for products they sell do not, of course, benefit from such barriers.

Dumping

Occasionally a nation will try to sell more of its products abroad by setting the export price lower than its domestic price, with the government reimbursing producers for the difference. This practice has come to be known as "dumping," and has been associated in the 1950s and 1960s with agricultural products produced by the United States and some of the other more highly developed nations. In their attempt to support prices of a number of agricultural products, the governments of these nations have been forced to buy the resulting surplus.[7] Then in an attempt to dispose of the surplus, the government sells it abroad at a reduced price or gives it away, usually to developing nations. The United States P.L. 480 program is a good example.

At first glance it might appear that such a practice works to the advantage of all concerned. Consumers of the developing countries receive free or low-priced food, which in many cases has helped them avoid starvation or at least severe malnutrition. And the governments of the developed nations have been able to put the surplus to good use. But there have been a couple of undesirable side effects. First, producers of comparable products in other exporting nations suffer a reduction in the demand and price for their products. For example, Canadian wheat producers do not

---

[7] A surplus results because market price is maintained higher than equilibrium price. This is just the opposite of the problem of shortages caused by price controls. For additional discussion, see Chapter 6 of the micro book.

greet reduced-price wheat sales by the United States with much enthusiasm.

A second problem, and perhaps even more important, is that producers in the recipient nations face a depressed market for their output because of the free or cheap products coming in under such programs. This in turn tends to retard the development of domestic agriculture in the recipient nations. We will consider this problem more fully in the next chapter.

One might argue, of course, that our immediate concern has to be with keeping people alive rather than with promoting a profitable agriculture in the developing nations. True. But we could do both by giving the people of these nations dollars or other currencies which they could use to purchase needed food in their domestic or world market.

The existence of unwanted surpluses in the developed nations undoubtedly has provided a strong incentive to give away or sell these products at reduced prices. Thus it is likely that farm income support programs in the developed nations would first have to be changed in order to avoid the problems mentioned above. One alternative would be to support farm incomes under a general negative income tax scheme rather than by supporting the level of farm prices. In addition to solving the surplus problem, government payments to individual farmers would be negatively correlated with income rather than positively correlated as they have been under past programs.

United States trade

It will be of some value to look briefly at the magnitude and characteristics of U.S. trade with other nations. The figures in Table 11–4 provide an indication of the magnitude of U.S. exports and imports. In most years since the Great Depression, the United States has exported a larger value of merchandise to other countries than it has bought from them. However, this pattern changed significantly in 1972, when U.S. imports exceeded exports by over $6 billion (1972 prices).

Also noticeable is the small quantity of imports relative to GNP. Most Americans, it appears, do "buy American." In fact, U.S. citi-

TABLE 11–4
U.S. exports and imports of merchandise, selected years, 1969 prices

Year	Exports (millions)	Imports (millions)	Imports as a percent of GNP
1930	$ 8,616	$ 6,807	3.4%
1940	10,852	6,915	2.7
1950	15,422	13,884	3.2
1960	24,147	18,270	2.9
1970	40,270	37,714	4.2

Source: *Statistical Abstract, 1969,* p. 783, and *Economic Report of the President, 1973,* p. 295.

zens consume a small share of their total goods and services in the form of imported items compared to most other nations of the world. We should not conclude from these figures, however, that Americans are more isolationist or distrustful of foreign goods than other people. For it is necessary to bear in mind that the United States is a large and diverse nation compared to most other countries. A good deal of the trade that takes place between regions or states in the United States would be considered international trade in other countries. It is worthwhile to notice, however, that the share of imports in GNP increased somewhat during the early 1970s.

Table 11–5 provides a little information on the major items traded by the United States. Notice in particular that manufactured items, including chemicals, machinery, and other manufactured goods, make up over two thirds of all U.S. exports. These general categories also make up the largest share of imports, although a somewhat smaller percentage.

TABLE 11–5
United States exports and imports, 1971 (millions)

	Exports	Imports
Food and live animals	$ 4,365	$ 5,531
Beverages and tobacco	710	875
Crude materials, inedible, except fuels	4,326	3,385
Mineral fuels and related materials	1,497	3,715
Animal and vegetable fats	615	172
Chemicals	3,837	1,612
Machinery and transport equipment	19,465	13,904
Other manufactured goods	7,147	14,932
Other transactions	1,535	1,476
Total	$43,497	$45,602

Source: *Statistical Abstract, 1972,* pp. 782–83.

It is possible to observe, of course, the same type of item being exported and imported, although not necessarily to or from the same country. For example, the United States may sell electric generating equipment to India and buy similar equipment from West Germany. It all depends on the preferences of buyers in the various importing countries. Also we should recognize that the large general categories in Table 11–5 include a great many diverse items, many of which are found only in exports and not in imports, and vice versa. Thus, we cannot use these aggregative figures to infer anything about the comparative advantage of the United States over other countries.

The figures in Table 11–6 tell us something about who the major

TABLE 11–6
United States trade statistics by continent and nation groups, 1971 (millions)

	Exports to—	*Imports from—*
Africa	$ 1,694	$ 1,237
Asia	9,850	11,783
Australia and Oceania	1,169	895
Europe	14,574	12,846
North America	13,557	15,790
South America	3,293	3,011
Communist nations, or areas	384	229
Developed nations	30,347	33,781
Developing nations	13,405	11,552

Source: *Statistical Abstract, 1972*, p. 778.

trading partners of the United States are. As we might expect, there is not as much trade with the developing nations as with the more highly developed, industrialized economies. Also note that U.S. exports to the developing nations are larger than imports from these nations. The opposite is true for the developed nations. It is interesting to note, too, that the United States buys somewhat   less from communist nations than it sells to them, although both figures are tiny compared to the totals.

A simple but often forgotten point is that from the standpoint of the entire world, exports must always equal imports during any given period of time. A dollar of exports by one nation must always be a dollar of imports to another, just as a sale by one person is always a purchase by someone else. Of course, for an individual nation exports need not equal imports during any given year.

A country is said to have a "favorable" balance of trade if it sells more than it buys from other countries, i.e., if exports exceed imports. It is perhaps unfortunate that this term came into such general use because it does not have much, if any, economic justification. As mentioned in Chapter 3, the error of this thinking is made clear by considering the limiting case where a nation sells everything it produces to other countries but buys nothing in return, leaving exactly zero goods and services for the people to consume— not a very "favorable" situation by most definitions of the word. Somehow people have fallen into the habit of thinking that foreign currencies, or gold, are more desirable than real goods and services.

Balance of trade versus balance of payments

In discussing international trade and finance, it is necessary to distinguish between a nation's balance of trade and its balance of payments. In the narrowest sense, the balance of trade can be thought of simply as the difference between exports and imports of merchandise. Of course, as shown in the lower part of Table 11–7,

TABLE 11–7
U.S. Balance of trade and balance of payments, 1972 (billions of dollars)

Exports of merchandise	+48.8	
Imports of merchandise	−55.6	
Balance of trade		−6.8
Income from investments abroad	+13.8	
Other income	+ 1.1	
U.S. private capital flow (net)	+ .1	
Income of foreign investments in U.S.	− 5.9	
Military expenditures (net)	− 3.5	
Travel and transportation (net)	− 2.5	
U.S. government grants	− 2.2	
U.S. government capital flow	− 1.7	
Remittances, pensions, and transfers	− 1.6	
Net		−2.4
Balance of payments		−9.2

Source: *Federal Reserve Bulletin,* April 1973, p. A72.

international trade also includes the purchase and sale of services. For example, during 1972, U.S. citizens spent $2.5 billion (net) in other countries on travel and transportation.

In addition to the purchase and sale of services, a number of other items contributed to the inflow and outflow of dollars. Perhaps most notable is the $13.8 billion income to U.S. citizens from investments in foreign countries. In part this was offset by the $5.9 billion income of foreign investments in the United States. In total, the outflow of dollars more than offset the inflow, giving rise to a $9.2 billion balance of payments deficit in 1972.

During much of the 1960s, the United States experienced balance of trade surpluses (exports exceeded imports) but balance of payments deficits. This occurred in large part because of the outflow of dollars from military expenditures abroad, foreign travel by U.S. citizens, and the purchase of plant and equipment by U.S. firms in foreign countries. In other words, the negative values at the bottom of the table more than offset the positive values plus the positive trade balance. In 1972, the negative values still offset the positive values in the lower part of the table by $2.4 billion. Moreover, the negative $6.8 billion merchandise trade balance added to the deficit, giving the relatively large balance of payments deficit of $9.2 billion in 1972.

Exchange rates

At this point you might ask, How do firms doing business abroad pay or receive payment for the items they buy and sell? An American seller of wheat, for example, would not want to be paid in English pounds because this money would be of little use in the United States. Conversely, sellers of wool in the United Kingdom need to be paid in pounds. This little problem is taken care of quite nicely by the financial institutions in the respective countries who are authorized by their governments to do business abroad. Some of the large New York banks have checking accounts in the larger London banks, and vice versa. Thus an English exporter of wool, for example, upon receiving a check from an American import firm drawn on a New York bank, presents this check at a London bank and receives payment in pounds. Ultimately the account of the U.S. import firm in its New York bank is decreased when the check is returned to the United States.

We must recognize, of course, that American dollars are not exchanged on a one-for-one basis with English pounds or other currencies. The currency of each nation has either an official or market exchange rate, or both, with the currencies of all other nations. For example, suppose one English pound is exchanged for $2.40 in American dollars. If a New York bank deposits $24,000 American dollars (in check or currency) in a London bank, the account of the New York bank in London is increased by 10,000 pounds.

The exchange rate, then, is simply the number of units of one currency that it takes to buy a unit of another currency. For example, if the rate of exchange between the West German mark and U.S. dollar is three to one, it takes three marks to purchase a dollar, or 33⅓ cents to purchase a mark. Or we could say that the exchange rate is the price of one currency in terms of another currency. For each nation's currency, there exists an exchange rate between it and the currencies of other countries.[8]

In order to fully appreciate the role of exchange rates in international trade, it will be necessary to study in somewhat more detail the import and export markets for internationally traded goods and services. After gaining an understanding of these markets, we will be in a better position to understand how exchange rates are determined and why they change.

Import and export markets for goods and services

Recall from Chapter 1 that in each market there is a demand for a good or service and a supply of that good or service. Also recall that we represented demand by a downward sloping line, indicating that people buy more when price declines (other things being equal). Similarly supply was represented by an upward sloping line, which implies that producers place larger quantities on the market at progressively higher prices.

It will be easier to understand international markets if we utilize specific examples. As the two countries, let us consider the United States and West Germany. Also let us consider two products: U.S.-produced feed grains exported to West Germany, and West Ger-

---

[8] For quotations of recent exchange rates see the *Federal Reserve Bulletin,* published monthly by the Federal Reserve System.

man-produced Volkswagens imported into the United States. Thus we will be dealing with two markets in the United States, one from the standpoint of U.S. importers of Volkswagens, the other from the standpoint of U.S. exporters of feed grains. Both the import price of Volkswagens and the export price of feedgrains are quoted in terms of dollars. The markets are illustrated by Figure 11–1.

FIGURE 11–1
Markets for imports and exports in the United States

(A) Import market for Volkswagens *(B) Export market for feed grains*

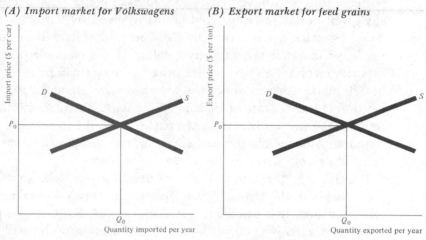

At first glance, the import and export markets appear no different from domestic markets discussed in Chapter 1. Both demand curves are downward sloping, indicating that U.S. consumers buy more Volkswagens when their dollar price declines and that German farmers buy more U.S. feed grains when the price they pay declines. Similarly, both supply curves are upward sloping, indicating that at higher prices more Volkswagens will be supplied to the United States and more feed grains to Germany. And each market has an equilibrium price and quantity, as shown on the diagrams.

However, the markets for internationally traded items are not quite as simple as domestic markets. The complication enters because of the need to consider the price of each currency in terms of the other, i.e., the exchange rate. First it is necessary to call to mind that in order to purchase U.S. feed grains, German buyers must first buy dollars in order to pay the U.S. exporter. Similarly, the U.S. importer of Volkswagens must purchase marks to pay for Volkswagens. And, as you might expect, the price that each has to pay for the other country's currency will have a bearing on the final price paid for the product.

An example might help here. Suppose a German importer wishes to buy 1,000 U.S. dollars in order to buy U.S. feed grains. If the exchange rate is four marks per dollar, the $1,000 will cost 4,000 marks. But if the exchange rate were 3:1, the German importer would only have to pay 3,000 marks for the $1,000. Thus at any given dollar price for feed grains received by U.S. exporters, the mark price per ton paid by German importers will be lower, the fewer marks it takes to buy a dollar. If, for example, the U.S. exporter receives $80 per ton, the price to the German importer will be 320 marks per ton under the 4:1 exchange rate and 240 marks per ton with a 3:1 rate of exchange. In a sense, there are two transactions: the first to buy the currency, the second to buy the merchandise. And the cheaper the currency, the cheaper the merchandise for a given merchandise price.

We could go through a similar exercise for the Volkswagen import market in the United States. In order to buy Volkswagens the importer must first buy marks. If, for example, the German price of a Volkswagen is 8,000 marks, the Volkswagen importer will have to pay $2,000 for the necessary German currency if the exchange rate is 4:1, and $2,667 under the 3:1 rate. In this case, the reduction in the price of the dollar (increase in the price of the mark) increases the number of dollars required to purchase a Volkswagen for a given Volkswagen price in the United States because the German currency has become more expensive.

As you might expect, then, a change in the currency price affects the markets for internationally traded goods and services because it affects the prices in these markets. This is illustrated in Figure 11–2. The original demand and supply curves are drawn for a given rate of exchange between dollars and marks, say four marks per dollar. If the rate of exchange should change to three marks per dollar, both markets will be affected.

Looking first at diagram (A), a decrease in the price of dollars relative to marks has the effect of decreasing the supply of Volkswagens for U.S. consumers, i.e., shifting the supply of Volkswagens to the left. In effect this means that U.S. consumers now must pay a

FIGURE 11–2
Effect on U.S. import and export markets of a decrease in the price of U.S. dollars relative to German marks

(A) Import market for Volkswagens   *(B) Export market for feed grains*

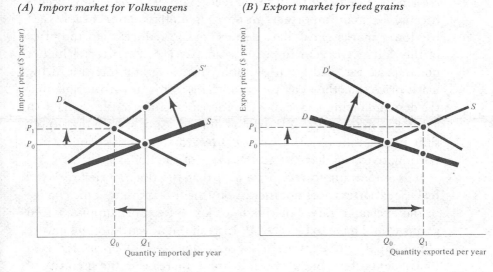

higher dollar price for any given quantity of Volkswagens imported. This occurs because the number of dollars required to buy the necessary number of German marks for a Volkswagen has increased. It turns out that the vertical shift in the supply curve is proportionate to the increase in the price of the mark. Hence in this example, supply curve S' would be higher than S by one third of the distance between the horizontal axis and S.

It is important to note, however, that the dollar price of Volkswagens in the United States has not increased by the amount the mark has increased in price. This would occur only if the demand for Volkswagens were a vertical line. Since this demand is downward sloping and likely to be relatively flat, the price of Volkswagens in the United States will increase a relatively small amount compared to the change in the exchange rate.[9] Notice, too, that the quantity of Volkswagens demanded in the United States decreases a relatively large amount because of the supply shift.

---

[9] Because domestically produced goods and services and items imported from other countries are substitutes for the imports of any one country, the demand for these imports is likely to be relatively price-responsive. See Chapter 3 of the companion micro book for further discussion on this topic.

Turning next to diagram (B) of Figure 11–2, we see that the decrease in the price of the dollar in Germany has the effect of increasing the demand facing U.S. feed grain exporters. This occurs because German importers can purchase dollars more cheaply, i.e., pay fewer marks per dollar. Because of the reduction in the price of the dollar, German importers can pay U.S. exporters a higher dollar price for feed grains without incurring any increase in the mark price that they pay for feed grains. This in turn means that the demand facing U.S. exporters increases (shifts to the right) with a decrease in the price of the dollar abroad. And, as with the supply shift in diagram (A), the vertical upward shift in demand is proportionate to the decrease in the price of the dollar.[10]

It is important to recognize also that the dollar price received by U.S. exporters does not increase by the full amount of the change in the exchange rate. For this to occur, the export supply of feed grains would have to be vertical. Instead the upward sloping nature of this supply curve gives rise to some increase in the price received by U.S. exporters, but also results in an increase in the quantity of feed grains exported.

To summarize this section thus far, a decrease in the price of the dollar relative to other currencies has the effect of reducing the supply of imported goods while increasing the demand for export commodities for the United States. Although we can expect some increase in the prices paid for imports and prices received for exports, these prices are not likely to change by the full amount of the currency price change because of the downward sloping demand for imports and the upward sloping supply of exports.

It would, of course, be possible to consider the same example from the standpoint of West Germany. Volkswagens become the export good, while feed grains are imported. Because the price of the mark has increased relative to the dollar (in this example), the shifts in West German import supply and export demand will be just the opposite of the U.S. case. In other words the import supply of feed grains from the United States shifts to the right (increases) while the export demand for Volkswagens shifts to the left (decreases) when the mark increases in value. It will be useful to con-

---

10 This material is fairly difficult to grasp, so it takes a bit of thinking.

struct diagrams similar to Figure 11–2, but now for West Germany, showing the effect of an increase in the value of the mark on the import market for feed grains and the export market for Volkswagens.

Consideration of both the U.S. and German international markets helps to make another important point: when the currency of a nation appreciates in value (the German mark in this example), export industries are harmed because of the decrease in the demand for their product abroad. On the other hand, import industries gain because of the increase in the supply of imports from abroad. The opposite holds true when a nation's currency depreciates in value (the U.S. dollar in our example). Now export industries enjoy an increase in demand for their products, while import industries face a decrease in supply of products from abroad and somewhat higher prices. This situation was illustrated by our Volkswagen and feed grain example (Figure 11–2).

Foreign exchange markets

Since an exchange rate can be defined as the price of one currency in terms of another, it is reasonable to believe that currency prices are determined in foreign exchange markets, similar to the way goods and service prices are determined in goods and service markets. Moreover, we can identify both a demand for and supply of currencies. In terms of our previous example, there would be a demand for U.S. dollars in West Germany in order to pay for the feed grains imported from the United States. Similarly there would be a supply of dollars in West Germany coming from the purchase of Volkswagens by U.S. consumers.

The demand for and supply of U.S. dollars in West Germany is illustrated by Figure 11–3. The price of U.S. dollars is quoted in terms of marks per dollar. The more marks per dollar, the higher the price of dollars, and vice versa. The quantity axis shows the number of dollars exchanged per year. Notice too that the demand for dollars is represented by a downward sloping line, indicating that more dollars will be demanded as the price of dollars declines. The supply of dollars is represented by an upward sloping line, indicating that the number of dollars supplied will increase as the price of dollars increases. Also there is an equilibrium price and quantity, corresponding to the intersection of these two curves.

FIGURE 11–3
Demand for and supply of dollars in West Germany

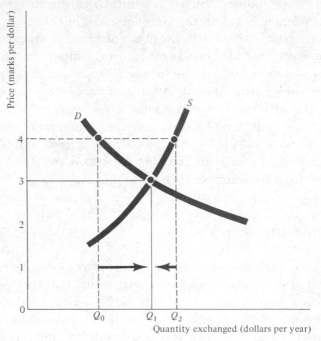

In order to understand the reason for the downward sloping demand for dollars and the upward sloping supply of dollars in Figure 11–3, we must go back to Figure 11–2. Recall that a reduction in the price of dollars from a 4:1 to a 3:1 ratio had the effect of increasing the export demand for feed grains and decreasing the the import supply of Volkswagens. The increase in the demand for U.S. feed grains resulted in a slightly higher dollar price of feed grains and a larger quantity of feed grains exported as the price of dollars declined. The result of this is that the total number of dollars demanded by German importers increased after the dollar price decline. In other words, in Figure 11–2, $P_1 \times Q_1$ is greater than $P_0 \times Q_0$, giving rise to a greater quantity of dollars demanded after the dollar price decline.

On the other hand, the decrease in the import supply of Volkswagens (Figure 11–2) resulting from the decrease in the price of dollars has the effect of reducing the quantity of Volkswagens imported but increasing their price slightly. In this example, the quantity of Volkswagens decreases relatively more than their price increases, so the total quantity of dollars supplied decreases as the result of the dollar price decline. In other words, in Figure 11–2, $P_1 \times Q_0$ is less than $P_0 \times Q_1$, giving rise to a smaller quantity of dollars supplied after the dollar price decline. Whether the nature of the demand for imported goods and services is such that fewer dollars are supplied as the price of dollars declines is an empirical question. The evidence seems to support the hypothesis that the import demand curves of most important commodities are of this nature.[11]

In the example depicted by Figure 11–3, the so-called equilibrium price of dollars is three marks per dollar. At the higher four-mark price, a greater quantity of dollars will be supplied per year than is demanded. As long as this price prevails, there will be a continual buildup of dollars held by German individuals, firms, or institutions. The resulting situation will be a surplus of dollars and continued downward pressure on the price of the dollar, similar to what happens in other markets when a surplus exists. As the price declines, changes occur in the import and export markets (Figure 11–2) which bring the quantity of dollars demanded closer to the quantity supplied.

We should be aware that shifts in the import demand or export supply can occur for reasons other than changes in the exchange rate. For example, inflation in the importing country can increase the import demand for products from abroad. Other things being equal, this will increase the supply of the nation's currency in the foreign exchange market, which in turn can result in a decrease in the equilibrium price of the currency. Thus it is well to keep in mind that changes in the exchange rate affect the import and export markets, and autonomous changes in the import or export markets in turn affect the foreign exchange market.

It is also necessary to bear in mind that the supply of dollars to

---

[11] Of course, it is not imperative that the supply of dollars slope upward. An equilibrium can be reached in the currency market even if the supply curve slopes downward, as long as the supply curve is steeper than the demand curve.

foreign currency markets depends not only on merchandise imports into the United States but also on such things as expenditure by U.S. firms for plant and equipment in other countries, expenditures by U.S. tourists, and U.S. military spending abroad. As mentioned in the section on balance of payments, the United States experienced a balance of trade surplus during much of the post–World War II period, but a balance of payments deficit for many of these years.

The post–World War II international monetary system

In the previous section we presented the process of adjustment that would occur should the actual exchange rate between two currencies be different than its equilibrium value. And in so doing we essentially showed how market rates of exchange are determined. However, it is necessary to qualify the preceding discussion by pointing out that during the major part of the post–World War II period, the exchange rates between the currencies of the major trading nations have been for the most part set by government decree rather than by freely functioning foreign exchange markets. A bit of background will be useful at this point.

In an effort to promote confidence and stability in the international monetary system in the upcoming post–World War II period, a conference of allied nations was held at Bretton Woods, New Hampshire in 1944. As an outgrowth of this conference, an international organization known as the International Monetary Fund (IMF) was established. Among other things, each member nation of the IMF agreed to maintain specified rates of exchange between its currency and all other currencies. This was to be accomplished by buying or selling its own currency in the foreign exchange market whenever the exchange rate deviated from the "parity rate" by 1 percent, or by making its currency convertible into gold or other reserve assets at the request of another member nation or official institution. As it turned out, countries other than the United States maintained or attempted to maintain the official exchange rate by buying or selling their currencies for dollars, while the United States attempted to maintain a parity between the dollar and gold or other reserve assets tied to gold by offering to sell gold to qualified buyers at a fixed $35 per ounce price. (We will discuss the role of gold and the problem of maintaining adequate reserves shortly.)

The IMF permitted member nations to alter the prices of their currencies in terms of gold (and other currencies) should they encounter a prolonged period of balance of payments disequilibrium. If a nation were running persistent balance of payments deficits, it would be likely to devalue its currency. More specifically, devaluation means that the nation increases the price of gold vis-à-vis its currency. For example, the United States devalued the dollar in 1971 by changing the price of gold from $35 to $38 per ounce, and again in 1973 by increasing the gold price to $42.22 per ounce. Another way of looking at devaluation is that it has the effect of decreasing the price of the currency vis-à-vis gold. If other currencies stay tied to gold, it reduces the price of the currency in question relative to other currencies. Recall that this is exactly the same situation we discussed in reference to Figures 11–2 and 11–3. This devaluation has the effect of reducing the supply of imports to a nation while increasing the demand for its exports. And this in turn increases the quantity demanded of the currency in the foreign exchange market while decreasing the quantity supplied, to bring the balance of payments closer to equilibrium.

Occasionally a nation revalues its currency upward against gold and other currencies, as West Germany, Japan, and a few other nations did in 1971.[12] This has an effect opposite to that of devaluation, in that it decreases the demand for the country's exports and increases the supply of its imported goods.

In practice, member nations of the IMF have adjusted the value of their currencies rather infrequently. Indeed the United States held to the $35 per ounce gold price from 1934 to August 1971. The maintenance of a rather inflexible system of exchange rates during the post–World War II period gave rise to a growing balance of payments deficits for the United States, shrinking U.S. gold reserves (from $23 billion in 1952 to $10 billion in 1972) and leaving an increasing number of U.S. dollars in foreign hands. During the

---

[12] In addition to West Germany and Japan, Switzerland, Austria, Belgium, and The Netherlands revalued their currencies upward against gold in 1971.

1960s it became increasingly apparent that a realignment of currency values against each other and against gold was the only permanent solution to the disequilibrium in the international money markets. Clearly the dollar was overpriced vis-à-vis gold and other currencies. Finally, in August 1971, the United States stopped the sale of gold for $35 per ounce and called for a meeting of IMF nations. As a result of this meeting, the dollar price of gold was increased to $38 per ounce. The currencies of the other major trading nations also were appreciated in value relative to the dollar and relative to gold.[13] The realignment of currencies in the 1971 meeting has come to be known as the Smithsonian Agreement.

It was soon evident, however, that the currency and gold price realignment coming out of the Smithsonian Agreement did not bring the IMF parity prices in line with equilibrium prices of currencies in the foreign exchange markets. Indeed the United States experienced an even larger balance of payments deficit in 1972 than in 1971. This culminated in yet another devaluation of the dollar in 1973, from $38 to $42.22 per ounce of gold.

But the second devaluation of the dollar still did not appear to bring the dollar price down to the foreign exchange market equilibrium. The disequilibrium seemed to be widest in the case of the dollar versus the West German mark and the Japanese yen. Even after the second devaluation, the governments of these countries were forced to buy billions of dollars in order to support the mark and yen price of the dollar. And each time the United States devalued the dollar, these governments (really, their taxpayers) lost large sums of money. For example, suppose the German government purchased one billion U.S. dollars at four marks per dollar in order to keep the price of the dollar from falling below this level. Let us say that after the devaluation of the dollar, the parity ratio became 3.6 marks per dollar. Now the people who sold the one billion dollars to the German government had the option of buying them back for 3.6 billion marks. If they did, the outcome was that the German government was left with 400 million fewer marks in its treasury after the U.S. devaluation than before it. The 400 million marks then represented a profit to speculators at the expense of German taxpayers.

---

[13] There were two exceptions. The Italian lira and Swedish krona each declined 1 percent relative to gold.

Needless to say, any government can be expected to soon grow weary of losing money of this magnitude just to support the price of another nation's currency. Hence it wasn't long after the 1973 dollar devaluation that most of the major trading nations of the world floated their currencies vis-à-vis the dollar, i.e., allowed the dollar to find its own level on the foreign exchange markets of the world. Although the 1973 float technically was a violation of the IMF rules, it had been done before. Canada, for example, had allowed the Canadian dollar to float for extended periods during the 1950s and 1960s, and Britain had already floated the pound in mid-1972.

The U.S. dollar, of course, was not always overvalued. Indeed during the time of the so-called dollar crises in Europe and Japan that we have just discussed, the dollar in some countries was undervalued by the official rate of exchange. This was true in many of the developing countries (especially those experiencing high rates of inflation), the Soviet Union, and its Eastern European satellites. For example, in the early 1970s the official exchange rate between rubles and dollars in the Soviet Union was roughly one for one. However, if one knew the right people in Vienna or Moscow, one could obtain about five rubles to the dollar.[14] Thus the official price of the dollar was set substantially below the price that would have prevailed in a freely functioning foreign exchange market.

The practice of maintaining an artificially low price of foreign currencies can be expected to result in a black market in currencies. For example, it is easy to see how much more a dollar will buy in the Soviet Union if you can obtain five rubles per dollar on the black market as opposed to the one for one official rate of exchange. By the same token, Soviet citizens have an incentive to buy these high-priced dollars if they can buy goods on their black market with the dollars that they couldn't buy with rubles.

Fixed versus floating exchange rates

The problems brought on by attempting to maintain official exchange rates different from the equilibrium rates established by

---

[14] This is not meant to encourage such transactions, particularly in the Soviet Union. The penalty for getting caught can be rather harsh.

freely functioning foreign exchange markets has prompted many economists to argue for a system of floating exchange rates. As mentioned, under such a system, the price of each currency in terms of other currencies would be allowed to find its own level in foreign exchange markets. Moreover the price of each currency would be allowed to change in response to changes in the demand and supply of the currency in question.

Yet there has been considerable reluctance to turn exchange rates loose. Those who favor a system of relatively fixed rates believe that such a system is more conducive to stability in the international markets than floating rates. As explained previously, a change in the price of a currency causes shifts in the demand and supply for imports and exports. It is argued that these shifts can be disruptive to an economy, especially if foreign trade accounts for a large share of its total economic activity.

In response to this argument, proponents of floating rates grant that a float initially causes shifts in trade patterns if the pegged rates are different from the free market equilibrium rates. However, this is mainly an adjustment that must take place in order to get the international monetary system's house in order. If rates had not been fixed, this adjustment would have taken place gradually over time. Once the currency exchange market prices approach equilibrium, changes will come mainly in response to changes in the demand and supply conditions of internationally traded goods and services. If the economies of these nations follow an unstable boom and bust pattern, the exchange markets also will follow a similar pattern. But this would not be due to an inherent instability in the foreign exchange markets.

A proposal known as a "crawling peg" has been suggested as something of a compromise between the Bretton Woods setup and a system of floating rates. Under such a system, exchange rates would be allowed to move a specified amount towards the equilibrium rate during a specified period of time. This system would be similar to floating rates in that market pressure would bring change in the right direction, the difference being that the adjustment period would extend over a longer span of time. The crawling peg would seem to be a reasonable compromise between the fixed and floating systems. Proponents of the fixed-rate system would not have to fear wild fluctuations in the exchange rate, while "free floaters" should welcome it as a step in the right direction.

Gold—The international money

Gold long has been used as an international money to settle accounts between nations. Perhaps the easiest way to see how gold is used is to consider a simple example. Suppose during a given year U.S. citizens purchase $900 million worth of goods and services from West Germany, while Germany buys $700 million from the United States. When the books are balanced at the end of the year, financial institutions in West Germany find they have $200 million more U.S. dollars at the end of the year than at the beginning. It is possible that these financial institutions will decide to hold these extra dollars as added U.S. dollar reserves. However, if the dollar reserves are deemed adequate or excessive, the German central bank may decide to exchange these dollars for gold.

Under the rules of the IMF, member nations were obliged to sell gold at the specified price. And this is what the United States actually did during much of the 1950s and 1960s. Foreign nations accumulated dollars because of the U.S. balance of payments deficits and proceeded to exchange many of these excess dollars for gold. Moreover, the more certain that foreign dollar holders became that the United States would have to devalue the dollar sometime in the near future, the more incentive they had to exchange dollars for gold. For example, by exchanging $35,000 at the $35 per ounce price, a foreign bank or firm received 1,000 ounces of gold. Exchanging the same $35,000 after the price of gold increased to $38 reduced the gold received to 921 ounces. Thus if one wanted to exchange surplus dollars for gold, it clearly was better to do it before devaluation than after. As the run on gold continued into the 1970s, the United States government suspended the convertibility of the dollar into gold in August of 1971.

We would also point out that the U.S. dollar (and to a lesser extent the pound sterling) has been used to supplement gold as an international reserve asset. In fact from the beginning of 1970 to October 1972, total international reserves increased from $78 billion to $152 billion, or almost 100 percent in less than three years, with most of the increase coming from U.S. dollars. During this period, the proportion of gold in international reserves decreased from 50 percent to 26 percent, while foreign exchange (mainly U.S. dollars) increased from 41 percent to 64 percent.

Because of the substantial increase in world trade since the end of World War II, the demand for international reserves also has increased. The supply of gold, on the other hand, grew to a much smaller extent during this time. Thus the market equilibrium price of gold increased accordingly, breaking the $100 per ounce level in the European gold market in 1973. At that time the official price of gold was $42.22 per ounce. Because the official price of gold was held substantially below the free market price in terms of dollars, a "shortage" of gold developed, i.e., a greater quantity of gold was demanded than was supplied, at least in reference to dollars.

It has been pointed out that the world gold "shortage" could be eliminated simply by freeing the official price of gold, allowing it to come into balance with the market equilibrium price, i.e., allowing quantity demanded to come into balance with quantity supplied. However, international monetary authorities also have shown a great deal of reluctance to set gold prices free. In part, this may be due to a reluctance to bestow capital gains on gold speculators and nations holding large gold reserves, such as the Soviet Union. But the usual argument against freeing the price of gold relates to stability. The concern is that a freely functioning gold market, where the price of gold changes in response to changes in demand and supply conditions, would introduce an added element of instability into international trade. Whether this kind of instability is worse than the instability resulting from infrequent government devaluations caused by extreme market pressures is an open question. At any rate, the IMF has decided to reduce the role played by gold in international finance. This brings us to the creation of a new international money.

Special drawing rights (SDRs)

In an attempt to "demonetize" gold, the IMF created in 1968 a new international money called special drawing rights (SDRs), sometimes called "paper gold." These SDRs were created to take the place of gold or other reserve currencies (mainly the U.S. dollar) in settling accounts between nations. The motive here was to create a true international currency that would be free from the influences of private supply and demand fluctuations (as gold), and from changes in domestic monetary policies (as the dollar or pound sterling).

Whether SDRs will eventually replace gold and other reserve currencies as the primary reserve asset is uncertain. In 1973, SDRs accounted for about 6 percent of the world's reserve assets. Whether this is a large or small growth during about four years of existence is a matter of personal opinion. One concern is whether SDRs can retain their value in terms of real goods and services and other currencies. This in turn depends a great deal on whether or not the growth of SDRs can be effectively controlled. Excessive growth in the supply of SDRs could become a problem if the IMF attempted to supply nations experiencing balance of payments deficits and liquidity problems with added issues of SDRs. And balance of payments deficits will continue to be a problem for some countries unless exchange rates are allowed to adjust to changes in the demand and supply conditions in foreign exchange markets.

Main points of Chapter 11

1. International trade is, in reality, trade between people who happen to find themselves within different national boundaries.

2. Trade allows people to specialize in what they do best, and hence increases their productive capacity.

3. The most noticeable basis for trade stems from differences in the natural endowment, such as climate, minerals, water, etc.

4. A nation or area will enjoy a comparative advantage in the production of a product if it gives up less of alternative products than do other nations or areas that produce the product.

5. By increasing the output of products in which it holds a comparative advantage and then trading these products for items it finds expensive to produce, a nation can enjoy more of both types of products.

6. Because nations or areas are not homogeneous, we do not observe complete specialization taking place. In other words,

because of increasing costs, a nation may lose its comparative advantage in a product as output of the product expands. Also as comparative advantage becomes smaller, transport charges may eventually offset the cost advantage, especially for heavy or bulky products.

7. There will be a private incentive for trade to take place as long as an imported item can be purchased at a lower price than it can be sold for in the importing country.

8. As international trade takes place, the people who produce goods and services whose prices are forced down because of lower priced imports suffer economic losses, at least in the short run.

9. In an effort to limit the import of relatively cheaper foreign goods or services, nations have imposed quotas and tariffs. Most of the rationalizations for the existence of trade barriers are, however, based on questionable economic reasoning.

10. Dumping refers to the situation where a country sells products on the world market for a lower price than exists in its domestic market, with the difference between the two prices made up by the government.

11. Imports account for only about 4 percent of U.S. GNP. The largest share of U.S. exports consists of manufactured products, and the largest share of U.S. trade is carried on with the more developed nations of the world.

12. The balance of trade refers to the difference in value of exports and imports of goods and services. The balance of payments includes the difference between exports and imports but also includes the inflow and outflow of money due to purchases and sale of services, remittances and pensions, grants to foreign countries, investment in other countries, and foreign investment in the country in question.

13. An exchange rate is the number of units of one currency that it takes to buy a unit of another currency, i.e., it is the price of one currency in terms of another.

14. A reduction in the price of the dollar in terms of marks has the effect of reducing the import supply of German goods in the United States because marks become more expensive to U.S. importers.

15. A reduction in the price of the dollar in terms of marks has

the effect of increasing the export demand for U.S. goods sold to Germany because dollars become cheaper to purchase.

16. The supply of dollars in the foreign exchange market is derived from the U.S. demand for imported goods, and the demand for dollars reflects the demand for goods imported from the United States.

17. The demand curve for dollars on the foreign exchange market is downward sloping, indicating that more dollars are demanded when the price of the dollar declines because of the increase in export demand for U.S. products.

18. The supply curve for dollars on the foreign exchange market will be upward sloping as long as the total dollar amount spent on imported goods in the United States declines with a decrease in the import supply of foreign goods.

19. During the major part of the post–World War II period, exchange rates in most of the major trading nations were established by government decree.

20. Devaluation refers to a decision by a government to reduce the price of its currency relative to gold and other currencies. This action becomes necessary during prolonged periods of balance of payments deficits.

21. The official price of the dollar was maintained above its equilibrium price for a number of years by the purchase of U.S. dollars by foreign governments and the willingness of the United States to exchange gold for dollars at a fixed rate of exchange.

22. In countries where the dollar is undervalued, a black market in currency tends to emerge.

23. International monetary authorities have been reluctant to set exchange rates free from controls, ostensibly because of concern over a possible increase in exchange rate fluctuations in foreign exchange markets. Yet infrequent devaluations by countries after prolonged periods of balance of payments disequilibriums also create instability. A crawling peg is a possible compromise between fixed rates and freely functioning currency markets.

24. Gold long has been used as an international money to settle debts between nations. The U.S. dollar and the pound sterling also have served as reserve currencies.

25. Special drawing rights (SDR's) were created by the IMF in 1968 to augment gold as a reserve currency.

Questions for thought and discussion

1. List some reasons why we observe certain countries or regions specializing in the production of certain products.
2. "By its nature, trade between two people, regions, or nations tends to benefit one party at the expense of the other." True or false? Explain.
3. Suppose country A is more "efficient" in the production of all the goods produced by country B. Would it ever pay country A to trade with country B? Explain why or why not.
4. Suppose the United States allowed the free importation of beef from Argentina. Who would gain from such a policy? Would anyone lose?
5. Suppose the United States decided to sell powdered milk to a developing nation at half the U.S. price of this product. How might this be done? Who would gain from such a policy? Would anyone lose?
6. Distinguish between balance of trade and balance of payments.
7. What is an exchange rate? What is the current exchange rate between the U.S. dollar and (a) the West German mark, (b) the Japanese yen, (c) the pound sterling, and (d) the Argentine peso?
8. Explain what happens to the import market in the United States for German products, and the export market in the United States for products sold to Germany, when the price of the dollar declines in terms of the mark? Utilize demand and supply diagrams.
9. Explain what happens to the import market in Germany for U.S. products, and the export market in Germany for products sold to the United States, when the price of the dollar declines in terms of the mark. Utilize demand and supply diagrams in your answer.
10. "The price of Volkswagens in the United States can be expected to increase 10 percent with a 10 percent decrease in

the price of the dollar relative to German marks." True or false? Explain.

11. Which industries in the United States would benefit from a lower price of the dollar in terms of foreign currencies? Explain how industries in foreign countries are affected by a lower price of the dollar relative to their own currencies.

12. Explain why dollars are demanded and supplied in foreign exchange markets.

13. *a)* Why would the demand for dollars curve slope downward?
    b) Why would the supply of dollars curve slope upward?
    c) Could the curve for supply of dollars in a foreign exchange market also slope downward? Explain.

14. Explain what happens when the official rate of exchange of a currency is above the market equilibrium rate.

15. Explain what happens when the official rate of exchange of a currency is below the market equilibrium rate.

16. Would you favor fixed or floating exchange rates? Why?

17. If the price of gold is $100 per ounce, how much are you worth if you are "worth your weight in gold"?

18. From the mid-1950s to the late 1960s, the United States lost about one half of its gold reserves. Why?

19. In what way is the introduction of special drawing rights similar to the introduction of a new money in a country? Why would control over the quantity of SDRs issued be of major importance?

12

Economic growth and development

In this the final chapter on macroeconomics, we will look briefly at the relatively recent phenomenon of economic growth. We say recent because from the standpoint of world history, several thousand years elapsed during which the economic well-being of most of the world's population remained at a relatively low level. Indeed in most nations of the world the largest share of economic growth has taken place within the past two centuries.

At the outset it will be useful to define rather specifically what is meant by economic growth. We will define economic growth as a long-run sustained increase in the per capita real output of a society. Occasionally growth is defined in terms of total output of a nation, but for our purposes, growth in the per capita context will be the most useful concept. For lack of a better measure, real output generally is gauged by one of the output measures discussed in Chapter 3 (GNP, NNP, etc.) adjusted by changes in the general price level. However, we should keep in mind the biases of these measures also discussed in Chapter 3.

Growth and the quality of life

Until fairly recently, most people thought of economic growth as a desirable goal. In fact throughout a large part of the post–World War II period, nations seemed to have been engaged in a kind of contest to see who could grow the most rapidly. The contest was especially noticeable between the centrally planned economies (mainly the Soviet Union, mainland China, and their satellites) and the nations having more decentralized economic systems characterized by relatively free markets.

This is not to say that economic growth has now become totally undesirable. Most nations still rank economic growth as a high-priority goal. But in recent years, in the United States at least, a growing number of people, especially young people from upper middle- and high-income families, have begun to question the wisdom of striving for a high rate of growth. They point to the growing amount of pollution, congestion, and social instability as evidence of the consequences of growth. Some have even suggested that a more desirable goal would be a no-growth economy, implying that the United States is rich enough already.

Upon closer examination of their argument, it becomes apparent, however, that the advocates of a no-growth economy really do not mean that at all. What they appear to be saying instead is that people now are consuming enough automobiles, appliances, luxuries of various types, but not enough of other things such as clean air and water, a chance to see the blue sky once in a while, and the opportunity to enjoy more peace and serenity. In other words, the no-growth advocates really want growth in the output of such things as pollution control devices and parks—goods and services that improve the environment.

Perhaps a reason for some of the confusion about a no-growth economy is that many things that people once considered "free" goods, such as clean air and water, blue skies, green grass, and the sight of a bird, now are no longer free. In an industrialized society many of these items become economic goods in the sense that alternative goods and services must be given up to obtain them. For example, if we want cleaner air and water around industrial cities, some of the resources that formerly were devoted to the production of industrial products now must be devoted to the production of pollution control devices.

There may be a few people who would be willing to give up some of their present consumption to obtain more quality in their environment. Surely there are more people, however, who would prefer to retain their present level of consumption and obtain a higher quality of environment through the growth of the economy. Indeed it seems reasonably safe to say that most people in the United States would prefer both more conventional goods and services and a higher quality environment.

Thus the question of growth versus no-growth turns out to be for most people a question of the most desirable mix of output. At this point it is not clear how much of other goods and services society is willing to exchange for a better environment even if they can have more of both kinds of goods through economic growth. So far the poor and lower middle-income people have not expressed a great deal of enthusiasm over the proposals of the environmentalists. Apparently, the poor are in no mood to give up much of what little they now have to obtain more quality in their environment. It's nice to be able to look at blue sky and clear water, but it's even nicer to have food on the table, a decent house, and clothing for the family.

Perhaps the main point to be made here is that there is really no contradiction between economic growth and quality of life. Indeed it is the phenomenon of economic growth that has freed man from a lifetime of struggle against famine, disease, and the elements, and allowed him to set his sights on a more comfortable and enjoyable existence.

This is not to play down the seriousness of problems resulting from economic growth. Pollution is a reality. So are the millions of people who have not shared in this growth, i.e., the poor. Of major consequence is our drawing down of the stock of nonrenewable natural resources during the 20th century, especially fossil fuels (coal, oil, and gas). During the past 30 years man has used more energy than he did in all previous history. Unless we can find alternative sources of cheap energy, the standard of living of people in the 21st century may indeed be lower than it is for people today.

Economics: The dismal science of the 1800s

For the most part, economic growth is taken for granted by people living today, especially those in the developed nations. But this was not always the case. After the world had experienced thousands of years of relative stagnation in per capita real output, few people, if any, living much over 200 years ago ever imagined the existence of such a phenomenon as sustained economic growth as we know it today.

After Columbus made his famous trip and the new world gradually opened up, it soon became apparent that new lands and resources could add appreciably to the economic well-being of the established nations. It was at about this time that economics began to emerge as a discipline. And a major economic issue of the time was economic growth. One of the first economics books, and perhaps still one of the most famous, is Adam Smith's *Wealth of Nations,* published in 1776. In the main, Adam Smith was rather optimistic about the chances for economic growth provided the government allowed markets to allocate goods and services to their most productive uses. He envisioned growing supplies of both capital and labor, leading to a growing level of real output over time.

About 25 years later a clergyman by the name of Thomas Malthus came out with a book, *Essay on the Principle of Population (1798).* To be sure, Malthus was something less than optimistic over the future of mankind. He is perhaps most remembered for his famous population growth example. Malthus argued that population has a tendency to grow geometrically over time (1,2,4,8,16,32, 64, etc.) unless checked by a shortage of food. And, according to Malthus, in the long run the shortage of food would serve as the ultimate check on population growth. Even if new lands were brought into production, it would only be a matter of time before the population grew enough to bring everyone down once again to a subsistence level.

Malthus, to strengthen his argument, also introduced his now famous "law of diminishing returns" in which he argued that as more and more labor is applied to a fixed amount of land, beyond some point the extra output attributable to an extra unit of labor will begin to decline. Because of the fixed amount of land in the world, the expanding population would insure that beyond some point, each additional person would not be able to produce enough food to sustain life. Consequently, a point would be reached where population growth would stop, as everyone (at least the masses) teetered on the edge of starvation.

To say the least, Malthus' ideas had a pronounced impact on the thinking of the time. It wasn't long before the optimism of Adam

Smith's ideas began to give way to the pessimism of the Malthusian doctrine. More and more economic writers took the Malthusian view that mankind was in for a rough time indeed. Because of the prevailing pessimism among economists, economics became known as the "dismal science" during a large part of the 19th century.

New technology and the unexpected dividend

Having the benefit of over 170 years of hindsight, we can now say happily that Malthus' dire predictions have not materialized, at least for the United States and the more highly developed nations of the world. Indeed, instead of famine the major agricultural problems of these nations have been overproduction and food surpluses. Why have these nations managed to escape the plague of long-run diminishing returns in the production of food? We know that their populations have grown considerably and that their total land areas have remained about the same or even declined. For example, in 1950 the total land in farms in the United States (50 states) amounted to 1,162 million acres. By 1969 this figure had been reduced to 1,064 million acres. Indeed in 1972 the federal government paid farmers not to grow crops on 62.7 million acres of farmland.[1]

It is interesting to note that the number of people engaged in the production of agricultural products also has declined substantially in the United States. At the end of World War II (1946), the U.S. farm population totaled 25 million people. By 1972 the farm population had been reduced to about 9.5 million people. These substantial reductions in both land and number of farmers become even more impressive when we consider that the total U.S. population increased from 141 million people in 1946 to nearly 209 million in 1972. Thus we see that in the United States, not only has a given land area supplied the food for a greatly increased population but the amount of land used to produce food and the number of farm people has in fact declined. For the United States, at least, Malthus couldn't have been more wrong.

But we are still faced with the question of why was Malthus

---

[1] U.S. Department of Agriculture, *Agricultural Statistics, 1972*, pp. 506, 637.

wrong. First, we should bear in mind that Malthus considered only two major resources in the production of food—land and labor. What he failed to consider was the host of new resources or inputs that have come on the scene since his time. Here we have in mind such things as new, improved varieties of crops such as hybrid corn, better and cheaper sources of commercial fertilizer, new and improved pesticides and herbicides, and the tremendous increase in tractors and equipment of all kinds. In addition, and perhaps most important, man himself has become a new and improved resource because of the increased skills he has acquired through research and education. These new, man-made resources, along with greater knowledge, have enabled mankind to greatly increase the production of food from a given land area.

Of course, we should not criticize Malthus too severely for failing to foresee the additional output that new technology has made possible. During his lifetime the primary inputs in the production of food were labor and land. Diminishing returns will indeed occur in any situation where there is the mere application of additional labor to a fixed amount of land. It is only the application of additional, complementary resources that makes labor and land more productive, thereby offsetting the phenomenon of diminishing returns. To be sure, the law of diminishing returns is still employed to a considerable extent in the study of microeconomics.

You may have recognized also that Malthus' pessimistic predictions about the future of mankind have been more nearly borne out in the underdeveloped nations of the world. In many of these nations food shortages and malnutrition have continued to be the major problems facing the people. Indeed, in some of these nations people are still perishing because of a lack of food. We will return to a more thorough discussion of the problem of achieving economic growth in the underdeveloped nations a bit later in this chapter.

Technological change

Our discussion thus far has centered mainly on the effects of new technology in the production of food, particularly in reference to the Malthusian doctrine of diminishing returns. We should be aware, however, that new technology has had pronounced effects on virtually every sector of the more highly developed nations. Indeed the developed nations are characterized by the widespread use of new technology.

The utilization of new and improved resources to achieve a larger level of output in the economy has come to be known as technological change. For a long time economists have been aware of increased output that could not be explained by the increased use of conventional resources such as land, labor, and traditional forms of capital. The additional or unexplained output was then attributed to the phenomenon of technological change. However, the more basic question still remains: What are the causes or sources of technological change? Using the phrase "technological change" as a label for the additional or unexplained output is really nothing more than giving a name to our ignorance.

In more recent years economists have begun to address themselves to the basic question of identifying the sources of technological change. There is still a great deal to be learned in this area, but at the present it is possible to at least make some general statements. At the most general level we can say that the basic source of new technology, or technological change, is new knowledge. By unlocking some of the secrets of the universe, man has been able to create new inputs or resources that are more productive than his traditional resources. Hence, it has become possible to increase output without increasing the use of traditional resources. Thus we observe an increase in output per unit of input because traditional measures of inputs tend not to reflect the improved quality of inputs or the completely new inputs that have come on the scene.

The production and distribution of knowledge

At this point it is legitimate to ask, What are the sources of new knowledge? The nations that have been most successful in acquiring new knowledge have done so through formal, structured research and development activities. Man has learned a few things in his normal day-to-day activities, but the contributions of learning by doing have been relatively small compared to the contributions of scientists and engineers.

A very important step in the acquisition of new knowledge by a society is the transmission of this knowledge from research workers to the general public. Knowledge that only exists in the minds of scientists or perhaps in scientific journals is of little value to society until it is disseminated to the general public and put to widespread use.

The dissemination or "trickling down" of new knowledge is in most cases a complex process. New knowledge seems to first find its way into professional journals, then into textbooks, most likely at the upper levels of school first, and then gradually out into society as graduates begin to utilize it. For example, the concept of hybridization developed by Mendel was understood only by professional geneticists not too many years ago. Now it is found in undergraduate biology texts and is common knowledge to plant breeders. As knowledge becomes more widely known and accepted, it seems also to become simplified, so that what was initially understood only by a few scientists and teachers later becomes understandable to more and more of the general public, provided, of course, the knowledge proves useful to the public.

Sources of economic growth

Although we do not as yet have a generally accepted theory of economic growth, such as the Keynesian theory of national income determination, economists have identified several factors that appear to be important in contributing to growth.[2] At the same time, we should bear in mind that a great deal remains to be learned about economic growth.

You will notice in the discussion to follow that the word investment is used repeatedly. We should stress at the outset that investment appears to be the name of the game as far as economic growth is concerned. By investment we mean the allocation of resources to the production of additional resources which themselves contribute to the increased output of future goods and services. In other words, in order for a society to increase its output of goods and services

---

[2] See for example Edward F. Denison, *The Sources of Economic Growth in the United States and the Alternatives before Us* (Washington, D.C.: Committee for Economic Development, 1962).

(achieve economic growth), it must increase its productive capacity. But we should also stress that investment per se may not necessarily lead to economic growth. Rather it must be investment that contributes substantially to the output of goods and services—what economists refer to as high payoff investment.

1. Investment in knowledge. From our preceding discussion, it should come as no surprise that investment in the production and distribution of knowledge is considered an important source of economic growth. Although our knowledge about the contribution of knowledge is still relatively meager, most of the evidence points to the fact that investment in knowledge-producing activities, i.e., research and development (R&D), has paid off handsomely, especially for the more developed countries of the world.[3] In fact, one characteristic that the more highly developed nations have in common is their substantial investment in research and development activities.

2. Investment in human capital. In recent years economists have begun to look upon education as an investment in human beings, i.e., the production of human capital. Perhaps most basic is the ability to read and write. We have evidence that achieving the equivalent of an elementary level of education as a bare minimum for everyone in society has paid off highly for the developed nations. In countries where a substantial share of the population is illiterate, we also observe a relative low level of per capita output of goods and services, hence a low living standard. Moreover, as the wealth and output of the developed nations increase, a larger share of their people tend to attain higher levels of education, which in turn results in still higher levels of per capita output of goods and services.[4]

3. Investment in nonhuman capital. Without knowledge and without tools, man is a very unproductive creature. Thus the production of machines, tools, buildings, etc., also is a major factor contributing to the output of nations. The more capital a person has to work with, the more productive he tends to be. At the same time, we should point out that the kind of capital produced will have an important bearing on the payoff of the investment. It is

---

[3] For a more thorough discussion of the economic effects of R&D, see Chapter 12 of the micro text.

[4] For a more thorough discussion of the economic effects of education, see Chapter 11 of the micro text.

becoming more evident that the highest payoff is achieved by producing capital that utilizes new knowledge. In other words the high-payoff investment (as far as nonhuman capital is concerned) appears to be in new or nontraditional inputs, such as new forms of power, agricultural and industrial machinery, transportation, and the like. The sheer multiplication of traditional inputs such as increased animal power, land, and physical labor has contributed something to output, but not to the extent that modern factors of production have contributed.

Of course, in order to create these new, nontraditional inputs and to use them effectively, knowledge must first be produced and distributed. Thus the three general sources of economic growth cited here are likely to be very complementary to each other. For example, the payoff to investment in the production and distribution of knowledge can be expected to be much greater when accompanied by increased education and investment in nonhuman capital. Indeed, much of the new knowledge that is produced requires new forms of nonhuman capital to be useful to society. Similarly, investment in education probably pays off more handsomely if accompanied by investment in R&D and in additional nonhuman capital. Thus we would expect the payoff to investment to be greater where all three areas are emphasized, instead of just one or two.

Costs of economic growth

First, we need to remind ourselves that two basic kinds of goods and services are produced in any society: (1) consumption goods and (2) investment goods. If a society insisted on producing only consumption goods and services, i.e., if people did not save any of their income, there would be no resources available for investment goods. And, according to the preceding discussion, there would be no chance for economic growth to occur. The fact that most societies have chosen to devote a portion of their resources to the production of investment goods means that they decided to forgo a certain amount of their present consumption in order to have more consumption goods in the future.

Thus in one sense we can consider the cost of economic growth as the consumption goods and services we have to give up in order to undertake investment. As members of the present generation, we should be thankful that past generations decided to forgo part of their possible consumption goods in order to produce investment goods, or we would probably still be living in caves, cloaked in animal skins and sustaining ourselves on roots and raw meat.

The fact that a certain amount of present consumption must be given up in order to achieve economic growth presents a serious problem to the underdeveloped nations. If the major part of a nation's resources are required to produce just the necessities of life—food, clothing, and shelter—there isn't much chance to forgo consumption goods in order to invest. And if investment is small, the resulting economic growth will tend to be small. Since the end of World War II, many of the developed nations have attempted to provide investment goods such as technical assistance (knowledge) and a small amount of machinery and other forms of nonhuman capital to their less developed neighbors, but progress has been slow. The fact that a large number of the people in underdeveloped nations tend to have a small amount of education makes it difficult for them to assimilate large doses of modern technology and capital.

In recent years there has been an increase in concern over what might be considered another cost of economic growth, namely the pollution, congestion, social unrest, and other problems that accompany an industrialized society. Part of the difficulty, which we alluded to at the beginning of this chapter, involved obtaining a meaningful measure of economic growth. If in fact the environment has deteriorated significantly over the years, then using GNP to gauge the economic well-being of society may result in an overstatement of economic growth. However, as we said, this does not mean that economic growth is undesirable. In order to obtain a more pleasing environment without giving up the consumption goods and services we now have, we must have continued economic growth.

Comparisons among countries

At this point it will be useful to compare the records of various nations in achieving economic growth. In Table 12–1 we present the 1960 and 1970 GNPs for 14 representative countries, ranging

TABLE 12-1
Estimates of average per capita domestic product in U.S. dollar equivalents, 14 selected countries*

Country	1960	1970	Average annual change, 1960–70
United States	$3,690	$4,737	$104.00
Sweden	2,425	4,055	163.00
Canada	2,785	3,676	89.00
West Germany	1,703	3,034	133.00
United Kingdom	1,778	2,128	35.00
Austria	1,167	1,937	77.00
Japan	605	1,911	131.00
Mexico	438	668	23.00
Brazil	272	362	9.00
Philippines	321	377	6.00
Thailand	127	181	6.00
Pakistan	109	149	4.00
Haiti	100	91	−1.00
India	97	94	−0.30

* All figures are in constant 1970 dollars. For Thailand and Pakistan, the figures in the 1970 column are from 1969, and the average annual change is 1960–69; for Haiti, the figures are from 1968 and 1960–68.
Source: *Statistical Abstract, 1972*, p. 813.

from the most highly developed to the least developed. The average annual growth in per capita GNP for the intervening period also is shown.

There are two major points to be gleaned from Table 12–1. First, notice the extreme variation among countries in the per capita output of goods and services. The people fortunate enough to be born in the nations on the upper end of the scale enjoy many times the annual total of goods and services available to the people of the poorest nations.

The second point to note is the wide variation among countries in the annual growth of per capita GNP shown in the last column. Again in this case, the people living in the richest nations have been able to achieve much larger annual increases in per capita output than the inhabitants of the less developed countries. Indeed during the 10-year period of 1960–70, the average Haitian and Indian citizen experienced a slight decline in output of goods and services. In this case population grew faster than total output. In terms of absolute growth, all of the nations at the lower end of the GNP scale, with the possible exception of Mexico, exhibited a rather meager increase in per capita output. In order for the poor nations to catch up, they must achieve a larger average annual absolute growth than their richer neighbors. Considering their small base values of per capita GNP, this requires an extremely high percentage rate of growth—something most poor nations have not been able to achieve. In a relative sense, at least, it appears the rich are getting richer and the poor are getting poorer, as far as nations are concerned.

Growth in the underdeveloped world

Because of the extremely low level of per capita output in the less developed countries (LDCs) together with their relatively small annual growth, the problem of achieving economic growth is both more critical and more perplexing than is the case for the richer nations. Of course, the general statements about the sources of new knowledge and the need to invest in activities that increase knowledge and education as well as the need for new forms of non-human capital to achieve economic growth apply to both the developed and underdeveloped nations. However, because of the critical nature of the problem in the underdeveloped nations, it will be useful to consider these in somewhat more detail.

First, we should bear in mind that the attainment of economic growth is a matter of life and death for many people in countries where the supply of food is extremely limited. Without food today, there is no tomorrow to enjoy the fruits of economic progress. It becomes apparent, then, that underdeveloped nations are faced with a dilemma. The acquisition of new knowledge, increasing the level of education and the production of new forms of nonhuman capital are long-run phenomena, taking perhaps several generations to bear significant results. Yet there is a critical short-run problem of staving off famine. An adequate food supply is necessary for people to be able to work and be reasonably productive.

To survive the difficult short-run future, most underdeveloped nations have attempted to adapt the knowledge and technology of the developed nations to their situations. These efforts have been moderately successful. Certain knowledge (such as the concept of hybridization, the technology for harnessing power such as electricity, the internal combustion engine, jet propulsion, the know-how for nitrogen fixation and chemical production, etc.) can be applied in any locality. On the other hand, certain technology, particularly that which is biological in nature such as new varieties of crops, must be developed in the area in which it is to be utilized. Varieties of hybrid corn that produce record yields in Iowa fare no better, and sometimes worse, than traditional varieties in Mexico and Argentina.

It is very important also to consider the profitability of new types of technology. It is a mistake to conclude that new resources which are profitable in the developed economies also will be profitable in the underdeveloped countries. A major consideration is differences in wage rates between nations. Laborsaving technology that is extremely profitable in countries where labor is relatively scarce and wages are high can at the same time be unprofitable in countries where labor is abundant and wages low.

Agricultural development

Agriculture is by far the dominant industry in underdeveloped nations of the world. It is common to observe between two thirds and three fourths of the total population of the LDCs directly engaged in agriculture. In contrast, farmers constitute only about 5 percent of the population in the United States. As a general rule, the poorer the nation, the larger the proportion of the population engaged in agriculture. This is not particularly surprising. The first order of business in staying alive is to obtain nourishment. Once food requirements are met and surpassed, some of the people engaged in food production can leave agriculture to produce such things as better housing, medical care, transportation, and the host of items that contribute to human comfort and enjoyment.[5]

This phenomenon of course has happened in the United States and the other more highly developed nations of the world.[5] At the time of the American Revolution the United States was as much an agricultural nation as most LDCs are today. But as the nation de-

---

[5] An exception would be a nation that remained agricultural but traded its excess agricultural commodities with other nations for industrial goods. Denmark and New Zealand are sometimes used as examples.

veloped, a progressively smaller share of the population produced food and a progressively larger share produced other things.

It is apparent, therefore, that agricultural development is of major importance in the overall development of the LDCs. Unless their major industry can become more productive, there is little chance of releasing people from agriculture to produce more of the other amenities of life or to trade agricultural products for industrial products produced by other nations.

Unfortunately there is no simple formula that a nation can follow to rapidly increase the productive capacity of its agriculture. The process is relatively slow and is likely to differ between countries. About all we can do here is to present some ideas that appear to have general application across various situations.[6]

The sources of economic growth presented in a previous section apply to agricultural development in particular as well as to overall economic growth and development. The key is making high payoff investments. But the question is where these investments are to be found. From past experience, we can say with some confidence they are not found in the production of more traditional varieties of crops, or more human physical effort. Although additions to these inputs provide some increase in food and fiber production, the increase will tend to be relatively small.

The investments that give rise to new nontraditional inputs, particularly new varieties of crops, appear to have paid off handsomely in many LDCs. Because plants can produce carbohydrates and protein more efficiently than animals, crops have been utilized much more as a direct source of food in the LDCs than in the developed nations. Unfortunately, because of differences in soil, day length, temperature variation, etc., it usually is not possible to relocate proven varieties of crops from one nation to another, or even from one locality to another. As a result investments first have to be made in research facilities that can develop new varieties suited for a particular area. The International Rice Research Institute in the

---

[6] For additional reading on the problem of agricultural development, see T. W. Schultz, *Transforming Traditional Agriculture* (New Haven, Conn.: Yale University Press, 1964); A. W. Mosher, *Getting Agriculture Moving* (New York: Agricultural Development Council, 1966); and Y. Hayami and V. W. Ruttan, *Agricultural Development: An International Perspective* (Baltimore: Johns Hopkins Press, 1971).

Philippines and the Rockefeller corn and wheat programs in Mexico, headed by Dr. Norman Borlog (a recent Nobel prize winner for his efforts), have been particularly successful in this endeavor.

But new varieties of crops with high yield potentials usually cannot reach their potentials, and may not even achieve the yields of traditional varieties, without increased fertilization. Thus investments are required in fertilizer production facilities, or imports of plant nutrients must be increased. In many parts of the world, irrigation water must be supplied in order for crops to approach their yield potential. North America and Europe are somewhat unique in that a large share of agricultural production can be carried on under conditions of natural rainfall. Many of the underdeveloped nations do not have this advantage.

The application of fertilizer and water to improved varieties of crops may also require a change in production techniques. For example, increasing the fertility of the soil, as well as adding water, usually intensifies the weed problem. So farmers must become better managers and in a sense become a "new input" themselves. Greater use of agricultural chemicals, mainly herbicides and insecticides, also may be required to control weeds and insects. After all, more plant food and greater yields produce a more favorable environment for yield-reducing weeds, insects, and plant diseases. The timing of planting and harvesting also tends to become more critical with the higher yielding varieties.

The gradual shift from a subsistence type of agriculture (where farmers produce mainly for their own use) to a commercial agriculture (where a greater portion of the output is sold) requires additional transportation and marketing facilities. So additional investments generally are required in these areas. In the United States and many other developed nations of the world, farmers have formed cooperatives for the purpose of marketing their products. Farmers in LDCs also are turning in this direction. Certainly there is not much incentive for farmers to increase production by adopting new varieties and other inputs unless they can be reasonably sure they can sell their added output for a profit. Although, if there are profits to be made in buying from farmers and selling in urban markets, we can be quite sure that entrepreneurs will show up to perform this service.

Industrial development

Although the LDCs by their nature are highly agricultural, the industrial or nonagricultural sector offers the greatest potential for growth. As implied in the previous section, the industrial sector must provide an increasing proportion of inputs utilized in the agricultural sector such as machinery, tools, chemicals, and fertilizers. One characteristic of a modern agricultural sector is that a large share of its inputs are produced off the farm. In other words, growth in the farm supply industry is an important determinant of growth in agriculture.

In addition to providing new, nontraditional inputs for agriculture, the industrial sector must provide many of the inputs for its own production of consumer goods. Industrial inputs such as machinery, tools, buildings, and chemicals are themselves the output of the industrial sector. Of course, as the economy grows, the industrial sector faces an ever-increasing demand for consumer goods of all types: housing, clothing, shoes, furniture, refrigerators, stoves, air conditioners, automobiles, radios, and TV sets, to name a few.

Since industrial technology is not likely to be as location-specific as agricultural technology, it is somewhat easier for industrial firms in the LDCs to draw upon the technological base of the developed nations. However, a major difficulty of transferring industrial technology from the developed to the underdeveloped nations stems from the wide difference between the two in wage rates relative to the price of capital. In the underdeveloped nations wage rates tend to be low relative to the price of capital. The opposite is true in the developed nations. Because labor is relatively cheap in the LDCs, production should utilize more labor relative to capital in order to minimize costs. As a result the production processes of the developed nations cannot (or at least should not) be exactly reproduced in the LDCs if they wish to utilize their abundant supply of labor and minimize costs. The same, of course, holds true for agriculture as far as the substitution of machines for labor is concerned.

The kinds of products demanded and produced in the LDCs also differ from those of the developed nations. Instead of expensive two-ton automobiles designed to cruise at 70 m.p.h. down a four- or six-lane expressway, they need relatively cheap, rugged cars that can maneuver down narrow, often unpaved roads. In general, their demand is mainly for relatively simple items that can be operated and repaired without a high degree of engineering skill.

By the same token, the manufacturing establishments themselves tend not to be large and highly sophisticated. Much of the manufacturing in the LDCs is carried out in relatively small establishments or machine shops, many employing no more than 5 to 10 people. Each establishment may produce a simple final product or a single component of a final product. Indeed the phenomenon of subcontracting is quite common in the LDCs. Basically it allows specialization of functions by employees without requiring the firms to be large. It is easy to underestimate the entrepreneurship of small businessmen in the LDCs. If there are profits to be made, someone is usually there to take advantage of the situation.

Another problem of industrial development in the LDCs is the mobilization of sufficient funds to finance business firms. The most efficient way to draw together funds, at least large amounts, is by a stock market. Without a stock market, firms have to utilize borrowed funds to a large extent, which in turn places relatively low limits on firm size unless the owner already is wealthy.

The entrance of multinational firms into the LDCs provides another source of financing industrial development. Usually these firms provide the plant, equipment, and management while employing domestic labor and raw materials. This kind of arrangement can work to the benefit of both the firm and the LDC. The firm taps a relatively cheap source of labor, and possibly raw materials, in producing a product that can be sold for a profit in the LDC itself or can be shipped to another even more profitable market. The people of the LDC, on the other hand, gain some additional industrial output or the means to buy such output on the world market.

In recent years some LDCs have become more nationalistic, purposely making it more difficult for foreign firms to carry on business in their countries. In certain cases the firms' assets have been expropriated by their host country, as occurred in Cuba and more recently in Chile. Whether or not the charges of exploitation and the like levied against the firms involved are justified is a question we cannot answer here. It appears, however, that banishment of a foreign firm by a host LDC does not, in general, further the economic development of the country in question. The country obtains some physical assets, which in most cases it could have purchased in the world market, but loses the management skills provided by the firms. The latter input is usually the most difficult to come by in an LDC. When the risk of expropriation increases, other foreign firms may not wish to "touch the country with a ten-foot pole," or may insist on a higher rate of profit in order to write off their assets in a shorter period of time. Of course, if a host LDC gives up more than it receives from a foreign firm, it is not surprising that the firm will not be welcome. But there is no reason why contractural arrangements cannot be worked out that can provide a mutual benefit to both the LDC and the foreign firm.

Infrastructure: Development and finance

In using the term infrastructure here, we have in mind a network of transportation and communication facilities, together with such public utilities as electricity, telephone, water supply, and waste disposal. Although the major cities in most LDCs (with the exception of the very poor districts) in general have modern and adequate infrastructures, the same usually is not true for the interior or rural regions. Such an unbalance of infrastructure contributes to the very uneven growth pattern observed in many LDCs. Their major cities become hardly distinguishable from New York, Chicago, or Los Angeles, while the interior lags a hundred years or more behind, not only in terms of per capita income but also in terms of public conveniences such as paved roads, public transportation, electricity, telephones, radio and television, waste and sewage disposal—services people take for granted in the large cities or in the developed nations. Understandably this situation in turn contributes to increased migration from the backward areas to the cities, further aggravating the congestion and unemployment problems of the cities.

Of course, it is one thing to say that the interior needs roads, bridges, electric and telephone lines, and railroads; it is quite another thing to supply these facilities. Although their construction usually is in the hands of the government of the LDC, they still require the use of scarce resources. In order to buy these resources, either domestically or abroad, the government must acquire the money. The question is, Where and how?

Most LDCs have a small number of relatively rich (and influential) families that certainly could afford to pay more taxes to provide more government revenue. However these families often have gotten to be rich because of special favors or tax advantages bestowed by past or present governments. And if the rich still enjoy considerable influence in the government, it is not difficult to understand why the government is reluctant to soak the rich.

But even if the government were to substantially increase the taxes paid by rich or high-income people, the total tax take may not increase substantially because the rich are relatively few in number. Certainly the added taxes would not meet the demand for infrastructure development. This leaves the poor (the vast majority of the people) and a small but growing middle class (if the nation is growing). Not even the most heartless of governments is anxious to tax the poor, which puts the major share of the tax burden on the middle class, usually the top-level civil service, management, and professional people in the large cities. But the ability to tax these people also is limited. For one thing, the income tax laws of most LDCs tend to have rather large loopholes. Also, the tradition of paying income taxes is not well established, so that tax evasion is a major problem. Moreover, an excessive rate of taxation dampens private incentive. Since these people are relatively mobile and usually can earn higher incomes in the developed nations, the LDCs certainly cannot afford to lose their services by taxing them out of the country. These people also are not likely to be very happy about paying a major part of the cost of infrastructure development in the interior. Certainly they are not likely to see much if any personal benefit from this public expenditure, unless they are planning to migrate to the interior, which is most unlikely.

Because of the problems of taxing income, governments of LDCs have turned more to taxes on internationally traded commodities. Certainly these taxes are the easiest to collect. All the goods are funneled through one or at most a few ports of entry, so evasion is relatively difficult. It is not uncommon to observe taxes on certain imports equal to their world market prices, especially on so-called luxury items such as automobiles and appliances. Of course, because the higher income people tend to buy these items, it is one way of taxing the rich. However, the low- and middle-income people are at the same time deprived of these commodities because their prices are driven up so high by the taxes.

Since exports also are easy to tax, they too provide a tempting source of government revenue. But because the LDCs are highly agricultural, exports are heavily weighted with these commodities. The major difficulty with export taxes is that they lower the price received by domestic producers of the items. As a consequence their profitability is reduced and output is less than it would otherwise be. In view of the importance of agricultural development in the LDCs, these taxes leave much to be desired.

As explained in Chapter 8, governments can of course spend more than they take in by tax revenues. Part of the deficit can be made up by selling government bonds and part by issuing new currency. In most LDCs the latter means of financing a deficit has been more popular than the former. And by now it is clear that large increases in the money supply result in high rates of inflation, which indeed is common in many LDCs. Of course, inflation also amounts to a tax, a tax on holders of cash balances, so the government still is left with the two alternatives of taxing or borrowing.

Funds for infrastructure development also may be obtained by borrowing (or gifts) from governments of developed nations or international lending agencies such as the World Bank. Loans and interest must of course be paid eventually, but payment can be postponed until the government of the LDC is in a better position to raise the revenue, hopefully from a broader tax base.

Education: Development and finance

Much of what we said about infrastructure development and finance applies also to education. People living in the major cities generally have access to at least average quality public or private schooling, again with the possible exception of the very poor. In the rural areas, if in fact schools do exist, the quantity and quality of schooling obtained by the people tend to be much lower than in the major city or cities. In rural areas it is not uncommon to see only one third to one half of the children in school, with the number falling to 10 to 15 percent for young people of high school age.

Nor is it uncommon to find two thirds to three quarters of the adult population illiterate, especially in rural areas.

We should be careful, however, not to equate illiteracy with ignorance. There is no reason to believe that the average level of innate intelligence (however measured) is lower for populations with a low level of schooling than it is for people living in the developed nations. Nor should we be so presumptuous as to believe that people with little or no schooling cannot learn. Granted, the ability to read facilitates further learning, but learning also can take place by oral communication and by observation. Experience has shown that illiterate farmers can and do pick up new inputs or techniques from their better schooled neighbors, from farm supply firms, or from extension agents if the techniques or inputs are profitable. Similarly, new factory workers tend to grasp what they need to know after a few weeks on the job. This is not to downgrade the importance of education. We argue only that economic growth can take place without waiting several generations for the major portion of the population to become literate.

The first order of business is to bring all children who are capable of learning up to the level where they can read and write with some facility; perhaps up to the equivalent of an eighth grade education in the United States. This should enable them as adults to learn new things more easily and also make it possible for increasing numbers to obtain the equivalent of high school, college, or professional training.

Investment in human beings, like investment in infra-structure, requires scarce resources, namely teachers and school facilities. Someone has to pay for these resources. If they are to be provided by the government, the government must first acquire the necessary funds. We need not restate the problems discussed in the previous section in regard to obtaining tax revenue.

Assuming that some resources are allocated to education, it may be another matter to obtain teachers. Since relatively few people have advanced in school through the equivalent of the high school level, few are available as teachers. Those who have completed the necessary training are likely to prefer life in the major city rather than in the countryside. Thus wages probably will have to be substantially higher in the interior in order to attract good teachers away from the advantages of the city.

Assuming that teachers and facilities can be provided, there has to be a demand for the education. Parents with little or no schooling may not be especially eager to educate their children beyond their level even if the education is "free." The problem is that the education will not in general be free to the parents, because after the age of 9 or 10 children become economic assets to peasant farmers. If the children are in school, they cannot be contributing to the family income, which is likely to be extremely low as it is. This problem can be reduced somewhat by dismissing school during times of peak labor demand (such as planting and harvesting) and holding classes when the children are less in demand at home. To ensure anything near universal attendance, schooling probably has to be made mandatory up to a minimum level such as the sixth or eighth year.

The cost of education increases as a greater proportion of young people go on to high school and college. In part this is due to more expensive (more highly trained) teachers and facilities. But even more important is the increase in forgone earnings (loss of output) that is incurred as young people attend school rather than enter the labor force. Although the absolute size of these earnings may be small relative to the earnings forgone by comparable students in developed nations, they often make a substantial difference in the amount of food and clothing that the students and their families can enjoy. Consequently the value of forgone earnings is likely to be even more important to young people in LDCs, particularly to students from rural areas, than to students in the developed nations.

In many developing nations, particularly the Latin American countries, a large proportion of college students hold full-time jobs during the day and attend classes in the evening. Although this practice reduces forgone earnings, it also reduces students' study time considerably and therefore reduces the quality of their education. Similarly, most college professors in these countries hold full-time positions in the government or the professions as well as teaching. Again, this limits the time teachers can spend in preparation for classes and in keeping up with new developments in their professions. The necessity for college professors to hold other jobs stems largely from the low salaries they receive relative to what they could earn in other occupations that require comparable training. Low salaries also deter capable people from entering the teaching profession, which in turn holds the quality of education below what it would otherwise be.

The agricultural adjustment problem

In the event that the LDCs can overcome the problems we have been discussing and start down the road of substantial growth, there are some other problems that will be encountered because of their growth. A major one is the agricultural adjustment problem—the movement of a substantial share of the population out of agriculture into the industrial and service trades.

As agricultural development occurs and the supply of agricultural products increases relative to demand, farm prices and incomes decline relative to nonfarm prices and income. This serves as an incentive for people to leave agriculture and take employment in nonagricultural occupations. The migration of farm people to the cities is a phenomenon observable in all of the developed nations of the world. In the United States the migration reached a peak during the 1950s, when close to one million people per year left their farms for the cities. At the present time in the United States, this adjustment has nearly run its course.

The migration from agriculture usually begins with young people who have just completed their educations and are embarking on their careers. The girls go in greatest number, with the young men following close behind. Next in line are the small farmers who find their meager incomes shrinking further as farm prices decline. Of course, in order to leave agriculture, one must find a job in another occupation. This is where the problem begins.

Although the industrial sector is likely to be expanding in a growing economy, it may not be expanding fast enough to absorb the large influx of farm people. As a result unemployment grows in the cities. Shanty towns made of tin and cardboard and inhabited by the poor, unemployed new arrivals from the countryside begin to spring up. It is unlikely that the already hard-pressed government can provide many public services such as waste disposal and health and education services. Because of the crowded and unsanitary conditions, disease and malnutrition problems are common. No doubt many wonder whether they should have left their former homes in the first place.

Some of the more fortunate and able-bodied migrants find jobs in factories and shops. Others find temporary employment, usually in the service trades. Selling newspapers, shining shoes, operating a taxi, and working as a maid or gardener are some of the common means of earning enough to stay alive while searching for more permanent employment.

In spite of low incomes in agriculture, some people choose to remain on their farms. Usually these are the older farmers, too young (or too poor) to retire but too old or unskilled to find employment in the cities. As a result they continue to work their small plots until they eventually pass from the scene.

What can be done to alleviate the agricultural adjustment problem? One big thing the government can do is to ensure freedom of entry into all occupations or training programs for all who have the necessary skills or capabilities. There is a natural tendency for unions representing the skilled trades to restrict entry into their respective trades. This is usually accomplished by regulating the number of people who can enter the training program, either apprenticeship or formal schooling. By so doing, unions limit the supply of labor and raise the wages of those lucky enough to be established members.

Powerful industrial unions also can make it more difficult for farm people to obtain work in the unskilled and semiskilled occupations. If these unions under threat of strike can obtain a union wage that is substantially above the free market wage, employers will attempt to substitute machines for labor. Even if the established union members can retain their jobs, the newly arrived and inexperienced ex-farmers will have a more difficult time obtaining jobs at the comparatively high union wage.

A similar effect can be created by a government-imposed minimum wage if it is above what would prevail in a relatively free labor market. Here again employers are motivated to substitute machines for labor. A high wage does not do a worker any good if he cannot find a job at that wage.

Sometimes governments of LDCs have made the agricultural adjustment problem worse than it need be by subsidizing the purchase of agricultural machinery, particularly for large farmers. The subsidy often takes the form of providing low-interest credit for buying farm equipment. In this case, the large farmers are induced to substitute machines for labor. As you can see, a combination of a relatively high minimum (or union) wages together with subsidized farm machinery squeezes the poor farm laborer or small farmer from two directions, leaving him unable to find employment in agriculture or in industry.

Governments could also take an active role in providing information to farmers on job vacancies in the cities. Many farm people probably migrate with the expectation of finding jobs that do not exist. If information were available on actual opportunities, or if farm workers could be hired before they migrate, the time spent living in slum conditions while looking or waiting for a permanent job could be eliminated for many, or at least shortened.

The population problem

Improvement in the economic well-being of the average person in a developing country depends on two factors: (1) growth in the total output of the economy and (2) growth in the population of the country. The per capita output of a nation can increase only if total output increases more rapidly than population. If population is growing at the same rate as total output, the economic well-being of the average person remains unchanged. Per capita output can be increased by a reduction in the population growth or by an increase in the rate of growth of total output.

An unfortunate characteristic of most underdeveloped nations is that they exhibit a relatively high population growth. As more and more people press against the land area and other resources of these nations, the pessimistic predictions of Malthus are more nearly borne out. Hence, in recent years there has been an increased awareness of the need for the underdeveloped nations to practice some form of population control.

The extent of the population growth problem in the less developed nations is illustrated in Table 12–2. Notice that the population growth rates of some of the representative developed nations shown in the left-hand column are less than half of the population growth rates of the selected less developed countries shown in the right-hand column.

TABLE 12–2
Annual population growth rates, 1963–70, 14 selected countries

Developed	Percent	Less developed	Percent
Austria	0.4	Brazil	3.2
Canada	1.7	Colombia	3.2
West Germany	1.0	India	2.1
Japan	1.1	Indonesia	2.8
Sweden	0.8	Morocco	3.0
United Kingdom	0.5	Pakistan	2.1
United States	1.1	Philippines	3.0

Source: *Statistical Abstract, 1972*, pp. 803–805.

Although we still have a great deal to learn about population theory, a few factors seem to be important in determining or influencing population growth. Taking into account migration between countries, a nation's population growth depends both on its death rate and on its birth rate. If the birth rate is larger than the death rate, obviously, population grows.

One of the important factors contributing to the spurt of population growth in the LDCs particularly during the years following World War II was the drop in infant mortality due to the availability of better medical care. Families that had 8 to 10 babies with the expectation of 4 or 5 dying as infants found their family size increasing as fewer died than expected. Of course, a lower infant mortality need not lead to a preference for larger families. But during the time it took parents to become adjusted to the lower death rate among infants, population grew rapidly.

Assuming that families eventually return to a so-called equilibrium family size, it is likely that this size will still be substantially larger for the LDCs than for the developed nations. Why? There probably are a number of reasons, both economic and noneconomic. We still have much to learn about the factors determining family size. However it does appear that one important economic factor is the price (or cost) of rearing and educating a child.

The price or total cost of rearing a child depends on a number of items. Most obvious is the cost of food, clothing, and medical care. Education also is a major item that includes out-of-pocket costs (tuition, books, etc.) as well as forgone earnings. For poor rural families in LDCs, the forgone earnings to the family become important rather early in life. As mentioned earlier, if a child is going to school he cannot be working in the fields. In fact, it is very likely that many children in LDCs turn out to be an economic asset to their parents rather than a cost. In contrast, children reared in cities, particularly in developed nations with child labor and minimum wage laws, do not have as many opportunities to contribute to the family income.

Another less obvious cost is the time spent by the mother in rearing the child. For a mother living on a farm in an LDC, this cost is not so important because she takes the child with her to work. But it is quite important for a highly educated woman in a developed nation. The reduced birth rate in the United States of late might be attributed to the increased employment opportunities for women outside the home, thus raising the price of children.

At any rate, it appears that the price or cost of a child is the least in the rural areas of the LDCs. And with a low price, we might expect that more will be demanded, which seems to be the case. The price of children in a country tends to rise as a greater proportion of the children are reared in cities. So we might expect some tendency for the birth rate to fall in the LDCs as people migrate from rural areas.

Recent advances in birth control technology have made it easier for parents to voluntarily limit the size of their families. Of course, this is no guarantee that parents will want to do so, especially low-income parents in rural areas. Considering that such action may constitute a short-run economic loss to these parents, we have little basis for optimism. If governments of the LDCs are determined to reduce population growth, they may have to institute policies that make children more expensive. These policies might range from removing existing incentives to have children, such as reduced taxes for large families, to more drastic means, such as placing a tax on children. It is interesting to note that the U.S. income tax law still provides an incentive to have children by allowing increased exemptions for larger families.

The foreign exchange problem

We argued that the key to economic growth in the LDCs is in the use of new, nontraditional inputs. However, in large part the knowledge and the facilities to produce these inputs do not exist in the LDCs. Thus it is necessary for the LDCs to either purchase these inputs from the developed nations, or import equipment and the technical know-how in order to produce them domestically. For most LDC's both lines of action generally are followed. But in either case, foreign currencies (or gold) are required to make such purchases. The needed foreign exchange is obtained mainly by selling to the developed nations.

What do the LDCs have to sell that the developed nations want to buy? A few of the more fortunate LDCs have petroleum, which is very much in demand in the developed nations and thus provides a good source of foreign exchange earnings. Other LDCs have rich mineral deposits which are in high demand in the developed nations. But for the most part the LDCs are agricultural. One might expect the LDCs to have a comparative advantage in agriculture vis-à-vis the developed nations. However because of the unproductive nature of agriculture in the LDCs, there is little surplus that can be exported. Some exceptions are the specialty crops such as coffee, sugar, tea, bananas, and citrus fruits. But in the case of livestock products and food and feed grains, the agricultural industries of the developed nations seem quite capable of satisfying their domestic demands, and even producing surpluses of their own.

Many LDCs therefore are caught in a situation where they are buying more from the developed nations than the developed nations are buying from them, as illustrated by Table 11–7. The inevitable result is a drawing down of the international reserves of those LDCs. Hence they must limit their imports of new inputs or facilities and live within their means. This in turn limits their ability to buy new inputs required for the development process.

In recent years some of the LDCs have been able to earn foreign exchange through the export of labor-intensive industrial products such as clothing, shoes, radios, and electronic components. South Korea and Taiwan have been especially successful in this area. However, this requires some development of the industrial sector.

It also requires a growing productivity of the agricultural sector in order to maintain food production with less labor. Of course, if the LDCs can buy some of their food and feed grains from the developed nations more cheaply than they can produce these products themselves, labor can (and should) be withdrawn from agriculture in order to increase the output of manufactured goods for export to the developed nations.

Thus we observe a rather curious and unexpected phenomena of the LDCs exporting manufactured products to the developed nations in return for agricultural products. However, this phenomena is not so surprising if we keep in mind that the manufactured goods exported by the LDCs tend to be labor-intensive and that the food and feed grains are produced in the developed nations under capital-intensive techniques.

This is not to say that the developed nations will someday revert to an agricultural status, with the LDCs becoming industrial. It is not likely that even the very productive agriculture of the developed nations can make much of a dent in supplying the demand for food of the two thirds of the world's population which resides in the LDCs. In order for the people of the LDCs to enjoy some of the fruits of their growing industrial sectors, most will have to increase the productive capacity of their agricultural sectors as well. Otherwise their agricultural output will continue to decline as people are drawn into the industrial sector. As a result more and more food will have to be imported, most likely at increasing prices which in turn have to be paid for by exports. In other words, a majority of their population will still be engaged in activities aimed at satisfying their demand for food.

Income redistribution

A common characteristic of most if not all underdeveloped nations is a relatively unequal distribution of income. We tend to observe the vast majority of people existing on a very low income and a relatively few people enjoying a lavish standard of living. In the main, these unfortunate situations have come about because of special favors or outright grants of land or property bestowed by past governments to a few privileged families or royalty.

In recent years governments of some LDCs have made progress towards redistributing income and wealth. In agriculture, land reform, whereby large holdings are split up into smaller plots and given or sold to landless peasants, has been a common device for redistributing wealth and income. It is also anticipated that an agriculture consisting of owner-operators will be more productive than one consisting of large holdings under absentee landlords. In the nonagricultural sector, increases in taxes on high incomes, the closing of tax loopholes, and higher excise taxes on luxury items have been used as redistributive devices.

Some nations have resorted to even more drastic means, such as the confiscation of property by the government. Usually this has come about in conjunction with a change in the political system, as in the Soviet Union, mainland China, and their satellites. Most people living in open or "free" societies abhor the purges or wholesale slaughter of people that took place in the Soviet Union and China in order to establish their political systems. The loss of personal freedoms in some Marxist or socialist nations represents for many an extremely high cost of income redistribution.

Although most of us desire peaceful and cooperative methods of income and wealth redistribution as opposed to violent and coercive means, its importance to economic growth should be emphasized. In a situation where a few are very rich and the masses are very poor, there is little incentive for those in power (the rich) to change the existing political-economic structure of the country. Those in power have much to lose and little to gain by change. As a result the very poor continue to live as they have done for centuries, while the rich, through income derived from property, are able to enjoy the fruits of economic progress of the developed nations.

Needless to say, this kind of situation tends to foster a great deal of resentment and hatred on the part of the masses towards the privileged few. Frequently the outcome of such an environment is violent revolution. Unfortunately, in the aftermath of such revolution the poor often find themselves suffering under just another kind of political and economic repression. In this case wealth and power may come from the "ownership" of positions in the military or the government rather than from ownership of physical property. It is not clear that the former is any more desirable than the latter. A landlord or property owner may have the power to influence a poor person's economic position, but generally does not have the power or the incentive to imprison or excecute a person on account of uncomplimentary things the person might say about his repressor.

Economic incentives

One of the lessons that many have learned, and many more have yet to learn, about the people living in the LDCs is that they respond to economic incentives as much as people living in the developed nations. An explanation sometimes given for the existence of the LDCs is that their people lack the ambition or the motivation to better their lot and prefer instead the "simple life." The stereotyped native sleeping in the shade of a palm tree often is used to represent this attitude.

Yet the more we learn about the LDCs the more apparent it becomes that the vast majority of their people, whether rural or urban, do take advantage of opportunities to increase their incomes. Farmers readily adopt new higher yielding varieties of crops, apply commercial fertilizer if it is profitable, and switch to crops that provide the greatest profits. By the same token, rural people migrate to cities in search of higher paying occupations and urban workers sell their services to employers who pay the highest wages. People in the LDCs, as everywhere, attempt to spend their incomes on goods and services that provide the most for the money. Trite phrases such as "the Protestant ethic" or "the work ethic" no longer can be used to explain differences in income between nations.

The desire to increase one's income is, of course, the ultimate prerequisite for economic growth. The existence of such a desire among the people of the LDCs provide a strong positive force for economic growth and development. At the same time, the desire for personal gain is often misdirected or controlled by various government policies. For example, an export tax on farm products or ceiling prices on food dampen the incentive of farmers to invest in output-increasing facilities or inputs, and hence retard the development of agriculture. By the same token, subsidized credit and minimum wage laws lead to a greater use of scarce capital and a reduction in demand for abundant labor, just the opposite of what we would like to see. Strict price controls and rationing give rise to privately profitable but socially unproductive blackmarket activities.

In the centrally planned economies, the opportunity for personal gain is reduced even more, although the desire for such gain on the part of the average person is likely to be as great as in any decentralized economy. In short-run national emergencies such as wars, people may respond to slogans and production quotas without economic incentives. However in the long run, most people are not likely to perform up to their potential unless they can see that increased effort will better their own standard of living or that of their families. A realization of the importance of economic incentives has prompted the Soviet government to institute more "material incentives" for workers in recent years, usually in the form of bonuses or prizes for increased production. Yet restrictions on ownership of private property, the absence of a capital market in which people can invest their savings, and scarcity of consumer goods, especially durables, still dampen the incentive to work. If there isn't much to buy with one's income, why struggle to increase it?

Economic stability

In the preceding discussion we argued that investment is the key to economic growth, particularly investment in people or facilities to produce new, nontraditional inputs for factory or farm. In a decentralized free market economy, a person must be reasonably certain that a profitable return will be forthcoming before he (or she) is willing to invest. In an economically unstable society, the uncertainty associated with the future is increased.

One common source of uncertainty in the LDCs is inflation, especially fluctuating rates of inflation, and the controls that usually accompany it. Inflation creates uncertainty because prices do not all rise at the same rate and, more importantly, the rate at which they will rise is unknown. If one borrows money at a 20 percent rate of interest, a rate not uncommon in the LDCs, it makes a big difference whether the future rate of inflation is 10 percent or 30 percent. In the former case the real rate of interest is +10 percent while in the latter it is −10 percent. If one could be sure the inflation rate would be 30 percent or higher, the chances would be good that the investment would be profitable. It does not take much skill to make money when borrowing at a negative real rate of interest. Of course, it is likely to be quite difficult to obtain a loan if other borrowers and lenders also expect the inflation rate to be much above the money rate of interest.

It is well to keep in mind that an inflation rate figure such as 30 percent is an average annual increase of all prices included in the price index. Certainly not all, or even any, prices have to rise by 30 percent.[7] Some prices may increase 40 to 50 percent while others rise only 10 to 20 percent. If the product to be produced is among the latter group and the inputs to be bought are among the former, the chances of making profits are diminished considerably. The imposition of government controls on prices also influences the profitability of investment. If the price of the product is controlled more tightly than the prices of the inputs, again profits are diminished.

If business is carried on in the international market, exchange rate fluctuations become important. If inflation is higher domestically than in countries where the product is sold, the local currency will probably become overvalued vis-à-vis other currencies and the product may become too expensive to compete in foreign markets. Of course, a substantial devaluation would have the effect of making the product less expensive to foreign buyers while increasing the price paid for imported inputs.

Thus you can see that inflation and changes in government-controlled prices make it extremely difficult to predict conditions very far into the future. One never knows if his investment will make him a millionaire or force him into bankruptcy. For people who like to avoid risk of this nature and magnitude, it is often wisest to buy consumer durables such as automobiles and housing. The prices of these items tend to be fairly responsive during inflation. They can be especially attractive if purchased with borrowed funds carrying a money rate of interest that is less than the rate of inflation.

Indeed, a very profitable investment, as far as the individual is

---

[7] You may have heard of the man who drowned while attempting to walk across a river that was on the average six inches deep.

concerned, can be the purchase of foreign currencies just before a devaluation. For example, in early 1971 the Argentine peso sold for about 500 to the dollar, while one year later one dollar bought between 900 and 1000 pesos. Thus one could have just about doubled his money by buying dollars with pesos and then reselling the dollars for pesos a year later. Although the purchase of consumer durables or foreign currencies may be the best thing the individual can do to protect himself during times of extreme inflation, such action certainly is not conducive to personal saving. Hence relatively few resources are available for investment, which in turn retards the country's growth in productive capacity.

Main points of Chapter 12

1. From the standpoint of world history, economic growth is a relatively recent phenomenon, most of it occurring within the past two centuries.
2. There is really no contradiction between economic growth and the quality of life. Unless society is willing to reduce its present consumption of goods and services, the quality of the environment cannot be increased unless growth occurs.
3. The optimism for economic growth and the future of mankind expressed by Adam Smith in his book *Wealth of Nations* was dampened somewhat by Thomas Malthus. In his book *Essay on the Principle of Population,* Malthus argued that mankind was destined to an existence of hunger and poverty as an expanding population pressed against the fixed land area of the world.
4. To strengthen his argument, Malthus also set forth his well-known law of diminishing returns, in which he argued that as more and more labor is applied to a fixed amount of land, beyond some point the extra output attributable to an extra unit of labor would begin to decline. And eventually population would grow until the masses teetered on the edge of starvation.
5. Because of the gloomy predictions of Malthus and his followers, economics became known as the "dismal science."

6. Malthus' dire prediction for the future of mankind has not
    been borne out in the highly developed nations of the world
    because of new and improved inputs which have comple-
    mented labor and land to increase man's productive capacity.

7. The term technological change describes the phenomenon of
    increasing output per unit of input. It occurs because quality
    improvements in traditional inputs or completely new inputs
    that have been adopted are not fully reflected in the input
    measures.

8. The most important determinant of economic growth is high-
    payoff investment. For the developed nations this has proven
    to be investment in the production and distribution of knowl-
    edge—in education—together with investment in capital that
    utilizes new knowledge.

9. In order to have investment people must be willing to save a
    portion of their income as opposed to spending it all on pres-
    ent consumption. This represents a major problem for people
    in the less developed countries (LDCs) because of their rela-
    tively small incomes.

10. Currently the annual per capita output of the richest nations
    in the world is about 40 times greater than that of the poorest
    nations. Also the annual growth in per capita output is much
    greater for the more highly developed nations, indicating that
    the poorer nations are falling further and further behind their
    more highly developed neighbors.

11. To a certain extent, underdeveloped nations have been able to
    utilize knowledge and technology from the developed coun-
    tries, although not all knowledge can be successfully trans-
    ferred between countries.

12. Agriculture is by far the dominant industry in the LDCs.
    Growth in agricultural productivity allows people to leave
    agriculture to produce additional goods and services that con-
    tribute to economic well-being.

13. Growth in agricultural productivity depends largely on the
    use of new, nontraditional inputs such as higher yielding
    varieties of crops, fertilizer, irrigation, water, herbicides, and
    insecticides. Each new input tends to be most productive if
    accompanied by other new inputs, i.e., a complete package of
    new inputs works best.

14. The industrial or nonagricultural sector offers the greatest

potential for growth in the LDCs. Because industrial technology tends to be somewhat less location-specific than agricultural technology, it is somewhat easier to transfer industrial techniques from the developed nations to the LDCs. However differences in input prices (labor versus capital costs) and differences in consumer demand between the developed nations and the LDCs generally require a modification of techniques that are transferred.

15.   The rural or interior regions of the LDCs are most lacking in infrastructure (roads, bridges, railroads, communications, and electricity). However scarce resources are required to build infrastructure. In order for the government to buy these resources it must levy taxes on a population that may not be accustomed to paying taxes. Taxes on exports and imports are relatively easy to collect, but distort market prices in the economy and may retard growth.

16.   The illiteracy rate in the rural areas of many LDCs runs as high as two thirds or three fourths of the population. The cost of schooling includes not only teachers and facilities but also the forgone earnings (lost production) of children in school. The demand for education also may be lacking because of the low educational level of parents.

17.   As agricultural development occurs and the supply of agricultural products increases relative to demand, farm prices and incomes in agriculture decline relative to nonfarm prices and nonfarm wages. This serves as an incentive for people to leave agriculture and take employment in nonfarm occupations.

18.   The agricultural adjustment problem can be eased by insuring freedom of entry into all occupations for all who are or can be become qualified. Subsidized credit for farm machinery intensifies the migration from agriculture, while high union wages and minimum wage laws make it more difficult for migrant farmers to find permanent employment in nonfarm occupations.

19.   The LDCs tend to exhibit higher rates of population growth than the developed nations. A contributing factor is the relatively recent reduction in infant mortality due to better medical care. Also children born and raised in rural areas tend to

be less costly than children reared in cities. Indeed many rural children are economic assets to their parents. Since most LDCs are highly rural in nature, the reduced cost of children provides an incentive for parents in these countries to have large families.

20. Imports of consumer or investment goods from the developed nations into the LDCs require foreign exchange, which can be earned by sales to the developed nations. Unfortunately there may not always be a market in the developed nations for what the LDCs have to sell. A recent development in some LDCs is the production and export of labor-intensive manufactured goods.

21. Land reforms and progressive income taxes are two common methods of redistributing wealth and income in the LDCs. The violent confiscation of private property which may occur when a new political regime takes power is another means of redistributing wealth or income, although a rather costly means in terms of life and personal freedoms.

22. People living in the LDCs take advantage of opportunities to increase their standard of living as much as people in the developed nations. The desire to increase one's standard of living provides a strong motivating force for economic growth. However certain government policies or ideologies can misdirect or stifle this force.

23. High and fluctuating rates of inflation create uncertainty about future economic conditions and tend, therefore, to dampen investment. Under these conditions the best course of action for the individual may be to spead much of his income on consumers goods (especially durables) or foreign currencies in order to hedge against inflation.

Questions for thought and discussion

1. What is economic growth?
2. In what way is economic growth a prerequisite for a cleaner environment?

3. Will GNP as it is currently measured reflect a cleaner environment? Explain.

4. Why have the gloomy predictions of Malthus not come true in the developed nations?

5. As economic growth occurs, it is common to observe an increase in output per unit of input. Why should this occur? Is it an indication that society is getting something for nothing? Explain.

6. Why has economic growth occurred in many nations of the world?

7. At their present rate of growth (dollars per year), how long would it take the poorest of the LDCs to achieve the present per capita output of the United States? Would you expect their absolute growth to increase over time? Explain. Do you think they will ever catch up to the United States and the other developed nations?

8. Suppose you decided to become an International Voluntary Services (IVS) worker and were assigned to a small rural agricultural village in Bangladesh. What kind of conditions would you expect to find before you arrived? What do you think you could do to help the people of this village?

9. Suppose in the course of your work in the village described in Question 8 you travel to a nearby town of 40 to 50 thousand people and observe a number of manufacturing establishments. You notice that much of the work, such as loading and unloading, bending and cutting of iron, etc., is done by hand. One of your hosts apologizes for his labor-intensive techniques, saying that the work should be mechanized as it is in the United States. What would you say?

10. What kind of tax system would you suggest for a highly rural LDC with one large city on a seacoast? After you have specified your system of taxes, explain how they would be likely to affect the economy.

11. What kind of an elementary school curriculum would you propose for the rural area of the country mentioned in Question 10? Defend your proposal.

12. Is elementary public education more or less expensive for the parents of children in rural areas than for people living in the city? Explain.

13. Why does migration of people from farms or rural areas to cities go hand in hand with economic growth?

14. Who tends to benefit from high union wages and minimum wage laws in the LDCs? Is anyone harmed by them? Explain.

15. It is sometimes argued that parents in rural areas have a comparative advantage in rearing children. Why might this be?

16. It is common to observe in stores nowadays many products manufactured in Korea, Hong Kong, and Taiwan. What kind of products do they tend to be? Why are they manufactured in these countries rather than domestically?

17. It has been argued that people of the LDCs are poor because they lack the initiative to better their living conditions. If this indeed is true, what kind of behavior should we expect to observe in regard to their responses to economic stimuli?

18. If you were a citizen of an LDC that was experiencing an inflation rate of about 50 percent per year, what would you do with the money you earned? Why?

Index

This book has been set in 11 point and 10 point Baskerville, leaded 2 points. Chapter numbers are in 30 point Baskerville italic and chapter titles are in 24 point Baskerville. The size of the type page is 26 x 45 picas.